A match may be made in heaven, but you still have to make it work here on Earth.

Fairy tales make for fun reading, but anyone who has ever been in a serious relationship knows that living "happily ever after" is a day-by-day project. Wouldn't it be nice if someone outside the relationship could point out the potential pitfalls between the two of you and show you ways to avoid them or work through them? That is just what noted Astrologer Bernie Ashman does in *The Magic of SignMates*. Stepping far beyond the typical lists of Leo gets along with these signs but is incompatible with these, he points out the destructive games any two signs are likely to play, gives strategies for overcoming them, and points the way to the rainbow, which is the happy ending of being real with each other every day.

The Magic of SignMates:

An Astrological Guide to Romantic Love

(Formerly Signmates: Understanding the Games People Play)

The Magic of SignMates:

An Astrological Guide to Romantic Love

(Formerly Signmates: Understanding the Games People Play)

Bernie Ashman

About the Author

Bernie Ashman has written for *Dell Horoscope, Astro Signs, Mountain Astrologer,* and *Welcome to Planet Earth* magazines. He has appeared on a number of television and radio shows and has lectured throughout the United States. He has also written the text for many astrological software programs. His other books include *Astrology, Psychology and Transformation, Sun Signs & Past Lives, Sun Sign Karma, How to Survive Mercury Retrograde* and *Roadmap to Your Future.*

Check out Bernie's website at *www.bernieashman.com*

Copyright©2022 by Bernie Ashman

All rights reserved. No part of this book may be reproduced or used in any form or by any means—graphic, electronic or mechanical, including photocopying, mimeographing, recording, taping or information storage and retrieval systems—without written permission from the publisher. A reviewer may quote brief passages.

(Formerly Signmates: Understanding the Games People Play)

ISBN: 9781944662-79-0

Printed in the United States of America

Published by Realization Press

Author photo by Keith Papke

Cover Design by Diana Henderson, CreativeType.biz

Other Books by Bernie Ashman

Astrology, Psychology, and Transformation
Sun Signs &Past Lives
Sun Sign Karma
How to Survive Mercury Retrograde
Roadmap to Your Future

Software by Bernie Ashman

Past Life Report: https://www.astrologysoftware.com/pro/win_writer/past_lives.html
Simpáticos: https://www.astrologysoftware.com/pro/win_writer/simpaticos.html
Earth Mandala Report: https://www.astrosoftware.com/EarthMandala.htm

Dedication

This book is dedicated to my own Gemini SignMate, Beth, in appreciation of her playful spirit and support, and to all individuals aspiring to find harmony and love in their relationships.

Contents

Introduction xv

Part I

The Twelve Players 3

    Aries (March 21-April 19) 4

    Taurus (April 20-May 20) 8

    Gemini (May 21-June 21) 11

    Cancer (June 22-July 22) 14

    Leo (July 23-August 22) 18

    Virgo (August 23-September 22) 21

    Libra (September 23-October 22) 25

    Scorpio (October 23-November 21) 29

    Sagittarius (November 22-December 21) 34

    Capricorn (December 22-January 19) 38

    Aquarius (January 20-February 18) 42

    Pisces (February 19-March 20) 46

Contents

Part II

Let the Games Begin.. 53

- Aries-Aries: The Daredevils 55
- Aries-Taurus: The Doers..60
- Aries-Gemini: The Movers and Shakers...........................65
- Aries-Cancer: The Initiators 70
- Aries-Leo: The Enthusiasts..75
- Aries-Virgo: The Energizers..80
- Aries-Libra: The Extroverts...85
- Aries-Scorpio: The Tenacious Ones 90
- Aries-Sagittarius: The Adventurers 96
- Aries-Capricorn: The Leaders...101
- Aries-Aquarius: The Eager Ones 107
- Aries-Pisces: The Imaginative Ones................................112
- Taurus-Taurus: The Economizers 117
- Taurus-Gemini: The Enterprising Ones.........................122
- Taurus-Leo: The Make It Happen People 132
- Taurus-Virgo: The Planners 137
- Taurus-Libra: The Romantics 142
- Taurus-Scorpio: The Passionate Ones............................146

Taurus-Sagittarius: The Jolly Ones 151

Taurus-Capricorn: The Builders 156

Taurus-Aquarius: The Surprisers 161

Taurus-Pisces: The Nature Lovers 166

Gemini-Gemini: The Thinkers 172

Gemini-Cancer: The Inquisitive Ones..177

Gemini-Leo: The Entertainers 183

Gemini-Virgo: The Scrutinizers 188

Gemini-Libra: The Live Wires 193

Gemini-Scorpio: The Detectives 198

Gemini-Sagittarius: The Travelers..203

Gemini-Capricorn: The Problem-Solvers 209

Gemini-Aquarius: The Brainy Ones 215

Gemini-Pisces: The Wishers and Hopers 221

Cancer-Cancer: The Homebodies 226

Cancer-Leo: The Industrious Ones 232

Cancer-Virgo: The Thrifty Ones 238

Cancer-Libra: The Plotters 243

Cancer-Scorpio: The Secretive Ones...248

Contents

Cancer-Sagittarius: The Restless Spirits..................254

Cancer-Capricorn: The Protective Ones 260

Cancer-Aquarius: The Hot-wired Ones...................265

Cancer-Pisces: The Intuitive Ones 271

Leo-Leo: The Directors..277

Leo-Virgo: The Broadcasters....................................282

Leo-Libra: The Socialites 288

Leo-Scorpio: The Negotiators 294

Leo-Sagittarius: The Confident Ones......................301

Leo-Capricorn: The Executives 307

Leo-Aquarius: The Spark Plugs 313

Leo-Pisces: The Actors...319

Virgo-Virgo: The Organizers 325

Virgo-Libra: The Allies 330

Virgo-Scorpio: The Thorough Ones........................336

Virgo-Sagittarius: The Seekers 342

Virgo-Capricorn: The Pragmatists 348

Virgo-Aquarius: The Resourceful Ones...................353

Virgo-Pisces: The Perfectionists 359

Libra-Libra: The Mixers..365

Libra-Scorpio: The Calculators...............................370

Libra-Sagittarius: The Gregarious Ones 376

Libra-Capricorn: The Reliable Ones 382

Libra-Aquarius: The Surprisers 387

Libra-Pisces: The Romantics..393

Scorpio-Scorpio: The Researchers..399

Scorpio-Sagittarius: The Motivators..404

Scorpio-Capricorn: The Power Brokers..................................410

Scorpio-Aquarius: The Determined Ones..............................416

Scorpio-Pisces: The Mysterious Ones......................................422

Sagittarius-Sagittarius: The Gypsies...427

Sagittarius-Capricorn: The Ambassadors...............................432

Sagittarius-Aquarius: The Freedom Seekers 438

Sagittarius-Pisces: The Ideal Weavers 444

Capricorn-Capricorn: The Strategists......................................450

Capricorn-Aquarius: The Anticipators...................................455

Capricorn-Pisces: The Conscientious Ones...........................461

Aquarius-Aquarius: The Rebels..467

Aquarius-Pisces: The Dazzlers..472

Pisces-Pisces: The Dreamers 478

Introduction

The Field of Play

When I began writing this book my hope was to inspire readers to never give up in finding a loving relationship. If only romantic relationships always had a beginning that predictably led to such harmony! Mystery and intrigue lead many of us to play the relationship game. Perhaps it's the excitement of unpredictability that romantic love offers that entices a person to avidly seek it in another.

The first edition of this book was published in 2000 by Llewellyn with the title, *SignMates: An Astrological Guide to Love and Intimacy*. In this second edition, I chose to give the book a new title, *The Magic of SignMates* because there is a magical attraction stimulated by the powerful, passionate force found in romantic love.

One of the aims of this book is to dispel the myth that certain signs can never be compatible or that some signs are always compatible with each other. Neither is true all of the time. With a lot of practice and patience, any two signs can learn to establish stability. Granted, certain sign combinations do bring out more of an intensity in one another on a regular basis. For instance, an Aries-Scorpio combination tends to be more tempestuous than a Virgo-Capricorn combination. Fiery Aries enjoys sparring with the passionate sign of Scorpio as much as Scorpio can test Aries' patience to the limit (as illustrated in the Poker Face game in part II). A long-term commitment can grow out of the Aries-Scorpio relationship *if* each can learn to negotiate with the other.

Even though earthy Virgo and Capricorn have a common need to create stability, this combination can find themselves playing the Working Harder Rather Than Smarter game. Each of these signs thrives on commitment and efficiency. The flowing ease found between a Virgo-Capricorn couple can be disrupted at times by conflict that tests the depth of the relationship. By the same token, the natural intensity found in Aries-Scorpio mates could do with a little lightening up once in a while.

There are no perfect relationships, so don't expect to find any perfect sign combinations in this book. Problems for many of us stem from being at a loss as to know

Introduction

how to deal with each other. Men are apt to be aggressive while women are inclined to be more refined and compassionate. Men are generally more detached from their emotions and concerned with hard facts and the bottom line. Women generally lean toward a holistic approach based upon emotions. Men usually do not show as much feeling in the bonding process. This is not the case when women communicate. Men and women often need to translate or reiterate the words spoken to one another to be clear about their true intentions. Many men need to learn how to get more in touch with their feelings. Women today certainly take on roles and express themselves in ways that in previous times were reserved for men only.

We really don't get much briefing on how to handle romantic relationships. In my opinion, romantic love is the most powerful motivating force in life. While career and family are key drives in their own right, they still fall behind the instinct in each of us to find a partner.

In his book *We*, Jungian Psychologist Robert A. Johnson states, "Romantic love is the single greatest energy system in the Western psyche." He goes on to say, "In our culture it has supplanted religion as the arena in which men and women seek meaning, transcendence, wholeness, and ecstasy."

Think about it for a second. What other experience do people continue to try over and over again, already knowing that in modern society the chances for success are slim? The risk of failing does not outweigh the alluring magic that romance promises to bring to each of us.

It is my hope that these pages will help you navigate your romantic encounters with more insight and create more effective ways to communicate.

Part I introduces the twelve Sun signs or players. You can turn to these chapters whenever you want to get a quick grasp of the psychological profile of each sign. Before moving into part II of the book (the games), you may want to use this first section as a reference to read about your own sign and that of your partner. You can always flip back to part I for a quick refresher course on a sign in which you are interested.

Part II is an in-depth comparison of each of the twelve signs to one another and identifies the games that can arise from these sign combinations. A game can best be defined as a repetitive pattern of negative behavior that interferes with the harmony of a partnership. It is an imbalance of energies that is created when one or both partners engage in thoughts and actions that are counterproductive or hurtful to them. Take, for example, the Missing the Boat game discussed in the Aries-Gemini comparison. This game arises when these two fast-paced signs continuously frustrate one another's actions

Introduction

and ideas. The challenge is somehow to acknowledge one another's needs and potential. The wires might be getting crossed due to Aries' desire to follow immediate impulses being at odds with the Gemini instinct to think before leaping.

The games that cause discord might have their basis in the conscious or unconscious drives of the players. A game often results when each person has a need or desire that conflicts with their partner's. Games start when the individuals involved don't deal with these issues intelligently; that is, they do not communicate openly to reach resolutions.

Each game represents a specific challenge to the success of a relationship. The games test the mettle of a relationship to continue as a growth experience.

The strategy section of each game shows how a game plan can be made an asset rather than a liability.

The rainbow at the end of each game describes the potential for harmony that can be achieved between any two signs. This is where you can realize your hopes of truly enjoying one another.

This book not only identifies issues, but is very much concerned with how to deal with them. In my opinion, a relationship is a living entity. It is a process of becoming that has creative force. The value in finding a strategy to deal with a game is that it can lead to clearer perception of your partner and a greater sense of togetherness. Another goal of this book is to encourage more communication between lovers because that is the best way to empower the relationship. Communication is often the bridge to enjoying more passionate sex and a greater sense of closeness! It is an essential way to develop real depth in personal relationships and in oneself.

Part I

The Twelve Players

The twelve Sun signs are the key players in these games. This chapter provides a comprehensive overview of your own and your partner's personality type according to your Sun signs. This handy reference describes the psychological profile of each zodiac sign.

The Sun in astrology points to your creative vitality and important ego needs. The Sun sign represents the areas of life where you want to shine. It is your quest for pride and happiness.

Your astrological Sun rules your heart. It is your center just as the real Sun is the center of your solar system. Romantic love plays dramatically on your heartstrings in tune with your individual Sun sign.

If you are not sure which sign you were born under, you can look this up here as the beginning and ending dates for each sign are listed. If you were born on the cusp (on the first or last day of a sign), you could be either of two signs. In this case, to be absolutely sure of your sign, you will need the help of a professional astrologer, who can determine this for you according to your birth time and place.

Aries (March 21-April 19)

The Ram

Element: Fire
Ruling Planet: Mars

Aries can dart past you at the speed of light. The Ram is a restless sign. They can seem like they are intravenously fed with caffeine. Lightning-quick impulses emanate from their soul. The one thing that Aries individuals fear most is boredom. They will do anything to avoid it—even wake sleeping dogs. The key phrase for Aries in traditional astrology is "I am," and those born under this sign project this image to the world from their first breath. "I am here!" they proclaim in a loud cry that echoes through a lifetime. This me-focused sign is constantly in search of ways to confirm their identity and has no compunctions about apprising the world of their findings.

A shadow of Aries is impatience. Another is not finishing what he or she started. When they begin to master these shortcomings, life seems more rewarding and people appreciate them more. No other sign is quite as direct and candid. Their bluntness can be either startling or as refreshing as a splash of cold water, depending on the psychological "climate" of those to whom it is directed. Give them their fair due and Aries of either sex can demonstrate remarkable bravery during a crisis. One good burst of adrenaline can transform them into champions or daredevils extraordinaire. They are often frightened into acting courageously. I am not kidding!

No other sign, except possibly Sagittarius, can be as embarrassed by twenty-twenty hindsight. The axiom "Fools rush in where angels fear to tread" could well have been inspired by this sign. When they learn from the past, it is a sign of high intelligence.

If they refuse to learn from mistakes, their life is made difficult. Like Peter Pan, Aries never really wants to grow up. However reluctantly, they do mature when taking on more responsibility. They lead well by being role models. Gloria Steinem is an Aries. Her willingness to challenge society's limiting view of the roles of women helped point the way to the fiery women's liberation movement.

Aries is a naturally competitive sign that hates to lose at whatever they are good at doing—and sometimes even at what they don't do so well! The ruling planet of Aries is fiery Mars. Anger is a natural component of Aries' character. So is the impatience to get something started. When Aries learns to finish what they started, they become more likable. When unfinished business looms in their path, they're as antsy as can be.

If you need motivation, spend some time in the company of this fireball. Let one coach you out of that lazy streak. They can get a fire lit that can awaken your creative impulses. Self-starting seems to be the birthright of this high energy fire sign.

Relationship Tendencies

In relationships, Aries can be a live wire. Their gung-ho enthusiasm to pursue a whirlwind relationship can be followed by "what am I doing here?" ambivalence. Their desire to explore their own agenda to the exclusion of anyone else's can be irritating. Sometimes it is the sudden change of agenda that angers others. Their need for attention is strong. However, it is this self-reliance that attracts people. Aries people are often attracted to active and boldly assertive individuals. Aries men and women are easier to be with when their career goals are reached. Each has tremendous intensity and passion to pour into work and love. Aries is called the warrior sign for good reason. Aries' characteristics are spontaneous action and courage.

The Aries Woman

She is apt to hurt your feelings once in a while by dealing a blow to your ego. Get over it; she does quickly enough. This is one nice thing about an Aries woman. She is often willing to move ahead and give you another chance. She might keep you in tow, dragging along your old kit bag of peccadilloes, if she's fond enough of you. Don't be scared away by her anger. Actually, it is time to worry when the Ram is too quiet. Those of us not born under this sign can get nervous when she holds back her anger. Let her vent to her heart's content. It may be uncomfortable for the moment, but it's good in the long run.

It is better to deal with the Aries woman directly. Don't wait for the "right time" to talk unless she specifically asks you to hold off. A tired Aries is best left alone until her battery is recharged; it quickly restores anyway! Aries people can be a lot easier to talk to when they have a chance to work off their stress through exercise.

The Ram can surprise you by suddenly lapsing into a sensitive mood. Don't be lulled into a false sense of security. It can disappear in a flash. The sharp sword of this Mars-ruled sign (remember, Mars was the god of war) can be wielded without warning. Let her be the warrior when needed. She will love you for this. Let her be assertive and she will respect you. The good news is that the Aries woman will let you be angry in response to her anger. She may even expect you to fight back. She respects this too! She actually thrives on this type of invigoration.

The sparring can become playful and lead to deeper communication. The female Aries is naturally competitive. It is an inherent part of her survival instincts. Contrary to popular belief, Aries can put their thoughts into words. If you can talk with emotion, you are more likely to get her attention. But get to the point fairly quickly before something else grabs her attention.

The Aries Man

He looks and acts like a displaced Stone Age hunter. The Aries man often appears a lot more insensitive than he really is at heart. His bark may be a lot worse than his bite. He believes in forging along a direct path through life. His patience is measured by how long he must wait until starting the next action. This is a fast-paced person. Keeping up with the male Aries is quite a feat. If you follow him in a car, you had best stay close behind because he is liable to rush through a red light and lose you in a jiffy. You are expected to match his speed. People can get tuckered out trying to do things with Aries. He has a tireless energy that does not stop until his tank is truly on empty. A little rest and he is off and running again.

If you want to learn how to be more self-motivated, just hang around an Aries man for a while. You can't find a better role model. He often picks and chooses his favorite areas of life to pursue in the fast lane. However, don't be surprised to find him relaxing at the beach or watching a ballgame at the house. He fully enjoys his leisure. Whatever you do, allow him the time he needs to passionately go after his interests.

He is a territorial creature. This comes as a standard birthright for the Aries man. He needs to know where his world begins and ends. In turn, you control your own turf. There's no guessing game here. He clearly defines the boundary line between your territory and his. The Aries man can spot a squatter as fast as a cat can smell a mouse, so let him have the illusion that he owns his own world.

He can be generous to those he loves. The Aries man will fight for you when someone else might lack the courage to do so. He can irritate you with his self-centeredness yet charm you by making you feel powerful and important.

Taurus (April 20-May 20)

The Bull

Element: Earth
Ruling Planet: Venus

They move with the greatest of ease. Comfort, especially creature comfort, is their birthright. Taurus, the Bull, moves with a gait that's steady and sure. Taurus is almost artful in its languid deliberation. It's as though they are moving in slow motion (and enjoying themselves) while the rest of us are rushing about our business in real time. This is a Sun sign that can appreciate beauty in all its forms. Venus, its ruler, must have created sunrises and sunsets by weaving easygoing Taurean magic into nature's panorama. Taurus' patience is as enduring as a great mountain, unmoved by the mightiest of winds.

One shadow of earthy Taurus is stubbornness. Another is excessive attachment to material things. Tempering these traits makes life more fun for them and the rest of us. If they don't gain some degree of control over these shadows, their life becomes one of great self-indulgence. They still might have fun, unless they lose a person or thing that they are attached to, like a tot with a teddy bear. This sign bellows like the dickens if threatened with giving up its beloved attachments.

In business matters practicality reigns. The instinct to invest money is strong. Business savvy develops before puberty for many of them. Taurus has an inner sense of the value of things. It's no wonder that the key phrase for Taurus in traditional astrology is "I own" or "I have." Possessions are gods to this sign.

The Bull can excel in music and art. Taurus is ruled by the aesthetic-minded Venus (as is Libra). The muse consciousness can dance, sing, and play music through the soul of this sign at an early age.

Relationship Tendencies

In relationships, Taureans can be quite faithful and reliable. Their stabilizing effect on others is well appreciated. Sensuality is a must in their lives. A lover must be inclined toward this kind of pleasure or be willing to be guided accordingly. Taureans don't seem bothered by the more fast-paced signs. The Bull will simply wait for others to slow down. Taureans enjoy life on their own terms. The Bull does not always compromise easily, but will do so to avoid extreme conflicts. Taureans are attracted to people who are relatively calm and possess a strong sense of managing finances. Persistence and an innate ability to find inner peace are the most predominant of Taurean characteristics.

The Taurus Woman

She is often attractive. Venus, the ruler of this sign, blesses the Taurus woman with an appreciation of beauty. She may not be as easygoing as others are quick to assume. She knows what she needs from life. Her determination to establish comfort and happiness comes as a birthright. She has a strong sense of color, and is a natural image consultant. Her clothes may seem to be fashioned exclusively for her body. She is a radiant sign that attracts relationships.

Since Taurus is an earth sign, a strong business sense is common. A Taurus woman knows how to make a living. Creating a budget is second nature to her. Lovers are fond of her practicality and worldly savvy.

The Taurus woman can be possessive and sometimes demanding, but usually she is quite fair. She admires individuals who follow through on their promises. Lying to her would be a tragic mistake. It offends her terribly. It is better to let her deal with the truth in her own way. Believe me, she can do this better than most of us.

Be gentle; she expects this. Be reasonable, and she will trust you. Be generous, and she will love you. She enjoys creating a romantic atmosphere with you. She may even agree to go camping with you in the wilderness. Celebrating anniversaries and returning to the place you first met are ways of showing her love for you.

Don't fault her for wanting to know about your views concerning ownership and money. She has business instincts and needs to believe that you truly value her. Her faith in you can fill you with the confidence to accomplish great things in life. She only asks that you cherish her and show it once in a while. Although communication means much to her, talk without action may be viewed as meaningless through her soft, Venusian eyes. She is a "show me" girl!

The Taurus Man

He walks firmly like he knows where he is going—whether he does or not. The Bull is persistent in reaching his goals and making his dreams come true. He expects the support of loved ones. He can be hurt or angry if you don't believe in him. He carries himself through life with confidence, that is, until he meets a situation that is bigger than he is. The Bull will then either try to charge through the obstacle or retreat to find a more comfortable path. Patience is a strength in the male Taurus. However, the Taurus man will act with swift impatience when his livelihood is threatened. There is an opportunistic dimension to the male Taurus that is like a sixth sense when it comes to financial opportunity.

Stubbornness does not endear the Bull to others. A lack of imagination or failure to be adventurous can irritate those they love. It is their willingness to care and make a person feel safe that adds great longevity to their relationships. He appreciates stability. His focus on his career can be nicely balanced with a calm home life. The male Taurus hates stress at home probably more than at work. A show of anger can be difficult for a Taurus to handle. Sometimes a lover will find an angry outburst the only way to get through the Bull's thick skin.

Taurus can honor a commitment with true sincerity. This is a sign that loves to build enduring things, whether it is a relationship, career, or house. They like people who are nurturing and who consistently maintain a loving atmosphere. Your Taurus mate can be a great chef in the kitchen, and it may seem like he knows just the recipe to capture your heart.

Gemini (May 21-June21)

The Twins

Element: Air
Ruling Planet: Gemini

They are the masters of duality. The Twins are curious to see what the world can teach, and what they can teach the world. Geminis only pretend to travel in a straight line. Their perceptions can take in an entire panorama in an instant. This sign can stop on a dime and change directions as smoothly as a champion Olympic skater. Geminis enjoy moving simultaneously on several fronts while they juggle multiple ideas effortlessly.

One shadow of airy Gemini is nervous anxiety. Another is a lack of concentration. Overcoming these tendencies makes life more user-friendly for them and more predictable for those of us who live with them. This is probably the most adaptable of all the signs. A common mistaken assumption is that Geminis cannot get to the depth of a subject. One area in which Geminis will not (and better not) compromise is in striving for mental or educational excellence! Those born under this sign make wonderful consultants or teachers. Geminis can paint word pictures that brilliantly reframe life for the rest of us.

Relationship Tendencies

In relationships, Geminis are diversified. They can be fun to be around because of their vivid imaginations. Geminis are attracted to people who communicate easily and intelligently. Geminis do not seek or honor commitments that interfere with their right to free thinking. Read this last sentence again; it may be the most important one in this section. In traditional astrology, the key phrase for this sign is "I think." The Twins won't completely reveal their thoughts and value intellectual freedom. This air sign can do two or three things simultaneously while many of us are still reading the directions. It is ruled by the winged messenger, Mercury. The mind is treasured by this sign. Thoughts are about as valuable as money in the bank to many of them. The main attributes of Gemini are mental imaging power and the ability to clearly translate life experiences into understandable terms.

The Gemini Woman

She thinks as fast as she walks—and I mean fast! The curious Twins open their eyes wide when learning adventures present themselves. The Gemini woman is an artist with words. She is adept at handling herself well in most social situations. She will not expect you to be as articulate as she can be, but she needs to hear you talk. Trust comes directly from the spoken word with this sign.

The rap on Gemini is that it is a sign lacking steady focus. The Gemini woman can be absorbed in one thing and, in an instant, be captivated by something else. This is a sign that needs multiple outlets. The more diverse her activities are, the more loving she will be. Gemini will not waste much time on people, places, or things that are not mentally challenging. Boredom is not a comfortable state of existence for this sign. It is best to keep learning with the Gemini woman. She really respects intelligence and open-mindedness.

Adaptability is an endearing feature of this sign. It comes guaranteed at birth. Geminis delight in being with people whose likes and dislikes are different than their own. It's true! They're probably excited by the mental adventure of being able to coexist with foreign entities. The Gemini woman expects to have her own unique ideas tolerated and accepted.

Geminis like to travel. Often the best time to really get to know them is when they're on the move, whether traveling around town or across the country. The Gemini woman is easy to get to know on one hand, yet complicated on the other. The duality of the Twins is important to acknowledge. She will extend a warm and open hand of love and friendship to you, but the other hand seems to be withheld. It may take years for her to truly reach out to you. If she does, consider yourself lucky. This is part of the hidden side of this deeply perceptive sign. The Gemini woman is even more mysterious than the man in this way. She'll let you read her to an extent, but she retains a secret set of books exclusively for her own playful imagination. Enjoy her dance of the seven veils, but don't expect her to discard them too quickly and reveal herself to you. Let her become known to you in her own way and on her own terms. She is a treasure worth waiting for—honest!

The Gemini Man

He is a fun-filled puzzle. The Gemini man has a way of performing that is not so evident until you really watch him in action over and over again. You almost need a hidden video camera to detect what's happening. His actions often run contrary to his thoughts, but he still manages to get the job done. He loves to teach, talk, discuss, consult, and converse some more. Show that you are listening and you may have a friend forever.

His judgment might be questionable. It is okay to confront him; however, he may not listen. He may not even hear you if his mind is moving too fast or is already fixed on a decision. Start a sentence with his name if you really want to get his attention.

President John F. Kennedy was a fine example of how powerful a speaker a Gemini can be. His words could inspire the nation as can those of others born under this loquacious sign. A Gemini man is capable of solving complex problems when he is really interested in doing so. He often loves to read. Show him you are knowledgeable about current events and news. He loves to engage in an occasional mental quiz. He can be cunningly assertive. You may not even realize you are losing a battle until after the fact. He hates to be accused of lying, although he's an expert at clouding the truth. He will often say he didn't understand what you needed or find another way of playing ignorant (or innocent).

The Gemini man is fun to have as a partner. He is witty and insightful. His love of finding diversified ways to have fun and to learn are stimulating. His way of communicating invigorates the psyche. If you want mental adventures, then you have found the right partner!

Cancer (June 22-July 22)

The Crab

Element: Water
Ruling Planet: The Moon

Moodiness. Yes, it comes standard with this sign. The moods of Cancer are what puzzle the rest of us the most about this intensely emotional sign. Deep introspection can eclipse the face of a Cancer. He or she may look depressed or sad one moment and happy the next. Don't become too obsessed with the downside; it can pass like a cloud over the Moon. I should say, don't become too fond of the happy face because it may suddenly vanish. The good news is that the phases of Cancer's moods change about as fast as those of its ruling planet, the Moon.

This sign can give the illusion of being timid. I advise you to never make this assumption blindly. Put Cancer to the test and the Crab can react ferociously if you threaten its security.

A shadow of Cancer is fear. Another is cast by unclear dependency needs. When Cancers can overcome these areas of life, their sense of security feels less threatened, and they are more generous toward others—in a big way! They give from the depths of their soul. This sign can be highly protective of loved ones. Feelings run deep. The key phrase for Cancer in traditional astrology is "I feel."

Privacy is paramount to many Cancers. They like to think that their secrets are safely hidden from the world. Home is a haven that Cancers must put their mark on—just like a cat. Cats instinctively mark their territory because it gives them a sense of home. Cancers can form a sacred bond with their dwelling, community, or with people. Doing so is a primordial instinct for this sign that probably goes back to the beginning of time!

Relationship Tendencies

In relationships, Cancers are sensitive souls. The emotional needs of this sign are subject to change at any moment. The moods of Cancer are complex. Their love of established comfort zones can be quickly overturned by the desire to initiate new experiences. This sign is sometimes more comfortable leading but at other times would rather follow someone else's lead. The hardest part is knowing which characteristics Cancer is playing out at any given time. Family is an essential need of the Crab. This can include children, but it can extend to plants and pets as well. If Cancer enjoys your company, the desire to draw close is evident. If you crowd Cancer's space, however, expect the Crab to withdraw into the warm protection of the sand. Cancers are attracted to people who share their vision of establishing roots and who support their security needs. The trials of this sign involve turning fears into strengths and developing the capacity to integrate the past into an empowering present.

The Cancer Woman

She can be an intense lover, but you must take the time to really get to know her. If a relationship starts too fast, expect it to slow down as she carefully processes what is happening. If a relationship with a female Cancer begins slowly, it may suddenly lift off. The pace of getting to know someone must be comfortable for her. Let the Crab dictate the speed of a budding relationship. This is an area where she sometimes likes to lead. Have patience. This is my best advice to you if you want to stay close to this sensitive woman's heart.

Her home is her temple. If she asks you to take off your shoes or to wipe off the soles of your shoes before entering, please do so! Her abode is a sanctuary. From what, you ask? The world! Indulge her in this regard. If you think she doesn't have serious rules about her home, my advice would be to tread lightly when you're there anyway. There are likely to be a few hidden rules that you'll discover as you go along.

The female Cancer has strong opinions about her own family. She wants you to like the relatives that she likes, but don't act too fond of the family members she doesn't like. You must accept her friends, even if you do not spend time with them. Relax. She will do the same for you most of the time. This is a nurturing person, but don't abuse her giving nature. Keep both of your dependency needs balanced and this can be a passionate and loving bond.

Remember this little tip. It isn't easy to leave a relationship with a Cancer partner. Why? Because you may have become spoiled by a Cancer partner's attentiveness. The memory of caring lingers long after he or she leaves, so be sure you want this relationship before getting too involved. A female Cancer's show of feelings can be heartwarming when she really pulls close. If you reveal your own vulnerability, this demonstrates your trust, and the depth of the relationship is enhanced. She will open her heart to you if you will communicate from your own heart. Show her your interest in establishing a family or home. She then will be willing to risk her sense of security to take a chance on you.

The Cancer Man

He is selective about what he keeps in his memory. The male Cancer has a habit of trying to forget anything unpleasant. He can be supportive when you need a friend the most. There will be times when he seems a little too invisible. If you trust him, it won't matter as much. If you don't, his vanishing acts of introversion will bother you a great deal.

His moods are omnipresent in his life. He never leaves home without them. His need to emote is strong. It would be nice if you were permitted to do the same. Some male Cancers fear emotional intensity in a potential mate. It can take quite a while for him to warm up to your desire to draw close. If he needs you, intimacy will grow more quickly. If you need him more than he needs you, expect it to take more time to really get to know one another.

The home is just as important to the male Cancer as it is to the female. The Crab is protective of his home turf. You will possibly see possessions given to him by previous lovers or by family members. He is attached to objects that hold positive memories. Don't ask him to give up anything from the past until you are really close.

The male Cancer can really be there for you during a crisis, but he may leave you for periods of time once he senses that you are more emotionally stable. His caring nature is not always revealed early in a relationship. He will hide it until he perceives that you can be trusted. His passion for you can be shown through his actions. He can please you physically, mentally, and emotionally like no other lover.

Your main concern may be to get a real fix on this person. His changing moods and feelings can keep you guessing about him. Clear communication is a great remedy for any confusion—if he is willing to talk. If you persevere in getting down to the real person, the rewards can be great. You can receive the very best the Crab has to offer.

Leo (July 23-August 22)

The Lion

Element: Fire
Ruling Planet: The Sun

The Lion roars in the jungle to announce that the monarch is present. Other animals, respectfully or fearfully, move out of the way. Leo, the lionhearted, commands attention when entering a room like a star taking center stage. Is it any wonder this sign is sometimes called the actor? The world is a stage for Leo. Even a shy Leo seems to believe in a divine right to be noticed. (Yes, there are shy Leos; I have met a few!) In traditional astrology, the key phrase for Leo is "I will." Their willpower is a force to be reckoned with. Leos commandeer life in a big way!

A shadow of fiery Leo is extreme bossiness. Another is an insatiable need for attention. When the Lion overcomes these tendencies, people appreciate this dynamic sign. Leos are ferociously self-expressive. Their creativity is intense. This is a passionate sign that does not always know where it is going but arrives at a destination and makes the most of it through sheer determination. Even though Leo can be stubborn, sometimes the Lion can be surprisingly flexible. It's their passionate love of living life to the fullest that makes them fun to be around.

This sign is the greatest of promoters. Leos can put a spin on anything to make it appealing to others. Marketing their own talent or helping others become more marketable is a trademark of the Lion.

Dramatics, humor, holding court—each have their place in Leo's repertoire. Appreciate these facets of Leo and the Lion will love you. The best way to argue with them is to create the illusion that they are winning. Then restate what you need. You will be surprised by their generosity. Leo is a kindly ruler.

Relationship Tendencies

In relationships, the Lion is a royal personage. Leos like to be perceived as passionate. Don't step carelessly on the Lion's ego. If you do, expect a loud roar. The Lion's ego bruises easily. This can be a very me-centered sign. It is ruled by the Sun, enjoying a central position in the make-up of our solar system. The Sun's rays bathe us in its glory. Leos like to think they do the same. Get the picture?

When Leos feel a sense of accomplishment in their chosen career or achieve an acceptable level of status, they are much easier to live with as lovers or partners. The Lion does not like to reveal any vulnerability. Leos would rather nurse their wounds in seclusion. A sure sign of trust is when they confess to their weaknesses. Such admissions strengthen Leos, even though it might make them feel defenseless. Once Leos start to complain about their wounds, expect this lament to become a never-ending refrain.

The Lion is attracted to self-confident people who enjoy having a good time. Leo's attributes are dynamic willpower and an all-abiding, limitless creative spirit!

The Leo Woman

She walks proudly. People often want to emulate her. She inspires them with her noble ways. A Leo woman can appear arrogant. (They are seldom viewed as being humble!) Knowing which life direction to pursue can take hold at an early age. She makes few excuses for her failures. Her successes are worn boldly like medals of honor for all the world to see. Her strength is confidence. She thrives on self-expression. Show your pride in her and you should find her to be a passionate lover.

If you know she is wrong, tell her directly. She doesn't always understand or listen to subtle comments. Yet, her sensitivity might surprise you. When she cries, the whole world can hear her (or so she hopes). Positive strokes make her pay attention to you. She can be forgiving if she truly believes you deserve this from her. She will even ask for your forgiveness if she has hurt you, that is, if she knows you will be receptive to her humbling herself in such a way. It's not easy for the queen of the beasts to make concessions or confessions for that matter!

The Leo woman will give you gifts. Be sure to reciprocate or at least show her your profound gratitude. She likes people with a sense of humor. It helps if you have the money to give her the lavish life she wants to live. She is quite independent. Her career is important to her. She is capable of acting out many different roles. The Leo woman needs to know she can live alone if circumstances demand this. Treat her to her favorite vacation spot. Take the time to laugh together. Take frequent breaks from work so you can really be with each other. She will stay by the home fires with you if you give her the love, attention, and respect that are her due. Long live the queen!

The Leo Man

Center stage was made for him—or so he thinks! It's as though the other eleven signs orbit around the Leo man. It seems that's how they see the world. Born actors! They are entertaining. People love their warm-spirited laugh. A sense of humor is a hallmark of their character.

When the Leo man acts like a dictator, people can be offended quickly. Leo's demeanor can shift rather unexpectedly. He really wants life to be on his own terms. That can make it difficult on lovers. Compromise does not always come easily. Usually the Lion will roar angrily before compromising—if he'll back down at all.

The Leo man can be wonderfully giving. He takes pride in his wealth and work. Compliment his generosity, and his mane will puff up and he will smile at you gratefully. The Leo man craves your loving affection even more than making love (he will never admit this). He is not always the easiest person to get to know. He talks about life in general terms rather than about himself. Eventually, he might hint at having feelings. He loves to be figured out by someone he truly cares about. (He will never admit this either.)

You can be as dramatic as you like; he'll be your adoring audience. Leo invented drama! It must be a primordial instinct with this sign. Be confident. If you are more successful in a career than him, don't brag about it. This rubs him the wrong way. He will be silently grateful to you for not trying to upstage him. Remember, he is the star. Everyone else gets second billing.

The male Leo will do anything for someone he loves. This is why a mate will remain with a Leo for many years. He will champion your causes, so be his cheerleader. He will tell you why you are the greatest. His creative energy can push you to new creative heights of your own. Long live the king!

Virgo (August 23-September 22)

The Virgin

Element: Earth
Ruling Planet: Mercury

"Perfection" is Virgo's motto. Is Virgo always a perfectionist? No, not in every area of life—only in those life arenas that command Virgo's compulsive attention. The attractions can be different from one Virgo to another. This is a sign with the in-depth perception tendencies of analytical Mercury guiding its every move. This is the same planet that rules Gemini—or is it? The winged messenger has more of an eye for detail in its rulership of Virgo, the critic of the zodiac. Gemini will let things slide by while Virgo can't keep those picky hands off them. The key phrase for this sign in traditional astrology is "I analyze."

Trying to attain perfection can produce a masterpiece. It is said that Michelangelo created his *Pieta* by cutting out from the stone what his discerning artistic eyes determined did not belong there. What was left was a breathtaking masterpiece. So what's wrong with perfection? Pitching a "perfect game" in baseball gives you hall of fame status. Perfection can bring one a greater salary in the workplace. It's when perfection becomes a constant end in itself that Virgo suffers, and so do those of us trying to live with this meticulous sign.

A shadow of earthy Virgo is negative thinking. Another is extreme criticism of self or others. When Virgos can overcome these tendencies, life is more forgiving of their actions, and the rest of us find it easier to accept them. The Virgin can have impeccable standards for excellence. Keeping expectations reasonable is wise. One thing you should always remember about Virgos is that they're never "wrong"—except by mistake!

Relationship Tendencies

In relationships, Virgo is a puzzling entity. Their dedication to those they love is authentic and admirable. With one hand the Virgin will stroke you with compliments and with the other can sometimes mercilessly point out your faults. It may help to realize that Virgo's criticism is often more from a primordial instinct, developed since the earliest days of our Virgo ancestors rather than from your leaving a spot on a washed pot or dish. You can protest all you want against Virgo's relentless analysis of the details of your actions. Good luck! It will not change this sign's behavior. Virgos can learn to be more sensitive in expressing your faults. Humility is usually what keeps Virgos balanced in relationships. Also, a service orientation toward others makes Virgos lovable. This sign is usually not given credit for being the great lovers they can be. Virgos will go out of their way to find out what pleases you in bed or in other areas of life. Virgos are attracted to people who can establish everyday routines similar to their own. They appreciate hardworking individuals. The attributes of Virgo are an uncompromising attitude toward excellence in work and an amazing ability to be organized.

The Virgo Woman

She can be as compulsively meticulous about herself as she is organized with everything else. Don't fault her for this. She is efficiency in motion. She is the perfect businesswomen. She can manage a business or department as well, if not better, than any other sign. You have to admire her intense desire to be efficient. A Virgo woman can work the rest of us into the ground. She's a tireless soul who may drop from exhaustion due to overwork.

There are no perfect people. She knows this. Forgive her for forgetting. Remind her that you are not perfect. If she tells you one of your habits bothers her, see if you can change your ways. It makes her love you. Don't try to change her, and she probably will not try to redesign you.

If you can work on a project together, it does wonders for the bonding process. She likes a hardworking partner. Don't be a workaholic because she may already be prone to this, and the tendency could do her in. The Virgo woman may appear to be a no-nonsense individual. However, her sense of humor can surprise you. It may be therapeutic to laugh at herself and others once in a while.

Her humility can be erroneously perceived as a lack of self-confidence. Don't take advantage of her giving nature because it will make her resentful. She loves cleanliness and order. You will need to accept this side of her. She can be overly critical of you about any area of life. It is her attention to detail and a powerfully discerning eye that makes her this way. You can and should tell her when she is tearing you down too much. By the way, she is very sensitive to criticism herself. Tell her how it makes you feel, and she is apt to stop.

She is a great problem-solver. She is a shoulder to lean on when you feel down and out, so offer the same to her. The Virgo woman usually has an innate understanding about and respect for commitment. She is nobody's fool. She will be the greatest of lovers if you treat her with respect and honor her intelligence.

The Virgo Man

He knows just how he looks without a mirror, but he is going to look for a mirror anyway. He can be a neat freak. Then again, a Virgo man might be messy. Yes, I said messy! It is his private rebellion against order. He will still probably be well organized at work. Disorder can make him nervous. It is instinctual for him to put things in order. Nothing might be wrong in your eyes but not so for this guy. The need to compulsively create order seems to be an innate characteristic almost like he has a computer chip implanted in his brain.

He can be attentive to your needs. He is a wonderfully supportive person. Even in the midst of his criticism, you can sense he cares about you. Commitments can make a male Virgo uneasy. He doesn't take them lightly. He needs to be really sure about a relationship before he gets serious. Don't fault him for second-guessing your love for him. He just wants to keep running it through his mental processors like you might put a load of clothes through a second rinsing to make sure you get all of the soap out. Perhaps you turned in a paper in school for a class or for a work assignment and kept reading it over and over to check for careless errors. The male Virgo does this incessantly with all areas of life. He can't help himself.

The Virgo man can put himself down too much. He will love you for encouraging him to think more positively. Make him chicken soup when he is sick, and he will love you forever. Be sure to tell him you don't plan on being his mother!

He doesn't give up on people or situations easily. His patience can greatly make up for his tendency to criticize. Tell him you will never be perfect, so he will know this

The Magic of Signmates

from the start. By the way, it doesn't hurt to tell him he will never be perfect either. His work is very much a part of him. He is apt to be devoted to it. He can still love you passionately even after he finishes running his perceptions of you repeatedly through his mental circuitry. The Virgo man can be courageous in dealing wholeheartedly with an issue in a relationship. This is a strong point that attracts lovers.

Libra (September 23-October 22)

The Scales

Element: Air
Ruling Planet: Venus

This is the most graceful of the twelve signs. Librans have a refined social poise that is especially endearing. This sign is as much at ease in dealing with public relations as a cat is while peacefully sunbathing. Librans can possess a delicate nervous system (as can the other two air signs, Gemini and Aquarius). Stress seems to do one of two things to Librans. It gets them to either take control of a situation through action or to become too afraid to make a decision. In traditional astrology the key phrase for Libra is "I balance." The balancing of the mental-emotional scales is a driving force in the life of Librans.

Librans seek peaceful solutions to problems. Knowing how to compromise is a birthright of this sign, but make no mistake about it, Librans can argue for a cause or opinion. They maker great lawyers and arbitrators.

A shadow of Libra is indecision. Another can be an extreme desire to please others. When Librans overcome these tendencies, life flows more freely and is full of greater spontaneity. Indecision is actually due to the talent of being able to perceive more than one side of an issue. Librans make great mediators. They can settle disputes between people with their way of making each party feel equally right. Neither is constrained by the confines of the other's discounting perceptions.

Aesthetic talent can be strong in this sign. The soul of Libra holds a passionate appreciation for art and music. The muse consciousness of Venus is as equally prevalent in Libra as it is in the other sign it rules, Taurus. In Venus-ruled signs, personal style is highlighted. If clothes could speak, they would sing the praises of these people.

Relationship Tendencies

In relationships, Librans maintain a socially active lifestyle. They will expect you to accept their peers and friends whether you like them or not. Librans are attracted to people who will be soul mates, partners in the truest sense of the word. Sometimes Librans expect lovers to be a mirror that will reflect and clarify their own identity. Librans are attracted to individuals who contribute to their own need to stay mentally objective about life. Passion and sensuality are important to Librans. Hidden behind this is a need to avoid getting too lost in the identity of a lover. When Librans feel another person is not taking away from their own identity, a relationship has a greater chance of success. The attributes of Libra are a sincere desire to create an atmosphere of harmony and an innate capacity to appreciate beauty in all its forms.

The Libra Woman

She can be exotic without really trying (though you will never convince her of that). Venus blesses each of the signs she rules with natural beauty. (Taurus is also ruled by Venus.) The Libra woman has a delicate nervous system. Don't force her to make decisions too quickly. She will become angry or stubborn if you are too pushy.

She is an expert social planner. She must be allowed to be on the go. Don't be jealous because she has male friends. Men love her. She will love you for trusting her to be herself. The Libra woman wants you to like her friends or at least accept them. She can make your own peers feel welcome. There is nobody as adept at entertaining your business associates; she will go out of her way to make each of them feel special.

Create a romantic atmosphere for her. She loves this. Give her flowers or gifts. Why? Because they make you her hero. She needs a hero. Let her be a heroine if she wants to be.

She is sometimes hard to figure out. Contrary to popular belief, she is not always sociable. Quiet time recharges her vitality. She can tire like a kitten or puppy that has been running wildly and suddenly stops to take a nap. She can arise just as fast to put her social agenda back into motion.

The Libra woman needs to hear that you appreciate her on a regular basis. Do this! It will keep you close. Don't become a hermit. If you do, you had better let her go and come as she pleases. The gods have granted the Libra woman extroverted instincts. She must share herself with the world. She is not as showy as Leo in getting attention. She doesn't need to take center stage, yet she is never far from the center of social awareness. People often look to her to make them feel better. When she is not in your presence, know that she is probably busy handling her social obligations whether it is having lunch with a friend or helping to plan a party.

The Libra woman knows what's going on in her sphere of influence. She is often active in organizations. Groups like her effervescent energy. She is graceful and energetic all at once. You will always share her with the world at large. Get used to it!

The Libra Man

He usually knows what he wants from life even if it takes a while to clarify decisions. Male and female Librans have it tough when it comes to making up their minds. Choices don't come easy. It's that knack for seeing more than one angle to a situation that makes decisions challenging. But there are times when this sign is powerfully decisive. Read this previous sentence again and remember it! When he really selects someone as a partner, he means it wholeheartedly. Work is another arena where the Libra man can be quite decisive. He really does not care for indecision in his work. It makes him feel uneasy. He often counts on his partner or close friends to give him feedback about his life strategies.

The Libra man often possesses a polished voice. Companies would love him to advertise their products on television or radio. He is convincing and genuinely likable. Why not believe him? His vocal cords are an important part of his marketing ability. He knows just the right resonance for any social situation.

Lovers find him charming. He is easy to talk to. Women can let their hair down in his presence. He has a grasp of all of life's polar opposites, so why shouldn't he understand women? The Libra man is easier to get to know if you go to his favorite places to socialize. Communication is like a ritual, and it needs atmosphere. A special meeting place can enhance your time together.

He will let you know if he disagrees with your opinions. He can argue ferociously if you tamper with his pet areas of expertise. He will just as quickly make peace if you simply acknowledge his perceptions and beliefs. In his heart he likes to please those he loves. Holding a grudge too long bothers his conscience. The Libra man will be there for you when you need his support. You must first let him satisfy all of his social passions. His attention can make you feel special. He will not make a commitment to you until he is good and ready to do so. Maybe it's because he doesn't want to make an embarrassing mistake, or it could be because he doesn't want to hurt your feelings if he decides this is not the right relationship. Then again, it may be he fears rejection, or it might be because he can't make up his mind! If you want to be with this person and he decides you are for him, then be ready to have an exhilarating ride together. Delight in introducing one another to your own special worlds.

Scorpio (October 23–November 21)

The Scorpion, Eagle, or Serpent

Element: Water
Ruling Planet: Pluto

When many of us hear the word "scorpion," we feel a little spooked or nervous as we might with snakes and spiders. Scorpio is probably the most misunderstood of the twelve signs. Sexy, promiscuous—these are labels often erroneously and carelessly assigned to this psychologically deep water sign. Although some of them might engage in secret love affairs, this is not a predominant trait of Scorpio. Their profound loyalty and positive bonding instincts are too often ignored.

A shadow of Scorpio is an unclear understanding of personal power—either assuming too little or compulsively wanting to overpower others. Another is manipulation. Transcending these shadows adds strength and charisma to those of this sign and can take them far in life.

It's hard to react with apathy toward the Scorpion. People are inexplicably attracted to the aura of mystery that surrounds this sign. We can be lovingly drawn to or repulsed by these emotionally intense individuals.

From an early age, Scorpios have a peculiar fascination with society's taboos. Topics often discussed in hushed tones pervade their thoughts. They can talk about sex and death quite openly. The ones who refuse to do so still have broad inner awareness of these matters. Even when they feign ignorance about one of these subjects (often due to being too embarrassed to discuss it), the look on their face betrays their understanding.

Scorpios tend to be somewhat reluctant to trust others, but when they do, it can be for life. It is difficult to break bonds established with them. They have an uncanny knack for regenerating a relationship even when it seems a crisis has signaled its demise. It's appropriate to mention here that another creature associated with Scorpio is the phoenix, a mythical bird that mysteriously rises from its own funeral pyre. So, this is something you can look forward to—as long as you aren't contending with a zombie!

We feel the sting of the Scorpion's tail when it is forced to make decisions against its will. Scorpios cannot be cajoled or otherwise manipulated. They master the art of negotiation as children. Parents often subconsciously consent to being manipulated by a Scorpio child's smile. Their hypnotic prowess, bolstered by staunch willpower, endures into adulthood and is unrivaled. Leo's willpower is easy to read; it comes straight at you like a charging Lion. The Scorpion appears to be fending us off with its claws yet dares us to engage in a long battle to stop it from doing whatever it wants. Scorpios have incredible patience (often lacking in fiery Leo). This sign will wait until you tire of resisting them.

Relationship Tendencies

In relationships, Scorpios are emotionally intense partners. Their intensity can be hidden deeply, but it surfaces in subtle ways. When those volatile, unconscious forces seem to be coming at you, run for cover. Summon some courage and let the Scorpion vent its venomous anger. That is part of Scorpio's unique process of gaining mental-emotional clarity. After they are through with their repulsive ritual, they are ready to carry on a civil conversation. Too many of us can be scared off by the thunder and lightning that precede the calm; these are primordial forces that date back to our first Scorpion ancestors. When Scorpios can forgive, and allow others to forgive them, they are wonderful to be with in a relationship. They are attracted to people with business savvy, and to those who are not prone to be frightened off by their passionate outbursts. The attributes of Scorpio are the capacity to turn negative circumstances into strengths, and a creative spirit born out of deep survival instincts. They are known for making the best lemonade from life's lemons.

The Scorpio Woman

Sexy. Reliable. Temperamental. Introspective. Compulsive. Which describes her best? All of the above can be right on the money! She has no desire to be predictable, yet she wants to be perceived accurately. She yearns for your understanding. Her moods are more stormy than even moody Cancer's! It's just that her outbursts are less frequent. Scorpion moods build over time like clouds borne by a slow wind that gradually darken the sky before a great downpour.

Moods are self-survival states of the Scorpio woman. She expects you to recognize and accept this. Don't interfere with this process unless she solicits your intervention. The hard part is that she wants you to figure this out for yourself. Remember, she is a water sign. These aquatic creatures have a nasty habit of muddying the waters so you can't see clearly into their depths.

She loves sex, but more important is what precedes the act: intimacy! It is not easy for the Scorpio woman to get close to others. She can be surrounded by people, yet only one or two of them really are privileged to know her. She usually prefers it this way. Her secrets are the essence of her power. You must earn her trust. Any attempt to overpower her is at your own peril. She will let you know if and when it is okay to gain any advantage. Another tricky quirk is that she expects you to compete with her. Competition is playful to her. It means she's the object of your attention, and it makes her feel important.

A love-hate relationship with a Scorpio woman is common. This is a passionate woman—make no mistake about it. Her anger may be conveyed by a cold quiet glance that cuts through you. Her hypnotic Scorpion eyes can cause you to become addicted to her. Watch out. She'll use that mesmerizing stare to make you do her bidding if you're not careful (but it can feel wonderful when she looks upon you favorably). Her penetrating x-ray vision can make you feel vulnerable to the core. Without her warmth, you're the loneliest person in the world—like a solitary soul aimlessly riding a city bus on a Saturday night. You need to wait for an invitation from the female Scorpio to share your life with her. Then, when you're "in," she is possessive of you. In turn, you will probably become possessive of her. The thread of an obsessive-compulsive behavior pattern weaves through her relationships. It's all part and parcel of the intense merging of souls that takes place in her partnerships. The sharing of power, wealth, pain, and, most importantly, love, make her a fascinating companion.

She'll take you on a joy ride to be remembered, one that's so exciting you won't want it to end. By way of Glory Boulevard, she'll show you around Heavenly Heights. Then you might swing by Fright Freeway and Terror Alley. Of course, you'll frequent some of her favorite spots: Cozy Cove and Ecstasy Lane. You won't find these places on any map because they're extremely private.

The Scorpio Man

He is the image of cool, quiet confidence. The key word emphasized here is "cool." The Scorpio man needs no introduction. People have already taken notice of him at social gatherings, or so he's given to believe. He often assumes this, not so much out of arrogance but from past experience. Charisma colors his personality. He is a great negotiator, and management positions often afford him the opportunity to display his ability to deal with crises. He doesn't really like stress but thrives on it. He can be a faithful partner. A common lament of the Scorpio male's mate is "If only he would talk more about his feelings." He will fight to protect you against danger and wants to be worthy of your trust. The Scorpio man needs this badly, especially when he doesn't trust himself.

He doesn't worship money in itself but loves what it can buy and, of course, the status it brings. Let him impress you with his gifts. He likes you to wear the jewelry and clothing he buys for you. Similarly, he will proudly show off what you give him. Money is often a key issue in relationships, and he is likely to be secretive about his finances. The more trusted you are, the more truthful about his finances he will become.

You will feel manipulated at times—count on it! Even when you call the Scorpio man to task about this, you will probably be cajoled into believing it's not happening. He is the artful negotiator. Stand up to him because he really needs someone who can. The mental exercises he puts you through will make you stronger, but you can't afford to let him diminish your power. He will make a big deal about loving you and yet may conceal why he loves you. This is the mystery of the male Scorpio. You must penetrate his guarded fortress. It is an inner maze much like the mythological netherworld of Pluto, Scorpio's ruling planet. The Scorpio man instinctively buries his emotions in his own sacrosanct inner world. He is waiting for a brave, trustworthy soul to explore his hidden dimensions. The interesting thing is he can be quite aware of how his feelings might impact those around him. He is impressed by those willing to discover and feel comfortable with them.

He is fully capable of forming a deep bond. This seems to come easier when he has achieved some level of self-mastery in his life. Self-mastery may be found by overcoming his emotions but is more often related to career success. He may be driven toward acquiring wealth, so he may seek a partner able to handle her own financial needs.

If you choose to be with a male Scorpio, you will be enthralled by the best in him and may feel either compassion or anger toward his shortcomings. This is a sign that can truly forgive and will at times look for your forgiveness. Your relationship will probably go through an exciting (and trying) rebirth or two.

Sagittarius (November 22-December 21)

The Archer

Element: Fire
Ruling Planet: Jupiter

An answer for the game show *Jeopardy* could be, "The sign of the zodiac known for being the traveler, gypsy, optimist, clown, and benefactor." The question is, "What is Sagittarius?" This fire sign walks a path of adventurous passion. The road to reaching a goal is usually more exciting to the footloose Archer than the destination itself. Sagittarians love to shoot quivers of arrows at a myriad of targets. This is a very eclectic and endearing sign unless taken over by dogmatism and self-serving versions of the truth.

Sagittarians' thirst for knowledge is insatiable. The key phrase for this sign in traditional astrology is "I understand." The Archer is on a never-ending quest for learning. They excel as teachers and consultants. I must confess that my own Sun sign is Sagittarius. Archers can have trouble with commitments that fall short of their expectations. Archers like to know how to back out of the woods of an agreement in case they decide to sprint in the midst of signing on the dotted line! Sagittarius will fight to defend its principles. Honesty means a lot to the Archer.

A shadow of Sagittarius is being too judgmental. Another is a rampantly expansive nature that can lead to wandering in circles. Sagittarius can expect too much from life. Its ruling planet, Jupiter, is the largest and weighs more than twice as much as all the other planets put together! Is it any wonder that this sign is known to exaggerate its potential? Sagittarians may think they are larger than life. That is a great mistake. When

Sagittarians begin to overcome these shadow tendencies, others begin to see them as more desirable mates. Dogmatism and judgmental behavior are really contrary to the Archer's natural open-mindedness. A willingness to agree to disagree brings greater tolerance to the Sagittarian mind. This fair-minded sign appreciates an inclination to live according to one's beliefs.

Relationship Tendencies

In relationships, Sagittarians are fun-loving mates. More serious, down-to-earth pragmatists can't really appreciate the Archer's free spiritedness. Make no mistake—the Archer can be intense when their concentration on accomplishments comes into clear focus. They may even leave a person behind as they pursue a job or relationship in another city, state, or country. They can be extremely motivated to put their values into practice. This is not to say there are times when the Archer doesn't practice what he or she preaches. Sagittarians court trouble when they promise more than they can deliver. The Archer is attracted to people who enjoy the chase and who love (or pretend to love) listening to them talk! Travel with the Archer and you will be regarded as a wonderful person. The attributes of the Archer are the ability to adapt to new situations and a positive attitude.

The Sagittarius Woman

You may prefer her to be a twentieth-century fox or a nineteenth-century peasant; you make the call. She's good at transforming herself. The Sagittarius woman is without a doubt one of the most independent individuals walking the earth. Don't expect her to ask you for permission before pursuing a new life direction when the spirit moves her (a frequent occurrence). Her social life thrives on spontaneous gusto. Her "let's live for today" attitude can mask a more serious side that's concerned with the possibilities of her future.

Although she loves to talk, she can also be an attentive listener. She's interested in so many things, including what's going on in your head. Tell her what you're thinking, and she will follow you anywhere. If you wander from the truth, however, she'll call your bluff. What she hates above anything else is to be lied to. She feels embarrassed if you catch her in a small white lie. She's not especially prone to this, however, since she is as candid as they come. She's used to telling it like it is.

Don't blame her for being late for dinner. A friend would not let her leave, or a sudden opportunity came up. Let her off the hook. She isn't going to change that much anyway. Besides, her innocent smile is more beguiling than her guilty countenance.

She will be your best friend and most passionate lover. Let her express her creative drives, and you will be allowed to venture into the depths of her soul. She may be self-centered, but she still knows how to make you feel special. It is one of her ways of giving—something she loves to do. Any sudden, demanding outbursts evaporate quickly. She wants to know that you won't be too bothered if she leans on you. Just as suddenly, her free spirit could either excite you or break your heart. You probably yearn for her to need you more than she does. Relax. Enjoy this high-spirited woman.

As a child, she could not wait to impress those who loved her by learning to walk. She is no different now. Respect her choices, and you are her champion. Take her self-doubts seriously, and she will help to heal your inner wounds and insecurities. She is a natural-born advisor. She knows the world loves and needs her for this. Don't doubt her version of the truth; share your own with her. You can argue and disagree. It doesn't matter, for in the end she will win. You may love her. You may want to leave her when she is not paying attention to you. Why do you remain? Because there are few like her who will take this much time to understand you.

The Sagittarius Man

He is talkative. His words reveal his love of talking about himself and everything he knows. Expect to hear about his travels to other cities and countries. A Sagittarius man is likely to experiment with various lifestyles. He brings this rich cultural background to his relationships. You might get the feeling that he is really from a wide variety of locations. At heart, he is a world citizen. It is probable that he will expect you to pack your bags on a whim—to follow him on a new adventure.

His loyalty to you is a short-term agreement (that's not to say he won't keep reviewing it). It is subject to change if his restlessness prompts him to explore greener pastures. He is honest more often than not. The Archer is fully capable of making a sincere commitment. Just don't keep reminding him about it! Let him live for the moment or day. Freedom and spontaneity are what drive this fireball.

You are unlikely to be bored with this adventurer. If he grows too attached to one lifestyle or belief system, however, he is not as much fun. He gets old before his time if everything around him remains status quo. Entice him to broaden his horizons. It is in his soul to do so. He subconsciously yearns to be deprogrammed from extreme devotion to one truth. You must learn to complement his philosophical outlook (changeable as it may be) with one of your own. He views life through an abstract lens (usually rose-colored) and sees the world as a huge playground. He looks for playmates. He can suddenly surprise you with a more sober side that is ready to take steady aim. He is a serendipitous planner. You will often be expected to do the real planning. He doesn't tell you this until the last second! Don't be too alarmed if you're all packed to go halfway round the world for a month, and you find out he didn't get any tickets. He might say as you're walking out the door, "Don't worry. We'll pick them up at the airport." His optimism can get out of hand.

He can inspire you to climb to new creative heights. You won't get a more positive force to cheer you on. He really can show you how to chase away your blues. Communication is his forte. He can obliterate obstacles in his and your way with the clever wiles of his positive thinking. His cockeyed optimism gets him into trouble at times. Lady luck comes through when he really has no right to be in her good graces. His incredible good fortune allows him to get away with more than most of us. We love and hate this about him. He is a great romantic. When you're groovin' to his unique way of celebrating life, you just have to forgive his foolishness. If you truly love your Sagittarian soul mate, he can do no wrong.

Capricorn (December 22-January 19)

The Goat

Element: Earth
Ruling Planet: Saturn

Serious, ambitious, cautious—get the picture? Capricorns are, part and parcel, all business first, but make no mistake about it they can play hard too! This is a sign that enjoys being in control. The Goat relaxes when life follows a preconceived plan. "Form follows function" makes a great Capricorn mantra for meditation. It is a pragmatic sign. In many cases, the Capricorn mind has mastered the art of political correctness.

Astronomers say that Saturn, the ruling planet of Capricorn, would be light enough to float on the ocean if it fell to Earth. Capricorns will never believe this. Levity does not come easily to this rock-hard, reality-based sign. The Goat is a "see-it-to-believe-it" sign all the way.

The key phrase for this sign in traditional astrology is "I use." Capricorns like to use their knowledge in practical ways. They often make great supervisors because they thrive on responsibility. Their sure-footed, down-to-earth modus operandi lacks spontaneity. Sometimes their fears do get in the way of progress. The Goat is embarrassed as all get out to fail at anything. From birth, Capricorns seem to march to their own anthem: "Don't bother doing a job if you can't do it with excellence."

A shadow of Capricorn is rigidity or recalcitrance. Another is bossiness. This is a sign that does not always compromise even when it would be in their own best interest to do so. Flow is a word that does not fit easily into the Capricorn vocabulary.

Caution surrounds Capricorn like the rings that encircle Saturn. "Nothing flows without a push" is more in keeping with Capricorn's philosophy. This can be a generous, yielding sign, but a person really needs to hold their ground when negotiating with Capricorn. The Goat knows the bottom line on just about any deal long before it actually begins, and they can detect any craftiness at the outset. So don't even think about it.

Career is usually a big part of life for Capricorns. Their perseverance to succeed is strong. These people don't give up easily. One of the Goat's greatest challenges is to rise above the rocky road of depression. Whether Capricorns will admit it or not, their self-expectations are high. This sign can project expectations and achieve success through others. They are perfectly content to lead a vicarious existence.

The higher Capricorns climb to reach a goal, the greater the risk of a fall. This is a life dilemma. Why? Capricorns become restless if not taking creative risks, yet they are terrified about not attaining success. The happiest Capricorns seem to find a way not to take life so seriously, especially as they mature.

Relationship Tendencies

In relationships, Capricorns are fairly predictable mates. They are either hungry for a commitment or ready to sprint away at the mere mention of deep involvement. This innate tendency is always with them. Contrary to popular belief, Capricorns can laugh with the best of them in social situations. This is probably a way of releasing stress. Those of this sign like to deal realistically with problems—unless they are too scared to bring them out in open discussion. Relationships go better for Capricorns when they have equal control in joint issues. Sharing leadership roles with them is wise. This sign is like a fish out of water if expected to always follow. It just doesn't work. Capricorns are won over by respecting their decisions. This sign must develop a sound strategy before proceeding toward a goal. When they are able to accept a commitment, Capricorns can be great partners. Take heart, though, if you haven't yet been approved as a family member because Capricorns can lighten up over time. Don't rush a relationship with the Goat. The going gets too rough for Capricorns if things move too fast. However, when Capricorns are ready to take that serious leap of faith, their chosen mate is expected to hop to it with them! Capricorns are attracted to people who realize that life can be a rocky road, so commiserate at every opportunity to earn your Brownie points. If you are too idealistic, you may not be trusted right away. The Goat loves those who are ambitious and agree that delayed gratification is okay. The attributes of Capricorn are discipline and an incredible ability to focus.

The Capricorn Woman

She can be a great lover and pillar of strength rolled into one person. She is capable of deep commitment. Her desire for shaping a relationship to conform to her standards is usually important to her. The female Capricorn is not afraid of responsibility. She needs to be careful not to spoil the rest of us to the point that we depend on her too much. She takes the lead easily in relationships. Her fears about life are often justified. She has clear forward vision. She is well versed in practical experience. Her wisdom is based on real hard copy—not light fiction.

People think Capricorns are always dead serious. Not true! The Goat likes to laugh. It is a great relief to find a moment to see the humor in life.

The female Capricorn will not allow herself to waste time. She does not appreciate partners who can't manage time efficiently. Work with her and she will grow to love you passionately. You must be reliable in the true sense of the word to get her to even like you. The flighty and the flaky get thumbs down from her.

Trust doesn't come easily for the Goat. In her book, you are guilty until proven innocent. She is often a firm believer that time will tell just how sincere a person is in a relationship. She believes in stable, enduring relationships. She is as intrepid as they come when she commits to someone. Don't expect her to scare away at the first sign of trouble. If she is pulling away from you too much of the time, don't pressure her. Let her be in control; she prefers this.

The Capricorn woman likes to feel successful. It doesn't matter if it is in work or love. She fears rejection as much as the male version of this sign. Make her feel important. Ask her what she needs to make her feel this way. Tell her what does the same for you. You are not dealing with an ordinary Goat! She has great endurance, which enables her to travel long and far to reach her ambitions and maintain her leadership role. The Capricorn woman is willing to admit her shortcomings and expects you to be open too. She hates to be embarrassed. Status can be important to anyone born under this sign. She merely asks that you help elevate her to the same level that you want for yourself. Why? Because she does this instinctively for those she loves.

The Capricorn Man

He has a serious expression most of the time. His forehead often wrinkles early in life, the mark of a conscientious worker. The Capricorn man is a beast of burden. He might possibly take a break during the workday, albeit reluctantly. He treats everything like it is business—yes, even relationships! He is time oriented.

Watches were invented for him (or so he thinks!). He is lost without structure. He's the master planner in action, focused from head to toe.

People can find him rigid in relationships. He functions in predictable patterns. Perhaps his greatest fault is not being able to admit when he is wrong. If he has slighted you, he will be nice to you again but will usually not come right out and say he made a mistake. Consider yourself fortunate if you are in a relationship with a Capricorn man willing to admit to his transgressions against you. He was probably taught at an early age by his parents and other authority figures to shoulder responsibility. You will need to watch that he doesn't try to take over your life. Although he would love to do so, he'll rue any such attempts if you have any leanings at all toward being a free-spirited individual.

His personal fears can put a damper on enjoying relationships. His approach to intimacy can seem devoid of feelings or lack spontaneity. When he loosens up, he can be fun-loving and make you feel special. The thought of failure terrifies the male Capricorn. "What will others think?" echoes through his mind. When he sees that a relationship with someone is steadily developing, he is a much more self-assured person.

This is the most strategy-oriented sign of them all. The Goat possesses a sharp mentality. He cannot relax and float easily in life until he slowly gets his toes wet. Act like you can live without him, and he comes running. Act like you need him and he might stop and ask why. "What is your motive?" he'll ask while peering at you through squinted eyes. He is wise beyond his years. In fact, when the occasion calls for it, he can assume the role of "wise guy." Sometimes he's too reserved or cautious, but he can learn to talk. He believes in tradition and wants you to share this philosophy. The male Capricorn is a testimonial to determination. His patience can win your heart. His coldness can break it. Either way, you can't help but love the fact that he has great, strong shoulders to lean on.

Aquarius (January 20-February 18)

The Water Bearer

Element: Air
Ruling Planet: Uranus

Aquarius is an individualistic sign. It is ruled by Uranus, the only planet that is tilted on its side, creating a unique orbiting cycle! Those born under the sign of Aquarius are just as unique as their wayward ruler. The Water Bearer's mental realm is truly inventive territory. This sign is sometimes mistakenly classified as a water sign. The water element is far too emotional for Aquarians. It has been said that the Water Bearer pours electricity rather than water. Electricity better describes the mental climate of this fast-thinking air sign, which can be as hair-raising as bolts of lightning.

The key phrase for Aquarius in traditional astrology is "I know." This sign is a master of the art of knowing. Tuning in to progressive trends quickly turns on Aquarian minds. This future-oriented sign can easily become impatient with the present state of affairs. Intellectual restlessness comes early in life. They are likely to rebel against institutions or people they can't influence to change. Could there have been any actor more appropriate than Aquarian James Dean to portray the rebellious youth in the film *Rebel Without a Cause*?

One shadow of Aquarius is aloofness. Another is rebelling for no good reason. They can be downright ornery! Overcoming these tendencies makes life less erratic and more fulfilling. There is nothing wrong with the mental objectivity that comes standard with this sign. The Water Bearer begins to wear on a person's nerves if he or she constantly holds others at a comfortable mental distance. Aquarians can hide any sensitivity behind the pillar of polished intellect. Emotions can seem a waste of time to them. It is better to find some middle ground between the mental and emotional worlds even if they never meet. Rebels can act on behalf of positive causes. These are the people who often question laws and authority that have outlived their usefulness to society. Aquarians are not always revolutionaries. This sign can be a sentimental reactionary with a fondness for the good old days. You will find some people of this sign reluctant to move ahead. They may not trust change.

Relationship Tendencies

In relationships, Aquarians are exciting mates. They love to surprise others as well as to be surprised. People may not always like the sudden changes on which some Aquarians thrive. They jump quickly from one experience to another. Their erratic tendencies can be confusing. They may stop abruptly to focus on a subject of interest. Then suddenly, without warning, the Water Bearer is ready to mosey down the road. Equality is next to godliness for these people. Experimentation can color their thinking about relationships. This is a sign that is easily bored, so it would be wise to keep these people guessing. Aquarians don't appreciate predictable people. Embrace their eccentricity and you may have a friend and lover for life. Aquarians are attracted to other unconventional and trendsetting individuals. The attributes of Aquarius are mental ingenuity and an insightful way of perceiving life.

The Aquarius Female

She has a courageous, devil-may-care attitude. Her fiercely independent spirit excites those adventurous enough to keep up with her. Intellectually, the female Aquarius can be full of surprises. Emotionally, she can be perceived as cold or distant. It is when she is pondering her future that people might get the feeling there's "nobody home." Actually, her mind is wandering to new vistas.

Don't limit her options. She is inspired by the hope of tomorrow. Today moves too slowly for many Aquarians. Her individuality and need for freedom should never be underestimated; they are awe-inspiring!

A lover tends to be attracted to her unpredictable nature. She is not for those who gravitate toward stability because she seldom functions in that mode. Her Aquarian genes are not programmed to be politically correct. She can be conventional when required, but she's more passionate about the unconventional.

She is quick to size up a situation. She may impulsively jump to false conclusions. If she's "done you wrong," let her get around to saying she is sorry in her own good time! The female Aquarius can forgive and forget, but she will rebel if you try to control her decisions. Her power is in her autonomy. Cut this off and you have taken her soul.

The Aquarius woman loves to surprise you. Her gifts can be unforgettable. Her icy stare is equally unforgettable; it can chill you to the bone when she is angry. Primordial memory tells her she has the right to be mad. She is impatient with obstacles. Rules were made to be broken unless they fit in with her free thinking. She can adjust to accommodate the needs of another person; just don't ask her to go too far.

The Aquarius woman naturally loves to experiment. She is blessed with an intellect that loves to think about a future filled with exciting changes. Time can pass too slowly for Aquarius. She loves relationships with people that can lift her mind beyond the limits of ordinary time and space. If you enjoy a person who doesn't like living two days in a row the same way, perhaps an Aquarius lover is the answer!

The Aquarius Man

He hates to be classified by any label. The Aquarius man can view the mind as an ancient icon to which he feels loyalty or as a seemingly futuristic symbol. He loves surprises about as much as the Aquarius woman. However, he is far less emotional than his female counterpart. Emotions lie comfortably distanced from his logic. There is no other sign that can look at life with such a detached gaze! The nervous system of the Aquarius man (and woman) is delicate. It's as though any emotional attachment will cause him to lose control over his life.

Individuality. Freedom. Yes, these words ring true for Aquarius. He can make you feel valued. His insights into your mind can make you feel understood. On the other hand, his criticism can make you doubt yourself. Then again, he can just as quickly build you back up again before you know what happened.

He has a love-hate relationship with the future. The inventor in him longs for the future, yet he can secretly fear that the future will tear away at the reality he so passionately has built to sustain himself. He inwardly feels a compulsive drive to keep proving himself in love and career. The strength of his convictions impresses others. He will fight to preserve your emotional happiness. It sounds like a contradiction to what was previously said regarding the Aquarius man's manipulative use of emotions, but it is true. Perhaps it is the need of the male Aquarius to find people who will emote for him. He doesn't like to appear vulnerable even when he admits to any weakness. Life can humble Aquarius to the point of making him vulnerable, but it takes a tornado-like crisis to open up his emotions.

His insight can benefit an employer or a lover. He loves to communicate. The Water Bearer can allow you to be yourself. He prefers that you are strong enough to be the individualist he believes he sees in you. When he communicates from the heart, you have to love him. He can be brutally honest. His logic has a raw, skin-and-bones rationality. His mind is as fast and vast as a computer. You will tire of his extreme intellectualization of life, yet you can't help but admire him as a friend. He values friendship. He wants you to like his peers. You will have little trouble getting him to accept the fact that you also need the companionship of others in your life.

What about his sense of humor? It's refreshing! It is probably dry and to the point and fascinatingly honest! He challenges life head-on and dares it to stop him from moving forward. He knows how to win your love. He hopes you will never tire of letting him do so. Living his life on his own terms exclusively can irritate you. Tell him where you need him to meet you halfway, and he will do so if he truly wants to stay in your good graces. He doesn't fear commitment as much as the intimacy attached to it. When he accepts responsibility, it is a serious matter for him. Although he longs to be close to you, he needs to maintain his sense of individuality. Maybe it's his gentle smile or eyes that speak from a frank knowledge that captures your heart.

Pisces (February 19-March 20)

The Fish

Element: Water
Ruling Planet: Neptune

Dreamy. Imaginative. Hypersensitive. These few words best capture the essence of this intuitive sign. Life does not really progress in linear time for Pisces as it does for the rest of us. Have you ever noticed how often Pisceans, especially in leadership positions, need an aide to keep them organized? Pisceans' sense of order extends beyond three-dimensional reality. Even if only an illusion, their life appears to follow a normal routine, and, believe me, it can be an illusion! Their inner landscapes are colored by the dreamy mists of their sign's ruler, Neptune.

Aesthetic impulses are ever present in Pisceans' mental landscape. The Fish will swim through turbulent waters to follow the promise of their creative consciousness. Pet causes can cause the Fish to forget food and drink. They are on a never-ending quest for ideals to inspire their goals. Pisceans can be deeply devoted to those they love and are known for idealizing the object of their affection. However, a passion for a cause or dream can strike Pisceans with short-term memory loss. Pisceans are pros at performing the disappearing act, but when in relationships Pisceans instinctively know how to please. Pisceans tend to put their mates "on a pedestal" and delight in fulfilling their every whim, provided they have not "gone out to lunch" or "gone fishing."

A shadow of Pisces is denial. Another is guilt. When Pisceans can overcome these tendencies, life is truly a more wonderful experience. No other sign is as good at denying what is really happening in any given situation. They need to conjure up their elusive courage to cross the fearful muddied waters to where they can see clearly. Guilt is forever coursing through Pisceans' conscience. A trickle of guilt doesn't hurt, but when waves of it keep pounding away, the Piscean mind becomes waterlogged. Everything becomes distorted in the deluge. Pisceans must find a way to get beyond this self-defeating stream of thought.

Relationship Tendencies

In relationships, Pisceans may be hard to understand because they function predominantly on the inner plane. This is a sign that relies greatly on intuition. The Fish may assume others are on the same page when, in fact, they may be reading another book entirely. Seeing others through rose colored glasses can make for some difficult relationships. Communication can really help them to see clearly enough to deal with your reality. Pisceans would much more prefer to observe than to deal openly with others. They are adept at being caring and compassionate. Commitments can be solid if they do not feel totally absorbed by others. Their ideals are lofty. Expectations of self and their mates are sky high! Often there is a murky divine discontent that runs deep through the soul of Pisceans where nothing in life can seem to match their perfect ideals. When Pisceans recognize that balance is important, they are easy to live with. Sound reality testing is a great teacher for Pisceans in relationships.

Pisceans can be attracted to intuitive people who are not afraid to live up to their highest values. Some Pisceans are attracted to practical individuals because they help to balance and ground their own emotional nature. Finding a partner in life can be perceived as a mission. The search for a soul mate might even be a driving force. The attributes of Pisces are faith and a sincere desire to put their intuitive vision to work in the world.

The Pisces Woman

She is hypersensitive. Her tears can well up in an instant. The Pisces woman is a true romantic. She is likely to first meet a lover under mysterious circumstances because this kind of fantasy-based reality makes sense to her. Her logic may seem less than clear because of the way she approaches conclusions. She can talk in perfectly symmetrical circles and spiral in to the point without getting the least bit dizzy. So, if you're at all prone to vertigo, hold on tight! She can believe in you like no other. When she loves you, it is because you fit into her vision of what love is supposed to be. You are better off if she doesn't expect you to save her. In fact, you can't! The Fish is out of the water when she's hooked on someone else to rely on. She is at her best swimming in the ocean of her own independence. She then has access to a vast supply of resources to share with others.

You may be her soul mate. Don't worry if you are not. She will gladly create a life that transforms you into her soul mate anyway. It might be held together by whimsy and fantasy with an occasional lark for good measure. Go ahead and humor her. Take your throne next to her in that castle in the air. She will love you for it! The Pisces woman is intuitive with a capital I. That is her birthright. They say you can't teach talent. Well, you can't teach intuition either. She has a direct communication link with the muse consciousness. Her love of art, music, and dance will intrigue you. She may be a practitioner or simply an aficionado of the fine arts.

Don't criticize her too much, or she will swim away to calmer waters. Her elusiveness will sometimes frustrate you. You want her to be direct, but she speaks in symbolic terms.

There are pragmatic Pisceans. These particular reality-oriented Fish might channel their intuition into their work or volunteer projects. She needs a cause, whether it be work, family, or to promote an ideal. Let her interpret your dreams or read your palm. Listen to her insights into your life. She knows how to make you believe in yourself. Her passion is intoxicating. She's a natural as an actress and is capable of acting out many different roles. Her undercurrent of discontent with life may surface in the form of moodiness. Nothing on certain days will be perfect enough. Relax. It will pass. She needs to talk about this. It's her way of getting centered.

The Pisces Man

The Fish swims through life relying on his intuitive sonar. He doesn't always care if it's wrong. He has faith that he will get back on course. Life is supposed to flow smoothly for him. He can bear a setback better than most. His luck will change when the time is right. A lover can become frustrated with his "holier than thou" attitude about right and wrong, but he can accept your differences if he falls in love with you.

To a male Pisces, commitment is a matter of interpretation. If he is really grounded, you will find him interested in a well-defined relationship. If you are with a Fish that believes in vague commitments, then you could be in for a long, emotionally exhausting ride. There are some Fish that must always know they can wriggle out of a relationship. In all fairness, though, we should recognize many Pisces men who can make fine partners. Communication is a must. Don't assume his dreamy, innocent eyes can always see into your mind. Speak. Listen. Get the thoughts flowing between you. Make it a regular habit. Pisces men and women are great watchers of life. Some of them find it truly exhausting to talk. Why bother explaining themselves? They can envision their life as an open book for all to see. This is another of their fantasies. Pisces is a water sign. Hidden feelings constantly course through their lives.

You can look far and wide and not find someone with more compassion for your problems and worries. Your Pisces man can have faith in you that moves mountains. He expects you to do the same in return. His moods signal times when he is immersed in his deep think tank. He can make you feel guilty in an instant. It's that "mind speak" look he puts on to tell you that you should have known just the right thing to say or do. If you haven't seen that look yet, just wait for it to appear. Believe me, it will! It's part of his inborn repertoire.

Are you searching for a soul mate? He wants to fulfill this desire if you have it. He longs for a mate to embrace his values. You are hoping that he will relate to your own. He can be malleable when it comes to pleasing you. At his best, he is inspired to be creative and happy. At his worst, he engages in escapist ploys. He will tempt you to bail him out of inner confusion. Be patient. Eventually the Fish will swim out of that dark cave where he got disoriented. Share with him your aesthetic likes and dislikes. He loves to compare notes in this area. He has at least one key cause, his life refrain. It can be devotion to work, a sport, or a hobby.

He can make you feel that he cares deeply about you. You might spend some nights alone while he is with his newest cause. Don't worry. His homing instinct is strong. He will return to you. Don't let him get too used to depending on you. When you're in love with him, it's hard not to cuddle him and indulge his every whim. You will never get tired of his romantic imagination. If he decides to really trust you, expect to have an exhilarating adventure.

Part II

Let the Games Begin

This section describes the Sun-sign combinations and the games associated with them. The games that you play can change from relationship to relationship. The Sun signs involved in a relationship point to the potential for particular games to be played. Remember, there are no perfect relationships. A partnership takes regular nurturing to sustain it. Even the most passionate or seemingly fated relationships require the efforts of both partners. The games here are designed to help you to better understand your romantic relationships. Perhaps they will aid you in finding ways to communicate more clearly.

Rather than seeing the various plays and ploys of the games as negative aspects of your relationship, view them as guides to greater self-understanding. There is no attempt here to make light of the problems and obstacles that lovers face. This book does not take a Pollyanna approach to solving love's dilemmas. I believe that it is healthy to seriously regard the commitment necessary for a long and successful relationship. Why? Because it can teach us not to take our partners for granted. Every day needs to be perceived in the light of opportunities to create harmony with a lover rather than problems. In many instances it is by working through the difficulties together that a relationship is strengthened.

The games really are designed to clear a path toward stronger bonding rather than to create distance between two hearts. Look for the deeper message of the games. They can be converted into assets. Conquering your differences with a lover can yield great power for the relationship. Integrating your individual needs into a partnership is worth the time. Accepting the needs of a lover takes even more time.

Some pain comes with growth. You may experience frustration, tears, and fears. Oh, yes, let's not forget yelling! You can add your favorites to the list. A lover attracts you for a reason. Perhaps it is because you are looking for someone with whom you can passionately share your life. Maybe you seek companionship. There are a hundred other potential reasons. You have probably run the gamut of every feeling and emotion ever experienced to be with a romantic partner. Physical attraction is just the beginning. The relationship "matrix" that you possess is multifaceted. The games discussed in this section of the book can help break down this complexity. They can provide keys to doors that seem locked. Sometimes you just need to be offered an alternative way of altering a behavior.

I once heard an Indian guru say that human beings only think they live intimately. He said that, in reality, people are like the stars in the sky. They only appear to be close together to the naked eye. In actuality, trillions of miles separate these celestial bodies from one another. The guru explained that, like the stars, each individual's consciousness is distant from all others! We only seem to be living in close proximity on this planet. I don't know if I fully accept his theory, but sometimes it seems that two lovers need to cross a universe to truly communicate and understand what each one needs from the other to establish greater closeness.

Remember, these games can play an important role in figuring out how you mesh with a particular sign. They help to identify where your relationship might need bolstering. Read slowly. Think each game through. See if it applies to your relationship. Don't fault yourself or your partner if you regularly play a game mentioned in your Sun-sign combination section. Give yourself permission to accept the behavior. It doesn't mean you have to like this side of being together. Just acknowledge it exists (if it truly does). It is better to accept the fact that the two of you play the game. Why? Doing so improves your ability to deal with the behavior pattern. Each partner in a relationship serves as a mirror for the other. Each partner has unique lessons to learn. Astrology can be a wonderful lens to focus on how two people enable a game to be played. Again, please don't blame yourselves. It takes practice and great patience as well as a sincere willingness to change a pattern.

Is this a new relationship for you? If your answer is yes, the games can help you to steer clear of snares that can be waiting to trap you. It is my theory that life is in many ways a setup. Relationships with certain Sun-sign types will pull you not only into the games you are destined to play but, more importantly, the ones you are meant to understand. Again, don't simply look at the games as negative pitfalls. They are situations that are apt to arise due to the Sun-sign chemistry of a relationship. It is my belief that the following games are highly likely to occur in the Sun-sign combinations that are discussed. Don't panic. Laugh a little. Be angry if need be. Contemplate. Cry. Do whatever it takes. Just don't judge yourself or your lover too harshly. Be harder on the problem than on each other.

Remember this as well: when in doubt, you can always Communicate (note the capital C!) with one another. Communication can do wonders to smooth over relationship issues.

Aries-Aries: The Daredevils

Aries + Aries = Fire Sign Theater

Here we have an equation that predicts the arena of action. Your Aries-Aries relationship is one of continuous adventure. Warriors both, you make a dynamic duo. You have one of the most energetic combinations of the zodiac. Passion is forever pulsating between your fiery hearts. Both of you probably hit the ground running when you entered this relationship. You may wish that you had discovered each other years ago.

Hit and Run Game

The games played in your Aries-Aries relationship center around impatience and competition. Neither of these tendencies in their own right necessarily means that your relationship is destined to fail. Please note that each game is based on behaviors that are the norm of the two signs' combined chemistry.

The *Hit and Run* game describes the way the two of you as Aries lovers might sometimes start something as individuals or a couple but not finish it. When you do this to one another or even together, it can result in havoc. Your relationship needs focus. You must find enough in common to bond you together. The two of you can move so quickly through life that you really don't see each other. You need to take a good look at where each of you stands in the relationship. Keeping pace with one another is no easy task.

Each of you could recognize a tendency in the other to abandon the relationship too quickly. Patience is a testy challenge. Let's face it. Your sign is not in the *Guinness Book of World Records* for patience. Aries people have probably started (but only started) more projects than any of the other signs. Finishing projects is tough for you.

The two of you can learn how to make this relationship work. Each of you has to feel the freedom to be true to yourselves. This is an urgent need. There are genuine territorial necessities that could infringe on your partnership. A me-first attitude is at the core of this relationship. Aries people love attention, don't you? Seeking it can be a force that drives you in search of another lover if your partner does not honor your needs. The excitement of receiving attention from a new lover is a type of high. You must somehow be able to keep your connection alive and vital if you want your hearts and minds to stay together.

One-Upmanship Game

Aries individuals hate to lose or at least don't want to be reminded of it when they do. The *One-Upmanship* game results when competitive urges are out of balance. Each of you needs to be a good sport in this relationship regardless of whether you win or lose. Don't ridicule the other if your opinion just happens to be right. Letting each other win once in a while really helps. Taunting doesn't bring you closer together.

Be the competitors you were born to be. Neither of you can hold back your boldness. Why should you? Be assertive with one another. Be direct. Get to the point quickly. Try to be sensitive when it is least expected. Sensitivity can't be faked. Each of you can spot insincerity when it rears its ugly head. There is too much of the warrior in the two of you to make a display of sympathy. It hurts your pride for people to help you too much.

Two Aries joining forces is a tough combo to beat. Disaster results when one opposes the other. Compromise is not easy, but it is wise to resolve to find pleasurable harmony. You need to generate the camaraderie of teammates occasionally. Putting your dynamic energy together toward a common goal adds a touch of the miraculous to your alliance.

Angry Red Planet Game

Sorry, Aries, but I couldn't leave this section without including an anger game. Your sign is ruled by Mars, the angry red planet. Anger is a key Aries expression. It can be communicated by pouting or more dramatically. Do you know what I mean? The *Angry*

Red Planet game occurs when one or both of you does not face up to the anger you feel. When you suppress your anger, it turns inward, and you either hate yourself or explode when you can't contain your feelings anymore.

You need to deal with your anger. You can't be afraid that your Aries partner will be scared away if you are too direct. Maybe you or your lover was taught that anger is an inappropriate behavior. Nothing is further from the truth!

Anger is a raw emotion that surges through every molecule of your sign. An Aries-Aries relationship must allow for anger to be expressed. It empowers you and even spices up your sex life.

Hidden anger turns to resentment. You know what follows next, don't you? Communication stops and that eventually leads to emotional distance. Beating one another up with angry outbursts is not the answer. Your fiery spirits must learn to deal with this vital part of your combined natures. Anger for an Aries can be a cry for recognition. It can be a plea: "Please don't ignore me." It wasn't wimpish passivity that attracted you to one another, was it?

Strategies

What is the strategy to make your Aries-Aries combo a winning team in these games? More often than not it involves time... and then some more time. Time out is sometimes a good idea too. First, each needs to learn how to identify the behavior patterns of the other. Aries people often don't like to take the time to analyze their relationships. The Ram would rather act first and think later. Aries partners need to stop and really look at what is right and wrong about the relationship. When each sees that the other will stick around for the good and the bad, trust deepens. Instead of acting out the *Hit and Run* game, you begin to have a more honest interaction that is bolstered by real staying power. You grow comfortable with the idea that your relationship will endure.

Two Aries people can understand their similarities because they share the same Sun sign. Paying attention to the unique differences adds a deeper dimension to your mutual understanding. Always respond to your partner in ways that reflect you are listening with an open mind.

The *One-Upmanship* game can be converted into a more balanced sense of competition. Expecting two Rams to never compete with one another would be asking too much, so what you need to do is create win-win situations, and that comes with practice. The opportunities for making one another feel more successful are endless. Use them to strengthen your relationship to its fullest potential. Taking a first step requires some humility and even sacrifice. Keep in mind that by making the first attempt, you pave the way for your mate to follow suit.

The *Angry Red Planet* game requires that one of you be big enough to forgive the other. Angry outbursts are often symbolic of the inner frustration that Aries is especially prone to. A cooling-off period may be needed before you can talk more civilly. There is nothing inherently wrong with anger. It is not always used just to badger or induce fear in others. Remember this: anger can be a healthy release of pent-up feelings that are fully justified.

The Rainbow

If you are in an Aries-Aries relationship, you can find life together absolutely wonderful. You are both energetic lovers. Each of you can inspire the other to reach new heights of passion in many areas of your lives. Protecting one another should come naturally. Each of you might be a bit self-centered. So what? It is a natural Aries instinct.

An Aries man can make the Aries woman feel important. He perceives her to be his competitive match. He quickly sees that making war with this kindred spirit is far less enjoyable than making love. The Aries man is exceedingly attracted to the Aries woman. He senses the heat of passion when they are together. She radiates a need to act on impulse, and her presence ignites a desire to make the most of the moment. She seems to know how to get his attention. He finds it interesting that she can use anger to bring the spotlight back to her. The warrior likes the way this feisty woman can stand up to his ideas. He finds her strength compatible with his own. He would like to get to know her better. He hopes he has read her correctly and that she is ready to join him in a quest for new adventures.

The Aries woman can make her Aries lover feel like a knight errant. She senses the two can make a powerful pact to stay together no matter how great the crisis. The Aries woman senses this is a relationship that thrives on stress. Aries individuals need tension to test their strength. The saying "if you can't handle the heat, get out of the kitchen" is an Aries bromide. She is aware of their strong sexual attraction. She wonders if it might be easier to talk after sex. The Aries man seems to be proud of his body just as she is of her own. The Aries woman hopes this male warrior will enjoy blazing new trails with her. It's not that she wants to set the world on fire. She only wants to be with someone who possesses the same fiery drive to fulfill a heartfelt need for meaning.

You may both be conscious of your appearance. A male Ram is less likely to admit this. Neither of you may like to seem too vulnerable. An Aries woman can become quite emotional. Sometimes it takes a bout of anger to really get in touch with her feelings. The same probably can be said for the Aries man. If his emotions are triggered, he can get mad pronto! The male Ram loves physical activity. It is best to encourage him to lead an active life. Once he works off some of that Aries energy, he becomes less explosive and more tolerant of differences.

Reinforcing each other's identity promotes the longevity of the relationship. What is the formula that leads to compatibility? It's simple. Allow each other to lead in the areas in which you love to lead as individuals. This will take some of the edge off when you have to work together.

Among my close friends are an Aries couple. It is always interesting to watch the two communicate. With what seems like brutal honesty to outside observers, the conversation can be likened to a no-holds-barred contest. Whether conveying compliments or criticizing blows, their words are direct. It's amazing to see how matter of fact they are after a big blowout. Rams need a good sparring match once in a while. It can even be quite playful like puppies or cubs tussling with one another.

Aries-Taurus: The Doers

Aries + Taurus = Productive Action

This can be a lively combination that makes ambitious goals practical. Two lovers of these signs can focus their creative energies together like a powerful laser beam. These signs are quite different in nature. Aries loves to move swiftly and spontaneously while Taurus is deliberate and wants to assimilate life more slowly.

One Step Forward, Three Steps Back Game

The games in your Aries-Taurus relationship are played by clashing your wills and testing each other's limits. When the Ram and the Bull are at odds, they can move into the *One Step Forward, Three Steps Back* game. Aries loves to rush forward while Taurus prefers to hold back. It could be that Taurus wants to move forward and Aries purposely sabotages the advance. You can test each other's limits in getting your own way. A fever pitch of frustration results when the two of you move in conflicting directions. The Ram can go on an angry rampage while the Bull stands fast with headstrong determination. Both of you can be territorial. The Ram does this to preserve its identity and freedom. The Bull is concerned with its comfort and possessions—don't mess with them!

Tug of War Game

Aries is probably more successful than any other sign in provoking Taurus to act openly competitive and angry. The *Tug of War* game symbolizes the way each of you tries to pull for what you want. The Ram and the Bull can lock horns with a vengeance! There can be much love shared, but an underlying current of resistance is ever present. Aries wants its own way while Taurus might become possessive. Aries may become resentful of the peaceful Taurean disposition that attracted the Ram in the first place. Sometimes both of you want the same thing but don't verbalize your needs. Aries can pick the wrong time to tackle an issue with Taurus. Don't ever challenge a tired Bull. That's when the Bull sets red! Taurus does better when rested. Aries can often rally to deal with intense situations even when near exhaustion. The Ram can forget that the rest of us may not be up for the fight. Aries' adrenaline keeps flowing, even when the gauge should show empty!

Blocked passion can result from this game. This condition causes each to hold back from the other, both emotionally and sexually. Each wants to be recognized as an individual, yet urgently needs to feel a sense of belonging with the other. This brings up a confusing question: "How did you ever get stuck in this cul-de-sac?" The road back to intimacy can appear to be many miles away.

Penny Wise and Pound Foolish Game

Aries and Taurus can be too self-absorbed. Finances and ownership issues can produce tension. Aries may grow tired of thrifty Taurean ways and go on a spending spree. Taurus may rebel against Aries by throwing economizing instincts to the dogs. Money can become a real bone of contention between your two signs. It can be difficult to build toward a common goal. Aries, out of boredom or anger, may undermine shared goals. Taurus may be obsessed with building a nest egg, until thwarted by Aries, who is caught in the act of shredding all the paper money.

The *Penny Wise and Pound Foolish* game can lead the two of you to take turns with making business decisions for short periods of time. Then, in the long run, you can both grow disillusioned with how few assets the relationship has produced. This normally threatens Taurus more than Aries. The Ram can see this more as just another challenge—a way to arouse their adrenaline to meet the demands of today. Taurus feels worried not only about tomorrow but the weeks (and years!) ahead. The immediate gratification of Aries does not ideally match the patience of conservative Taurus. The drive in Aries is aimed at meeting immediate goals (right now) so that you can be ready for new challenges by midnight! The two of you can burn through resources quickly if you fall into shortsighted behavior, and your expenditures can turn into a blaming contest as time goes on. You might accuse each other of being careless. Aries doesn't really enjoy restraints on their spending. As a form of rebellion, Taurus can be enticed into wild spending, especially if tired of being the banker in the relationship.

Strategies

Your Aries-Taurus games are played in poor light, shaded by resistance to change. The fear of giving in too easily to one another sometimes keeps you two lovers from communicating effectively. In the *One Step Forward, Three Steps Back* game, the Ram and the Bull need to learn how to encourage each other to first be successful as individuals. Individual success will take the stress out of your partnership. Trust comes with each small achievement in your individual lives. If this doesn't happen, your two signs often will thwart the progress of the relationship with outlandish behavior. The relationship will not work without both taking responsibility for shared growth. You need to regard each other as members of the same team.

The *Tug of War* game is symbolic of Aries' determination opposing Taurus' stubbornness. What a game this is! There is no winner. Both of you tire from exhaustion. This game produces a cosmic stalemate, so a compromise point must be reached. Neither has to fully like the way the other lives, but there must be mutual acceptance and respect. The Ram's energy must be allowed to run its course. Let the Ram get tired first, and then Taurus' suggestions start to make sense. Before this, Aries just thinks that Taurus' ideas sound like pure bull. Aries would be wise to indulge the needs of Taurus once in a while. Generosity increases the flow of goodwill between you, and that nourishes your relationship.

The *Penny Wise and Pound Foolish* game can easily be turned into an abundant lifestyle for both of you. Self-indulgence sooner or later irritates one or the other of you. Aries must learn to stay on a budget in order to really be with Taurus. Taurus has to be willing to occasionally splurge on life's adventures. This give-and-take makes life more peaceful. Instead of rebelling against each other, the Ram and the Bull can combine their resources creatively. Much more is accomplished when you work together.

The Rainbow

Your Aries-Taurus relationship exudes sensuality because this is a combination of signs ruled by Mars (Aries) and Venus (Taurus). You can experience great sexual pleasure together. If you feel each other's love, you should achieve intimacy. This can be a sexually liberating union because you ignite spontaneous sparks of passion in each other.

The Aries man can be stopped in his tracks by the sweetness and earthy beauty of a Taurus woman. He feels at ease with her practical approach to life. Regardless of age, she is often more mature than he. Her grace mystifies him just as his youthful directness captures her imagination. He senses that this Venusian woman immediately has his macho ways pegged. He wants to charm her as so many others before him have tried. She enjoys the attention. The Aries man detects that this woman with soft, comforting eyes seems to be genuinely interested in his ambitions. She loves his courage and impetuous actions. She also likes to see him slow down and really smell the roses. Her beautiful feminine spirit captures the heart of the warrior. He is drawn to her stubborn strength because it feels tangibly real to him. The Aries man hopes she will walk or run with him toward new territories where they both can feel renewed.

The Taurus woman never really knows what to expect from the Aries man. He tramples through her life like a stampeding buffalo. His energy lifts her out of any comfort zone that soothes her. She is happy and dismayed almost in the same breath to have this warrior man in her life. She can be ready at a moment's notice but prefers to have advance warning. He loves stress while she worships sunsets. She has to admit that his impatience with complacency intrigues her. The Venusian woman sees that if she waits long enough this fiery lover will see that she is worth the wait. She wonders whether this enthusiastic man has long-range goals. She is put at ease when she hears him talk about his plans. This comfort-seeking creature can't help it. Her destiny depends on reliable paths, though it might be fun to throw a drop of that caution to the wind and take a spontaneous headlong dive into adventure. After all, this macho man doesn't have the only claim to feeling the call of the moment.

An Aries woman is intrigued by the calmness of the Taurus man. However, she has no desire to be controlled by him and will make this known early in the relationship. The Bull's possessiveness is due to his love of having her near. He really does not like to share her time, but will yield to humor her. The Aries woman feels the immediate attraction between her and this Venusian man. She imagines their two hearts felt a special attraction to each other. Their chemistry could eventually become as complimentary as wine and roses. She only needs to know that this man with business savvy and a soothing voice will not interfere with her drive for spontaneous freedom. You can't blame this feisty woman. She has been like this since her first breath. Life filled her with a sense that she must run to her destination. This Taurus man gets further with her when he makes room for both of their worlds. There is plenty in common. She thinks they could learn to stretch far enough to enjoy the fruits of what each creates as well as the treasures that are part of their joint efforts.

The Taurus man is taken aback by the directness of the Aries woman. She walks as though she has a steady direction, yet he is fascinated with the way she alters course in midstream. This isn't his way of doing business. So what? She ends up on her feet. He appreciates the breeze she blows into his life; her ideas whiz past him like comets. Their minds seem to connect in the most fun-loving of latitudes.

These two can meet halfway. In contrast to this warrior woman who definitely cruises at a higher speed, the Taurus man prefers to take his time. He thinks they make a fine duo—lovers who can share a purpose to be happy and satisfied in every way. He wants to spend more time with this free-wheeling woman. He probably could pick up the pace if she would be willing to shift to a lower gear once in a while.

Your relationship may be rich in love as well as money. Aries has the energy to pursue a goal. Taurus has the sense to manage and invest resources. It is a distinct possibility that you will build a solid life together. You can be proud of each other. Conflicts can be resolved with wisdom to add longevity to this partnership.

Aries-Gemini: The Movers and Shakers

Aries + Gemini = Excitement Plus

These are two fast-moving signs—Gemini represents quick thinking and Aries symbolizes impulsive action. Two lovers of these signs can lift one another to exhilarating heights. The courage of Aries can inspire Gemini to act on ideas. The insightfulness of Gemini can help Aries learn to look before leaping.

Roadrunner Game

The games played in your Aries-Gemini relationship are connected to inaccurate perceptions and foiling one another's decisiveness. When your two signs are unsure of each other, the *Roadrunner* game can ensue. This game resembles a children's cartoon from decades ago in which a coyote relentlessly chased a roadrunner only to become the victim of his own traps. Aries and Gemini can never outsmart each other for long. Their frustrating battles benefit neither opponent. In this game, both of your signs are provoked into negative behavior that wastes a lot of time. Communication is tainted with information meant to be misleading. The speed of your sign combination can cause you to jump to conclusions based on false assumptions.

Missing the Boat Game

Aries likes to shoot ahead at full throttle. A "full speed ahead" effort comes naturally to this spontaneous-combustion fire sign. On the other hand, Gemini, a highly intellectual sign, prefers to use reason to chart the way to a destination. Gemini (ruled by the winged messenger of the gods, Mercury) moves continuously along a zigzag course. Navigating by dead reckoning, in a straight line, is perceived to be boring. However, when Gemini becomes really excited about a plan, the Twins ride waves of energy together like sister ships to the same ports of call.

When you keep one another from leaving the pier (taking action), you're engaged in the ploys of the *Missing the Boat* game. These are missed opportunities. Aries can lack the initiative here to push Gemini to move. The Ram can be so self-centered that there is little thought given to moving forward together. Gemini can talk Aries out of acting swiftly. Remember, you are two fast-moving individuals. You can move even faster when working in harmony or as a team. When each has goals or views that directly oppose the other, you take the wind out of each other's sails. It can feel like the boat is dead in the water and, at worst, is shipwrecked. Gemini becomes bored, and Aries becomes angry if kept at a standstill for too long. You may suffer from the doldrums. You have a sign combination that can't bear to let the winds of time pass by. Why? Inaction is perceived as a letdown. Tremendous disappointment comes with this game. Taking advantage of opportunity is your sign combination's mark of distinction. Each can easily blame the other for holding up progress. The assertiveness of one can block the other. There can be times when one talks the other out of taking a risk that might be advantageous. Aries needs the freedom to act boldly. Gemini must at times be able to put an idea into action to realize the validity of the thought. Holding each other back causes friction. Many times each of you really wants the other to go for it! Discouragement from pursuing goals can cause a lack of confidence. There are instances when one of you might show anger by negating the other's hopes and dreams. This is not endearing behavior.

Scatterbrain Game

Aries and Gemini can make each other nervous wrecks! It can be hard to really hear what the other is saying. Your signs, which are ruled by Mars (Aries) and Mercury (Gemini), indicate the need for dramatic communication in the relationship. Finding a common bond that will give your relationship a sense of togetherness can be challenging when you're playing the *Scatterbrain* game. There must be a willingness to work together that sometimes is just not there.

When headstrong Aries stomps off in one direction and aloof Gemini sprints in the other, a great emotional distance separates them. Fiery Aries can make the already fidgety Gemini even more uneasy with a sudden need to blaze a new trail. Gemini can make Aries uneasy with the ever-present need to change course at every fork in the road. You can feel divided over the needs or whims of the other. Your two signs sometimes try too hard to solve problems too quickly. Each can unrealistically expect instant results from the other. The ability to listen to one another can grow quite strained.

Strategies

What can be done to solve the riddle of your Aries-Gemini games? The *Roadrunner* game requires Aries and Gemini to acknowledge one another's ideas more sincerely. Taking the time to listen is easier said than done for your sign combination. It almost takes a referee to call a foul when one of you is not playing by the rules of the game. Each needs to recognize and heed the need to communicate. Each of you is likely to be very intelligent. Intense thinking is part of your nature and is one thing you have in common. A willingness to share this intelligence is the challenge. If you show that you are listening through your actions, it will help you both to win this game!

The *Missing the Boat* game can be solved by both Aries and Gemini advocating for one another. This game is not that hard to convert into a win-win situation. Each of your signs responds quickly to attention. Mutual support of each other's goals is a powerful way to score winning points. It can take courage and attentiveness to align your assertive energies. Shared ambitions for the relationship get a real boost when the individual needs of your two signs are fulfilled.

The *Scatterbrain* game may point to a need for emotional distance from each other. A little breathing room may restore mental clarity. There is an intense nervous energy that keeps recycling through your sign combination. This energy needs to be directed into both individual and joint creative pursuits. Picking times when you both feel mellow to discuss touchy subjects is a good rule of thumb. Otherwise, it may seem like one of you is throwing a lit match at gasoline! Travel can help you process your relationship's dynamics. It would be wise to give each other some slack when it comes to solving mutual problems. In some instances, there are no quick answers to a situation. Neither of you can always be the champion of the other, so it is smart to not expect it.

The Rainbow

Your Aries-Gemini relationship thrives on surprises. Neither of you takes time to stand still, do you? Why should you? You are an opportunity-seeking combination from the start! Imagination constantly pulsates throughout your romance. Listening to one another's ideas is stimulating.

An Aries man is entertained by a Gemini woman's intellect. Her ideas seem to somersault magically through the air and reactivate thoughts that he has put on the back burner. This Mercurian woman moves with great versatility. The Ram can move fast too but is not as agile in changing directions. He believes she can keep up with his impulsive actions. He is aware that it is not wise to tire out this woman by endless starts that lack follow-through. He is energized by the enthusiasm of the Gemini woman, who is eager to learn.

The Gemini woman's imagination is captured the moment the passionate Aries man steps into her life. The Ram's direct landing in her path gives a start to the Gemini woman's mind. She perceives his impatience and tendency to act impulsively. She hopes he can show some patience in matters of the heart. He resembles a displaced hunter in search of adventure. She is moved by his bold advances. Her perceptive mind thinks it would be interesting to match wits with this fast-paced man. The Mercurian woman likes the way he motivates her. She would like to get to know this fireball better, that is, if the two of them could slow down enough to talk. Conversations on the run seem to suit both of their styles. She knows that life together will never be dull. How could it be when these two restless souls constantly run circles around one another?

A female Ram can love the way a Gemini man deals with her demands. She can be mesmerized by his perceptive second-guessing of her every desire. She is surprised to see how her own straightforward style is slowed a bit by his inquisitive eyes. She isn't used to stopping in her tracks to reevaluate a decision. This Mercurian man seems to delight in poking holes in her ideas. The fiery woman likes the attention of this coolly intellectual man. He fans her fires with exciting thoughts. She thinks they make enough electricity to ignite others into serious action. It seems they could go far down the road of love together.

A Gemini man can be energized by the Aries woman's need for immediate action. He can both love and hate her assertive leadership. His male ego suffers once in a while when she fires a direct hit. The Mercurian man notices that the two of them enjoy life in the fast lane. They are equally equipped to deal with each other's intensity. Each can rush forward to take advantage of opportunities without a backward glance. He is drawn to the Ram because she takes love by storm. He would like very much to experience firsthand the eternal fires that burn in her passionate eyes.

Your first encounter may have been unusual. You may have met while waiting for a taxi or through a chance encounter at a resort. Difficult circumstances can challenge the early stages of your relationship. One or both of you can have ties to other lovers. In overcoming the early obstacles to being together, such a relationship can take off like a jet plane. You are likely to find each other sexually fascinating. Each can arouse the other's erotic instincts. Your desire to surprise one another adds zest to your romantic interludes. Both Aries and Gemini are resourceful when it comes to finding ways to keep the vitality in commitments. You both may enjoy bringing stimulating experiences into one another's life. There is a lively rhythm to your partnership. Few outside observers may understand it. Who cares? It doesn't matter as long as you do!

Aries-Cancer: The Initiators

Aries + Cancer = Fiery Emotion

You can fuel each other's passions in a heartbeat. You can have quite different ways of achieving your personal goals. Aries moves directly to blow obstacles out of the way. Cancer cautiously picks and chooses when to act. Aries rushes to take the first step while Cancer patiently waits for the right time to launch a plan. Aries can inspire Cancer to act on impulse, and Cancer can influence Aries to become more reflective.

Border Wars Game

The games played in your Aries-Cancer relationship have their roots in the need for space and in establishing trust. You can easily expose one another's territorial needs. Declaring your turf is something that probably occurred rather suddenly in your relationship. The *Border Wars* game surfaces when you refuse to recognize the privacy needs of one another. Aries often more obviously shows anger over this while Cancer may choose to mask those feelings. Fighting over what each of you sees as vital to your growth and happiness can become exhausting. Your hearts and minds can seem to be miles apart if you don't meet each other halfway. These border skirmishes are more likely to happen if either of you compromises too much to please the other. You may believe that privacy includes the right to focus on your own goals. Distracting your partner away from serious projects or hobbies will not win admiration. Whether one of you needs a night out with your pals or wants to enjoy a brief retreat with a book, honor it. Give each other the freedom to feel safe together even if you take short detours down separate paths.

Hide and Seek Game

The *Hide and Seek* game could just as well have been called the *Now You See Me, Now You Don't* game. You may not always have a clear sense of each other's real agenda. Be frank! It will keep you on the same path together. You will drift apart when you don't take the time to state your true intentions. Each of you can fear the other as the relationship grows closer. Try not to push your partner away. There is a tendency to run when you feel your secrets are being discovered. It's when you feel free to reveal your inner self that this relationship flies the highest. Let at least a bit of yourself be discovered. The fear of emotional closeness can make you suddenly feel like strangers. The funny thing is that you may be calling out to be found but don't know how to admit the truth. If you don't stop and let your guard down, your partner isn't going to know your needs.

Moody Blues Game

The chemistry formed by crossing a Mars-ruled sign (Aries) and a lunar-ruled sign (Cancer) is going to produce heated opinions; count on it! To outside observers you may appear to be a calm couple. Those who really know you might buy you boxing gloves as a gag gift. You may have sensed an intense emotional energy between you when you first met.

There's nothing wrong with anger. It's only when it becomes a constant interruption to the flow of your partnership that the *Moody Blues* game becomes a problem. Moods will come and go in this relationship. Don't let an occasional mood swing in your partner disturb you. Be patient. (Isn't that so much more easily said than done?) You may be pushed to the brink of sanity when you are too demanding of each other. If you try to force your viewpoints on each other, you will feel angry and hurt. Aries sometimes unknowingly (and at times knowingly) wounds Cancer with blunt remarks. Cancer can ruffle feathers by not including Aries in big decisions that affect both partners. Moods and the blues become a regular event when you don't acknowledge one another's decision-making power.

Strategies

How do you turn these games into winning points? You can tone down the *Border Wars* game if you don't infringe too much on each other's need for privacy. A little give-and-take goes a long way toward keeping you close. Let each partner define individual needs in the relationship. Neither of you can expect the other to always be ready at a second's notice to drop everything for the other's needs. Trust becomes stronger and clearer in a mutually supportive atmosphere. If you allow your partner to move toward realizing personal ambitions, it will accelerate your growth together.

To rise above the *Hide and Seek* game, you need to come out of the closet and let at least some of your innermost needs be known. Hiding your feelings only builds a gulf between you. Nobody can be truthful all of the time. There is a bit of denial in all of us. It's only when you conceal too much of yourself that communication becomes difficult. It's hard to talk to someone that you don't really know even if you live with them. Talk more and you will be a happier duo. It's often more painful to hold back your real feelings than it is to reveal them!

In the *Moody Blues* game, tolerance of each other's differences may be part of the answer. Moods can sweep in suddenly. Moodiness may be caused by situations that don't even have much to do with one another. A bad day at work may cause you to have a shorter fuse than usual. Make it clear when a mood swing is due to a problem outside the relationship. Why? It takes a lot of the heat out of a potential argument. If you clearly identify why you feel the way you do, it will lead to quicker resolution of disruptions caused by sudden mood swings. You can be tempted to be critical of each other because it is a convenient way to release pent-up anger. If you feel an inner explosion, you may need to go for a walk or to use this energy productively. If you do launch an attack on your partner, remember the magic words: "I'm sorry." They will still work in the twenty-first century. An apology isn't a sign of weakness; it is a sign of strength. This game tests you. You won't figure it out in one day. Master the arts of listening and talking. It takes practice, and, yes, more practice.

The Rainbow

Your Aries-Cancer relationship is nourished by a desire to challenge one another to go after enterprising goals. There is an initiating spirit deep in your souls. Encourage your partner to go forward with confidence. Courageous action makes life together stimulating.

An Aries man can be stopped in his tracks by the intense gaze of a Cancer woman. Her intuitive eyes can play upon the heartstrings of the adventurous Ram. He is bemused by the quiet ways of this mysterious lunar woman. She has a reflective mental nature fueled by intense emotions. The Aries man notices that when he approaches this woman too quickly, she retreats into privacy. He is quick to see that the Crab may appear to be easily scared but can quickly become the pursuer. She is a complex woman who, for some strange reason, makes him want to understand her. She is completely aware of her feelings, but his own emotional understanding is not as deep. No matter, she still seems to like his bold assertiveness, that is, as long as he doesn't plunder her personal space.

A Cancer woman's heart may skip a beat when an Aries lover suddenly lands into her life. She is in awe of his ability to briskly push ahead as though life was a race against time. The lunar woman wonders if the Aries man ever pauses to think before he leaps. He has probably learned that hurried actions do not always get good results, or has he? She knows a good thing when she sees it. He advertises himself as a catch, but she wants to know if he can talk about his inner world. The outer one has probably already been circled over and over again. She thinks it would be fun to travel through life with him whether for a short jaunt or a long expedition. She has a few tricks to keep him from wandering too far from home.

The female Ram can arouse the passion of a Cancer man even if he is timid in showing his intense emotions. She excites him and may be the catalyst to elevate him to new creative heights. An Aries woman can alternatively be mystified and exhilarated by the Cancer man's mysterious persona. He appears to be crab-like when he hides in his shell, but, at the same time, he can be forceful when he finds what he wants. This fiery Ram would like to blow him away with a direct blast of her passion. He seems like a sensitive soul whose feelings reach to the core of the earth. His face is as animated as that of the man in the Moon even when he doesn't say much. She certainly enjoys being swept off her feet when he feels a burst of confidence. She needs to be overwhelmed by her lover once in a while. It reminds her that love is not stationary.

The Cancer man is quickly attracted to the Aries woman. She speaks directly to his heart and mind. Her bold gaze makes his own eyes light up. He thinks she is intense, and the Aries woman's warrior-like presence arouses his passion. He finds her enthusiasm contagious and finds it difficult to slow down when this action-packed woman is nearby. Yet, she may be surprisingly timid if he tries to discover her secrets too soon. He observes that she is more trusting of him when he talks honestly about himself. They are similar in the sense that both like to get on with the show once they see what they want. His moods seem to swing with greater intensity now that he has met this fiery

The Magic of Signmates

woman. However, the Cancer man doesn't feel that he is unusually distracted; to him, his emotions are like love chimes blown by the wind. He usually doesn't want his life to be turned upside down, but in this case he is anxious to make an exception.

You experience a high when you feel truly *together* sexually. Recognize emotional highs and lows in each other, and tune in to the right time to make love. You soon realize it's important to experience being in love because it translates into true passion. Nobody is telling you this is an easy relationship. Your ability to endure the storms shows you to be dynamic lovers. You can form a bond that is hard to break. When you no longer doubt how far you have come together, it is probably the sign that you have arrived.

Aries-Leo: The Enthusiasts

Aries + Leo = Anything Is Possible

You don't like to wait for things to happen. It's more like you happen to life! People can't help but notice when you enter the room. Patience isn't your first response—is it? Aries ignites the creative energy of Leo like few other signs. Leo can push Aries to new courageous heights. You desire the attention of each other rather dramatically. There's no need to be concerned if you talk loudly to make a point. You are meant to be heard over the noise of a crowd. When you grow too quiet together, people probably feel that something must be wrong, or that they said the wrong thing. Your public will be more at ease when you are outspoken. Your friends can get a real energy lift by being in your company.

Stress-aholic Game

The games played in your Aries-Leo relationship center around an inability to slow down or a tendency to be too pushy regarding personal desires. If the two of you get too caught up in your own drive to succeed, the *Stress-aholic* game can result. Each of you can feel a spontaneous calling to go in new directions. There can be a tendency to catch your partner by surprise with a quick turn. This can be exhilarating and fun; however, it can wreak havoc on your stability as a couple. There is a competitive drive in each of your signs that brings out your passion for life. Slowing down does not come naturally in this relationship. Life may seem like it is meant to be lived in a hurry. Your friends and work peers can admire the intensity the two of you pour into getting a job done. You can lose touch with each other when you don't take the time to stay on the same page.

You may push each other to move too fast. Rather than listen to each other's needs, you may assume that you know what is best for your partner. Some stress is a good thing because it keeps life from getting dull. A compulsive need to move in too many directions at once may leave little time to focus on each other. Always staying busy can be a type of high, but frustration can occur when you feel that your partner is too distracted to pay attention to you.

In Your Face Game

Neither of you responds well to bossy behavior. The *In Your Face* game plays out when you don't let one another think independently. Rather than talking, one partner barks out orders. If communication becomes a one-way street instead of a flowing, two-way dialogue, you may react angrily and refuse to cooperate. Aries and Leo are naturally resistant to being told what to do. Arguments will be a regular event if you infringe on each other's freedom of choice. You don't function smoothly as a couple when you lack clearly defined individual plans. If you try to force one another into decisions, the situation will be explosive.

You both thrive on being the center of attention. This means you need your own stage on which to perform. When one of you regularly tries to occupy center stage to the exclusion of the other, it causes great emotional distance. You have a lot of power in this relationship. It is better directed at constructive projects or outlets than at each other. When you feel like equals, you are at your best. When one of you dictates the agenda, the balance is lost. You will feel an underlying tension when there is a power struggle. If you don't share the leading roles, this game is going to be evident in your everyday life together.

Me First Game

A power struggle is found in the *Me First* game. You don't like to come in second when you expect to win. It's a natural instinct that is promoted by being together. If you can't take turns winning, you will not enjoy feeling that your partner always makes you lose. Advocating for each other builds your self-confidence. Quite the opposite happens when you don't support the roles in life each chooses to adopt. When you don't show you are proud of each other's accomplishments, happiness is a stranger.

Aries wants to be the champion in every endeavor. Leo demands recognition, whether doing so blatantly or by acting hurt if accolades are withheld. Your hearts are at odds when you don't give each other positive strokes. Do it often! It's when one of you feels the world is not a big enough place for you both to shine that this game can come between you.

Strategies

How do you solve the dilemma these Aries-Leo games present? In the *Stress-aholic* game, find a pace in your relationship that works. Remember the old saying, "Rome wasn't built in a day." Your relationship doesn't need to fulfill all of its potential this instant! You were fire signs before you met. You are still fire signs in the relationship. The nature of fire is to get to the finish line as quickly as possible. Learn to take a break now and then as individuals and as a couple. If you get burned out through hectic schedules, your sex life and quality time suffer. It's a given that you will become bored if life moves too slowly. Nobody should ever tell you to not lead active lives. Trips to the health spa, outings with friends, going out to dinner, a quest for challenging careers, and an active family life don't need to be sacrificed. This is a relationship that thrives on activity. Your restless spirit motivates others to take action. You have a huge amount of creative energy that needs to be expressed. Be sure to make enough time to be together without too much outside interference. You must get enough of a handle on your time to be able to concentrate on one another. If you do, you will really feel like partners in love.

The *In Your Face* game can be neutralized by not *expecting* (note the emphasis) your partner to follow your lead. Each of you is a natural leader in your own right—that is to say, leadership is your birthright under your respective signs. You empower each other when you recognize your partner's individual talents. Encourage. Promote. Cheer a little. You will draw out each other's best. Forcing your own beliefs reveals a lack of faith in one another. You don't have to agree on everything. Tolerate your differences and you will be a powerful, forceful couple. It is unrealistic, actually bordering on the ridiculous, to predict that you will always see eye to eye. Often your unique opinions fuel your passion and creativity. Believe in your partner's diversity, and you are at your best.

The *Me First* game is not all that hard to convert into a winning point. At first glance it may seem difficult, but you only need to refocus this dynamic energy. What you have together is hot stuff. I didn't say that it is perfect. A drive for recognition is human, but to receive all of the attention and give little or none back is not going to make you happy. Relinquishing power to someone you love is not a show of weakness; it is a strength.

You show your true talent and creativity if you let each other win or share the lead. If one or both of you is in the habit of getting in the other's face to make demands, try a different tack. It requires a little trust combined with a touch of faith. Let go and let your partner call the shots. It will surprise you to see that you will likely win even more cooperation by allowing your partner to share the spotlight. It takes a lot of pressure off if you let one another express your best talents. When you rise to your highest potential, the relationship as a whole prospers.

The Rainbow

Your Aries-Leo relationship can skip merrily through life with a feeling you made the right choice. There is not much time to look back at the past because the present is taken up with your active lives. You will summon opportunities to come your way. Luck is never far out of your reach.

An Aries man feels special thanks to the attention lavished upon him by the Leo woman. Her belief in him makes him ready to fight any battle. The Aries man senses that the Lion shares his dynamic energy and ability to blaze new trails. The Ram recognizes that the fire in her heart is like his own. He wonders if she is as impatient as he is to explore all dimensions of their relationship. He appreciates the way she accelerates his creative drive. Since meeting her, he thinks less in terms of what he can't do and more about what he is going to accomplish. She has immense willpower. He realizes that he had better not be too pushy with this proud woman in whose eyes he sees proof that they are a well-suited couple. His eyes shine with the same conviction.

A Leo woman can be won over by the ferocious pursuit of her heart by an Aries man. His self-assuredness elevates her own self-confidence. She thinks they will probably spar because passion has a way of eliciting a fiery response. She is attracted to the Aries man's directness. She hopes he can be more subtle when it comes to feelings. She is not timid in matters of the heart; it's just that it takes so long to get over a broken one. This fire starter looks as though he enjoys creating sparks. She likes to hear him talk as though he understands the dues that love can cost. It's hard to deny how refreshed he makes her feel. She may tell herself that this is no time for fear, not when two bold beings can tempt fate by throwing caution to the wind.

An Aries woman can be amused by the way a Leo man shows no fear of her passion. His response to her directness might make her laugh and drop her jaw at the same time.

The female Aries knows they bring out each other's competitive spirit, and she delights in the lively atmosphere that surrounds them. His humor makes her see the lighter side of life. She perceives that he likes the way she carries herself, and that taking a risk is what makes the world turn around. She senses that they are in for a passionate explosion, but it's the aftermath that interests her. Will they discover the sheltered valleys where their feelings reside? It seems that they had better have fun first and let the chips fall where they may. It seems to be a formula that makes them want to play the game of love with one another.

A Leo man can find that the intense emotional nature of the Aries woman arouses his creative spirit. Her apparent lack of fear of his roar is spellbinding. The Lion enjoys the way she humors him and lets him lead. He takes notice that she responds angrily if he plays with her feelings. The ground shakes when they walk together, alerting others to their presence. The Lion senses that the Ram knows this is not a relationship for the meek of heart. He realizes that she can push him to go after his dreams, and he thinks it would be exciting to return the favor.

When you accept the power each of you brings into this relationship, there is no end to your accomplishments. Others may envy or be amused by your show of passion for each other. Your determination to blaze new trails keeps life exciting. Aries is pioneering. Leo likes to take risks. Put this together and you can add a vast richness to one another's horizons. You know how to make each other feel important, and it doesn't take long to figure this out. You probably felt a romantic spark the moment you first met. The world you create together has a promise of material and emotional wealth. Negotiate with each other fairly, and you will never be far apart in spirit. Admit when you are wrong, and problems are more apt to be nipped in the bud. The Ram and the Lion can build a relationship that can survive any crisis. Show that you are paying attention, and your two hearts will be as one.

Aries-Virgo: The Energizers

Aries + Virgo = Restlessness

Aries is ready for the next challenge while in the midst of the previous adventure. Virgo has an inquisitive mind with an impulse to move nervously back and forth to meet the deadlines imposed by multiple challenges. The main difference here is that Aries is inclined to let someone else finish what it starts while Virgo is bothered by leaving work undone. This may sound like a challenging Sun-sign combination; it is. Aries can motivate Virgo to stop worrying too much about the details and to move forward. Aries does well to listen to Virgo's advice to consider consequences before rushing ahead.

Tornado Game

The games played in your Aries-Virgo relationship are associated with not really listening to each other and with negating one another's opinions. The *Tornado* game is born when one or both of you is preoccupied with excitement over a new opportunity. It could be because one of you is nervously focused on getting a job done right. The two of you experience a speeding up of your minds that can rival any funnel cloud. When Aries becomes nervous for too long, the stress felt is intense. Aries' anxiety levels increase dramatically when Virgo worries. You can cause each other to worry without even knowing you're doing it. In this game the two of you lose your awareness of the big picture. Each of you becomes so absorbed with the details of your individual lives that the relationship lacks a clear sense of direction. If nobody steers the ship, it drifts at the mercy of the waves. A whirlwind of ideas is produced by the natural chemistry of your sign combination. The blending of your plans and thoughts is challenging to harness at times. Some Aries-Virgo couples panic. Constant yelling and screaming will be a barometer that something is out of balance. If you choose to write off your partner's complaints, resentment will build. Because you can move decisively to solve problems together, it may be difficult to perceive that there is even anything wrong. It can be tempting to hide from the truth. Don't be afraid to clean out the closet once in a while; there is nothing in there that bites!

We Can't, We Can't Game

This game finds the two of you lost in negativity. Your minds have become absorbed with doubts about your individual and shared potentials. It's amazing how far a little encouragement can go. It's equally startling how a lack of faith can stop even fiery Aries in its tracks. Dependable Virgo's confidence can suffer from the fallout caused by negative reactions. Attaining a "we can" attitude will take that much more practice if the two of you have indulged in too many doubts for too long.

Your minds have a bad habit of first thinking about what could be wrong with the relationship. It may be true that you need to address an issue or two. If you start from a negative perspective, the work is nearly impossible to accomplish. Furthermore, it's not much fun being together. It is tiring to be continually reminded of your mistakes or faults. The lack of a positive attitude regarding your shared potentials makes it difficult to find a sense of unity. Even passion is blocked, and sex isn't quite the same. You can feel something is wrong with your connection. Finding your way back to a positive connection will require genuine effort, but it can be done!

Nine to Five Game

When life falls into a dull routine, the two of you may lack the stimulation you need to feel energized. Both of you can delight in exposing one another to new ideas. But when your everyday life together becomes too predictable, you can become irritable. Your minds seem to lose that edge when you don't make new plans. You can enjoy a sense of curiosity in exploring new business enterprises or hobbies. If you are tied down to the same schedules, day in and day out, it takes the passion out of you. There will be times when you really do have to focus on major projects or take care of serious business. When you forget to even think about spicing up life with travel or other social events, you can lose appreciation for one another. Your sign combination thrives on new activities. Take a chance and throw some of that caution to the wind. Let the initial excitement that brought you together in the first place find its way back into your relationship.

Strategies

How do you rise above the challenges of your Aries-Virgo games? In the *Tornado* game, the two of you can follow your own interests but need to keep each other "penciled in" on your schedules. Make big decisions together. Sometimes it's easy to get so swept away by the momentum of a new direction that you forget to include your partner. Aries can ride a wave of enthusiasm to new creative heights. Although Virgo is not known for the same fiery intensity as Aries, Virgo's mental power can suddenly propel this earth sign forward. In an Aries-Virgo relationship, there is a common need to put ideas into motion. Aries usually leaps into action. Virgo may first analyze an idea but is still capable of moving with great intensity. The *Tornado* game usually is more disruptive when you are not communicating clearly. You probably assume that you are being understood, but you will not always be able to read each other's minds. The excitement that change brings to you is worthwhile because it keeps your hearts and minds alert. If you pay attention to what each is pursuing, you are not likely to drift apart.

In the *We Can't, We Can't* game, you might need to retrain your minds to think more positively. It takes practice. Channeling your energies into constructive projects together can guide you out of the maze of negative thinking. A little belief in your partner brings out your best. A bit of hidden anger may lie at the root of this game. Old issues that have never been discussed may get in the way. Resentful feelings can keep either of you from seeing a more positive picture. Addressing previous issues can pave the way to greater happiness. Sometimes it only takes one failed experience together to convince a couple that future endeavors will turn out as badly. It requires courage to think more positively. One successful venture together can turn this around. Often the weight of one small success tips the scales in the favor of a more positive outlook.

The *Nine to Five* game only requires that you free your imagination to explore stimulating options. If you just give yourselves a chance, it is easy to make life more exciting. Although everyone needs routines to establish stability, allowing for new experiences recharges your romantic instincts. The same schedule can dull your passion and creativity while changing your daily patterns can bring in a ray of sunshine. Your relationship can benefit from spontaneity. Surprising your partner with a gift or going to an unusual place pays dividends.

The Rainbow

Through your Aries-Virgo relationship, you can learn to be loyal to each other's goals. The push you give each other to go after your dreams can make your hearts grow fond of one another. You can be good partners in business and love.

An Aries man can appreciate the steadiness of a Virgo woman. She is entertained by watching him run in circles around her while she moves systematically ahead. He hopes his impulsive actions won't disturb this well-organized female. The Ram is surprised to see that this woman can switch from being a serious-minded worker to being a fun-loving lover. He learns quickly that she responds to those who show a serious interest in knowing the real her.

The Virgo woman is moved by the Aries man's determination to move mountains. He always seems to be in a hurry to be somewhere. She wishes the Ram could occasionally enjoy the moment before allowing himself to be enticed into the next chase. Her perceptions are governed by primal instincts that have developed into fine powers of discrimination. Her common sense tells her that he is a risk and a half. The Mercurian woman would rather listen to mischievous whispers that coax her to let go and take a wild ride. After all, does she always need to know exactly where her feet might land?

The Aries woman is attracted to the Virgo man's sense of self-assuredness when he talks about his accomplishments. She tries to build his confidence so he will be a match for her. He may be aware she is doing this, and does he like it! The flame-throwing logic of the Ram certainly burns right through his normally reserved thoughts. The Aries woman immediately sees that this coolly rational man is enthralled with her take-charge spirit. She is glad to see that he can take the lead. She becomes confused if she always must be the initiator. She is delighted to see that he is an attentive lover. She brainstorms ways to break him free from his thoughts so that he can be a free spirit.

The Virgo man meticulously tries to analyze the Aries woman. He hates to admit it, but her unpredictability turns him on. Most of his world is labeled but not this complicated woman. He wishes she wasn't so direct at times. Then again, he likes the way she makes her ideas known. He gets the message that he needs to be fast on the draw if he is going to capture this woman's interest. She seems to want his patience to be balanced with assertiveness. He observes that this outgoing feminine spirit is happier when he is acting rather than thinking.

This is a particularly good match sexually. Fire and earth often enjoy each other's bodies. It's often true of your two signs. You know how to awaken each other's sensuality. If you are clever enough to choose careers or businesses that don't prove to be too exhausting, the time spent together is filled with passion.

You can give a boost to one another's wealth. Problem-solving can bring out your best talents. When you put your heads together, few couples can match your ability to find a way out of a jam. You will find yourselves working together late into the night to overcome obstacles. You are a strong duo in a crisis and are great allies when taking on new challenges. You share inventiveness in blazing career trails. You can offer each other tips from your experiences that could save you many steps in climbing the ladder of success. What you need the most is time. When you tune in to the habits and reasoning powers of one another, the days together are not so tedious. They are downright enjoyable!

Aries-Libra: The Extroverts

Aries + Libra = Active Social Life

These signs are opposites. What does this mean? Opposites can attract or repel. There is a grain of truth in both words of the previous sentence. You are well matched for one another. Your signs appreciate attention. The two of you can put ideas into motion with great zeal. The get-up-and-go of Aries frees Libra from the tendency to carefully weigh options indefinitely. Libra's strategic instincts help Aries to take a more sober look at decisions before rushing ahead. These two signs together are fast on their feet!

Masquerade Game

It is fun to go to parties and to be playful with each other. You encourage many different facets of your partner's personality to come out. Just be sure that when you are talking about serious matters that you show your real selves. If you hide too much behind the images that you project at each other, you could find yourselves playing the *Masquerade* game. This game involves getting lost in an outward definition of yourselves. It becomes too important to hear the approval of others. You might even try too hard to impress each other as something you are not. If you hide behind too many different personas, you can confuse one another. Be brutally honest when you want to be understood on the deepest levels.

Another dimension of this game is that your social urges can become so overwhelming that you spend little time together. One or both of you can be driven to entertain people. There is nothing wrong with this. It's only when you go too far in seeking the applause of others that you can lose your balance. If you can't accept each other at face value, the depth you could have in your partner will be lost. There is some denial in every relationship, even ones that have worked successfully for years. Nobody faces reality all of the time. This game means that at least one of you is swimming in an ocean of denial. When you don't reveal your deepest needs, it can be difficult for the two of you to connect on the deepest of levels.

Warmonger Game

Libra is not seen as having an angry disposition. There is a diplomacy in Libra that is artistic. Aries can probably push Libra's buttons more than any other sign. With its cool and matter-of-fact way of looking at things, Libra can upset Aries' desire for intense reaction. The *Warmonger* game is played when you have lost all reason and objectivity. It occurs when you fight for your own ideas or goals with little awareness of those of your partner. Compromise is thrown out the window. Aries can provoke Libra by simply not listening. Libra can infuriate Aries by refusing to be pushed into doing something. The last thing Aries wants at this time is a well-calculated, rational explanation for not going along with Aries' plans. This game produces a lot of tension. Neither of your nervous systems benefit from this behavior. The desire to follow angry impulses tends to dominate your minds when you follow in the footsteps of this game. It's not anger that is the problem; it is lacking the insight to find a resolution. Clarity comes when you can cool down enough to see alternative points of view.

Haste Makes Waste Game

I cooked with a great chef from India several years ago. One of his favorite sayings was "hurry spoils the curry." There is a false sense of urgency in the *Haste Makes Waste* game that interferes with the flow of communication. The upbeat tempo of being together can hit full stride occasionally. As a matter of fact, it's off the Richter scale! Your commitment can be in question due to a lack of patience. Your fondness for each other will lessen if you get too pushy. Time is your ally, not your enemy. If one of you becomes worried because the relationship is not moving fast enough, don't pout. The more you discuss your needs, the better. Even if you have been together for years, there can still be a tendency to lack patience with each other's decision-making processes. Let's face it, Aries and Libra show their opposition in decision-making more than anywhere else. Aries often will act first and think later. What does Libra do with decisions? Libra wants to get back to you later. This produces a great dilemma. It can look like a major obstacle (or even Mount Everest). The sooner you tune in to the way your impulses function differently, the happier you will be.

It could be that your careers make your schedules that much more hectic. You may forget to plan enough fun time together. A routine of all work and no play is stressful. It may be that one of you is under a lot of pressure due to circumstances beyond your control. Talk to each other! Alert each other when you are running on empty. It may help your partner understand why you lack patience.

Strategies

How do you get through or around the challenges presented by the Aries-Libra games? In the *Masquerade* game, you need only to remember to be your true selves. This sounds easier than it is to put into practice. If you are persistent, the truth will emerge and honesty will come naturally. You can be entertained by your lively and dramatic personalities. Enjoy your partner's humor and playfulness. It may even be that being a bit theatrical is your way to let go of stress. Find bits of quality time to communicate the goals you have as individuals and as a couple. It will come through for you when challenges come your way. You probably feel that in many ways you are well matched. You are a natural complement to each other's identities. You can act as a mirror of clarity when you take the time to discuss issues thoroughly. When you individually ask the question "Who am I?" it could be reassuring to feel you have found a partner who really understands how to help you find the answer.

The *Warmonger* game asks you to find the middle ground from which you can get a clear view of shared and individual needs. This game is symbolic of the passion that is at the root of your relationship. Frustrated passion can turn to anger and must find an outlet. Your sexual relationship will suffer when you hold a grudge; it's better if you release the anger. Anger without resolution is an endless merry-go-round of traps. It's hard to run away from each other, isn't it? Do you notice that in your heart you usually want to come back and work it out even when your mind says no? It's getting your hearts and minds on the same wavelength that is so difficult. Talk even when it's tough. With practice, you will break through your resistance. After all, it's closeness you miss, isn't it?

Someone has to take the first step. It doesn't matter who gets the ball rolling, though it will be appreciated if it isn't always the same person.

The *Haste Makes Waste* game isn't that difficult to turn around. You probably need to stay out of each other's pet projects. Doing so will relieve a lot of pressure. You each need to lead in your own arenas. There are always going to be tasks, hobbies, or social events you can do as a couple. Patience. Remember the saying, "Walk a mile in my shoes." It applies here. You need to walk in your partner's shoes. Take a moment and try to look at your relationship from each other's perspective. If you can't figure out how to do this, then ask your partner to help you tune in to his or her world. You can't work through an issue any faster than both of you are willing. Remember, your way of reaching decisions is quite different. Aries will often follow an inner call to action. Libra listens to different perspectives and is often aggravated by the demands of others. It could be that Libra wants to please Aries but is worried about offending the mother-in-law at the same time. Patience—I know it was already said! You two were never meant to move at a snail's pace (more like the speed of e-mail!). You only need to show you are listening; that's a big part of the art of listening. It is still true that actions speak louder than words, so please try to show that you are getting the message!

The Rainbow

Your Aries-Libra relationship guarantees that neither of you will ever feel lonely. It symbolizes the meeting of two enterprising spirits. You may find that you are the most compatible of spirits. You can sometimes anticipate each other's thoughts and actions. Isn't this true?

An Aries man is easily captured by the Libra woman's graceful charm. The Ram quickly is attracted because she makes him feel important. The Aries man feels the heat of passion from the first glance into this Venusian woman's eyes. Her demeanor suggests that she seeks a true soul mate. The Ram knows they could complete each other in the quest for love. He strives for the patience to let this woman enter into the relationship under her own terms. In some ways he wishes that he had found her yesterday, but in the quietness of his heart is true wisdom; there is no real rush. In meeting, it almost feels like they have always been together.

The Libra woman understands the Aries man's need to act out his primal instincts. After all, he reminds her of the sleek hunters of a distant era. The Libra woman can't help but notice the gallop of the restless Ram. He seems to be constantly on the go regardless of whether he has a destination. He is on a constant adrenaline rush or at least on ready alert. She wants to be pursued by him at first, but she enjoys responding with a chase of her own.

An Aries woman arrests a Libra man with her direct gaze. Her eyes don't just meet his—they join in a midair collision! There is an instant recognition that this could be dangerous, but neither wants to heed the warnings. She likes his inviting face. He is the best of hosts. Her feelings blow hot and cool when near him. Why? When his mind is caught between two possibilities, it causes her usually fast mental impulses to downshift. The Aries woman finds it easy to reserve a tender place in her heart for the Venusian lover. When they joust over differences of opinion it is exhilarating. When one or the other says enough is enough, the merriment begins anew.

The Libra man has a sense that the Aries woman notices him. It's in her face. Her demeanor doesn't blatantly suggest that she wants him to pursue her, but she doesn't send a message to stay away either. She seems to see right into his dilemma from the outset. Measuring the dos and don'ts, shoulds and should nots is enough to give this man a migraine headache. She immediately tests to see if he can make a decision about her. He knows the score and pushes himself to make a first move. To his surprise, she inches a bit closer to make it easier. He is intrigued by the heat in her eyes. This could be a love that lifts them both to high levels of fulfillment; at least that's what he senses.

There is an attraction between Aries and Libra that will defy any odds to explore a love relationship. Sex is intensely erotic. You both delight in making the other leave the body through pleasure. Both of you possess a desire to keep up with each other's sexual energy. You may even talk more easily after sexual encounters. You offer each other opportunities to be accepted just the way you are—with no strings attached. It could be quite refreshing to be in the embrace of someone spontaneously in touch with your next step. There can be delight in being with the sign opposite you in the zodiac. After all, at least you have found someone with the same urgent quest to find love who perhaps answers a part of your life's puzzle.

Aries-Scorpio: The Tenacious Ones

Aries + Scorpio = Dynamo of Energy

These are two signs cut from a similar mold. Each needs to be emotionally excited in order to pursue a dream. Aries is spontaneous while Scorpio, the Scorpion, is more cautious. Both of you like to leave your mark on your creations. Aries will ask Scorpio to be bolder in displaying feelings or in following a vision of truth. Scorpio pleads with Aries to understand that there is an honest reason for shielding intentions. This bargaining back and forth starts early in the relationship. Whether this sign combination stays together for a few seasons or through several vintage years, the art of negotiation is a key to success.

Poker Face Game

The games played in your Aries-Scorpio relationship appear to be power standoffs. Upon closer examination, they are usually more associated with tendencies to manipulate and to hold back anger. The *Poker Face* game arises when the two of you keep a few cards face down. One thing about an Aries-Scorpio couple is usually predictable: there is always a card hidden somewhere. Why does this happen, or, better yet, why does either sign feel the need to hide the true agenda? Trust is tricky to define. In other sign combinations, partners may find it easy to bare the soul to one another; not so here! This is not to say that Aries and Scorpio cannot reach deep levels of trust, but each feels it must be earned! Another tricky area to explore is how to prove you are worthy of trust. Aries may suddenly change the requirements in midstream. Then, there is Scorpio's philosophy about truth and honesty. If Scorpio is able to lay out a road map that Aries can follow, the Scorpion is the voice of wisdom personified. In other words, there is no map for this game; it is a guessing game.

I recently worked with an Aries-Scorpio couple who were in divorce court. The Aries woman never knew how much her Scorpio partner earned. Money issues can become a real problem in this game. These two individuals had little feeling of ever being in a union. Most purchases were not made together. In this game, unspoken information keeps people apart.

One bluff after another is directed at one another. There is no winner, and both of you will feel cheated. It doesn't really do that much good to blame each other. A feeling of being deprived of love is the end result. Somehow, those hidden cards need to be turned face up. Bad habits are hard to change. There is an underlying power struggle over possessions and money. This is a winnable game, but it takes a lot of tenacity (which you both possess) and the willingness to surrender your fear. Wow! That's a big one, isn't it? Why are you reluctant to speak frankly? It's hard to trust someone you don't really know.

Battering Ram-Biting Scorpion Game

This game probably sounds like it is all about arguing and fighting for your own way. This is partially true but isn't the whole picture. The *Battering Ram-Biting Scorpion* game represents the innate drive in each of you to fight for your rights. You both seek to achieve equality. When this game surfaces, it points to an imbalance of power. Are you really trying to empower one another? All relationships go through at least temporary skirmishes, but this game is a long battle that may rival a one-hundred-year war! At least the exhaustion and turmoil it produces has that impact.

Passion is forever present in an Aries-Scorpio romance. You are going to walk through the minefields of one another's deepest emotional intensity. It takes time and practice to deal with each other's likes and dislikes. Negotiating from a place of equal power makes you both feel like part of the royal family. If one of you usurps too much control, your partner feels a slap to his or her self-esteem.

Arguments don't necessarily mean you are in the wrong relationship. Tiptoeing around tough disagreements isn't the answer. The problem in this game is that there is a tendency to avoid listening to each other. When one of you launches an all-out offensive, the other responds with a counter-offensive. If you two could only direct this incredible heat toward shared projects. Hurt feelings are at the root of this game, often from discounting one another's ideas.

Erupting Volcano Game

When you hold back your anger or resentment too long, the *Erupting Volcano* game shows its face. This game is driven by anger that is repressed until it becomes poisonous. When it is released, neither of you may know what to do with it. The first impulse may be to run away. It can be scary or at least unsettling to hear someone blasting away at you because you "ruined" your partner's happiness. This game is often caused by not listening. It can be healing to finally let out your true feelings.

It is typical in the *Erupting Volcano* game for two people to irrationally accuse each other of being the source of the problem. The challenge is for each person to accept responsibility. Even if one of you makes it this far, the other may not be so willing to accept responsibility, which might make you erupt even more! This can lead to a series of eruptions back and forth. It doesn't really matter how long it takes. The key question is whether the two of you can chill down enough to look for solutions. Controlling your reactions to each other is no easy task. A great gulf will be created between your hearts if you follow the impulse to blame or say hurtful things to each other.

Strategies

How do you steer clear of the debris embedded in these Aries-Scorpio games? The *Poker Face* game requires that each of you deal fairly with the issues. It can inspire you to be the best swashbuckling problem-solvers you can be. Does this sound impossible? It isn't! You only need to trust yourself enough to show your hidden cards. Seeing that the fear of being truthful is more painful than being truthful can be a revelation. You can still keep a secret or two; however, it is imperative to be honest regarding the big issues. Financial planning is easier when there are no hidden agendas. It doesn't mean all of the money and property have to be communal. You can discuss ways to maintain your personal financial autonomy. It can feel like death to Aries not to get its own way; Scorpio realizes this early in the relationship. Aries likes to lead while Scorpio would rather be a manager. However, Scorpio doesn't like to be bossed around anymore than Aries. The *Poker Face* game is a strategy to manipulate situations through not sharing plans. Either Aries or Scorpio can be a guilty party. Eventually, the direction of the relationship grows vague. You can nip this pattern in the bud. Can you guess how? State your individual vision for the relationship. Put it into words. If this is too agonizing, try writing it down. You need to let your partner read what you write! First listen to each other; then you can start bargaining. You must repeat the following mantra during all of this collective bargaining: "We need a win-win strategy." You two can turn your poker faces at more appropriate targets. The world of business is a good one.

The *Battering Ram-Biting Scorpio* game can be won over to your mutual advantage through fighting fair. Direct your heat at the real problems, and be harder on the problems than on one another. Be clear about what you need from your partner in order to reach a truce. You bring out a competitive spirit in one another; it's part of the Aries-Scorpio chemistry. Love and passion are powerful undercurrents in this game. You realize you are not getting the love you want when you are bold enough to see why you are mad. It's okay to argue. It's worse when you find it useless to talk anymore. Keep the dialogue going. The Ram's horn is not as sharp nor the Scorpion's bite as painful when you acknowledge your partner's power. Let each other be strong, and you become a more stable alliance. There is a promise of longevity when you two join forces to take on challenges in a cooperative way.

The *Erupting Volcano* game requires humility and ability to ride the emotional storms to win. If you push one another's most reactive buttons without really trying, there must be a lot of passion in this relationship. If you learn to say what is on your mind sooner rather than later, so much the better. It is true that Scorpio processes thoughts more than Aries. This doesn't mean that processing implies that you never share your innermost thoughts. Scorpio needs to interact in a visible way once the Scorpion has thoroughly digested a situation. Aries is known for wanting to deal with circumstances here and now, but this doesn't mean that Aries has the answer. You can combine these strengths into a happy medium. Help each other get to the truth. You can't force your partner to agree with you; great resistance will be the response. There will be less erupting if you don't discount each other's opinions. You won't always agree, so finding better ways to disagree is important. Let your individual voices be heard. The hardest thing about romantic relationships is staying cool enough to really hear your partner's words. So much of the message gets lost in the translation if you are angry. It is better to talk directly because it takes the poison out of this game from the get-go.

Rainbow

Your Aries-Scorpio relationship is filled with new understanding. Self-examination is a by-product of being together. Curiosity about what makes each of you tick is almost destined to occur if it hasn't already.

An Aries man is stopped in his tracks by the penetrating gaze of the Scorpio woman. She already seems to know him. The Ram instinctually perceives a similarity between them. He can't really put his finger on it but thinks that perhaps it is their intensity and ability to fight through obstacles. He likes the touch of the Plutonian woman. She holds him possessively but strikes him as knowing when to let go of a hot iron. The Aries man would rather see this relationship as a refreshing new experience. He is already attached to the magnetic currents that flow between them. She certainly deepens his reflections about his ambitions. She seems to know much about his inner and outer worlds.

The Scorpio woman is blown away by the Aries man's swift movement. She isn't sure whether life was meant to be lived this fast. The Ram impresses her as someone who doesn't take no for an answer very lightly. She would like to be saying yes, that is, if he will respect her territorial freedom. The Plutonian woman can see right away that each of them likes to get their own way. If he can compromise, so can she. She has a burning desire to know what drives him. She wonders if he knows how close in spirit they truly are. She thinks time is a great teacher. It could very well show him how to draw out her deepest feelings. It does not matter how long it takes in her opinion for them to decide if each other is worth the trouble. The journey should be a lot of fun, with a tinge of mystery.

The Aries woman is moved by the charisma of the Scorpio man. She may not move to get close until she is convinced that he won't bite. It's not that she is afraid, it's only that he might be scared away by her boldness. The Aries woman sizes him up to be such a private sort. He comes out of the shadows when talking about his ambition. She notices that he is more comfortable talking about tangibles while his feelings seem to be off limits. The Aries woman will break down the door if she is ready to get on with a relationship. Her patience will run out with someone who slows down to a snail's chase. She has a macho persona that can stand up to the testiness of this deliberately poker-faced hombre. What's interesting is that it doesn't take him long to see that he needs to either put up or shut up. The Ram wants to make room for the Scorpion if he is ready to take the risk with her.

Let the Games Begin

The Scorpio man is intensely curious about the Aries woman. She senses his presence and power but conceals that she is impressed. This really intrigues him. Crossing the path of the Aries woman gets him to take another look in the mirror to see if he has lost his touch. After a reassuring glance at himself, he discovers that this is a playful feminine spirit. He experiences intense feelings when in her company. She knows how to bring out his assertiveness. He is aware of his own attraction to living on the edge. She seems like someone who has traveled that route before and doesn't need to jump for the experience. Life with this woman isn't all that complicated. He is trying to muster up the courage to let his inner and outer selves spontaneously express themselves.

You will never feel unchallenged by each other's intellect and competitive desire to be successful. Your signs are naturally compatible because you both know what it takes to realize your potential. In a peculiar way, you are incompatible because each of you has mental chips or circuitry that are as different as night and day. It is the attempt to combine your forces that makes life interesting. If you don't run away from your partner at the first sign of conflict, you tend to become more confident when the next obstacle comes along.

Chances are there will be those who are jealous of your love for one another. Don't listen to their criticism. Your best allies will see into the deepest part of your union. Don't be squeamish about the fear you can cause in each other by proclaiming your individual truths. Your personal insights will, at times, be like a light shining into the hidden recesses of your partner's mind. Don't run. Learn from what you see and fear. There is an awakening that comes forward through knowing one another. This is nothing to fear; rather your understanding guides you to look toward the light of positive thinking. It is here that you find the wisdom to forgive and the ability to surrender to the truth!

Aries-Sagittarius: The Adventurers

Aries + Sagittarius = Life in the Fast Lanes

The two of you take no prisoners in the pursuit of excitement. You can talk each other into trying just about anything under the Sun! You are both fire signs, which means there is a relentless push to be mentally and physically on the move. Aries' zest can keep up with Sagittarius' zeal to learn and explore. Sagittarius' quick mind is well equipped to match wits with the challenging competitiveness of Aries. Your shared sense of humor helps you get through the stressful times. An endless search for activities to occupy your minds is another theme you may have in common.

Rugged Individualists Game

The games played in your Aries-Sagittarius romance center around self-absorption and the intense desire to fast forward through life. The *Rugged Individualists* game features extreme independence, which could get out of control. Harnessing your individual aspirations is like holding back Niagara Falls. Frank Sinatra's song "I Did It My Way" describes the essence of this game. You choose not to heed your partner's rights. It could be a matter of losing awareness of the relationship's boundaries, which leads you to push too far along your own paths. Even the creation of ground rules to guarantee greater togetherness meets with rebellion. You can grow weary from trying to convince each other who is right. The more brash you are when trying to prove a point, the more the protest intensifies.

This game can derail your sense of commitment. Commitment takes a willingness to reach mutual acceptance. In the *Rugged Individualists* game, your attitude is "every person for him or herself." The price is a lack of stability. Fire is a self-centered element. Don't worry. Fire signs are meant to show everybody else how easy it is to promote oneself. There are limits that this philosophy must adopt, that is, if you want to hold on to each other through thick and thin.

Fools Rush in Where Angels Fear to Tread Game

The two of you can easily throw caution to the wind or even the stars. Aries and Sagittarius hate to be confined. You are freedom seekers from the root of your soul. Tempting fate to take a risk now and then is your shared birthright. Many of the other signs admire your fortitude and even envy those moments when you choose reckless abandonment. In the *Fools Rush in Where Angels Fear to Tread* game, you can influence one another to take unnecessary chances. Business deals can make you mad at one another if they are not thought out in advance. If you believe in spontaneity rather than forethought, you may regret many decisions with twenty-twenty hindsight. The frustration you can cause each other leads to trouble.

The sense of adventure that you bring to one another is exciting. You can keep your lives exciting through activities such as camping, cross-country driving, searching for lost treasure, and so on. If you do a little planning, you may find that you save a lot of time. Aries and Sagittarius individually can easily take chances that many others fear to try. As a couple you run a greater chance of defying the odds to make something happen. It could become tiresome to repeat mistakes with your partner because neither of you considered the consequences.

Tomorrow and Tomorrow Game

Aries and Sagittarius don't find it natural to do today what could be done tomorrow. They can, with practice, master the art of being disciplined. In the *Tomorrow and Tomorrow* game, there is a tendency to disappoint each other by not following through on promises. The attention span of Aries, whether short or long, is easily distracted by new projects. Affable Sagittarius has a similar problem. The Archer can be so expansive, promising more than can possibly be delivered. These signs find it easy to put off a project with the thought that it will be done later. Yet, when a deadline arrives, the result will be the same: "I am not done yet."

The failure to fulfill promises may not be intentional as much as it is caused by the inability to be pinned down to a time frame. When it becomes a regular pattern, procrastination leads you to stop believing that your partner can deliver on a promise. You can perceive one another as being irresponsible. Remember, the fire-sign habit of trying to pack as much as possible into a day may prohibit prioritizing tasks. It is possible that one of you will feel that the other is selfish, only focusing on his or her own needs and ignoring your own. Commitment can scare some fire signs. You may feel that it is next to death to follow a schedule. In this game, one or both of you is making the statement, "I don't answer to anyone." You can alienate your passion for each other by acting in ways that don't back up your words.

Strategy

How do the two of you handle these Aries-Sagittarius games? The *Rugged Individualists* game challenges you to bend at times. You can't expect to always get your own way. There is no relationship that truly can survive without give and take. The Ram and the Archer must show their individuality; this is a given. The trick is how to coexist as individuals and still interact like a couple. It can be done! You will find you're even stronger when you learn how to empower each other. Building a stable relationship will come with practice. If you make a mistake and find yourselves backtracking into old behavior patterns, don't panic. Don't make accusations. Don't blame. Simply start again to find middle ground.

You can discover certain projects that, when done together, can build more of a team spirit. Include each other on major decisions. Announce your schedule or priorities once in a while. If you communicate your plans, there is less tension. You two already are individualists. Don't try to change each other. What you are doing is responding to the real needs that each of you possesses. Show that you are listening. You will not sacrifice your spontaneity by planning ahead. As a matter of fact, you will get even more mileage out of your impulses because there will be less chance of wasting time and energy. It takes strength to change this game into a winner. Why not use that competitive fiery spirit to bring your relationship closer?

In the *Fools Rush in Where Angels Fear to Tread* game, the two of you need to beware of walking too near the edge. Sound reality testing is part of the remedy to this game. Nobody needs to tell you to play it safe. The adventurous side of you two will ask for a voice when life is too slow. From a practical standpoint, your cash flow could increase by making planned business decisions. It might be wise to listen to the advice of your partner or friends if you embark on a major risk. Aries likes the thrill of danger or uncharted territory. Sagittarius, through blind faith or endless optimism, will climb mountains just for an exhilarating experience. You can mix the love of the unknown with a careful look at the stakes for your actions. This is better than a shortsighted leap that leaves you with a mess to clean up. Remember, your romance will not suffer if you embrace the wisdom of looking ahead with a degree of foresight. Then leap!

The *Tomorrow and Tomorrow* game asks you to live as much for today as tomorrow. Your commitment to finish what you start only deepens your connection. You will probably find that you feel more productive when following through on your promises. Rising above the tendency to procrastinate will win mutual admiration. It improves your sense of togetherness. There will continue to be a part of you that refuses to give in to the expectations of others. That's fine. Be sure you don't do this to each other. An element of compromise is a key ingredient to steering clear of this game. There is something else to consider. If you are reasonable in what you ask of each other, it takes the pressure off responding to a request. Give your lover enough time to work with you. Patience is testy for two fire signs. You both are ready to move ahead whether the other is ready or not; isn't this true? People will put off doing what they can get done today as a way of rebelling. This is why you must be reasonable in your expectations of each other. Focus on helping one another be successful. Use it as a guide to keep you on the right path.

The Rainbow

An Aries-Sagittarius duo is one of those rare examples of people in love with life. Adventure seeking imbues you with vitality and youthfulness. Your friends can find you delightfully refreshing. Your laugh is deep and reflects the happiness you find together.

An Aries man is spellbound by the Sagittarius woman's way of looking at reality with childlike innocence. She is not naive—quite the contrary. She is not impressed by seriousness. The Ram takes notice that this Sagittarius woman, who radiates dazzling idealism, can get the job done in a flash. She can instantaneously transform herself from the role of parent to businesswoman to pleasure seeker. He is swept off his feet by the Archer's vision. Inspired from the depths of her soul, she can shoot an arrow farther than the eye can see or the mind can fathom. Her persuasive voice combined with her spontaneous humor and keen awareness of world events have him following in fast pursuit.

The Sagittarius woman accepts the stormy, combative presence of the Aries man reluctantly. Is he more trouble than she needs? This is sometimes her first thought. She gives in only because she convinces herself that he can't really be so direct all of the time. The Archer learns later that the Ram is as straightforward as they come even when he tries to act shy. If for some reason he speaks in eloquent circles (like a Ferris wheel), watch his actions. He is quick to go forward whether or not his movements are announced. Aries' primordial rhythms make him a swashbuckler. He is sometimes scared into his courage, such as when meeting an outgoing Sagittarius woman. Make no mistake about it: when she sees the fighter in him, she doesn't run!

The Aries woman finds the Sagittarius man to be charming. He can shoot himself in the foot one moment yet offer startling insights a moment later. It strikes her that the Archer understands romance. The male Sagittarius also promises more than he can possibly deliver. The Ram is amused by this theatrical show. She loves his humor and lighthearted spirit. He seems to enjoy the chase as much as the catch. His impatience for instantaneous gratification in life matches her own. She thinks this man shares her own anxious desire to live each day as though it was an hourglass running out of time. Their minds and hearts appear to meet at the most inspiring of places.

The Sagittarius man is attracted to the blunt directness of the Aries woman because it reminds him of his own. She has a look of courage that he doesn't see in everyone. He believes that the Aries woman's feistiness is heartfelt. The Archer likes to fire arrows at far off destinations. The Ram certainly has a gusto for embarking on high adventure that matches his own. The two can leave the past in the dust. Romantic energy is never far from your restless imaginations.

Sexually speaking, it is fun to delight one another. There will be times you feel dead from your self-imposed schedules. Travel to romantic getaways brings out the real romantics in you. Passion is more alive when you develop a kingdom big and generous enough for your potential to be used to its fullest. The two of you don't expect life to only give you part of what you desire. When the cup isn't merely full but overflowing with the experiences you seek, your happiness together reaches its most exalted state.

Aries-Capricorn: The Leaders

Aries + Capricorn = Taking the Lead

Others will find you a self-assured couple. Ambition is in your hearts and souls. There are few challenges you will fear when you are inspired to attain desired aims. Aries motivates Capricorn to go beyond its cautious thoughts. Capricorn helps focus the impulsive energies of Aries into more concrete expression. You can take one another to new positions of power. You are the support behind one another's drive to rise to prominent status. The initiating themes in both of your signs are strong. Aries moves abruptly forward out of a need to prove that the first step can be taken. Capricorn launches a plan to ensure the security of the future. You may become a result-oriented duo due to enjoying the sweetness of success and prosperity.

On My Guard Game

The games played in your Aries-Capricorn relationship feature control issues and a tendency to thwart one another's goals. In the *On My Guard* game, it is difficult to let your partner into your world. Trust is lacking, and you are uncomfortable in letting your guard down. Sometimes your uneasiness may be due to a power struggle. A sense of competitiveness can come between you. One of you may feel inadequate due to the success of the other. Jealousy can be at the root of this game. Fear is another possible dimension; it may scare you to let your lover get too close. You may not be ready to reveal old wounds that were inflicted before you even met. It may be that hurt feelings caused by critical remarks cause one or both of you to pull back. It is not unusual in a relationship for there to be times of closeness followed by periods of distance. The difference found in this game is that the two of you stay at an arms-length away emotionally, which can block passion. You may sense that your partner is holding back, or that you are reluctant to really open up. The love you give and receive is trapped.

I Am the President Game

There may be instances when you can't agree on key decisions. The *I Am the President* game finds the two of you undermining one another's efforts. You both can be great leaders. Letting each other feel in control when doing a joint project may become touchy. It is not natural for Aries and Capricorn to be followers. Aries is more prone to question authority. Capricorn can have difficulty delegating jobs to others. Capricorn's motto is: "If you want to get the job done right, then do it yourself!" Power struggles can dominate your life together. It is never that far from your minds to question the motives of each other for making a particular decision. Do you have both of your interests in mind? If you don't recognize your partner's ideas as being as important as your own, discord will result. You are both executive types and need to know that you are on equal footing in the relationship. When you sabotage one another's need to lead, resentment will build.

Freeze Frame Game

Losing control does not come easily in an Aries-Capricorn romance. It can be slow to establish a commitment because each is looking to the other to make that bold first step. Who is going to go first? Even after you live together in a committed relationship, you may still ask, "How deep is our love?" and "Did we ever really let go to each other?" The answer may truly be yes, but it is difficult to convince yourselves of this. Developing stability is challenging if you don't have much faith in the foundation. Faith starts with commitment. Aries can dedicate great love and energy to a partner who shows appreciation. Capricorn will show great generosity to a lover, indicating longevity is probable.

Both Aries and Capricorn have a fear of fear itself. Aries must eventually launch a frontal attack on what it fears. Capricorn must somehow learn to stop making mountains out of molehills. Capricorn's fears can swell from the size of a mustard seed to that of a blimp. Cracking through the iceberg of fear takes courage. Honesty with one another comes after seeing you will not be rejected for being yourself. It is nearly impossible to make big changes in your natural way of being. The funny thing is that if Aries becomes too much like Capricorn or vice versa, neither is happy. You are not attracted by your similarities but by your differences! Problems arise when you look for too much of yourselves in each other. You tend to freeze when your expectations are rigid.

Strategies

How can you meet the challenge of your Aries-Capricorn games? The *On My Guard* game can be neutralized through exhibiting trust. You won't gain anything by holding back. You must convince yourselves that it is worth taking the risk to talk openly about what you need from each other. Be assertive. One of you must get the ball rolling. Waiting for the other to make the first move wastes time. Both of you must state your deepest needs. This game is a lot harder than it looks. Rock star Tom Petty was right on the mark in his song, "The Waiting." It is "the hardest part." Opening up the lines of communication becomes easier with practice. Aries and Capricorn don't find it easy to show vulnerability. Your two signs often have survived difficult circumstances to prove your abilities. People often test your capabilities, don't they? Why do this to each other? Give one another the benefit of the doubt. You may have decided to make others earn your trust. That's okay, but sooner or later take a chance with one another and really talk "straight." An underlying fear of being rejected can be at the heart of this game. Somehow, you must create an atmosphere that's safe enough for dialogue. Build a haven or cocoon, which doesn't mean a perfect world but a place that allows you to talk freely from your hearts. With practice and patience, you can see that letting down your guard doesn't mean you will be crushed. You could find yourselves getting angry at one another when you start really talking. Ride out the waves. It is probably bottled-up passion—anger stuffed into a bottle. Eventually, the waves will settle, and you can get to the heart of the matter.

The *I Am the President game* asks you to become more respectful of one another's personal need for power. There will be a time when one of you will assume the lead because you know more about an area of expertise. This is not the time to question your partner's authority unless you are being asked to swallow a plan you can't possibly find palatable. It is important to realize that, even if you are the expert on a subject, your partner may still have a different perspective. Aries and Capricorn can have trouble seeing life from this vantage point. Flexibility is your sword to cut away the traps of this game. Use it regularly, wisely, quickly, and perceptively; it's too bad it couldn't have been used yesterday!

You both will seek promotions and multiple life roles. Capricorn attracts responsibility as much as Aries frantically pursues paths leading to self-mastery. Your worlds are not so far apart. You need to build a bridge that carries you back and forth from one another's terrain. Empower what your partner seeks to accomplish by lending your support. Pay attention to your own ambitions and keep an eye on those of your lover. You will be handsomely rewarded with wealth and passion. The two of you go further when self-fulfillment surrounds your lives.

The *Freeze Frame* game is thawed out when you come closer to the fires of self-honesty. Honest self-assessment is the first step to warming your hearts. Your commitment is only as deep as you are willing to make it. Aries and Capricorn are a good match for each other. You have the strength to deal with one another's bossiness, which is a good thing. The fear that the relationship may fail need not stop you from taking your love to a higher level above the clouds of doubts circling in your heads. It takes work to define how you want your relationship to work. Business is as vital as sex. Your expectations of one another don't have to be decided in a day but do need to be addressed. Make sure any plan can be amended or revised so neither of you feels a need to filibuster. You can dodge any glacier in your path if you put your heads together. The energy you expend in resisting one another's control can be dynamically channeled into creative pursuits. It is often your strength that collides. Figuring out a way to stay out of each other's air space just enough to allow for spontaneous action is within your reach.

The Rainbow

In an Aries-Capricorn relationship you may immediately be impressed with each other's poise even if you both are scared to death! The two of you can leave many other couples behind your tracks as you pursue your goals.

An Aries man can see that the Capricorn woman is steady and strategy oriented. She cares about others yet maintains her focus on her life accomplishments. Her eyes reflect a strong awareness of reality. He thinks the two of them can accomplish great things. She seems to appreciate his initiative. He notices that this Saturnian woman usually finishes what she starts, which is in stark contrast to his tendency to leave projects undone. The Ram gets the message that he had best act responsibly. Once the job is done, this wise woman shows her fun-loving nature and lets her hair down. That's when she lets out a sigh of relief. She has incredible focusing power, and the Aries man would like to be on the receiving end of her serious passion.

The Capricorn woman finds the Aries man to be decisive and assertive. She needs a partner who is able to lead because, frankly, there are times when she tires of carrying the load for others. The female Capricorn senses that the Ram may rebel against duty and responsibility. If he will just honor her right to coexist as a leader, she will cut him a little slack. The Saturnian woman likes this lively man. His striving to get ahead is not so different from her own. He doesn't always bother with pleasing city hall. She would like to pick up tips from him on how to minimize the demands imposed on her. Life with this man appears to speed up her adrenaline. He can talk her into delegating work to others so she can have more fun with him. She could get used to this lifestyle.

The Aries woman likes to see a take-charge mentality in the Capricorn man though she doesn't care to be controlled by anyone. The Aries woman is inspired by the ambitious instincts of the Saturnian man. He seems to learn well from experience. She sees that he is a doer. His reluctance to show all of his cards doesn't bother her. The Aries woman is quick to enter a relationship. She doesn't waste time wondering if something can work. She notices that his caution evaporates when he warms up to her passion. Conversations gradually go from the impersonal to the personal. He has a responsibility-filled past. She would like to fly off to a place where time is not a constraint. She thinks it may be fun to be the object of each other's complete focus. Aries and Capricorn hearts really could be united much more quickly if there were fewer outside distractions.

The Capricorn man doesn't really know how to deal with the Aries woman. He is instantly attracted to the Ram's eagerness to explore life. The male Capricorn needs this kind of partner because he is inclined to look at life through sober eyes, seasoned by a time-tested, realistic philosophy. She defies time. She can be as time management oriented as he is when needed but is not as ruled by the clock. Her passion is in her swift mind and movement. The male Capricorn hates and loves the way she resists his control. His one big question is: "Am I big enough to let her have her power?" Whatever his answer, she will make up her own mind anyway! She doesn't really wait for permission from the Capricorn man to do her thing. Her boundaries are not really open for discussion, and they both know this from the start. She loves his affection and attention. His passion is serious, yet he may even learn to become playful once he lets go.

The Magic of Signmates

Aries and Capricorn spar more openly when they fall in love and gravitate toward speaking more freely. It's when they don't feel free to argue or to be individuals that storm clouds predict tough weather ahead. When you know you are a winning combination, you like to show the world you are happy. Not much can interfere with your commitment once you break through to a level of trust that allows you to ride out inclement weather. You can accentuate your individual potential. As a couple, you can confidently make decisions. Once you clearly define how to work together, you will create many opportunities for abundance. Neither of you likes to lose at whatever you do best. Aries is usually franker in showing this side; it is not so obvious in Capricorn, but make no mistake about it, defeat is painful. Your competitive power takes you to the heights of success. It can be rewarding to share in each other's victories.

Aries-Aquarius: The Eager Ones

Aries + Aquarius = Lickety-split Unpredictability

Speedy Aries and lightning-quick Aquarius team up to be a formidable couple. Bring on the future, please; you live there most of the time anyway. You can walk (or more likely run) hand in hand, ready to greet the next sunrise. You quickly tire of the current scenery. It takes a bullet train to keep up with you. Ex-Beatle John Lennon said that New York City was the only city that could keep up with him, and the same could be said for this sign combination. Action-oriented Aries complements the experimental side of Aquarius nicely. Aquarius' fascination with the mind fits in with Aries' enthusiasm for mental tests. Both love and hate stress at about the same level. You can't live with stress and can't live without it. Oh, where is the happy medium? You race through life together, trying to attain a balance between extremes.

Don't Crowd Me Game

The games played in your Aries-Aquarius romance fall into two categories. One is caused by your fierce independent streak. The other arises from great impatience with anything that resembles confinement. The *Don't Crowd Me* game occurs when the two of you don't want to answer to each other. Breathing room is vital to your well-being. Here the problem develops when you abruptly drop a bombshell that you want to be left alone without giving much notice. You want to retreat to the solitude of your sanctuary with a book, a mixed drink, a meditation pillow, or whatever else comforts you. That's fine unless you need to go all the time! It can be a convenient way to run away no matter how much the experts say you need a place to retreat. Not communicating for prolonged periods of time isn't resolved by constantly slipping away. Sooner or later, you need to talk through issues. Aries demands territorial rights and free speech. Aquarius pleads for free thinking, not always free speech because Aquarius may not be ready to talk. There are times when one or both of you needs to cool down; this is a must with you two. The anger that Aries or Aquarius can feel leads to agonizing mental anxiety. Your challenge is to determine how to balance your desire to be close with your need for space. If all else fails, Aries will try to provoke mentally detached Aquarius into a response. Aquarius will attack Aries' weak points to get the Ram to communicate. You both know how to get the other to talk. The question is whether you will do it. Also, remember that in this game if either of you is too demanding, the other will choose to fight or, as in this case, flight.

Nineteenth Nervous Breakdown Game

The two of you can work each other up into such a frenzy that the *Nineteenth Nervous Breakdown* game finds birth. So many sudden starts and stops in trying to work together cause your nervous systems to wear down. Communication breakdowns make it difficult to resolve issues. The speed with which you move makes it difficult to accurately perceive one another. The vision of your lover in your mind may be more out of focus than you realize. Surprise can be a wonderful part of romance, but too many surprises can be irritating. You may find that it's delightful to announce last-second changes in plans, yet such deviations can often cause havoc. This is especially true if you both have busy schedules. Change adds excitement, yet too many sudden departures from plans when it regularly only benefits one of you is not going to thrill the other. The tendency to be too self-focused is a trait of both Aries and Aquarius. You are role models in showing others how to swiftly achieve unique goals. If you want to be lovers with a future together, you will need to give advance notice of major revisions. You will feel more appreciated if your partner treats you with consideration. Otherwise, you will be disappointed because you are not sure you can depend on one another.

Lost Direction Game

If Aries and Aquarius lack a sense of direction, something is quite wrong. Aries starts to run in circles with a panic-stricken look when lost. Aquarius begins to resemble a ghost and feels uncomfortably invisible if disoriented. The *Lost Direction* game is played when you don't have a course to sail as a couple. You may even have well-defined personal goals yet not be on the same page as far as pursuing the future together. It could be strange not to be able to solve this puzzle. You look at each other and see two great minds. You share passion, excitement, and high hopes that you will find the best of everything together. You can plan your own life with a minimum degree of confusion, but when the two of you try to put your plans together, they don't mesh. If you force these two worlds to unite, you realize that it's like trying to pound a square peg into a round hole. Your individual universes are exhilarating, but your ability to share your partner's dreams is swept away by the all-consuming drive to pursue your own potential. The path together becomes slippery when you don't carefully compare notes, doesn't it? The irony here is that you are two potent forces as individuals and even as a duo when you shift gears at the same time. It's being in sync that is out of your reach.

Strategies

How do you turn these Aries-Aquarius games into winners? The *Don't Crowd Me* game demands sensitivity from each of you. If you invade the space of your partner too much, learn to back off. If you allow your lover the breathing room needed, life will be more fun. If you don't give each other enough space, Aries will angrily declare a need for solitude while Aquarius will give you a cold shoulder to drive you away. If you respect your partner's need for space, your partner is apt to come back that much faster. It is essential that neither of you run away. The retreat-to-the-cave theory works better when you truly use it to recharge your energies. A cooling down period is good for the psyche. Escaping responsibility or dodging conflict only makes problems loom larger. It is not as difficult to break the ice on a hot issue if you don't put discussing it on hold for too long. Practice good communication habits. It is okay if you need to pick a more convenient time to talk. The trick is not to forget to get around to talking!

In the *Nineteenth Nervous Breakdown* game, make it a policy to advise your partner in advance if you are going to make changes in your schedule. You may even need to give one another a day or night to claim as your own. Just don't forget to plan at least one day, night, or week that belongs to the relationship. It is unrealistic to expect everything to go according to schedule. In an Aries-Aquarius relationship, you can forget that! You thrive on the unexpected and on spontaneous ideas. That's why you need to create a little of the expected. Freedom doesn't mean that you always get to do your own thing. Don't worry. You can build a life together that doesn't require sacrificing your own goals. You may come to appreciate the benefits of not worrying one another to death. You may have more sexual fun and greater energy for creativity.

The *Lost Direction* game signals that all is not well with your communication skills. How can two people so driven to move forward with such force lose their way when trying to walk together? Take the time to pay attention to your partner on a regular basis. It will save you from having to stop to see where you got lost. Which turn did you miss? If only you had stopped to ask for directions or, better yet, asked each other about your shared destination. The two of you can put a future direction together that is big enough to include both of your worlds. Have fun putting together the blueprint of what you need in order to feel content. Give each other equal freedom to determine what's best for the relationship. Participate together in joint goals. Share your individual visions; it will help you to discuss your communal dreams. You may be surprised to find out you want some of the same things but never took the time to say so.

The Rainbow

Your Aries-Aquarius relationship is the essence of what it can be like to be with someone who enjoys your intense desire to live life to the fullest. There is an impatient streak that makes the two of you leapfrog right over boredom. You are lovers with an eye for new directions that are breathtaking and opportunity producing.

An Aries man is spellbound by the free spirit of the Aquarius woman. Her electric vision delights him and makes him curious about her. The Ram likes her vast visionary insights; she keeps him on his toes. Aries and Aquarius will probably have heated battles, but the Ram finds that love is not as productive without them. Freedom permeates this liaison like light does the Sun. The Aries man knows that he and this Uranian woman have quite a wild ride ahead of them. He is ready to get on with it!

The Aquarius woman perceives that the Aries man has a macho image to maintain. She confidently knows she can reach his more sensitive side—when the time is right. Not everyone has the courage to get the Aries man to feel. His pride to accomplish stimulates her own creativity. She will let him be charming if he will acknowledge her independence. She feels the two make an unpredictable pair, and that's fine by her. She prefers someone who is not too stodgy. Their minds appear to meet at some of the most interesting places. She wonders if he also feels like his mind is racing. It's refreshing to be with someone able to understand that love is a risk worth taking. The Uranian woman knows that a door can open and shut in a hurry. She hopes he will grab her hand so they can get through the passageway of opportunity together—the sooner the better.

The Aries woman is moved by the Aquarius man's cool intellect, which is colored with an intense need for self-expression. His mind is what initially attracts her, though he may think it's his passion. She is excited by the way he challenges her. She knows he will not retaliate even if she manages to outsmart him. The Ram isn't afraid to pursue the Uranian man's heart. She isn't so sure if she wants such an unpredictable approach from him. He seems worth the trouble. It's hard for this daredevil woman to turn down a chance to share this man's radical vision. His thinking is futuristic and his uncanny knack to maintain a sense of direction fascinates her. She thinks a ride with him would be exhilarating and full of endless surprises.

The Aquarius man is reluctant to approach the Aries woman. He will never admit this. He wants her to think that he is impervious to fear. She knows his strengths and senses his frailties. She finds his weaknesses to be endearing, but he thinks she is attracted to his strengths. He likes the way the Ram handles herself. She flatly tells him her likes and dislikes. He sees a way to accommodate this outspoken woman. He becomes attached to her upbeat personality. The Uranian man isn't worried about fitting her into his life as much as how to land on her turf without crashing. Life together will require a wider fast lane, or so it seems to the inventive Aquarius man. It strikes him that her quick impulses to act will fit right in with his lightning-quick ideas. They can figure out how to hit the brakes later!

This is a match that seems to be made in heaven: Aries, the warrior, and Aquarius, the unconventional thinker. The two of you want your freedom to be respected. It is highly likely you will push one another into new growth. You detest prodding yet admire its results. Each of you likes to know the other cares, and you appreciate seeing dramatic evidence of it. You may ask inconvenient favors of each other as a test. You know what's going on but do your best to comply anyway. You want to "win" one another's heart. A sea of love connects your two worlds, and it is through navigating the waters with a spirit of cooperation that you realize that you are not envious of each other's possessions. A third world is there to create, the one you long to share. Take your time in building it. It is not exactly the same as the one you live in as individuals. It is a brave new world, one that requires your clearest vision, forgiveness, and the determination to fight for it.

Aries-Pisces: The Imaginative Ones

Aries + Pisces = Fondness for Mystery

Aries normally isn't evasive, but the Ram can show a much less straightforward side when in a relationship with a Pisces. Intuitive and emotional Pisces influences fast-footed Aries to be more sensitive to the invisible forces of the universe. Does this sound too mystical? Then think of it another way. Aries becomes more enthralled with fulfilling its imagination when in the company of the dreamy Fish. The "doer" in Aries is good for Pisces. Why? Aries instills a drive in Pisces to bring ideals into the world of reality. Pisces reminds Aries that the universe is a much bigger place than the mundane world. Life borders on the unusual when this pair of signs falls in love. It is a bit of a magical mystery tour; a bit of the romantic in each is easily awakened.

Paradise Lost Game

The games played in your Aries-Pisces relationship orbit around two key themes: disappointment of one another's unrealistic expectations and difficulty in facing reality. In the *Paradise Lost* game, you may overly idealize one another. It is not easy to maintain life on a fantasy level. Even when a relationship starts with a passionate explosion, it settles down into day-to-day concerns, including the need to communicate. Expectations can be extraordinary between Aries and Pisces. Neither of you truly wants to disappoint the other. Perfection is impossible to accomplish since there are no perfect people. You want each other to be something that is not humanly possible. The romance will sour if you become too critical. Sooner or later each of you will notice behavior in your partner that you want to change. In some instances you may be correct. The problem in this game occurs when you demand the impossible. Each of you will make mistakes. It is inevitable that the Ram will anger the Fish by being insensitive. It is highly predictable that the Fish will offer a plan that, from the Ram's perspective, lacks logic. Aries can say hurtful things when thwarted. Pisces can lapse into silence to irritate Aries, waiting for a quick reaction. Be reasonable in the dreams you want to pursue together. You won't find a shared message that sings to your hearts in this game.

Hiding from Reality Game

If the two of you refuse to deal with decisions realistically, the *Hiding from Reality* game can result. Denial overshadows your clarity. It could be the fear of taking responsibility that causes this behavior. Your sense of commitment may seem vague, and communication may be lacking. Why do you feel the need to hide? Perhaps being honest with each other is challenging. There may be an underlying fear of being hurt. Aries acts strangely when trying to conceal the truth. Doing so runs contrary to the Ram's need to blurt out observations. Pisces would seem the more likely candidate to be the cause of this game but may not deserve all of the blame. While Pisces may hide real feelings better than a possum playing dead, Aries can run as fast from the light of reality as Pisces can drift toward idle fantasy. Each is far from helping to solve the dilemma of this game. Sometimes an Aries and Pisces couple may go for weeks and months without really addressing an issue. Eventually they float into a reef of trouble. There are instances when Aries and Pisces hide more from themselves than each other. Denial keeps your hearts at an agonizing distance.

Treading Water Game

The Ram and the Fish can thwart each other's momentum. This can bring on the *Treading Water* game. Have you ever had a dream in which you try to run away from a pursuer but can't seem to move or can only move in slow motion? In this game neither of you can make progress in your personal lives or as a couple. What is wrong? You may have unresolved emotional issues. Many times this game is caused by hidden anger. Aries will go into a more introverted mode in order to avoid stepping on sensitive Pisces' toes. Pisces will often choose to tiptoe around conflict rather than risk awakening the Ram's temper. Contrary to popular belief, Pisces can tap into its own angry streak, but will the Fish appear visibly angry? This may be the question of the century! Fire (Aries) and water (Pisces) can produce steam! The two of you could dilute each other's sense of direction. People of this sign combination can fall deeply in love. The details of everyday living are what seem to throw you off course. Aries and Pisces speak languages from different worlds.

Aries understands people who act upon their intentions. Whether or not the Ram likes your actions in the end, it is secondary to his or her thankfulness that you act upon your ideas. Pisces may seem to appreciate your frankness, but this disguises the Fish's inner anger at your audacity, which is where things start to get confusing. Not all Pisces are the same! Many are willing to undergo the trauma of emotional storms to tempt others to speak their minds. Aries may hold back from Pisces' sincere request to reveal the truth. It can be hard to recognize that this game is even being played and may take quite a while before both of you are aware that the relationship is stuck.

Strategies

How can you rise above the challenges of these Aries-Pisces games? First, remember that it may take a lot of practice. No, let it go on the record right now that it *will* take tons of practice! Harmony is not as elusive as it appears. One of the difficulties in Aries-Pisces relationships is that it is not always easy to measure how far you are from resolving an issue. The answers could be so close that you can cut them with a knife, but would you even know there is an issue? Awareness is vital. Tuning in to each other's longing to be loved and a sincere desire to be a good lover are good places to begin. In the *Paradise Lost* game, it is less necessary to prove something to each other than it is to truly perceive each other. Passion, sex, and falling in love start a process of discovering great depths about your partner; it may be more than you ever bargained for. There is nothing wrong with wanting paradise. In some ways, every relationship is searching consciously or unconsciously to escape to Utopia or Shangri-la. What you both need to keep in mind is that this is a transitory state of being. If you keep communication flowing, there is a chance your relationship will maintain a clear perspective. You may not always be there for each other in the way you desire, but you can come through enough of the time to believe in the value of your commitment.

The *Hiding from Reality* game requires you to face down secrets and fears. No one can expect to face reality all of the time. However, you can't drown in denial either and expect to live a balanced life together. It takes more energy to conceal the truth than to put it on the table. More energy is consumed in running away from an issue than in dealing with it. You must let the truth set you free! Defining your relationship will be less of a struggle if you deal with this game. The more you commit to being each other's most trusted ally, the less darkness there is to confuse you. Bring on the Sun by slaying emotional distance. Asking for the love we need is scary. Some of us have been betrayed in the past. You will never know the highest potential of love waiting for you both if you don't come out from your favorite hiding places. No one can really force you to pursue greater love. You must take that first step. Aries must welcome the challenge in order to leap. Pisces must find the faith to leap. You are not jumping over a cliff but into a more secure place in each other's arms!

You will find yourselves less waterlogged by the *Treading Water* game if you pool your resources. The unity you want is destroyed by pulling in opposite directions. The problem may arise from the way the two of you embrace challenges. Aries is the initiator and dives in feet first. Pisces will swim in circles at first (like a merry-go-round) before taking the plunge. The amazing thing is that, if left to your own devices, you still may finish a task at about the same time! The sense of direction or momentum you seek requires inspiration. It is vital to find that shared belief in your relationship. If observable or unspoken anger has collected, a certain degree of wisdom is needed to address the situation. Anger will turn into moods in an Aries-Pisces romance. Pay attention to moods because they reveal it is time to deal directly with an issue. Don't run away from a heated exchange; it's the signal you are about to uproot the problem. If you must wait for a cooling down period to really talk sensibly, do so, but remember it isn't always nice and neat when you settle an issue. Let it get a little "down and dirty." You don't want to hurt each other. You are trying to remove the obstructions to giving and receiving love.

The Rainbow

Your Aries-Pisces relationship can be a source of great joy. Did you feel a special possibility when you first met? Did you meet under mysterious circumstances? Whether the answer to these questions is yes or no, it won't take long to realize you may have plunged into deep water fast.

An Aries man can be fascinated by the intuitive flare of a Pisces woman. He is charmed by the way she walks away from him but, at the same time, tempts him to move closer. Her ideals and feelings are worn like ornaments. The Ram is attracted to her openness. The Neptunian woman is hard for the Aries man to forget. She touches the essence of his being, and he knows this to be true.

The Pisces woman admires the look of experience in the Aries man's eyes. He has certainly fought a war or two. She is not afraid of his strength. Rather, she wants to show her own valor. She senses his attraction but wonders if her inner world will attract or repel him. The Neptunian woman likes to see that he can say what's on his mind and in his heart. She believes that one without the other is only half of the story. She would like this to be a story with a happy ending. She intuitively realizes that, if they put their best foot forward, anything is possible.

The Aries woman sees the Pisces man as a challenge. His face reflects her innermost feelings, but his inner world is hidden from everyone. She muses that if the two of them believe in each other, their greatest goals can be attained. She wants to pursue him because he captures her romantic dreams. Love has a wonderful rhythm in an Aries-Pisces relationship. She likes to look into his caring and sensitive eyes because it shows her the possibilities that life with him may offer. It seems to her that they could share an inspiring dream that propels them forcefully ahead.

The Pisces man is moved by this warrior princess who has come into his life. She brings passion to the recesses of his innermost worlds. He is excited and surprised to find that she has unlocked the door to his heart so forcefully. The Neptunian man appreciates the lively intensity in her eyes. It is refreshing to meet someone with the courage to live the dreams that he feels.

Aries and Pisces can be the greatest of lovers. Staying in touch with the ever-changing moods of this romance is an adventure. You will need to be part psychologist, student, and listener to understand all of the dynamics brought into manifestation in this relationship. If you want an easy relationship, this may not be the one. If you want a feeling of endless love (with a few ups and downs), you may have chosen the right partner. Aries will enjoy leading Pisces down new and adventurous paths. Pisces takes Aries on intuitive journeys that offer beauty and a taste of the unusual. When you freely share your views of reality, the chances are better you will find the unity you seek. It may not always be paradise, but it will be a life together of mutual growth with a dependable partner.

Taurus-Taurus: The Economizers

Taurus + Taurus = Show-Me Kind of Couple

The two of you won't believe in something until you see its real potential. You are good together in managing what you own. Though it's true that all Bulls are not the same, you have a natural affinity for one another because you were born under the same Sun sign. If you want stability, you probably have found it. You can display solid business savvy. A mutual appreciation for comfort and beauty is probable. You inspire one another to be determined and patient in fulfilling your ambition. You tend to become motivated when you both sense an opportunity to secure your present and future. Working together with a spirit of unity takes you far together.

Bullheaded Game

The games played in your Taurus-Taurus relationship orbit around stubbornness, fixed values, and possessiveness. The *Bullheaded* game shows its face when the two of you lock horns over differing points of view. Your sign is known for its tendency to live life on its own terms. Two Bulls can become inflexible when negotiating with one another. If you fight solely for your own position, it will be difficult to reach common ground. This game usually is caused by losing sight of how to form a win-win proposal. Neither of you can expect to always get your own way. Finding ways to communicate without power struggles makes life together more enjoyable. You could find that passion fades when you bicker over inconsequential details. You need to stay open to alternative ideas but fail to do so. A strong leaning toward your own priorities holds back clear communication. An unwillingness to listen to your partner keeps you at a distance. The comfort you seek as a couple is elusive. Getting you to change your mind once your radar is fixed on an idea is almost as impossible as relocating Mount Everest!

All Dollars and No Sense Game

If the two of you become too earthbound in your thinking, the *All Dollars and No Sense* game can manifest. This game typifies the tendency to become so absorbed in business that you miss out on romance. Your perceptions are so locked into making ends meet that you create a bottom line with little pleasure. Your interactions are colored by material concerns to the exclusion of each other's feelings. You may ask, "Where is the love?"

There is nothing wrong with living an abundant life. It's only when you sacrifice too much to acquire the good things in life that you may fall victims to this game. You may need to examine what you value. The relationship may be lost to career drives. Instability arises if you sacrifice the balance between your public and private lives. The momentum to get ahead or to rise in status can lead you to lose perspective. This game may lead you to refuse to adopt a strategy that would include greater romance in your lives.

I Want to Own You Game

Possessiveness is always a potential problem in a Taurus-Taurus relationship. When one of you feels too restricted by the other in making independent decisions, you will know you are caught up in this game. Affection and attachment in their own right are harmless. As a matter of fact, you may be delighted that your partner feels so attached to you. The Bull needs to feel ownership much like a cat that marks people as its own by swishing its tail over them. Allowing for personal autonomy may seem threatening. You may fear losing your partner if you give him or her the freedom to pursue personal paths.

The mistake that is often made in this game is to apply your philosophy about business to the way you relate to one another. The two don't mix all that well; it is like adding water to a gasoline tank. Your romance will seem like it is running on fumes, not on high octane. Passion fades when you perceive a lack of trust. Without faith in each other, you will sense your relationship is not as deep as it could be. As a matter of fact, you are floating near the surface, and your discussions probably steer around the real issues.

Strategy

How can you climb above your Taurus-Taurus games? In the *Bullheaded* game, you simply need to be determined to adopt a more supple way of communicating with each other. When each of you *sees* you can gain from a decision, negotiations become much easier. Otherwise, what do you risk? War! Resistance! You are probably already well versed in the saga of what happens during a standoff. Frustration can be sidestepped by practicing true communication. Demands will not lead the way to victory. Taurus is a lot more apt to go along with the program when participation is not forced. You can elicit support for an idea by reciprocating the favor for your partner. Get good at this! It really does open the door for creative energies. Love will seem less mysterious if each of you feels empowered in decision-making processes. Inflexible perceptions need to be traded in for more elastic ones. Try it; you may even learn to like it. When you see the increased flow of feelings in your partnership, the rewards will be obvious.

The *All Dollars and No Sense* game needs you to value your quality time spent together as much as the intense work you put into your career. There are times when you can't exert much control over your schedules. The two of you may have enormous responsibilities as parents or caretakers, which means you have to find a day here and there just for you. It is easy for you to forget to pencil your partner into your schedule. The work world itself can consume your energy. Even if you love your job or career, don't lose the focus on your relationship needs. Even great success in the business world can be a distraction. The other side of this is true too. Poverty can put great pressure on any couple, especially the security consciousness of Taurus. Wherever you fall on the wealth scale, this game is still a possibility. Somehow you need to keep in front of your mind the reasons you wanted to be together in the first place. A renewal of your commitment (or vows) from time to time may be wise. Honoring your relationship by going to special places can be a reward that you need to ensure your longevity.

The *I Want to Own You* game is a matter of not trying to assume too much control. You will fall more deeply in love if you encourage greater freedom. You know when trust is there or it isn't. Experiment a little. Let go. It takes more energy to try to dominate someone than it does to empower each other. Each of you can show your talent in leading in your own areas of self-mastery. There is no need to get into a long-term power struggle. Power games are tiring and usually don't make either of you happy, do they? You have picked the wrong relationship to expect your partner to give in to you. You reach a state of mutual admiration through recognizing each other's rights. Focus your intense power as a duo into projects and investments or into changing the world. You have the capacity to convert the traps of this game into insightful energy that empowers you both.

Rainbow

Your Taurus-Taurus romance is adorned with many fine attributes. The relationship has a pragmatic radiance that guides you to make sensible decisions. You can add to each other's wealth in many ways. The allure of the sensual is never far from your minds.

A Taurus man finds the Taurus woman well suited to his material and romantic aims. Each has a need to settle down and to find permanent roots. The Taurus man is looking for confidence and appreciates her ability to massage his ego. She knows how to stand her own ground yet can stand by the side of her male lover as he proves his worth to the world. The female Taurus is not exactly timid when it comes to making her own way in the work arena. She is as determined as her male Taurus counterpart, which pleases him greatly.

The Taurus woman loves to receive the attentions of the Taurus man. A performance takes place when these two meet. Acting upon physical attraction is as big a deal in the relationship as seeking financial security. Each responds to a primordial calling that drives these pleasure seekers to passionately unite. There is wisdom in Taurus when it comes to the value of things. Down to its very bones, Taurus knows how to survive a financial crisis better than most. When it comes to a conflict in your romantic life, you can grow panicky. The love of balance and stability is at the core of your Venusian hearts.

Taurus lovers must make a pact to conquer their differences quickly. Neither can put up with the agony of fighting endlessly to make a point. There is a tendency not to surrender to an adversary easily. When two of this sign are in a relationship, one or both must become talented in dispelling the darkness of discord. You must be willing to value the beauty of being together more than having your own way. Make no

Let the Games Begin

mistake about it, you have a true treasure in each other. Don't lose sight of the love you have discovered and worked so hard to maintain. Take it out of the safety deposit box. Express your love daily to keep it alive. Rather than focusing on money and possessions, use your security to support the bond that you so energetically share.

Taurus-Gemini: The Enterprising Ones

Taurus + Gemini = Solid Thinking

This sign combination lends itself well to being a productive duo. Making good use of resources is likely a trademark. A get-down-to-business mindset is never really that far out of sight. The powers of concentration found in Taurus, especially when pursuing tangible results, can keep Gemini focused on getting a job done. Gemini's quick grasp of situations while in the midst of a process offers great insight to one-step-at-a-time Taurus. If Taurus is materially comfortable, this sign is more apt to enjoy romance and the pleasures of life. Gemini's mental invigoration often inspires romantic energies to come alive.

Anxiety Prone Game

The games played in your Taurus-Gemini relationship are connected to disrupting one another's concentration and to intentionally unclear communication. Taurus doesn't like surprises. Everyday existence needs to be logical and to provide reliable structure. Gemini prefers life to be unpredictable. This sign might even pull a few tricks to undermine everyday routines. When the two of you disturb one another's natural rhythms, the *Anxiety Prone* game occurs. Taurus isn't happy when its stability is threatened. Sometimes it doesn't even take such a threat to upset this creature-comfort sign. The inability to control Gemini can get on Taurus' nerves, or figuring out Gemini's next move can bother the Bull. Gemini doesn't exactly rebel against authority. Rather, Gemini skirts around or over the issue altogether. Gemini doesn't like to waste the time it takes to deal with a dictator! Gemini's spontaneous, multidimensional, and aloof movements can irritate Taurus.

What might Taurus do to upset the fragile nervous system of Gemini? The Bull may initiate a self-absorbed and unannounced drive to launch a business venture. Leaving Gemini out of decision-making processes is a good way to poison the relationship. Communication is next to godliness for Gemini. Your relationship needs to expand to make room for two considerably different ways of engaging the world. Taurus and Gemini filter what they see differently. Both walk with determination, but Gemini can change directions swiftly and not lose its way. This doesn't work as well for Taurus; taking a turn too quickly results in a nasty spill. Talking keeps you walking together even if you choose divergent paths. If you don't talk, this game can find you seeking time apart just to regain your energy. You are in a relationship with a sign that has the capacity to excite you. You are also attempting to relate to someone who can upset your mental equilibrium. It's not that Taurus always prefers life to move slowly or that Gemini always wants to make points a beat more quickly. Your minds filter reality differently. This game presents a challenge: Can you identify the warning signals that you are about to blow your partner's peace of mind out of the water?

Double Messages Game

When communication contains intentionally misleading information, you may be in the middle of the *Double Messages* game. The purpose of your conversation isn't to enlighten one another but to confuse or to distract each other from your true intentions. Taurus can make even romantic relationships part of the business playing field. This is a dreadful mistake. Gemini may hide its agenda in order to protect its ability to express multiple sides of its personality. The game may even start out as an innocent display but end up with one partner purposely misleading the other. This is a power game that can come between you. Each of you is trying to preserve your own turf. Setting up a smoke screen keeps real motives camouflaged but isn't a big problem unless you start to sense that a gulf of emotional separation is taking over. When there are so many secrets, you may start to forget what the truth is. The natural Taurean tendency to keep life simple and the natural Gemini instinct to paint clear word pictures are in hibernation. You may sense your companionship is out of tune. It is difficult to get back on key if you are not playing by the same rules.

Hearing What You Want to Hear Game

In the *Hearing What You Want to Hear* game you choose to be selective listeners. You may miss key facts. Taurus can slip into the game in order to avoid unpleasant situations. The Bull can run from conflict as though it is a plague. Gemini will at times prefer to back away from tough issues in order to gather its mental faculties. Taurus will retreat to delay responding to life's demands. When the two of you discuss important things, you may tune out whatever doesn't fit into your vision of your partner. You may become angry when your ideas or suggestions are run through a litmus test. A desire to share your resources is diluted by doubting your partner's faith in you.

Strategies

How do you turn the tide of these Taurus-Gemini games? In the *Anxiety Prone* game, it is vital that you identify what each of you does that makes the other nervous. You may not be able to change your behavior completely, but some adjustments may help. Sometimes you only need to show your partner that you are at least trying. Your efforts will lessen the tensions of this game; it works in this instance! Be patient. It takes practice to tune in to each other's needs. You will minimize disappointment if you include one another in major decisions. The trust you develop is a good antidote for this game. There is little need to fight for a majority of the controlling interests in the relationship. You will need to stay away from hidden agendas. Giving advance notice of a plan is more stabilizing. The more balance you maintain, the greater your joy and passion.

Your signs are cut from very different molds, but there are a few common elements. Each of you, in your own way, values beauty. You share a drive to build a life together that has a promise of growth. The enterprising spirit you both possess can be forcefully channeled into business ventures. You certainly can add stability to each other's life by supporting individual serious ambitions. Pour your energies into your similarities. Don't become hypnotized by your differences. Be aware of them but don't let them rule you. Your true power lies in your ability to use your resources.

In the *Double Messages* game, giving clear clues about your goals is a prerequisite for a healthy relationship. You don't have to confess every secret, but it is a good idea to mention those that will upset your partner. Honesty takes courage. It is scary to think our most cherished dreams may be rejected and more convenient to hide our true motives, but does this lead to the result you want? Give clear messages. Learn to negotiate from the truth rather than trying to conceal from fear. This doesn't happen overnight. Old habits are hard to break. Mutual empowerment occurs when you rely less on this game. It is a key that each of you be able to perceive that your personal goals can be realized in this relationship. It only takes a little encouragement to get back on the right highway. Say what you mean, and mean what you say. Honesty isn't all that painful; it is the path to harmony.

The *Hearing What You Want to Hear game* echoes less loudly in your relationship when you are willing to flow with life's ups and downs. Conflict is more threatening or unsettling when you don't face up to it. The art of listening is not as easy as it sounds. You can be a spin doctor who colors what you think you hear with what you want to hear. Communication will be your ally if you are willing to consider both sides of an argument. You will have opposing perspectives occasionally. If good communication patterns are established, it will become easier to integrate new ideas into your relationship and to work together to conquer this game.

The Rainbow

Your Taurus-Gemini relationship is elevated to the highest of levels when both of you sense that your potentials are being utilized. A commonsense approach accompanied by a steady-as-you-go outlook propels the two of forward.

The Taurus man doesn't readily know how to size up a Gemini woman. He watches her with curiosity. Her spirit perplexes and delights him. She seems easy to control, but her powerful intellect can detect any trap. The Bull finds he gets further by allowing this Mercurian woman the freedom of movement that she needs. He is fascinated by her intense desire to learn. She draws closer when he focuses on open-ended discussions. The Bull notices that she likes to keep her options open. He wants to explore those romantic avenues with her.

The Gemini woman is captivated by the attention of the Taurus man. She knows her movements will never be quite totally understood. Her passionate heart is lit up by his willingness to let her be. She loves his strength but knows that she must sometimes defy it. The Mercurian woman perceives that he both loves and hates her defiance. She likes the softness in his voice; it reminds her of a peaceful landscape. She prefers his sensitive side over his business persona, though his ambition measures up to her practical needs. This Mercurian woman likes to know that her imagination and reality-testing actions are appreciated by this earthy Venusian man.

The Taurus woman senses that a Gemini man can lead her into trouble. He can lift her spirits with his refreshing ideas and disappoint her if he can't find a place for his ideas in the world. She will overlook all of his apparent shortcomings if he honors her need to be valued. She is as solid as a rock when it comes to business. The Mercurian man can be pragmatic, which is wise if he wants to win this woman's heart. She knows a good deal when she sees one. The Gemini man strikes her as an adventurous investment. Her heart entices her to go after this lively, alert man.

The Gemini man finds the Taurus woman to be a creature worthy of study. She can seduce him with her innocence and empower him with her ferocious desire for love. It isn't winning that drives her as much as seeing her ideals find creative expression. She seems to be both a goddess and an earth mother. The duality of the Gemini man worships this about her. On one hand, he likes complex people. Then again, the clear simplistic beauty of her mind and spirit never grows old. He is drawn to the way this woman carries herself with elegance even during the most stressful of times. She has a calm passion that seems to come alive as trust deepens.

You can support each other's unique missions. You are not always going to see eye to eye, but the strength you find in resolving your differences makes you an invincible couple. You will not always find the other signs willing to break through your defenses. It is possible that your relationship will endure. As a couple you can fulfill a vision that your lives will be filled with love and wealth. You will never really possess each other's spirit. Taurus is too stubborn to let this happen while Gemini is never really constrained by mental or physical limitations. The freedom you ignite in each other is your underlying coat of arms. Your partnership can be a testament to fulfillment. Your passion for each other reflects your willingness to support each other's path. You are a beacon of hope, support, and faith for your lover. Don't let the light go out. When you put your secrets on the table and reveal your true thoughts, you make a pact that is very, very real.

Taurus-Cancer: The Cautious Ones

Taurus + Cancer = Playing It Safe

Your two signs have a natural affinity for each other. Taurus is comfortable with the nesting instincts of Cancer. Similarly, Cancer finds the no-nonsense side of Taurus trustworthy. These signs welcome a certain degree of stability. Both can accept the wisdom of "saving for a rainy day." This is not a duo that readily puts all of its eggs in one basket either. Business savvy is likely. Budgeting resources are usually instinctual for this sign combination.

Muddy Waters Game

The games in your Taurus-Cancer relationship center around not reading each other's needs clearly and a lack of trust. Together, earthy Taurus and watery Cancer can make mud. The *Muddy Waters* game typifies the emotional and mental confusion that can occur. Taurus looks for instructions that are easy to read and follow. Cancer has the power of intuition at its beck and call. When the two of you work together, it can feel like you are on different pages or that you are reading from different "how to" manuals. Inertia can result if you aren't careful. The two of you can lose momentum for individual or joint goals. Taurus' first concern is whether an idea makes sense. To Cancer a project or idea doesn't always have to be logical as long as it's clear how to get the job done. Material gains motivate Taurus to take the initiative to move forward. The Bull also weighs whether the result is worth the energy required. Cancer is motivated by its need for emotional security. It's not that this sign is above the material world. Material possessions and money become important once

Cancer resolves to go out in the world. In this game you somehow do not speak the same language; you go around in circles because you seem to be speaking in foreign tongues. You may be sincerely trying to communicate, but you are simply not interpreting what your partner needs or says accurately.

Digging Up the Seed Game

You may be tempted to continually question how deep your love is. A hearty discussion to see where each of you is in the relationship is one thing. Compulsive worrying about the relationship's health could result in the *Digging Up the Seed* game. A lack of belief in your commitment is at the root of this game. The seed can't grow if you will not leave it alone. Your relationship needs to be constantly nurtured to make each of you confident in what you plant together. The storms that come through will not be so threatening to your stability if you practice good communication habits. This game is more likely when the give-and-take in the relationship seems to be out of balance. Taurus' trust is nurtured by not asking this sign to carry all of the responsibility. Cancer automatically becomes trusting when its nurturing attributes are not abused. It's when Taurus or Cancer feels it is being taken advantage of that these signs start to look intensely beneath the surface of things. Weeds of discontent can surface. You may project your own problems onto one another. Blame can close off your hearts. Passion and love will dry up if you can't find a way back to more fertile territory.

Playing It Safe Game

Taurus and Cancer are not signs that enjoy confrontations. The Bull likes to proceed with a deliberate demeanor. Cancer, the Crab, prefers to crawl slowly and cautiously. Neither wants to face the anger you may provoke in one another. It doesn't mean you are always passive people, but you influence each other to choose your battles carefully. The *Playing It Safe* game depicts how you could sidestep important issues. Denial is preferred over facing a problem directly. A problem can be blown out of proportion if you put off finding a solution. The more combative signs could learn a lesson in patience from you. This game does not reflect your patience but your avoidance behaviors. Running from the truth only leads you into the shadows. Sooner or later you both must come out into the light. Why? It gets lonely hiding in the dark. You may find that you lack closeness and warmth in your relationship.

Your commitment may become a blur due to a lack of definition in what you want from your partner. Rather than basking in the glow of intimacy, you are left in a damp, miasmic atmosphere.

Strategies

How can you resolve these Taurus-Cancer games? The *Muddy Waters* game only requires that you listen to your partner more attentively. This sounds easier than it really may be. You filter your experiences in different ways. Taurus is more comfortable with what it *sees* as realistic and plausible. Cancer finds comfort in intuition because of its ability to sense the future. You need to tell each other how you really view a situation. Listen carefully. There are likely to be vast differences in your reasoning. You do share a strong need to be valued for being yourselves. When you understand your own points of reference as individuals, it will help to create a mutual roadmap. Emotional confusion will sometimes require that you briefly step away from one another. You may need to do this so you can regain your objectivity. Don't panic. Remember that if you get lost in the woods, the first thing to watch out for is fear and irrational thinking. In this game, you may want to remember not to jump to erroneous conclusions. You might not be as lost as you think. If you can calm down, the path back to togetherness may not be that far away.

The *Digging Up the Seed* game calls on each of you to reach for a little extra faith. Often a crisis can really test the depths of your love. If you have established solid communication habits, an unexpected emotional storm won't blow you out of the water. It is easier to believe in each other if you feel your own ambitions are given equal time and consideration. Make it a constant part of your routine together to positively reinforce each other's key needs. Really being there for your partner when his or her spirits are a bit down boosts your relationship. This is an inexpensive but valuable strategy. It is one thing to tell each other you care, but showing how much you care may be even more important. It doesn't take as much time as you think to erase negative patterns. Pay attention to the inner calling directed at you from your lover. Responding to these needs is as vital as material necessities.

The *Playing It Safe* game is rectified by not being too cautious. Life doesn't wait for us; it is a train that's always on the move. Relationships have a pulse all of their own. Don't take it for granted that you can wait forever to take care of unfinished business.

Everyone experiences at least some fear when first meeting someone. You may still be trying to take that leap of faith even after months or years of being together. Remember that old saying, "It takes two." It's true here! It's not enough that one of you is willing to move forward. You both need to find that trust and level of commitment. Time is sometimes the answer. Your relationship may need time to really learn how to move in unison. There is nothing wrong with taking it slow. The two of you can figure out when it is time to change your tempo. Talk honestly and eventually you will find a pace that quiets your fears.

The Rainbow

In your Taurus-Cancer relationship you gradually open up to each other's ideas and dreams. The gifts you can offer one another deepen with time. You can move from caution to sheer delight in being with someone who showers you with affection.

A Taurus man is not really sure how to approach a Cancer woman. She appears harmless enough, but her eyes seem to penetrate his innermost thoughts. He feels less self-assured in her presence until he *sees* that her desire to know him stems from curiosity about how he thinks. The Venusian man likes the way this lunar woman does business. She has a level-headed way of carrying herself. He thinks they could make the world spin in their favor.

The Cancer woman wants to see if the Taurus man's emotions are as steady as the image he projects (and protects). She doesn't want to scare him off as she tunes in to his feelings. He looks as though he wants to run but doesn't because he is fascinated by her. The Cancer woman eloquently leads conversations. She wants him to talk. Why? She listens to the male Taurus with an ear for small talk and for the truth. His romantic voice makes her want to know his inner world. He certainly has the business world figured out!

The Taurus woman wonders if the Cancer man will ever boldly sweep her off her feet. When he does, she wonders whether she can fulfill his romantic fantasies. Her instincts tell her if he has the passion she needs. She wants him to be the answer to her dreams and to fulfill her desire to reach out and truly touch someone. She is hesitant to reveal this side of herself, thinking he may flee before he really knows her. The promise that they can fulfill each other's dreams makes her want to stay close.

The Cancer man *sees* the Taurus woman as having the "right stuff." She smoothly handles herself and the people she meets. He can easily imagine this Venusian woman as his lover. Her sensuality is apparent. Her appreciation for beauty touches his heart. The Cancer man notices that his moods don't bother this stable woman. She takes things in stride. He likes being near her because she seems to read his innermost being with few words spoken. He will go out of his way to make her happy. He *sees* that she responds well to a romantic atmosphere.

It isn't unusual for people of your signs to get along. You can find ways to make each other feel important. Celebrating the milestones you reach as individuals and as a couple can be a source of delight. Material security isn't what takes you to the highest levels of enjoyment, though you can accumulate the best that life has to offer together. There is a vast richness available in being by one another's side. The passion you experience may seem secondary to the safety you find in your partner's presence. You both seek security. Your home is probably of great importance. The decisions you make have power. They are based on real hands-on know-how that doesn't come from playing it safe. When you release this intensity into the world, it responds positively. You must be clear about your intentions from the time you first meet. Your sincerity leads you past the islands of doubt you must navigate. Your most passionate desire to sustain a commitment leads you through all of the tough times. When breaking free from the hold of doubts and fears developed in the past, Taurus and Cancer can truly put something together of lasting value that others either admire or envy.

The Magic of Signmates

Taurus-Leo: The Make It Happen People

Taurus + Leo = Steam Engine That Can Climb over Any Obstacle

A stick-to-it drive can find the two of you hanging in there when many others may find the going too tough. This is not a relationship that is excited about changes—at least the ones you can't control. There will be occasions when the two of you will be thrilled by exotic vacations. A high-energy social life is quite possible. Your tendency is to build a stable platform from which to act out your creative roles. Knowing you can count on one another is reassuring. Lucky hunches can have tremendous payoffs. You don't always wait for good fortune to be delivered on a silver platter to you. People often remember you long after meeting you. Your friends are apt to be loyal and your adversaries jealous of your success.

Tales of Power Game

The games played in your Taurus-Leo relationship are associated with power and a desire to impress through wealth. Taurus and Leo can try to outwait one another on key decisions. If this becomes too extreme, the *Tales of Power* game can be born. The Bull and the Lion ferociously defend their positions. You will find it is easier to move a mountain than to change your partner's mind once it is made up. You won't get too far if you try to force the issue. A stubborn streak can dominate your interactions. Learning new communication tricks doesn't come easily, especially if you become attached to this game. Compromise may be hard to reach. If one of you is intent on getting your way, the other will push that much harder for his or her own point of view. Instead of pouring your great energy into joint ambitions, you spend a great deal of time feeling defensive. Resolution is difficult if you refuse to see things from your partner's perspective. You will not experience the great follow through that can be displayed by your sign combination. Rather, you will be party to frustration and anger because you see that you accomplish so little. This is a strange paradox. Taurus loves to watch Leo's pride in completing a mission. Leo is motivated by the sense of self that Taurus finds in showing its highest potential. In this game, your two signs are locked in a behavior pattern that doesn't bring out your best.

Luxury, Luxury Game

Taurus and Leo like to show they have reached success through what they can buy or display. Be careful not to try too hard to impress one another or others. The *Luxury, Luxury* game plays on insecurities that cause you to go far beyond your budget. Ego strength is a good thing. A healthy ego simply means you have enough gusto and confidence to pursue your greatest ideals. However, indulging in activities only because they flatter your ego may trap you into wasteful behavior. Spending money on each other is okay in itself. Buying a gift to express appreciation for your partner is wise. This game represents the problems caused by an inflated ego. One or both of you may believe an outward show is more important than how you really feel about one another. The depth you could tap into is lost to superficiality. Your values may need to be reexamined. There is another side to this story. You can feel neglected because your partner is too preoccupied with what he or she owns. Personal ambition can become unbalanced. A compulsive desire for success, or to get to the top, may lead you to alienate one another.

I Can Do It Better Game

The competitive side of your relationship can be playful and humorous. Be careful with how far you take it. The *I Can Do It Better* game can cause hurt feelings. Each of you is out to prove that you can outshine the other. This provokes real tension if you start to step on each other's favorite forms of self-expression. Neither of you likes to lose. In this game you are not doing great things for your partner's self-esteem. Your competition can concern career, sexual performance, creative talent, etc. You don't excel in the passion category if one of you continuously comes out on the short end. Showing vulnerability is not natural in a Taurus-Leo relationship. You instinctively challenge one another. This game can develop into a bad habit of rubbing each other the wrong way. You end up with bruised egos and estrangement of the heart. This game leads to disruptive behavior that can suddenly interfere with your fun plans.

Strategies

What can the two of you do to stay away from these Taurus-Leo games? For starters, in the *Tales of Power* game realize that when one of you has most of the power, the other doesn't have enough. The idea is to achieve mutual empowerment. Let each other lead in his or her areas of expertise. It will keep Taurus out of Leo's mane and Leo out of the way of the Bull's charge. The two of you are happier when you know you belong to the same team. Short skirmishes are okay; it's those long, drawn-out wars that frustrate you. Respect each other's right to disagree. It's unreasonable to want your way all of the time. Learn how to work out your issues. Assertiveness is all right, but you need to see when you are being too aggressive. You will make more love when you feel powerful and proud. Your individual goals must stay alive because they fuel the heartfelt desire to work together. Power is not a bad thing. You will find it a thing of beauty when you use it in a balanced manner. Your two signs don't budge from an idea easily. It is a matter of winning one another over. "Win-win" is the best policy in this game. You can't go wrong when you have your partner's best interests in mind, can you?

The *Luxury, Luxury* game may be a cry for attention. Even boredom can lead you to want to buy bigger and more extravagant items. Managing your money as a couple is not all that difficult. You stand a good chance of making a lot of money together—at least enough to live comfortably. If your lavish spending really puts a cramp on your savings, tension will break out sooner or later. Stay tuned to the big picture. What are you trying to accomplish together? It is limiting to be obsessed with impressing each other and others. Winning your partner's heart is probably a lot simpler than you realize. Giving equal attention to each other is a good starting point. Enjoying the finer things in life is something you have in common. You each seek material comfort. Taurus can enjoy owning a vast array of resources to put to practical use. Making money work is Taurus' joy. Leo can market skills as well as any sign out there. The Lion likes to have the buying power for investments and to exhibit a lively, fun-filled existence. Extreme poverty does not mean you will appreciate each other more. This game just indicates that you need to take a good look at compulsive urges to spend or to impress.

The *I Can Do It Better* game is put to rest by being clear about how you express your competitive spirit. There is a vivacious and passionate force at work in this relationship. You probably already know this about yourselves, don't you? What you may not always perceive is that you may be crossing boundary lines. You enhance intimacy by acknowledging your partner's strengths. You are not a couple that is going to quit when challenged. Don't expect your partner to be quiet if you act as though you can outperform your partner in his or her area of expertise. With practice, you can learn how to stimulate self-confidence in one another. Being a cheerleader for your lover will be enjoyable when you are applauded in return.

The Rainbow

Your Taurus-Leo relationship can elevate you both into positions of authority and power. Use your energies wisely. You can make a strong statement about yourselves through what you create together. You can be surprised by the love you receive when you generously give. You will find that this relationship offers a package of unexpected gifts. When Taurus and Leo first meet, you recognize that something magical is possible.

The Taurus man likes the way the Leo woman brings out his self-confidence. She does not feel intimidated by his strength, and makes it clear that his charm is well received. He is attracted quickly to the radiance and assertiveness of the Leo woman. She exudes power and seems to know where she is going. He likes her outgoing personality. A passionate fire burns when he looks into her *eyes*. He feels an attraction that emanates from a shared need to take control.

The Leo woman is fond of the way the Taurus man understands her need for attention. He seems willing to go the extra mile to please her. She perceives quickly that the Venusian man has a keen sense about money. Her heart is warmed when she *sees* his generosity. The passionate fires between them are delightful.

The female Taurus doesn't know what to make of the male Leo. He is a tower of power. If he will share the throne with her, her heart readily opens. Her desire for material status finds a willing admirer. She just wants to be sure he doesn't usurp her territorial rights. She appreciates his passion for life and better yet, for her. The Venusian woman likes how he projects self-confidence. She only hopes he will not overshadow her own pursuits with his own interests. The potential to realize big dreams tempts the Venusian woman to come closer. She sees that he likes to be a winner. The Taurus woman is delighted to discover that he knows how to make her feel like a champion. When he shows he can share the stage with her, she opens her heart to him.

The Leo man is amused by the way the Taurus woman can dodge his advances. She steps forward but, at the same time, holds him at arms' length. The Lion realizes he must at least give the appearance of relinquishing some of his power. The Taurus woman is moved by this gesture of goodwill but knows deep down in her soul that the Lion will need a push to treat her as an equal. She will need to spar playfully with him to show her own strength. He likes the way this woman makes him feel. He is in awe of her diplomatic way of putting them both first. The Leo man needs a woman with the fortitude to be herself. This earthy woman can stand up to anyone's test. He likes that about her!

People can easily see you as a couple who knows how to achieve what you want. You are apt to spar along the way but usually will champion each other's causes. Your partner will want your unconditional love, whether or not you can give this on a daily basis. The hunger to be loved by each other intensifies with time. You can form an alliance that will lead to great accomplishments. Sex is as creative as your romantic imagination. You delight in being predictable and, at the same time, in being surprisingly unpredictable. You so badly want your partner to figure you out that you keep dropping clues about your secrets. Perhaps the biggest secret you keep is that you can't imagine life without one another. That doesn't mean you can't live or go forward without this relationship, but the treasures here far outweigh the challenges. You are not in an easygoing relationship. When you try to please your partner, it is often an all-out effort. When you want attention, you may need to wave your hands wildly. When you seek support, it must be clear and obvious, not subtle. When you want to feel the deepest levels of trust, it must be real and meet the tests of reliability. Time will test your endurance as a couple. A time will come when you know that nothing can come between you.

Taurus-Virgo: The Planners

Taurus + Virgo = Logical Thinking

These two signs combine into a sound, reality-testing duo. Both are earth signs, yielding a productive, organized working team that is task-oriented at heart. The resourcefulness of Taurus goes well with the analytical nature of Virgo. Virgo's thoroughness, which leaves no rock unturned in the search for details, is received positively by practical Taurus. You have the potential to assume equal responsibility and to enjoy little conflict. Dependability is a cornerstone in this relationship.

Earthbound Game

The games played in your Taurus-Virgo relationship are connected to a lack of imagination and getting stuck in routines. If you become too attached to the mundane, the two of you can run into the *Earthbound* game. You may need to get out of a rut. The hardest thing about this game is that you may not realize you are in it. There is nothing wrong with stability, but too great an attachment to the material side of life can prevent you from fulfilling other life paths. You will become numb if you don't bring new experiences to the relationship. The same schedule can dull your minds. Romance will wane if you don't allow for a little spicy variety. The earthiness of Taurus and Virgo can lead you to doubt the validity of taking risks. A new path can ignite greater vitality. One or both of you could resist change, which is why you are not open to alternative ideas. The strengths of earth signs are commitment and the ability to finish what you start. A weakness is the unwillingness to adopt a more flexible approach. It's the latter that's the culprit. If you don't trust your intuition or spontaneous impulses, you may block greater passion. If you negate each other's insights, you are impeding the vitality that can be the answer to this game.

Work and More Work Game

If you indulge in work over play, the *Work and More Work* game will be your reality. Ambition is a good thing, but this game involves carrying the work principle way beyond the call of duty. The two of you are probably not afraid to make the effort needed to accomplish your life aims. Daily responsibilities can be shared with a spirit of cooperation, yet your signs can become focused on projects to the point of negating fun. Your social lives in this game may be close to nonexistent. Making time for each other is essential. Watch out for a tendency to make excuses for not taking a vacation or relaxing. Taurus grows grumpy when not allowed to relax and enjoy the comforts of life. Virgo becomes irritable when not getting enough rest and relaxation. Habits are not easy to break. A broader perspective of living is neglected here. Reaching your milestones will be satisfying. Make sure you don't lose sight of your partner along the way. If you don't allow time to enjoy each other or to "smell the roses," you are shortchanging yourselves. The investment you make in a balanced life will yield immense dividends.

Reward Us Later Game

The practicality of the earth element can entice the two of you to not ask for enough pleasure and abundance as seen in the *Reward Us Later* game. The tendency in this game is to sacrifice too much of your time and energy. Your belief in frugality may lead you not to buy things that are not practical. Your pragmatic nature can rub off on one another and convey a message that life is serious. You don't need to throw out your common sense. If you limit yourselves to a narrow view of enjoyment, you may miss out on some invigorating opportunities. Taurus can believe in saving to the extreme, holding back on buying items that may pave the way for new possibilities. Virgo can become so hypnotized by the work ethic that there is little awareness of expanding the horizons. You both may need to see that you merit being rewarded now rather than later. Your planning abilities are an asset; perhaps it is time for a refreshing new game plan!

Strategies

How do you get past these Taurus-Virgo games? The *Earthbound* game requires you to not limit yourselves only to what is logical. Allow your intuition to speak. Trust your imagination. Spontaneity may not be your first impulse. It may take some practice to not be so suspicious of change. You won't break out of the same old lifestyle overnight. Bring in new experiences because they sharpen your mental faculties. You will find there is greater passion when you allow for a few surprises. You may be holding each other to rigid expectations. Let go. Encourage one another to take that class or other new opportunity. If you always travel to certain places or eat at the same restaurants, change the pattern. Don't see this as a disruption as much as a way to liven up your time together. Taurus can relax into routines as much as Virgo. This means you will need to be determined to go beyond your normal daily rituals. Your enjoyment of a refreshed relationship can lift your spirits.

The *Work and More Work* game takes a commitment from the two of you to take a break now and then. The drive to make ends meet and to get ahead is strong in any earth sign relationship. You probably need to remind one another to work less. Setting limits is likely to be a necessity. Scheduling a day each week to be together may be wise if your schedules are filled to the brim. There is a possible tendency to keep pushing until a job is finished. You don't like to leave loose ends, do you? Virgo is especially compulsive about maintaining a sense of order. Unfinished jobs can be perceived as a mess. Taurus loves beauty. A finished product just plain looks better, so you sometimes feel a sense of urgency to complete a task or mission. You can still learn to enjoy the journey as much as the destination. Work can seem like pleasure to two earth signs as in the saying "different strokes for different folks." Time away from the work world may show you other dimensions of each other to appreciate.

The *Reward Us Later* game is essentially about not valuing yourselves enough. If you don't reward yourselves in the here and now, who will? "Saving for a rainy day" is Taurus' mantra. "Be prepared for the worst" is Virgo's motto. Put these two ideologies together and you have delayed gratification. You can be patient in acquiring what you want, but don't put off being good to yourselves when it isn't required. You can be harder on yourselves than anyone else will ever be. Don't make life a punishment. Taurus loves self-indulgence. Virgo can get into the swing of things once its sense of humor and desire to have fun are primed. Sometimes you need to focus on celebrating your relationship. Splurge on yourselves once in a while.

The Rainbow

Your Taurus-Virgo relationship is well prepared to handle whatever challenges come your way. A solid, logical framework permeates your partnership. There can be passion and great days of joy.

A Taurus man finds that the Virgo woman understands his world. He notices her likes and dislikes are not so different from his own. He recognizes that she has great presence of mind and remembers facts and events even when she is in the middle of a crisis. He is attracted to her attentiveness. Their sense of reality seems to be similar.

The Virgo woman sees the Taurus man's sensual demeanor. She senses he is not as calm and cool as he wants her to believe. His concern over material accomplishments conforms with her own drive to be successful. She wants him to know that she enjoys his charm but needs to be respected for her own capabilities. It appears that this Venusian man is the type of romantic who remembers special occasions. She likes this!

The Taurus woman knows she might need to train the Virgo man in how to love her. She admires his thoroughness in work and knows her patience is needed in waiting for him to learn about play. She hesitates to reveal her affection until he shows his softer side. He looks like he can melt, but he doesn't thaw quickly. The Venusian woman trusts his sensible thinking.

The Virgo man is moved by the Taurus woman's tenderness on one hand and admires her firm grasp of the hard facts on the other. He knows that his negotiation instincts will not impress her but that his sincerity and authenticity will move her. She already knows his mind is work-oriented. He perceives it isn't wise to make her feel she will be competing with work for his attention. The male Virgo has passion, and if anybody can pull this out of him, it is the Venusian woman.

Often this is a sexually compatible sign combination. If you can avoid being distracted by worldly ambitions, you will enjoy much physical pleasure. Ownership is a by-product of being together. You tend to collect and purchase shared items. You can open doors for one another by offering good advice. Be careful that your wisdom is being solicited. You are lovers with a well-defined purpose. You like the steps to be clearly marked, yet taking a detour off the beaten path is stimulating. When you encourage your partner to take a leap of faith, you could revitalize the relationship.

Let the Games Begin

The stability you create makes you both feel secure, but it's the unexpected that entices you to take a new glance at each other. If you can steer clear of endless routines, you will discover hidden dimensions within yourselves. Allow your partner to express his or her unique qualities even if they conflict with your own. You won't always understand why your partner chooses a particular form of self-expression. Your similarities won't make you kindred spirits; it is your tolerance of the unique qualities deep within your souls, sometimes beyond the reach of your conscious minds, that will show you how to reach out with a renewed, passionate embrace.

Taurus-Libra: The Romantics

Taurus + Libra = Love of the Best Things Life Has to Offer

There is a desire to be self-indulgent when these two signs form a partnership. Each is ruled by Venus and seeks comfort and ownership. Both are people oriented. A key theme is finding a negotiating strategy that is satisfactory to you both. Earthy Taurus provides grounding for the intense thinking capacity of Libra. Airy Libra offers objective input for the things in life that cause Taurus to react too personally. This is a relationship that appreciates beauty in all of its forms. Each of you is trying to keep life simple. Confrontation does not excite you.

Please Fulfill Me Game

The sensual side of life is well known to both of you. Physical attraction probably got the relationship off to a fast start, and expectations grow after the initial meeting of your two hearts. The *Please Fulfill Me* game occurs when the two of you ask for more than is realistic. You are left with a feeling of emptiness if you look for too much of what you lack in your partner. It is tempting to paint pictures based on your imagination. Nobody can possibly come through for you all of the time. The fulfillment you seek is not in one another, but you can help the other complete part of the puzzle. Taurus and Libra hungrily seek balance. The scales are tipped too far to one extreme in this game. Be fair in your judgment of the relationship. When each of you is not pulling your own weight, it adds great tension to the partnership. Problems can arise over money and ownership. This is often due to unclear perceptions of each other. Your dependency needs could use an alignment. This game can manifest in another way. You may ask for unrealistic amounts of attention. Inner clarity cannot be substituted with vicariously living life through each other.

Indecision Game

You feel like fish out of water when you are hooked by one another's inability to make a decision. The *Indecision* game frustrates you like nothing else can. Taurus likes clear simplicity. Libra likes a well-thought-out strategy. This game makes you think you are talking in foreign languages. You may wonder how this could happen. You may be trying too hard to please one another. It is less painful to make up your mind than to agonize over what is right or wrong. Trying to please people outside of your relationship can interfere with reaching a resolution. You can feel like you are trying to get an amendment passed by one hundred noisy members of Congress! Procrastination is the flip side of this game. One or both of you may purposely postpone the outcome because you don't want to face the consequences. Avoiding the unpleasant choices may seem easier, but in the end it only causes trouble. When you are reluctant to be direct it can cause confusion and indecision. Hiding your true needs makes it difficult for your partner to know how to negotiate with you.

Hole in the Pocket Game

Spending money in the pursuit of happiness may lead you to play the *Hole in the Pocket* game. The drive for excess may be due to not getting the love you desire from one another. Taurus and Libra can, at best, bring out great sensibility. At worst, these signs can encourage overindulgence in food, drink, sex, etc. Your excesses are symptoms that something in the relationship is off target. You both want to be adored or at least appreciated. It could be that unhappiness in work causes the two of you to look elsewhere for happiness. It's hard to stay on a budget when you compulsively crave fulfillment. Instead of supporting one another, you may unconsciously undermine the real love you seek.

Strategies

How do you rise above your Taurus-Libra games? In the *Please Fulfill Me* game you need to be more honest with yourselves. You will be much more content when you let your partner off the hook. Someone leaning on you with sky-high expectations creates tremendous pressure. You will feel liberated if you keep your dependency needs in balance. Neither of you can really be totally responsible for the other's happiness. It's an illusion to think otherwise. When you attain personal fulfillment, you will have a great deal of energy to share with each other. It is when you focus on what you lack that you think that truth or answers lie with someone else. It's not that you will never need to depend on each other—quite the contrary. When you come from a place of abundance, you will attract what you seek. This game can be subtle in that you might not be aware that this is what you are acting out. It's tempting to deny that you expect the unrealistic. If you are able to talk clearly concerning what you need, that's a good place to begin. A shared sense of power will elevate the love you feel; even your sex life will benefit.

The *Indecision* game can arise from not seeing both sides of an issue clearly. It's hard to choose one option over the other. Taurus will surge ahead when clear about how to proceed. Libra can sprint ahead when it sets the true path. The trick is to get on the same track. Compromise can get the ball rolling. In some instances, you may be able to pursue both options. Alternating which one of you "breaks" a deadlock is another way to win at this game. It takes courage to make a decision. Overcoming the fear of making a bad decision is a part of the journey. Learning to live with a choice is not that difficult. You can always make revisions later. The two of you will be happier when your minds are at work and your actions deliver results. There is a result-oriented mentality in your sign combination. You will have more faith in one another when you see that you can create opportunities by acting on your thoughts. A lack of faith can be the underlying issue. Belief in your decision-making power comes with practice.

The *Hole in the Pocket* game occurs when the risk-taking side of your relationship is out of control. A craving for happiness must somehow be satisfied. You can only buy so much fulfillment through pleasure. An honest self-evaluation is needed. It could be that your individual goals must be redefined. Your inspiration could use a tune-up. Perhaps a refreshing new perspective is the road to pursue. The greater the abundance you find within, the less will you chase after it in the world, though there is still a strong possibility your job or other roles may need a change. This game is a cry of desperation that all is not well and sometimes a plea for more attention. Are you ignoring each other's needs? If you are, this game fills the vacuum. To change the scenario, you must fill the empty places with real meaning. Start with honest communication. You can be a dynamic duo, taking well-calculated risks. You can increase your cash flow when you focus your business savvy on the same financial statement.

The Rainbow

Your Taurus-Libra relationship leads you to try to bring each other the essence of pleasure. You want peace and stability. When you treat one another with fairness and recognition, you are well on your way to a happy destination.

A Taurus man is quickly drawn to the Libra woman. Her graceful movements are poised and polished. The Libra woman is not really performing, though he may think she is trying to entertain him. Her intellect is refined from experience. Her voice is as beautiful as her demeanor. The Venusian man thinks they can create wonderful music together; each seems to appreciate beauty.

The Libra woman can't help but notice the Taurus man's smooth delivery of words. His self-consciousness is masked behind an air of self-confidence. The Libra woman reads between the lines and quickly tries to decide how to handle him. She is touched by his intense, passionate attention.

The Taurus woman is drawn to the Libra man. His intentions seem easy to decipher. The Taurus woman would like to be his lover if he will just indulge her pet likes and dislikes. She wants to possess him a little but not be possessed by him. He knows how to make love to her, but does he know how to love her? Time will tell. If she grows possessive, he will expect the world! On the other hand, if he turns out to be her true love, it's all worth it!

The airy Libra man zooms quickly into the Taurus woman's life. She sends a message that her boundaries must be honored. He adores the sensuality of this goddess. He wants to have her in his life and sets out to charm her with his beckoning call. He waits to see if she feels his passion. If she opens to him, he is ready to claim her as his true love. He knows this is just the beginning but hopes it will be so much more. He believes their love will last forever. Both hope he is right!

You are self-indulgent and delight in showering each other with gifts. It's your way of making each other feel special. Such a display makes you happy even when you see through the charade. You bring each other abundance, but too much of a good thing may take you down the wrong paths. Know when enough is enough. You can paint new realities together. You can repair shattered hopes and live out real dreams here. People want to share in your happiness because it revitalizes their spirits. You have many acquaintances because others want to vicariously experience your happiness and see if it is real. Some will be disbelievers and others believers. It doesn't matter what others think, does it? As long as you are content in each other's arms, that's the only truth that counts.

Taurus-Scorpio: The Passionate Ones

Taurus + Scorpio = Deep Plunge into the Unknown

You have met your opposite because Taurus sits exactly across the zodiac from Scorpio. This doesn't mean the two signs are completely different. There may be a sense that part of what one is missing can be found in the other. Taurus has a down-to-earth approach that is grounding for the emotionally introspective Scorpio. While Taurus may not perceive the underlying currents of a situation, Scorpio can detect them with its sensitive radar. With this sign combination, it is likely that you are intensely passionate lovers. Each influences the other to sample many pleasures.

Borrowing Game

The games in your Taurus-Scorpio relationship are associated with how you conduct business and deal with emotional extremes. The *Borrowing* game occurs when you don't appropriately honor each other's material possessions. Nothing is more painful for Scorpio or Taurus than to see that their possessions aren't properly used by others. Taurus can get quite upset if Scorpio assumes ownership of what is only meant to be a loan. Scorpio becomes angry and moody if Taurus becomes too possessive of what is intended to be a temporary situation. The Bull and the Scorpion can face off regularly over material differences of opinion. These are the two money-oriented signs of the zodiac. If the two of you don't carefully define your philosophy about how to handle business affairs, this game can become prevalent. If you don't share bills equally or fail to at least clearly communicate mutual expectations, it can lead to disastrous consequences. A power struggle can become upsetting and pull you apart. Money issues will cause hard feelings if left to be dealt with later.

Damned Emotions Game

When Taurus and Scorpio find it difficult to express feelings about conflict, the *Damned Emotions* game can manifest. You are going to elicit powerful reactions from each other. This happens frequently when people of opposite signs form a romantic liaison. Taurus will stubbornly hold back hurt feelings while Scorpio is the master of hiding what it doesn't want others to see. The Scorpion builds power by keeping projects a secret until finished. The problem is that Scorpio may treat emotions the same way. Rather than communicate directly, watery Scorpio may choose to sidestep issues. When you hold back strong emotions for too long it eats at the core of the relationship, like rotten fruit that has fallen from a tree. These powerful, restrained emotions may be unleashed at each other under seemingly unrelated circumstances. Your passion will suffer as will feelings of intimacy. There is a sense that something is wrong. In not addressing a problem, you create new ones. This can become a poisonous game that blurs your clarity. The depth of your relationship is not as deep as it could be. The trust you are searching for will seem just out of your reach. There can even be a feeling of loneliness because you are not connecting to the soul of your partner.

Odysseus and the Sirens Game

The *Odysseus and the Sirens* game points to the compulsive behaviors that can be expressed when the two of you lose your balance. Odysseus was the mythological hero who escaped destruction by the voices of the three sea nymphs. The sea nymphs were part-bird and part-human creatures who could cast a spell upon those who listened to their song, causing a ship and its crew to run aground on the rocky coast. Odysseus had himself tied to the mast of his ship and stuffed the ears of his crew with wax as the ship neared the treacherous coastal waters so they could not be enticed by the sea nymphs to self-destruction. As the story goes, Odysseus and his crew did not succumb to the siren song of the sea nymphs. What does this story have to do with you? Your siren song is the temptation to live life near the edge. It throws off the equilibrium of your relationship if you chase after extremes. Desire can cause reckless behavior. A disregard for limits can be self-defeating. You may overindulge in any of the following: spending, eating, work, or sex. You awaken intense energy in each other. In this game you direct your energy in the wrong way. The love you want to realize can be lessened if you get lost in wayward behavior. Opposites have a great capacity to bring out each other's best. The other side of the coin is true as well. This game is never really intentional. It is a subconscious plea for love, acceptance, and fulfillment.

Strategies

How do you solve the dilemma of these Taurus-Scorpio games? The *Borrowing* game only requires a more conscious understanding of your use of other's resources. There is a degree of truth to the axiom that your two signs, in particular, bond quickly to the tools you choose to use. It's this deep connection to resources that can lead to losing sight of whose materials you are using. You must honor each other's material possessions if you want peace of mind.

Money can be a source of joy or contention. Sharing your finances makes your hearts grow fonder. You don't endear yourself by holding back from your partner. You probably need separate bank accounts—plus a joint one! You both have instincts about how to make your own wealth. You will not always want to rely on each other's ideas about money. It's not in your sign chemistry to be agreeable on these matters. You will have a greater tendency to share when you feel free to make individual acquisitions. Be honest when borrowing from your partner. When you lend money, make it clear that it is a loan. Say that you expect to be paid back or want an item returned in its original condition. When borrowing, don't assume that you now own the item or that money doesn't need to be repaid. How you handle the business in this relationship is vital. Romance is affected by the respect you show for one another's property.

The *Damned Emotions* game asks you to let go of your anger and fear. Your relationship is probably stronger than you give it credit. You will not like what you hear if you let hidden feelings out of the box, but keeping a lid on your problems is not the answer. Try to let each other talk without interrupting and take turns stating your case. Don't defend your position. You are only trying to clear the air so you can resolve your differences. Remember, hurt feelings don't always go away quickly even after letting them out; however, this starts the process of honest communication. Don't make wild accusations, but express what your partner's actions or statements do to you. Practice talking. Practice something else a lot harder: listening. It's so tempting to react with anger. Patience is truly a virtue, and no one has all of the patience in the world. You can convert this powerful dammed up energy into creative avenues. You will be pleased with the increased passion and love shared if you move in a positive direction.

The *Odysseus and the Sirens* game is complex but can be brought into balance. This will take great *honesty* (note the emphasis). Many people prefer not to discuss compulsive drives, but there is another way to look at compulsions. A person with obsessive drives makes a strong statement that he or she is powerfully alive! The behavior may look quite the contrary. When you overdo sex, stimulants, television, work, and other avenues of escape, what is the underlying message? Perhaps you are trying to tell each other something but choose extremes to send the message. If you can identify the root causes of your compulsive behavior, you can take a key first step in transcending them. You might want more love than either can give. It may be necessary for you as individuals to pursue more meaningful goals. It may be that you block your partner's vital drives. The good news is that, as in the *Damned Emotions* game, the negative energy can be overcome. Is it faith you require? You may need to cultivate more positive thinking. Composting self-destructive energies into growth-promoting soil is within your reach. It's good to remember that the same focus we put into negativity or limiting behaviors only needs a similarly intense desire to put it elsewhere. Your Taurus-Scorpio games become empowering when you accept the challenge of taking them to a higher level. You can do it!

The Rainbow

Your Taurus-Scorpio relationship reveals your innermost desires. The two of you don't exactly go halfway when tasting life's pleasures. You seek opportunity with a healthy respect for what it takes to be successful.

A Taurus man is impressed by the quiet intensity of a Scorpio woman. He is sure that she reads his thoughts. He isn't sure whether to be comforted or intimidated by this, though he loves the way her attention lights up his zest for life.

The Scorpio woman sees the male Taurus as capable of dealing with her ambition. The female Scorpio searches for clues that will reveal how business savvy he is at the core. It's not money in itself she seeks but a lover and companion who can match her strength.

The Taurus woman cautiously views the Scorpio man's sense of self-mastery. She wonders if he will try to master her. It's not his intense desires that bother her as much as his assumption that the world is his for the taking. She wants to test whether he will continue to adore her after she trusts him. Is he really all that sweet once the fires are lit? She sure hopes so!

The Scorpio man is drawn to the alluring power of the Taurus woman. She is sensual and speaks quietly yet authoritatively. He knows he had better not take advantage of her generosity. The male Scorpion hopes his female Taurus lover has a forgiving heart. One thing is for sure, he would like to join forces with this earth spirit whom he can't seem to get out of his mind.

Your love for one another will be tested by the challenges you face as individuals and as a couple. When you don't take your agony out on your lover you will enjoy ecstasy. You will fight with passion. It's your birthright to do so. Taurus wants tranquility as much as Scorpio looks to maintain its inner certainty. The two of you make solid allies. When you know you can count on each other's strength, no obstacle is too difficult to conquer. Tell the truth. You need each other but may find it hard to verbalize. You expect your partner to continually prove his or her trustworthiness. In time you can reach out to one another with spontaneity. You enjoy physical love because it makes you feel wanted. The meeting of your minds cuts through any darkness. You so much want your partner to be the person you have searched through life to find. If you reveal your inner selves, it becomes apparent that you are soul mates. It's not the fear of losing each other that is endearing but the knowledge that you will come through for each other. You can form a loving partnership that can accompany you through rain or sunshine.

Taurus-Sagittarius: The Jolly Ones

Taurus + Sagittarius = Luck in the Nick of Time

These two signs enliven and enlarge each other's good fortune. There is no real conflict between earthy Taurus and fiery Sagittarius on the surface. When you further investigate, the saving tendencies of the Bull don't exactly match the "let's live for today" thinking of the Archer. Taurus stabilizes and Sagittarius energizes. The Bull may need the Archer's enthusiasm to pursue a new path. Sagittarius could benefit from Taurus' inclination to think before acting on a whim. This sign combination can move with a consistent and decisive clarity when experiencing a high degree of harmony.

Serve Me on a Silver Platter Game

The games played in your Taurus-Sagittarius relationship are linked to denial and false optimism. The *Serve Me on a Silver Platter* game ensues when the two of you believe that you will get results without really trying. Missed opportunities can result. You can demonstrate faith that provides little foundation for the desired result. It's great to believe in yourselves. If you don't put an idea into motion, it won't get off the ground. Denial is usually at the root of this game. You don't want to face reality. Opportunity may come to your door, but it will be lost if you don't open the door. The self-indulgence of Taurus and Sagittarius operate to the extreme here. Laziness or inertia can set in if you don't flex your muscles and pursue your ambitions. Wasting time will grow frustrating, and not taking advantage of opportunities could cause you to lose faith in one another. You may be ready to celebrate on a moment's notice. First you have to do the work; then you can rejoice. There may be a tendency to exaggerate your wealth and fame. This could lead you to want to be served. Rather than resting on your laurels, whether true or imagined, don't forget the journey to success requires a first step—then several more!

Fixation on Limitation Game

When Taurus and Sagittarius lose sight of how to achieve abundance, the *Fixation on Limitation* game awaits. You two don't do well when you lack the faith or vision to obtain the resources you need for happiness. You need to avoid a poverty consciousness or settling for too little. You cannot afford to surrender to a negative attitude. It may be that a setback for one or both of you has put you on this downward trail of thinking. Meditating on the negative will not take you to the positive road. Your relationship feels the blues when you can't see a more expansive future, doesn't it? An impoverished Bull, whether in terms of money or comfort, is not a happy Bull. An Archer who can't afford to buy the newest arrows on the market isn't going to be happy with a quiver of outdated ones. Sagittarius' distress is apparent when it loses all hope of overcoming a challenge. Somehow you have to regenerate positive energy. You may unrealistically want too much too fast. It is possible that the two of you are doing just fine materially but for some reason refuse to see it. If this is true, you will tend to be hard to convince that life is already good. Resisting a change in attitude will keep you trapped in this game.

Everything Will Get Better Game

When the two of you deny there are any problems, you could find yourselves playing the *Everything Will Get Better* game. Taurus abhors dealing with conflict as much as Sagittarius. The Bull likes a level playing field without hidden traps. The Archer likes terrain that holds the promise of adventure. There is optimism in this game, so what can be wrong? The problem is that no solutions are sought for real issues. Every unpleasant issue is conveniently tucked away. In reality, things are not getting better; concerns are just hidden from sight. Sooner or later, old problems will cast a haunting shadow. Rather than grow by working through difficulties with one another, silence reigns. A sobering dose of reality will eventually show that all is not well. Your sense of closeness will grow more and more fragile if you refuse to address issues. You don't have to spend all of your time working on the relationship, but if you don't fix what needs repair, there will be unfortunate consequences.

Strategies

What does it take to turn these Taurus-Sagittarius games to your favor? The *Serve Me on a Silver Platter* game requires that the two of you focus on a strategy to ensure that you finish a plan. If you make little or no effort, you can't expect to get the result you want. You will disappoint each other less if you show more determination to go after your dreams. Taurus is often willing to work toward a goal if the true value of the endeavor is visible. When Sagittarius is inspired, its follow-through is much more dependable. You can encourage each other to initiate the steps to success. A pattern of laziness can be easily changed; moving in a new direction can ignite a takeoff. There is nothing wrong with wealth, but affluence is not the point. To leave this game behind in your tracks, you simply need to act with enthusiasm. Discipline may not excite either of you that much. Even though Taurus is an earth sign, comfort is considered a worthwhile pursuit. Sagittarius is a fire sign but may prefer lounging when its philosophy is "life is a beach." Your two signs expect life to come to you. Eventually it will—when you pursue your ideals and dreams with a clear intent.

The *Fixation on Limitation* game is a contradiction to the core meaning of your signs. Taurus must believe that life is good and plentiful to maintain creative intensity. Sagittarius is like a leaky balloon when its expansive perspective is lost. Belief in the power of positive thinking helps. Your relationship has great vitality when life is seen as a series of options for growth. You are like wilted flowers when the rays of hope disappear. Nurture one another with good ideas. Faith in yourselves may sound corny, but you will need it to reach the higher ground. Wealth comes to you when each of you radiates fulfillment and happiness with your individual lives. You can figure your way out of any jam. Creative frustration need not make you suffer. Use this as a challenge to find the right outlet. Your upbeat energies make people want to reward you.

The *Everything Will Get Better* game is based on denial that you cannot afford to allow. It is convenient but not productive to put off decisions. Taurus resists decisions that provoke tension. Sagittarius dislikes choices that appear to be confining. Commitment can free you! Yes, when you decide to take control of a situation, you no longer have to worry about whether it will control you. Life gets better when you stop denying there is anything wrong. All relationships have to face differences of opinions occasionally. Adversity can come in the form of unexpected bills or conflicting schedules or the inability to reach a compromise. The list is endless. You don't need to have all of the answers. Talking together will show you how to clarify your issues. It's okay if you don't agree on everything—honest!

The Rainbow

Your Taurus-Sagittarius relationship establishes a soothing rhythm. Each of you wants to make the other feel highly valued, and you desire to feel cherished. The joy you share can be perceived by others. Your overflowing enthusiasm and belief in the vision you have of tomorrow elevate you far above everyday ups and downs.

A Taurus man experiences a mixture of delight and uneasiness when he encounters the Sagittarius woman. He knows he can't corral this free-shooting Archer. He is touched by her bubbly personality and optimism and intrigued by her descriptions of her travels. He is at ease with her friendliness and energized by her directness. He can learn to live with her straightforwardness if she can tolerate his need for stability.

The Sagittarius woman sees that the Taurus man is as solid as a rock. She wonders if he can keep up with her pace (though she does enjoy snuggling with him). She senses it would not be wise to underestimate this man's stamina and ability to accomplish whatever he sets out to do. The Archer's heart is captured by the way that the Bull notices little things about her. Such a person is hard to find these days. Perhaps they could find a place called happiness together.

The Taurus woman is startled by the sudden entrance of the Sagittarius man. He strikes her as a wild stallion, enjoying free rein over his own territory. The Venusian woman isn't anxious to lay any claim to this adventurous man. She is entranced by his stories of travel and adventure. She wishes she could say she has been there and done that, but the Sagittarius man has walked in so many climes—some of which she has never heard of before. The female Taurus has the power to tame his wildness. She must decide if it is worth the challenge, though she must admit that she can't stop thinking about this free-spirited soul. Is it his irresistible smile, his wonderful stories, or his cute way of explaining his viewpoint that intrigue her? She can't help but want to be near him when he makes her feel that she is as awe-inspiring as his dreams.

The Sagittarius man enjoys the sweetness of the Taurus woman. She kisses like it's for keeps, even if it isn't. This wild rogue lives in the present but feels a connection to a primitive world that calls him to the gates of adventure. The male Sagittarius also understands the world of reality. He really hates the demands of contemporary life but grudgingly puts up with it. She very much adores the Archer's primeval energy. He wants to meet her in the real world where she needs to know she can depend on him.

You can become deeply attached to each other. Taurus and Sagittarius both appreciate simple truths, though it may not be so obvious at first glance. When you find the ways to communicate to one another's mind and heart, it becomes hard to separate you. You can help each other attain great things with your faith. Nothing will delight you as much as knowing you have such a positive spirit in your corner. When you don't run away from the down times, when you appreciate the good ones, you will not take each other for granted. This is a love story that can become deeper with each scene. The two of you have to keep writing a script that is big and eclectic enough to allow you to continually grow. You bring a wealth of ideas to each other. Perhaps it's the magical way you make one another smile that keeps you close. Maybe it's the awe that you feel when watching your partner excel. Whatever the reason you are together, it probably isn't the entire story anyway, is it?

Taurus-Capricorn: The Builders

Taurus + Capricorn = Reliability

People know when they ask you to do something, they can count on you to do it. Consistency and dependability are qualities you look for in each other. You probably are a steady-as-you-go couple most of the time. You like individuals who follow through on promises. The precision of your decisions paints a stabilizing present and a rather predictable future. Your values may have an old-fashioned ring to them, and a healthy respect for the past is likely. You may surprise a few people with an upbeat tempo when you celebrate your milestones. Life is wonderful when you are good to yourselves.

Tree That Won't Bend Game

The games played in your Taurus-Capricorn relationship are tied to a lack of flexibility and being too tight with your assets. If the two of you refuse to budge when discussing matters, the *Tree That Won't Bend* game visits you. The Bull can dig in its heels adamantly when holding its ground. What about Capricorn? More of the same. The Goat can be as obstinate as they come once its mind is made up. The two of you will know when you are locked into this behavior. Your sentences become shorter and shorter, and you become more determined than ever to prove your point. This could be your way of expressing anger. You simply don't cooperate. This isn't all that harmful if it lasts only for a day or two, but if disagreements fall under the category of "irreconcilable," you have trouble. You will become resentful if you give in to your partner all of the time. Your two signs can show remarkable patience, which is a good thing. You will get tired of fighting these battles, and of waiting each other out in this game. Your passion can grow as dull as a rusty knife that hasn't been sharpened in years. Taurus often sees acceptance as directly connected to the intimacy process, which means that if the Bull gets its way now and then, its heart opens. With Capricorn it is another story. The Goat incorporates negotiation right into the love process. It doesn't mean that Capricorn won't forgive if you get the Goat to the compromise table. Capricorn finds power and passion through success. If this sign senses that it will lose power by agreeing, it will hesitate to do so. If you both cannot find suitable common ground on issues, eventually it will seem like you live on separate islands even if sharing the same bed.

Scrooge Game

You are two earth signs. This doesn't automatically mean you are tight with money. The *Scrooge* game indicates you may have definite reasons for not sharing what you have with one another. It might be that you want to retain your personal autonomy and one way to do it is to hold on to your money. Taurus is more at ease with a few dollars tucked away in the bank or under a pillow. The Bull can covet other's possessions. Capricorn likes to control its own destiny through ownership, and at times through its partner's possessions. Perhaps you have issues about giving. The main thing to keep in mind is what this game can do to your relationship, whatever the reason you choose to hold back your resources. Some people who are afraid of losing what they have are even more attached to their wealth. Believing in lack rather than abundance is going to contribute to this behavior. You might not feel loved if you sense your partner is not generous. There are no hard and fast rules here. The true bottom line is to ask whether your hearts are broken over not feeling valued.

Tortoise That Doesn't Win Game

In the fable, the tortoise wins the race. He defeats the much swifter and overconfident hare through persistence plus tremendous determination to finish. The *Tortoise That Doesn't Win* game points to being stuck in a mire of inertia. Taurus possesses a masterful way of showing patience. Capricorn excels at carefully laying down a well-structured life. This game reflects a tendency to lose spontaneity from your lives. It may become difficult to pursue new goals together. Your shared imagination needs a tune up. There is nothing wrong with taking it slow, but when you act like sticks in the mud, life loses its magic. The surprises you once delivered to each other need reactivation. You might be fighting new experiences because of great energy being poured into careers. There might be such a focus on one area of life that the others are being neglected. Your passion will be a few quarts low if you don't keep life a little exciting. You don't have to become mountain climbers or race car drivers, but you may need to consider inserting variety into your agenda occasionally. This game is sustained by not having enough momentum to break through thought patterns that keep you from greater growth.

Strategies

How do you put these Taurus-Capricorn games to rest? *The Tree That Won't Bend* game asks you to be amenable to new possibilities. Flexibility will take as much determination as you put into being successful in work. It is your individual strengths that are in opposition. Taurus is not a sign to take lightly when its determination is heartfelt. Capricorn's conviction to stick to a plan is almost impossible to influence. You need to appeal to each other's common sense and even compassion to get this game out of your path. Until you learn how to deal with one another, you will be facing this dilemma over and over again. It's like an old vinyl album, turning round and round on the turntable, letting out a screech every time the needle passes over one of its scratches. You will know beyond a shadow of a doubt you are running right back into this nagging behavior. This is a key lesson in your relationship. Conquer it and you will have greater passion and joy. Taurus' and Capricorn's hearts are joined when both respect the other's decision-making capability. You will win a friend and admirer if you show a willingness to change. Forget about changing your partner! It's like trying to turn rock into flour; it's impossible. You are wiser to acknowledge each other's power. It can hurt your pride to admit when you're wrong, but it is a boost to your commitment when you go beyond needing to be right or wrong. You are the Mr. and Mrs. Right for each other when you put each other in the winner's circle.

The *Scrooge* game isn't just a matter of sharing money. Giving your time to one another may be as important. Taurus doesn't really like to change its schedule suddenly but will do so if you clearly express a need for help. Capricorn is more rigid in adjusting a routine. The Goat defines itself through its schedule. If you lay out a solid explanation of why you need him or her to alter plans, a miracle can take place; you may be penciled in (not in ink just in case you really don't need your partner), whether reluctantly or generously. "Give" is the key word. When you back each other wholeheartedly, interesting things happen. Your sexual relationship intensifies. Trust becomes as deep as the Pacific Ocean. It isn't that hard to make your relationship click. You must stay cognizant of the fact that you both have a prerequisite for a serious relationship. What is it? You offer each other emotional and material support. It isn't that you are overly materialistic, but earth signs can't get away from the fear of losing power and status through poverty. Your partner must share your need to feel secure emotionally, which rests upon an underlying instinct to find reliable assets in the material world. The character Scrooge in Charles Dickens' classic story, *A Christmas Carol*, was not happy until he learned the art of giving. What you receive will increase when you give because the act of giving awakens your partner's desire to give in return. If that was too much of a mouthful, then think of it as a simple formula: Giving=Receiving. If one of you does all of the giving and the other all of the receiving, the formula is negated. The Giving=Receiving formula applies to both of you!

The *Tortoise That Doesn't Win* game will take your enthusiasm to bring new experiences into your lives. Stability is fine, and unpredictable events may not appeal to you, yet a surprise now and then by suddenly changing your schedule energizes you both. When your lives become too predictable, you can grow numb. Immobility can lead to less creativity and may deflate your romance. You can simply plan a candlelight dinner or use the *Yellow Pages* to put your finger on tonight's recipe. Find ways to elevate your love back to the place it occupied when you were still learning about each other. Rekindling that spark is easier than most people think. Even if you have just met, don't let this game come between you. It is when people take each other for granted that such behavior can show its face.

The Rainbow

Your Taurus-Capricorn relationship is as planning-oriented as they come. It is possible that you channel most of your planning into work and rebel against being organized anywhere else in your life. The two of you can bring out the best in each other by not making stiff demands. Building a creative life together can be satisfying.

A Taurus man likes the way the Capricorn woman carries herself. She appears able to balance many responsibilities and somehow knows how to proceed. He senses playfulness hidden behind the sensibility of the female Capricorn. He is in love with the way she can make him feel important without being overly flattering.

The Capricorn woman isn't sure how to show affection for the Taurus man. She sees he likes to be adored, but she doesn't want to spoil him. His fondness for romance touches a place in her heart that few have been able to reach. She wants to take it slow in getting to know this Venusian man. She likes to see that he has ambition. She needs a partner who is willing to let her test the furthest borders of her own self-expression. She wants to feel the loving arms of this sensuous person around her.

The Taurus woman likes to look at the Capricorn man because he seems to project permanence. He seems older than his years, regardless of his age, yet she detects a youthful vigor when he forgets about his worldly ambitions and responsibilities. So many people lean on him that she doesn't want to seem like another clinging vine. The Taurus woman likes the strength of his hands. She doesn't want to be forced to follow his lead. She wants to see if he is strong enough to not be intimidated by an equal partner. She is already falling in love with him. If only he has the sense to add to her romantic fire rather than snuff it out with his demands; she wonders about this thoughtfully, curiously, and hopefully. She is intrigued by the look in his eyes that suggests that he wants to share future milestones with her. She has her own ambitions and is anxious to show them to this wise man.

The Capricorn man is taken by the femininity of the Taurus woman. Her warmth is perceived as unconditional acceptance of him, but his vintage knowledge about doing business in the world colors his view about matters of the heart. His reality-based mind believes that the female Taurus is too good to be true. He wants to get close to her but does so cautiously, that is, until he is certain his ambition will not bother her. He realizes that this Venusian woman needs to perceive him as a sharing individual. He does his best to convince himself he can be this way to please her. Does he ever want to receive the passion she can offer him!

Taurus and Capricorn relationships have sustaining power. You display a rugged determination to make the best of what life puts in front of you. Capricorn can value a more old-fashioned approach to romance. Taking the time to create romantic atmospheres delights Taurus. Capricorn has primal instincts to honor tradition that date back to the beginning of time. It would appear to be a match made in heaven. Keeping your romance above reproach will take steady attention to your partner's need for support, even when it is not convenient to do so. Talk with a willingness to listen, and you will never be that far away. Be there in the most visible ways possible. Your partner needs to know you will remain close during the good and not-so-good times.

Taurus-Aquarius: The Surprisers

Taurus + Aquarius = Perseverance Plus

The traditional astrologer would say these signs conflict. They can powerfully attract—and often do! Contrary to popular belief, Taurus and Aquarius often get along. It comes down to putting up with each other. This duo shares natural electricity. When the two of you are able to harness your sometimes divergent themes, great things can be accomplished. Your ability to be a breath of fresh air for your partner can make this an exciting relationship. Taurus helps Aquarius moderate excessive drives to be in the fast lane. Aquarius ignites innovative vision in practical Taurus. It's the way you bring different values to each other that makes for interesting times.

Different Just to Be Different Game

The games played in your Taurus-Aquarius relationship center around rebellious behavior and fixed ideas. The *Different Just to Be Different* game shows the tendency not to agree only for the sake of disagreeing. You can bring out contrary behavior in each other. Taurus isn't usually rebellious. The Bull definitely taps into this dimension when learning it from the greatest teacher of all, Aquarius. Each of you makes a statement that you want your uniqueness respected. When you don't feel that it is, you can act out with individualistic behavior. It may be that one or both of you doesn't feel support for your goals. This game occurs because of a desire to step out on your own. Giving each other the freedom to explore personal ambitions and hobbies is smart. You may even thrive on having peers outside of the relationship. You don't have to feel the same way about each other's friends or group affiliations. If you pledge allegiance to the right to personal autonomy, the relationship stabilizes. You will find the more you stand in your partner's way, the greater the rebellion. Don't fear your partner's need to pursue his or her ambitions. The freer you both feel, the more energy comes into your relationship.

I Shall Not Be Moved Game

Your obstinate side reveals itself through the *I Shall Not Be Moved* game. Taurus won't give in easily if it believes in an idea. Aquarius is just about as determined to hold its position no matter what happens. Taurus-Aquarius rhythms can move at cross-purposes. Aquarius may want to move more quickly in a direction than Taurus is ready to do. Taurus tends to want to move at a pace that suits its current mind set. It might not always be slow, by the way. Taurus will charge like a bull when excited by an event or hunch. Aquarius is not always the one in a hurry. This is an unpredictable air sign that may hit the brakes and send you sailing through the air. When the two of you become fixed, it's like trying to pull up a two-ton anchor with your bare hands. You can become angry and frustrated by holding on to this game. You may become disappointed to the point that you may do fewer and fewer projects as a couple. It could interfere with romance in that you do not want to go out of your way to please each other. Hard feelings settle in and make for a bumpy road ahead.

Which Way Do We Go Game

Taurus and Aquarius can lose their sense of direction by failing to communicate their plans in a clear and concise manner. The *Which Way Do We Go* game can have several different causes. One may be that you are hiding your agendas and secretly pulling each other your own way. The problem is that you are no further from the shore than you were several days ago. Another version of this game is when the two of you feel such a need to pursue an individual goal that you try to stuff it into your shared goals. As a result, your ship constantly changes directions at sea with no real destination in mind. You are more or less (probably more!) drifting, hoping for a gust of wind to make the choice for you. This is not the way for two determined people to accomplish anything. Taurus does not panic immediately when its compass is broken. Anxiety sets in when its plans are about to be foiled due to poor planning. Then the Bull becomes angry. With Aquarius, a loss of direction is akin to death. A fast and compulsive search for the right highway is an instantaneous reaction. When lost, Aquarius screams (probably silently), panics, screams again, and then becomes calmly objective. How Aquarius does this is anybody's guess. The Water Bearer has been doing this and getting away with it for centuries, so who are you to question its wisdom? Taurus will start to ask questions if tired of following panicky Aquarius. Anxiety-ridden Taurus may watch Aquarius jump ship and wait at the shore. You don't like to be around each other when you are dazed and confused. Blaming one another won't help you to find your footing, though isn't it tempting to do so?

Strategies

The *Different Just to Be Different* game can be dealt with by encouraging personal autonomy as needed from time to time. Space can truly make the heart grow fonder. Try it and you will like it. The more in love with your individual lives you are, the more love you will make with one another. Your partner will definitely ask you for your full support in this partnership—count on it! It's inevitable. Your partner wants your support, not out of neediness but because he or she feels uplifted by your attention. You are different and make an exotic combination. Your similarities aren't what drew you so passionately into each other's company, though it is good to have some common goals that solidify your relationship. Allowing for idiosyncrasies adds spice to your relationship. You are a more energetic duo when you know nobody is looking over your shoulder to see if you are following orders. It is probable there will be a need to hang out with your own friends as much as socializing as a couple. You are attracted to your partner's unique qualities. By not questioning the exploration of new paths, you win the heart of your lover.

The *I Shall Not Be Moved* game is a question of who will blink first. Staring one another down does not win points. You could need to compromise to end this game. You both like to win once in a while. Fixed attitudes need to be traded in for more pliable ones. You can accomplish great things together when you put your incredible force behind the same idea. You become immovable when you try to force each other into something. Learn how to negotiate in a way that makes you both come out winners. Letting down your guard helps. The position you are defending is probably not worth the struggle. It would be wise to let each other off the hook. It may be that you both have the right answer in your own way. If this is the case, then why not "walk your own walk?" You can still join forces on other projects. Sometimes when one of you loses an argument, you later see that it worked out for the best anyway. Flexibility is a useful tool. Talking rather than endlessly fighting about issues is a good idea as well.

The *Which Way Do We Go* game is a matter of communication. It may even evolve if your partner wants to accompany you on your journey. Maybe you can meet a mile or two up the road after each of you gets your own explorations out of your system. In this game you need to confess your true goals. It's all right if an individual goal conflicts with your shared ones. You can't expect to travel constantly toward the same objectives. If you feel lost in the middle of a decision, you may need to get out of each other's space briefly. Come back later and your minds may be clearer. You have a tendency to be so attached to the outcome that you try to confuse your partner. You will become disoriented and dizzy if you think about the same thing over and over without making up your mind. You need to get hold of yourselves. It may help to distract yourselves from a problem until you calm down. In any event, neither of you enjoys putting energy into plans that go in circles. The shortest distance between two points is a straight line. You sail straight ahead when you talk directly about what you want. Do it!

The Rainbow

Your Taurus-Aquarius relationship was never meant to be predictable. The sudden opening of new opportunities captures your attention.

A Taurus man knows he will never be the same after romancing an Aquarian woman. He is excited and scared all at once. His common sense says no, but the quick beat of his heart utters yes. The Bull knows he will be jumping over fences to keep up with this unpredictable woman. He is even willing to throw out his practicality if this happens to be an unconventional version of the Aquarius woman. It's the excitement of finding a new reality that takes the Venusian man down this road.

The Aquarius woman is fascinated by the Taurus man's relaxed way of doing business in the world. She wonders if his wild side will come forward. It's not that the female Aquarius can't be conservative or traditional. She can be whatever it takes to express herself, though there is a spirit of freedom within her that can scare any man, especially a reserved Taurus. This free spirit is drawn to his boyishness regardless of his age. Her heart yearns for intimacy with him. If only his comprehension of the world could be truly expansive enough to understand her on the deepest of levels. She sure hopes so!

The Taurus woman is enchanted with the Aquarius man. He seems to be rugged, visionary, and sensitive all at the same time. He seems to know how to make a living even if distracted by his pet projects. She likes the youthful way he talks about his hopes and dreams. She notices he even likes to hear about her own future plans, especially the ones that coincide with his. The Taurus woman decides quickly if this man will ever totally understand her need to feel secure. He doesn't have to say he will support her, only that he won't make her feel uneasy by sudden whims to try almost anything for the thrill of it. She is excited about joining him on an exhilarating ride.

The Aquarius man is enthralled with the Taurus woman. She represents all that he wants in a partner. Her sweetness and stability puzzle him but at the same time intrigue him. Is she really always this way? Something tells him to not try to take advantage of this gentle spirit. She has already made it clear she can stand her ground if he can read between the lines.

You are a duo with a capacity to move forward ferociously. The love you share is reflected through what you create. You are apt to bring one another emotional and material wealth. Resolving your conflicts becomes easier with a lot of persistent practice. Don't be too hard on one another. Your individual frustration when life fails to respond to you on your own terms arouses your anger. Your relationship is in a league of its own when it comes to quickly making a dream come true once you tune in to it. There is a hint that you want instant gratification. Who is to say it doesn't work for you? People may regard you as a role model when it comes to making your partner feel valued. When you pay attention to your unique, individual goals, magic surrounds your relationship. Passion stays alive when you don't try to remake each other in your own image. The way you can motivate your partner to boldly try new endeavors probably keeps you close. The ups and downs you face together teach you to lean on each other's strength. You are happier if you don't try to always walk alone. When you ask for support and receive it, you know you have found someone special. Even when you are not able to be physically present for your partner, just knowing you care warms the heart. The irony of a Taurus-Aquarius romance is that you may never find someone able to break your heart as much, yet there are few who probably will love you like this! It's the latter that leads you to put up with the former. You can form an alliance that is hard to break due to its resilience. Enjoy it!

Taurus-Pisces: The Nature Lovers

Taurus + Pisces = Appreciation for Beauty and Love of Serenity

These are the two most complacent of the twelve signs. This doesn't mean you don't have any drive to succeed. It indicates you must find the inspiration and focus to make your dreams come true. Romanticizing life is in your sign chemistry together. A love of the arts is probable. Your relationship may have begun in mysterious or unexpected ways. Taurus is a sobering influence for idealistic Pisces. The intuition of Pisces entices reality-based Taurus to trust the higher mind. When all cylinders click in this romance, it can be a source of inspiration for you both and those you touch.

Don't Make Any Waves Game

The games played in your Taurus-Pisces relationship feature behavior connected to passivity, dependency, and unrealistic hopes for fame. The *Don't Make Any Waves* game occurs when the two of you dodge the need to address situations directly. The desire to remain complacent wins out over grabbing the Bull by the horns or the Fish by the tail. Taurus prefers life to continue with few disruptions. Taurus finds beauty in sunrises and sunsets and enjoys peaceful interactions with others. Pisces is attuned to tranquility in its own way. The Fish searches for calm waters that soothe its sensitive emotional nature. All of this dreamy energy does not create solid communication. You may find that reality is a few decibels below consciousness. In this game the two of you skirt around issues to the point that clear communication is blocked. No confrontation doesn't mean that everything is peachy. Taurus and Pisces don't like the messiness of anger, yet getting your feet wet in conflict resolution deepens your sense of commitment. Denying that you are unhappy is not wise. You don't need to reach for perfection. A mistake or two is not devastating. It may be that you both are afraid to speak up for fear of losing the relationship. Taurus is strong enough to survive a little commotion. Pisces can let go of hurt feelings and release the past. Each of you is not relying on your strengths. Fear and denial are playing on the chords of your weaknesses.

Helpless Victim Game

The *Helpless Victim* game can enter your relationship when one or both of you tries to illicit sympathy by pretending to be helpless. It forces the other to assume the role of savior. The balance is far from the center in this game; it's tipped to an extreme. This behavior can be used to manipulate your partner into making a decision. Taurus can pretend to lack the volition to achieve a goal in order to get someone else to do the work. Pisces is the master of using helplessness to get others to feel sympathy. This isn't the same as asking directly for support. You can drain each other of valuable energy if dependency requirements are vaguely defined. It's okay to need each other. It isn't productive to your relationship not to talk honestly. You are probably unclear about how to ask for what you need. The assertiveness to be yourselves is hidden from view. You can confuse one another by beating around the bush instead of getting to the point. If you rely on this game too much, your partner may not respond to your cry for help when you really need a lift. Remember the story about the boy who cried wolf one too many times. When the wolves really came, nobody paid any attention to the boy's plea for help. Be sure you don't end up in this predicament.

Visions of Grandeur Game

The ambition of earthy Taurus combined with the imagination of watery Pisces can lead to climbing the highest mountains of success. The other side of the coin is not as pretty. If Taurus' compulsive drive for wealth joins forces with the fantasy world of Pisces, it could lead to an unrealistic belief in their shared potential. The *Visions of Grandeur* game describes a loss of perspective. It's good to have ambition. Taurus is lost without it. Pisces must have an inspiring ideal to express its devotion, whether it be to a material or emotional cause. This game is nourished when the two of you lose sight of reality. You need to carefully assess a plan to determine if you have the time and resources to invest. If your bid is too high, you will be disappointed with one another. You can put fanciful ideas into each other's head that need a lot more careful planning than you realize. Miracles have been accomplished even when the odds have been heavily stacked against you. Just make sure how much you want to tempt fate. Walking near the edge of the cliff may not be necessary.

Strategies

How can you put these Taurus-Pisces games to rest? The *Don't Make Any Waves* game will require assertiveness and the willingness to talk honestly. Saying what each other wants to hear is not as productive as communicating what you need to hear. The two of you must not be so timid in dealing with your differences. It doesn't have to be a shouting match; you can use kid gloves if necessary. The main thing is that you get into the habit of saying what is on your mind. Why? If you don't, it fogs your perceptions of your partner. It can even weaken your sex life. If your intensity is hidden, passionate fires are put out by the waters of emotional confusion. The tender loving care you want from each other doesn't need to be sacrificed. You will find even greater love and care when you are real with one another.

The *Helpless Victim* game is a poor replacement for equal dependency needs. When one of you leans too heavily on the other as a regular pattern, it causes all sorts of problems. One problem is that the person doing the rescuing has little time for anything else. Also, resentment is going to settle in sooner or later (probably sooner)! Caring about each other is wonderful, and so is lending support to get through the demanding times. Yet, it grows old if one of you always asks for a life jacket. Taurus gets tired of footing the bill as much as Pisces can get irritated when its faith in someone is abused. When Taurus acts helpless, it seriously undermines the Bull's self-esteem. When Pisces expresses a helpless demeanor, little energy is left to find creative outlets. Your expectations need to be clarified. Certainly the boundaries must be redefined so that you won't cross too many miles into your partner's territory. Taurus is usually more aware of where the middle ground may lie, though the Bull can lose sight of it when portraying feigned neediness. Pisces always needs to keep an eye on the middle ground. The Fish can drift into giving too much away or feeling sorry for itself. This game can be converted into a winner if you are determined to put an end to it. Adopt a ground rule or two. One is that you must start with what you will do, or will not be able to do, for each other. You can ask for your partner to put an equal amount of time, energy, and resources into the relationship. An organized approach may be required to get the ball rolling because this game is not always easy to get a handle on. You will need a little bit of structure to keep yourselves from returning to this scenario over and over again.

You can turn the *Visions of Grandeur* game to your favor by keeping in mind what is possible to attain. There is nothing wrong with having high-minded goals or dreams. The sign chemistry you share romanticizes your vision of life. You want to lift one another to higher levels of fulfillment. Stay with a formula that will guarantee success. You don't need to pretend to reach or go beyond your aspirations. You will feel greater admiration and love when you stay grounded to reality. Your individual and shared visions need not be limited. You will have a greater chance to reach your destinations if you set out on a course with a strong foundation.

The Rainbow

Your Taurus-Pisces relationship is one of many splendid colors. You may inspire the creative talents in one another in a way that few other romances can. Your dispositions run along similar veins. Taurus often exhibits a patient attitude in dealing with everyday living. Pisces hopes its dreams will be realized while putting up with the hassles of life. It is true that your signs have different points of reference in making decisions. Taurus is pragmatic while Pisces is intuitive. Each of you can get the results wanted and can integrate unique qualities into your romance in an exciting way.

A Taurus man wonders how a Pisces woman gets things done. Her way of proceeding with a plan appears to have no preconceived order. The Bull is fascinated with the way this intuitive woman can happily rely upon something other than logic. What that something might be, he doesn't know and is not so sure he wants to. After all, her voice delights him, and her poetic words strike a pleasing chord within him. This Neptunian woman has a glow that shines like a sunset though sometimes storms gather on the horizon. She seems to know him better than he knows himself; he isn't used to having anyone see to his very core. He hopes this water spirit, born under the idealism of Pisces, understands the value of money. He can't help himself. Ownership is as dear to him as breath itself.

The Pisces woman finds the Taurus man to be reliable. She questions whether he will be able to accept her hidden inner world which is the source of her strength in the outer world. Samson had his hair; this Neptunian woman has her intuition. The female Pisces likes the Bull's stabilizing energy. She doesn't want him to think her unable to match his ambition. She dreams that they might merge with a life direction that lifts each of them to their greatest happiness. Faith is the daughter of her intuition, which is her true strength. In time she hopes he will see her real self. It's not that she can't be successful in her career and with her finances. Worldly success seems to be a product of her creative passion. She perceives that Taurus sees the things of this world as an end in themselves. To her, tangible objects are the means. She wants to find the place where her East meets his West. In other words, this feminine spirit longs for the unity of their two hearts in spite of their birth influences.

The Taurus woman is touched by the attention of the Pisces man. His smile plays upon her heart strings. She loves the way he wines and dines her. The Venusian woman hopes this Pisces man will not get lost in his causes. He is a drifter when his idealism and devotion to his beliefs take him away to the unknown. It's not that she wants to keep him from his heartfelt goals. She only wants to be his source of inspiration. She is ruled by Venus and wants to draw close to her partners. It is her birthright to request from the deepest part of her being that he be her soul mate. This Neptunian dreamer, whether a writer or accountant, is intensely emotional. The Taurus woman is serious about business. She is relieved to see that between his escapes to other lands, this sensitive soul manages to keep his feet planted on the ground that comforts her. His feelings for her are invited because they match the love she wants to give.

The Pisces man knows that he better not take the earthy, spirited Taurus woman for granted. She will call him on this. She will let him get away with a few things but not with undervaluing her. He loves her affable and fair personality. He is moved by her willingness to believe in him. The Neptunian man has strong intuition, probably inherited from his Piscean ancestry. He is nostalgic about the past but knows he must live in the present if he wants to have this Venusian woman in his life. He is afraid to love her because he discerns she will likely love him back. He is uncomfortable with surrendering to love but loves to be in love. He knows that she senses this in his inviting face. He sees the bottom line. She will probably demand his time. His heart wants to reach out to her. He wants to be in the hands of a strong and dependable partner—one who will hold him to his promises yet wish him well when the night spirits speak to him, calling him forward, away from the familiar, to test the waters of his own faith.

Let the Games Begin

    You can find yourself getting attached to the dreams you pursue together. The individual paths you choose will benefit from the self-confidence you derive from your romance. A passionate spark is lit from the moment you meet. You can keep it burning through mutually accepting one another's values. There is warmth here you may find missing when you become too self-absorbed in your own milestones. The two of you will enjoy the attention received in this relationship. You can offer one another a vast array of support. You feel like true soul mates when you make the effort to tune in to each other's inner and outer worlds.

Gemini-Gemini: The Thinkers

Gemini + Gemini = Few Uneventful Moments

You are ready to skip through life, merrily, merrily all the way. There are few couples who can keep up with your mental energy. Ideas travel back and forth at the speed of light. Mental stimulation is a must. You like to move on multiple fronts as much as possible. Boredom has no place in your lives. Reading and learning are probably fond interests. Restlessness is a perpetual challenge, which can be mastered if you keep several intellectual outlets open. Looking for alternative ways to solve a problem is at your fingertips. The power of positive thinking is your best ally.

Intellectualizer Game

The games in your Gemini-Gemini relationship are associated with avoiding the expression of feelings, losing focus, and dishonest communication. The *Intellectualizer* game arises when the two of you live in your heads rather than in your hearts. Your sign tends to analyze feelings rather than experience them. When you choose this type of communication, it creates emotional distance. You have a strong natural tendency to think, and your mental processes can't help but get excited (often unexpectedly!) when in each other's company. If you avoid emotions, it makes for a very dry existence. You can get so mentally buzzed that you don't even realize that emotional exchanges are not happening. This isn't to say you lack passion—probably quite the contrary. It's just that you are well trained in ideas and thoughts. Concentrating on feelings could mean taking time to yourselves away from the rest of the world. Even then, you can initiate mental processes so fast in each other that you will still need to make sure you talk heart to heart. Communication is often what many couples have trouble developing. You already possess the natural ingredient for a wonderful connection to each other. It will take a bit of practice to get good at using "I feel" rather than "I think" statements.

Dual Exhaustion Burnout Game

Your sign isn't ruled by the winged messenger, Mercury, for nothing. It means your thoughts are constantly migrating to new horizons. While many people are fixated on one idea, your mental sparks fly like a helicopter's blades. You want to have your hand in many projects simultaneously. Shorthand was probably invented because of your sign. After all, why waste so much time writing the whole mess down when you can abbreviate it with a few strokes? This restlessness to indulge in your curiosity might lead to the *Dual Exhaustion Burnout* game. This game can manifest in a couple of ways. You may tire your partner's mind by throwing out more information than can be processed. The central nervous system can feel like it has burned out when you try to keep up with one another's life pace. Another side of this game is that when the two of you embark on a path together, you may find that your minds "short out." You could go so fast in multiple directions that you lose your sense of direction. A mentally invigorating atmosphere is at work, maybe even while you sleep! When automobiles first were converted to a dual exhaust system, the belief was that it would give increased power. However, as time went on, the single exhaust system was refined to give maximum power. When you combine your energy, it can be as focused as a laser and can cut through anything in your way. What is the key? Focus your aim with your partner's long enough to get the desired results.

Forked Tongue Game

When you don't say what is really on your mind, you just might be playing the *Forked Tongue* game. Gemini is often not given the credit for its mental strength. You both have Mercurian power running through your heart and soul. This makes it imperative to be up front with your partner. No, don't give each other a lie-detector test every night. You do need to keep each other abreast of the latest breaking headlines about your personal goals. When you don't, anger sets in along with mistrust and a few other little nasty reactions. Somehow, you need to straighten yourselves out so you can be honest. You may be afraid that your partner will negate your ideas if you share them. Keeping too many secrets causes great anxiety, and it cuts down on the support you can give one another when you might need it the most. Trust is going to be a quart low if this pattern becomes too pervasive.

Strategies

How can you jump over the hurdles these Gemini-Gemini games present? The *Intellectualizer* game requires a willingness to let your mind take a break in order to allow your emotions to come across. The saying, "the mind is a terrible thing to waste," seems right out of a Gemini catalogue. You have a wonderful gift: you insightfully see how to interact with each other and how to explore the world at large. It isn't easy at first to change old habits, is it? Flexing the heart muscles can be more taxing than the mental ones in your case. Letting your partner into your inner world of emotions can be scary and downright awkward if you aren't used to doing it. Nobody said you need to get good at this overnight. It might be hard to imagine right now, but a step into the shallow end of the pool will eventually lead you to the diving board. You may not even know how much you live in your mind. It's like when you first learn to meditate. You may sit and struggle as your mind continues to resist the concentration exercise. Whenever you try to train your mind to quiet down so that other dimensions of yourself can be discovered, you meet resistance. So, be prepared to start over a lot. The key thing to remember is to keep trying. Eventually, you can quiet your mind long enough for your heart to speak.

The *Dual Exhaustion Burnout* game will occasionally take your willingness to focus on one thing at a time. When talking to each other, try to avoid overwhelming your partner. It is tiring to be bombarded by too much stimuli. You will find you hear more of what you say to each other if you slow down your delivery. When you take on a project or cause together, don't forget to rest. You will get more done in a shorter amount of time if you don't cram too much into your schedules. Be good to yourselves. Your nervous systems will thank you for slowing down. By focusing on fewer objectives rather than wildly proceeding ahead, you may achieve more favorable results. It's ridiculous to tell Gemini not to do more than one thing at a time. Just don't try ten at once! Your health will even benefit if you go to the trouble to plan before you jump. The truth is that you can get away with more than most by not adhering to a strict schedule. You are going to resist too much structure. The excitement of running into surprises is what keeps you mentally fit. It will create less anxiety for you to live spontaneously, but you would be wise to give your partner a warning when you are about to make a major revision around the next bend.

Rainbow

Your Gemini-Gemini relationship was never intended to suffer through dull days. The two of you may even live by a philosophy that goes something like this: "I am ready to set my mind free in new worlds of learning." You have a vast array of information to share with each other. When a Gemini man meets a Gemini woman, he is quick to see he has found a kindred spirit. You may both feel like you were sent by that gallant champion of the intellect, Mercury, to help the rest of us who are hungry for new experiences.

The Gemini man perceives that the female Gemini is linked to the same type of internal computer system as his. Even the brain synapses seem to carry impulses at the same speed. He wonders if she escapes through free association as he so often does. He asks himself, "Have I found my soul mate, or is this too good to be true?" Her eyes reflect deep passion, but he wonders if she can really let go of her heart. He wants to find out as soon as possible.

When first encountering the male Gemini, the female Gemini tests his intellect with a few questions. She wants to know if he can be sincere to the point of saying what he really thinks. She is turned on by his mental prowess. The Mercurian woman is as reserved as the Mercurian man in deciding how much of her inner emotional landscape should be revealed. The female Gemini notices her male counterpart showing off his wit with colorful, entertaining short stories. She doesn't want to hear his sales pitch. She prefers to hear the intensity behind his entertaining words. She wants to listen to the greatest miracle of all, the expression of his feelings.

You have a knack for finding the news. To other people, you may even be a popular topic of discussion. Don't let this concern you. People find you stimulating. Your circle of friends must be wide enough so the two of you don't feel hemmed in. Each of you needs enough mental latitude to explore whatever appeals to you. You are talented advisors, consultants, and teachers. Communication is your hallmark, and it takes you far. Ride it together to the most thrilling destinations. Your relationship is one of individual and joint discovery. You are not happy when life is stagnant. There is a calling from within your souls to respond to the most exhilarating experiences you can find. Become lovers of the heart and mind. When you touch both in each other, there are few challenges that

The Magic of Signmates

will seem insurmountable. Lead each other to the truth within you. When you speak with the passion of conviction rather than saying what others want to hear, you capture each other's hearts. The thrill of becoming lovers may bind you together. When either of you thinks you have the other figured out, you know you still have a long way to go. You are not meant to understand every final detail in your lover's mind. It's vital to feel the pulse of your partner's needs. Don't fail to listen to that ancient guide, Mercury, as he shows you how to perceive the love behind the words that slip from your partner's lips.

Gemini-Cancer: The Inquisitive Ones

Gemini + Cancer = Strong Attachments

These two signs can probe to the bottom of any mystery. Gemini's sleuth-like mind combined with Cancer's tenacity can penetrate through the maze of any brain teaser. In short, you can figure anything out! The trick is to set your mind to it. Gemini is known for the power of its mind. This persuasive air sign can turn linguistic cartwheels and use the exact accent needed to make a point. Cancer is not recognized for being articulate, but this sign can fool you! Cancer can use its watery emotional force to take you right out of your game. The Crab can quietly (and even not so quietly) move with deceptive speed to outmaneuver whomever it must conquer. Cancer's ambition is sometimes hidden but not from itself. Gemini shows Cancer how to be more mentally detached. Cancer tells Gemini that it is okay to feel as well as think. Together the Crab and the Twins are quite a duo. Cancer will sometimes wonder if they are relating to one or two people as the twin-like Gemini personality becomes bubblier when familiarity breeds fondness.

Walking on the Moon Game

The games played in your Gemini-Cancer relationship derive from mental disorientation, unbalanced dependency needs, and being too judgmental. The *Walking on the Moon* game arises when the two of you can't concentrate together. You can feel like your minds are lost on the Moon. Your perceptions of one another are unclear, which is likely due to unfinished business. Perhaps an issue on both of your minds still lingers in the air. Each of you can sense something isn't right. If you don't talk about what is wrong, your confusion only grows. This game may find you emotionally bewildered when you try to talk. You may seem to fog your partner's perceptions. The harder you try to discuss an area of concern, the more blurred your vision becomes. It's like when you first spray window cleaner on a dirty windshield. At first, the window looks even dirtier, but eventually it starts to clear. When you begin to talk about an emotionally charged issue, the feelings can be so strong that you both back off from getting to the heart of the matter. This can be a continuous cycle that becomes frustrating. Your passion can begin to wane if you stay stuck in this predicament.

Clingy, Clingy Game

Gemini is more free-spirited than Cancer as a general rule. Cancer will display more spontaneity and a desire for space when its self-confidence is awakened. Gemini likes to draw close to someone who stimulates its thinking but within certain parameters of mental freedom. Intellectual freedom warms Gemini's heart. Cancer might become overly attached to a person out of genuine love. You may get to a point where it feels almost too good to have your lover nearby. When Gemini doesn't trust a person, this sign becomes suspicious and usually wants more distance. Cancer retreats into its shell when it doesn't feel secure. In the *Clingy, Clingy* game you act from the fear of loss rather than from what you perceive to be genuinely yours. Gemini doesn't like to be held so close that its freedom of movement is infringed. Cancer can also feel smothered. The Crab can become uncomfortable if someone wants too much of its body, mind, and soul. When you don't allow for personal freedom to be expressed, the vitality and shine of your relationship isn't as apparent. It will feel like living through the perpetual twilight of an Alaskan winter. The coldness in your hearts will hurt. Resentment comes when you become too demanding of one another. You cling to doubts rather than certainty.

Torpedo Game

Communication must stay aboveboard. If you go underwater to undermine one another's ideas and fire angry words at each other, you are in the midst of the *Torpedo* game. Usually, a judgmental mindset lies at the root of this behavior. One or both of you may be attached to your own views regarding a hot topic of discussion. It's better to openly disagree. Agreeing to disagree may be your best course of action. Gemini likes to speak its mind and may simultaneously come at Cancer from the north, south, east, and/or west. The Crab will feel under attack if the shots come from every direction.

Cancer doesn't appreciate it if someone does not stay focused on one point at a time. Gemini is adept at jumping back and forth in an argument, but most would call this approach scattered. Gemini laughs at this because it believes its mental acrobatics are articulate. Cancer can fire back with a retaliatory shot faster than most think possible. When this emotionally intense sign gets angry, look out! What occurs in this game is not so much the fighting itself but how you fight. It is better if you battle aboveground, so you can work this out. Hidden motives need to be made visible. It may be that hurt feelings are making it hard to patch up your disagreement. Old wounds won't heal if they stay buried. You express your anger through a game like this. Someone must make the first move to talk.

Strategies

How do you sail clear of these Gemini-Cancer games? The *Walking on the Moon* game will take your understanding. Gemini's air and Cancer's water at times intertwine in ways that ask for your patience. Your individual goals may get tangled in the strings of your shared plans. Separating out your own needs takes discrimination and clear communication. You can have everything if you go about asking for it with objectivity. The mental and emotional depths you can arouse in one another are awesome. If you are causing confusion in each other, it could be that you are not going deep enough. There could be a tendency to get caught up in so many details that you lose perspective. Stay aware of the bigger picture. If your emotions are too magnetized, step back and take a breath or two. Let the emotional waters calm down. Balancing your mental and emotional intensities comes with exercising them. You can solve any problem when you tune in to each other's mental frequencies. Air signs such as Gemini perceive situations quite differently from water signs like Cancer. It doesn't mean either is "right" but that these signs offer divergent ways of putting it all together.

Processing information and feelings are not the same for Cancer and Gemini. The Crab takes longer to digest what it hears because it filters everything through its powerful feelings. Gemini takes in information and labels it almost as fast as it utters a response, sometimes in the same breath! You will find romantic beaches and create a loving atmosphere when you take the time to talk. You may even need to educate your partner on how to interpret your language. You are not speaking in a foreign tongue, but what you say still may require further elaboration. You will feel closer when you know that you are heard.

The *Clingy, Clingy* game indicates your dependency needs must be clearly defined. Neither of you is going to be comfortable if not given the space that makes you feel free. You need to state what causes either of you to feel insecure with each other. If there is fear, you need to eradicate it. It might not be fear of losing your partner as much as other worries. In identifying the source of your fear, you are most of the way home to each other's heart. When Gemini clings to Cancer, the Crab gets nervous. It isn't sure which way to move to please this fast-thinking, analysis-oriented air sign. Cancer's clinging ways will make the Twins want to run in separate directions to confuse the Crab. Why create these dilemmas for your partner? Get at the real reason, or, better yet, talk from the heart. Cling to what you love in each other, not what scares you. It takes so much energy to hold on to your fear. Fear doesn't love you, haven't you noticed? It betrays all of us faster than a black widow spider eating its mate. When you cling to your anxiety, you hold on desperately to your partner. Let go and trust each other. Better yet, communicate because it gives your partner a good reason to hold on to you. Talk clearly. It's amazing how much you can stay out of this game by not making your lover read your mind.

The *Torpedo* game is neutralized when you come out into the open with your expectations. Judging your partner is not endearing. Your sex life certainly suffers. It's hard to feel passion toward someone who holds an interrogation light over your head or launches a surprise attack. You need to move from being on the defensive to being on the same team. You will feel better when firing at what you want to accomplish together and not at each other. Repressed anger will find a way to the surface; count on it! Gemini gets extremely nervous when locked into hiding strong opinions while Cancer becomes moody. Nervousness and moodiness do not make for a sunny forecast, do they? Anger is better expressed in the present so you don't pay the price later. Unexpressed anger eventually will come calling. Before it comes knocking on your door, beat it to the punch, and get your feelings out into the open. You will be happier when you tolerate alternative points of view. There will often be more than one solution to a problem and multiple choices to make in planning your future. You can count on it!

The Rainbow

Your Gemini-Cancer relationship can take you to places you might never discover on your own. For better or worse, Gemini inspires Cancer to change directions. Cancer dredges up emotions that Gemini may not want to face but that force Gemini to grow.

You don't always make life easier for one another, yet you can open exciting doors for your lover.

The Cancer woman's penetrating presence startles the Gemini man's heart. He wonders if it is her gaze that is as brilliant as the full Moon or her desire to know his heart that quickens his pulse. This male traveler of the intellect (taught under Mercury's tutelage) notices the little things. He appreciates this woman's generosity yet senses she will be demanding (of what he can't decipher). His mind is thrilled by the depth with which she explores the subjects she admires. Everything about her, including her gait, has a distinct rhythm, just as his thoughts create a constant beat in his mind. She seems to be serious about her plans for a home. He listens with great curiosity though his idea of home is in the world of ideas. He thinks she would be a warm spirit to come home to. He loves her passion and dares himself to come closer.

A female Cancer sizes up the male Gemini quickly. It will be impossible for him to be focused unless he loves what he is doing. The Crab likes the mental intensity of this airy man. She hopes he will be careful when listening to her most cherished dreams. The Cancer woman is fond of his mental ingenuity. She hopes his heart holds a place for her. Why? He lifts her out of her inner shell by persuading her that life must be experienced. He beckons her to travel with him by airplane, car, horse, boat, hot air balloon, or whatever else strikes his fancy. She knows that some of these journeys are better left just for him. She hopes he will grant her the same favor since some of her paths will not be for him.

The Gemini woman talks quickly to the Cancer man, hoping that he will be so distracted that he will not notice she is analyzing his every thought. Her intellect is honed by Mercury's wit and insight and her powers of discrimination are keen. She tests this watery soul in front of her. She is attracted to the male Cancer's passion. In matters of the heart, he can be thorough and attentive. Even in love-making his attentiveness can delight her. If he grows attached, she knows that she will need to call upon her wits to maintain her freedom. This man's warmth may be more than she bargained for. Make no mistake about it, she knows this but enjoys being with this emotional man. She likes the fact that he takes the sacredness of her high-flying and thirsty mind seriously.

The Cancer man finds it hard to read the Gemini woman. On one hand, she seems easy to draw a bead on and, on the other, she is wonderfully complicated. He is not even sure why she is so complex. Perhaps it's her Mercurian eyes that beam with curiosity and penetrate his innermost thoughts maybe even better than he does! Her perceptiveness fascinates the Crab. He wants to reach out to touch her but isn't sure how to reach her deeper nature. He loves her light spirit and outspoken candor. He knows that idle chitchat masks her real depth. He wants to know the real person behind that mask or at least thinks he does. Her words spark his passion and even make him take a deeper look at himself.

The two of you can rise to the top of the world when you gain insight on how to ride the energy of this relationship. You can delight the lover in one another by being dependable friends. You have a lot to share. The inspiration to follow similar paths will tighten your connection. The freedom you feel to express your minds fuels your resolve to be together. Listen to the aspirations that come from deep within each of you, and there will be plenty to celebrate.

Gemini-Leo: The Entertainers

Gemini + Leo = Fun in the Sun Liveliness

When teaming up, these two signs form a highly creative duo. Gemini's communication power blends wonderfully with the dramatic promotional energy of Leo. Each of you can exude great confidence in this romance. Be careful of what you ask for since you will probably get it. Your passion was likely to have been awakened the instant your eyes first met or will explode if you are just now crossing paths. People are attracted to the love of life and mental energy you both project. Others may rely on your belief in them. You can excel together in business or in play, and both are tempting. You can be stimulated by the wide range of choices that each of you will bring into the other's life.

Outflank You Game

The games played in your Gemini-Leo relationship emanate from trying too hard to outsmart one another and from a weakening of that incredible imagination that propels you both. The *Outflank You* game transpires when you try to outdo one another. Gemini can live so much in the head that it becomes a pattern to cleverly sidestep Leo's demands. The Lion with its proud roar can by sheer force outdistance even the range of that incredible Gemini mind. Why do Gemini and Leo even play this game? It's probably a power play as much as anything else. Gemini retains power through keeping its mind free of those who want to control it. Leo fights to preserve individuality by drawing a line around itself which bears a sign that says: "No admittance without my express permission." There is a competitive spirit in fiery Leo that matches that in Gemini even though this air sign usually prefers to forego competitive struggles. Gemini doesn't like to waste the time that long, drawn-out strategies involve. To let you in on a secret, Leo doesn't like them either! The Lion doesn't mind sending others out to fight the battles while it moves on to other interests. You will eventually ask yourselves, "How did we get here?" Unfortunately, the willpower and stamina of Leo may lead it to choose to keep going with this standoff. Losing is not acceptable. When provoked enough, Gemini will hold on to these cards if the dealer is still bluffing. In a way, you are both probably waiting for the other to wave the white flag. Gemini doesn't want to be seen as a pushover. Leo, in showing off its creative ability to keep one step ahead, can go on like this indefinitely. The result is you don't enjoy the finer moments of being together. This game channels most of your passion in the wrong direction.

Head in the Sand Game

It is hard to imagine a Gemini-Leo partnership down for very long. When you lose your creative intensity the *Head in the Sand* game is the culprit. It takes major obstacles in your paths to derail your ferocious drive to get ahead. If one of you grows despondent indefinitely, it might bring the other down with you. The tireless energy of Gemini or Leo can keep trying to pull a partner out of low times. In doing so, both of you may need a recharged battery. It runs contrary to your natural energy flow to lose your momentum. You two must have at least one major plan before you. The rest of us are counting on your inspiration! It could be that too much time is going into work to the exclusion of play. Exhaustion can contribute to this game. You don't have the energy left to have fun. Forgetting to pace yourselves makes you grow irritable. You need to watch out for blaming each other. Mutual incrimination is this game at its worst. You may lose sight of what you are all about. Watch those accusations. Gemini becomes anxious when its intellect is stuck in low gear for extended time periods. Mercury's sign becomes eerily aloof when feeling the blues. Leo is tough to be around when it loses that competitive edge. The Lion must find the part of the jungle that is its property; then the Lion is less inclined to be bossy and moody. When Leo feels its power has shrunk, its roar is off key and bothersome rather than loud and playful. It's really a cry for help, but the Lion isn't good about admitting a need for assistance. You two are miserable when not feeling mutually empowered.

Talk but No Walk Game

The ability to put a plan into action is a fine trait that can be displayed when you hit on all cylinders. The *Talk but No Walk* game is one in which you both advertise great things but fail to follow through on them. Gemini can put out fine public relations statements. Leo can publicly broadcast its future plans. When Gemini doesn't get off the mental fence and Leo is content to keep ideas on a conceptual level, you both can become frustrated. You are doers who, for some reason, may not be doing. The cause can be a lack of focus. Gemini can spew a stream of incredible ideas as its mind opens up. Leo's enthusiasm may be short lived. Fire signs are better starters than finishers; however, when Leo's attention is totally captured, it can make it to the finish line with enough breath to go right on to the next challenge. The trick is to hold the attention of your two restless signs. When you interfere with each other's personal goals, you can expect a firestorm of anger. Be sure not to grow jealous of your partner if he or she is a step ahead of you. It can be a real disappointment to see your partner is not happy for you. If you panic because your actions don't bear fruit, this could lead you to sit by the sidelines rather than walk into the fray. If you lose your cool and don't talk about it, this game will be prolonged.

Strategies

How do you resolve these Gemini-Leo games? The *Outflank You* game beckons for your openness to each other's point of view. It is so tempting to think we are Right with a capital R. It's okay to defend your position. In a Gemini-Leo relationship, it is inevitable that your ideas will fuel a few fights. You never really saw each other as "yes" people, did you? You can keep circling one another's minds with a passion for your own ideas. When you come to terms with alternative opinions, you will receive more passion from each other's heart. In this game, the negotiation strength of your sign combination is turned on one another. Can you imagine the powerful creative force you could put forward if you aimed this energy at more appropriate targets? You must talk. It doesn't have to be as eloquent as Shakespeare or as exciting as Tom Clancy's novels. Gemini often lets go of its defensiveness after connecting with its thoughts. Leo will usually be slightly less obstinate if you appeal to its humor and generosity. If this doesn't work, tell Leo to cut out the playacting and Gemini to snap out of it. The shock treatment might work on either of you. You can escape from this game by seeing where and how you contribute to it. The good news is that if you confront it successfully once, ending the game gets easier the next time. Use Gemini's ingenuity and Leo's fortitude to outflank this game!

The *Head in the Sand* game means that life isn't as much fun as it used to be. You are not the type to sit and wait for opportunities; you can kick open new doors to walk through. If you are working too much, you may need to get out on the dance floor or explore hobbies. Take a trip to a fun location. You need to breathe life back into your deflated passion. Your romance is young at heart regardless of your age. When your spirit feels old and tired, it is a sign that you need to revise your game plan. The script you are reading has lost its punch. Write a new one! Inspiration is about one half of a breath away for Gemini. Leo needs to take a long, deep breath and focus on the self-confidence in its heart. Sadness is a state of mind. Perhaps one of you has experienced a setback. Get your mind off your worries long enough to rewrite these mental files. A small amount of success does wonders for you. Be determined to change negative energy but do so wisely. You don't want to fight yourself. Concentrate on what you want to do rather than what you aren't doing.

The *Talk with No Walk* game can be turned into a *Talk While You Walk* game. You need to spend more time on planning a blueprint that will ensure you get out of the starting gate. Gemini's electric and contagious ideas network to other ideas (a family tree of ideas). Thoughts are even stronger with action. Leo can advertise like no other. Even if Leo is shy, this sign can discover a self-promoting style if it works at it. A fire sign like Leo finds greater creative insight when it is smack-dab in the middle of a project. Leo's closing power blows others out of the way. The Lion's creative intensity is poetry in motion. Gemini has a way of weaving ideas behind its actions that can be spellbinding. When you are stuck at first base because you don't have the courage to steal second, not only do your fans grow impatient, so do the muses. The saying, "the proof is in the pudding," applies here. You are a twosome who needs to see that your world is expanding. You were never meant to be satisfied with staying at home within your own borders. The world will tempt you to impress it with your gifts. Delight each other. How? Strut your stuff!

The Rainbow

Your Gemini-Leo relationship dances to a tune that few others even hear. Your joy in being together can shine in your faces. The pride you have in your partner elevates his or her confidence. Your romance can send a creative blast of gusto through all the people you reach out and touch. You attract attention through being the real you. Gemini's words and Leo's theatrics make for high times.

A Gemini man exchanges fast glances with a Leo woman when first meeting. He is stopped in his tracks by her air of certainty. He wonders if she is always this confident or simply acts that way. He senses that she is a person of action; she makes a definite impression on him. "Who is this?" he asks himself. He wishes that he could connect with her. He hopes to see her again if only she will remember him.

The Leo woman is impressed with the ideas of a Gemini man. It's not that her own thoughts aren't as exciting. She is happy to meet another person with a fast mind. Her risk-taking side is attracted to this fast-talking Mercurian man. She is amused that he knows so many people and is knowledgeable about so many subjects. He becomes passionate when he discusses his interests. She looks to see if he is interested in her own pet subjects. She hopes he will want to understand the source of her passion, which is the desire to express herself through a variety of roles.

The Gemini woman finds the Leo man to be a fun-loving pal. She takes her time in deciding if he is a long-term lover or a short-term interlude. Either is okay with her as long as he doesn't have too many expectations of her. She is a good match for the Lion. She will face him directly and not back down. The Lion adores this but won't admit it. She may even roar playfully with him to try the experience. The Gemini woman will let this strong-willed man into her life as long as she is sure she can escape from his domain when needed. Her fleet-of-foot mind appreciates the fiery heart of the restless Lion.

The Lion is mesmerized by the Gemini woman's eyes regardless of their color. Her eyes seem to pierce his soul like the eyes in a portrait that follow you as you walk by. The Leo man is hypnotized by her stare. He thinks she is singling him out; he doesn't realize that she can do this to anyone though she isn't anxious to offer this revelation. The Leo man is attracted to the youthful laugh of a Gemini woman. She doesn't act serious but can be quite sober in realizing her own goals. He knows that he had better not forget this point because she has already made this as clear as a Hawaiian sunrise.

You are a special pair. Enjoy the gifts you offer to one another. Let each other occupy center stage. There is more than enough recognition and applause for both of you. Those moments when you remember the details of what makes your partner happy keep you as close and snug as can be.

Gemini-Virgo: The Scrutinizers

Gemini + Virgo = Finely Tuned Attention to Detail

Both signs are ruled by analysis-oriented Mercury. Even though Gemini is not as compulsive about order, it is still nervous about getting things done without leaving too many loose ends. Virgo is always ready on a fraction of a second's notice to edit the actions of the rest of the signs. These two signs can be extremely precise in carrying out plans. Airborne Gemini encourages Virgo to let go of the heavy baggage that keeps this earth dweller so attached to pragmatism. Lift off for Virgo takes great effort because it likes to view life at ground level. Gemini benefits from Virgo's organized thinking, which is as powerful as a radar system. Gemini's tendency to restlessly roam in several directions is under the watchful eyes of Virgo.

Not Seeing the Forest for the Trees Game

The games played in your Gemini-Virgo relationship center around paying too much attention to the little things, resulting in negativity and worry. When Gemini and Virgo grow overly protective in order to preserve a too-narrow focus, it can be the beginning of the *Not Seeing the Forest for the Trees* game. Mercury masterfully teaches each of these signs how to spot flaws. Be careful when you use your powers of discrimination that you don't lose sight of the big picture. When you are overwhelmed by the details in this game, it distracts you from a broader purpose. It's nice to notice the trees, but don't try to replant them; you will never get out of the woods! You could be working on a project together and decide you don't want to try it again. You could be right if it was a miserable experience for both of you. Your perceptions can be so lost in irrelevant details that you are worn out. Refusing to weed out what is not important can waste a lot of your time. Your attention to the finer points is a talent. It becomes a problem when you compulsively comb over something more than needed.

Litterbug Game

Negativity even sounds like a nasty word, doesn't it? The *Litterbug* game describes the way you might dump harmful debris on each other. You may even be harder on yourself than your partner. Either option is not a winner. Old habits can be hard to change. If you have been engaged in negative thinking for quite some time, it may take almost as long to get a positive framework in place. The most difficult thing about a lack of optimism is that the opposite type of energy is glad to fill the vacuum. The old saying, "the absence of darkness brings the light," unfortunately can become "the absence of light brings the darkness." Neither of you gain much as players in this behavior. Criticism can be a constructive thing, but it certainly is destructive when you beat yourself up or take out your irritability on your partner. Clean up your mental highways. It won't get better with more negative thinking. Doubt can be hypnotic. Its only real power is that which we give it over us. In this game, the two of you are caught in a cycle of negativity. You will need to really work together to jump off this merry-go-round of limiting logic.

Worry Warts Game

It could appear to you that a job will not get done without worrying. Why doesn't this theory work? In the *Worry Warts* game, you are not so easily convinced that worry doesn't get the job done better. If you could watch yourselves in a movie, showing you worry-free, you would stare in disbelief or laugh or cry. It can be argued that some of the greatest creativity in this world comes from people who worry painstakingly over details. Their energy was poured into their masterpieces. It is a fine line between the kind of worrying that makes things flawless and that which won't allow us to stop thinking about it. You don't need to be perfect. Perfectionism is the sure way to fall into this game. Gemini is not as mentally clear and full of vitality when run down by excessive concerns. Virgo is running off much less energy when preoccupied with problems. What you focus on influences your thinking in some respects. Dwelling on the downside of life can't do anything but take you further down. Gemini and Virgo feed on positive and negative signals from each other's minds, maybe faster than any other sign combination. This is due to being born under Mercury's tender, loving care. If most of what you receive are anxiety signals, your positive energy can't break through the busy worry signal.

Strategies

How can you break free from these Gemini-Virgo games? In the *Not Seeing the Forest for the Trees* game, you need to relax more in order to stop being overly analytical. You can still do masterful work and don't need to intentionally make errors. You don't have to feel responsible for the world's details, do you? You will have more fun if you keep your eyes on the larger picture. Keep the enlarger lens ready if you slip into the world of too many parts. Putting a large puzzle together is challenging (you know, the ones that contain about one thousand pieces). You start by searching for the first few pieces that will fit together and branch out. You are easily roped into doing this, maybe even for other people. Gemini gets antsy if it sits still for too long. This sign doesn't like to focus on one thing indefinitely. Gemini would rather use its well-developed intellect on a series of projects. Virgo is mistakenly described as being excessively passionate about details. When it comes to duty, this is usually true. A bored Virgo isn't quite as effective as an enthusiastic one. This game plays on your nerves. The trees are more fun to look at than the details they symbolize. When you see the forest, you seem to have the time to picnic under the trees. Work gets old if that's all you are doing. You will make better love when you don't get bogged down by inconsequential details.

The *Litterbug* game can be cleaned up by making a sincere effort to think positively. It has been said the greatest of miracles is an altered perception. Transformation starts with a first baby step, not with a long jump. This is certainly an easier way to think of change than believing you have to grow by leaps and bounds. People who start too fast often regress anyway. Keep it simple. It might sound silly, but you need to meditate on positive thinking to get through this game. Keep a list of positive words in your pocket if you must. Make sure you put them into your vocabulary. An overkill of positive energy is okay. Be as compulsive about going toward the positive as going toward—now, what was that—oh, yes—negativity. Anyway, have a strong intention to turn this habit around. A lot of your mental power is trapped here. Be ready for an explosion of passion and creativity in your romance. Negative thinking has no power. We only think it does and there lies the problem. You need to believe in the power of positive thinking. It sounds so corny, but it works. Creatively visualize yourselves to be the gurus of positive thought. Well, it may take a while before you make it to the top of the Himalayas, but as the old wise men of the past have said, enjoy the journey!

The *Worry Warts* game is another side of negativity. This game has to do with feeling too responsible for others or with making everything come out just right. You don't need to be perfect. Let's say it again, together this time: "I don't need to be perfect." Learn to walk away from imperfection, but stay and complete whatever you do for a job or in parenting or wherever you need to be on top of your game. There is probably a lot you could ignore and still find that life is fine when you wake up the next day! Gemini can worry Virgo to death by making sudden changes. Virgo wants to glue Gemini to a chair in order to pin the restless one to a decision. Virgo can squeeze the life out of spontaneity to make sure everything will go smoothly. This drives a Gemini to climb walls or to scream, "Stop!" Worry means you have doubts. What are you doubting? Trust yourselves. It helps. When you give your best, leave the job or task where you finished with it. Don't bring it home. Set some mental limits. It's not easy, but it's not impossible, and it takes effort. You can retrain your mind when and where you will permit yourself to worry.

The Rainbow

Your Gemini-Virgo relationship looks for excellence. You don't believe in leaving things half done though sometimes it doesn't hurt to do so! The powers of the mind are at your disposal. When you feel are in the driver's seat, the world responds to your passion. You delight in the heights you go to before each other's loving eyes. Romance is work. You may realize this better than many. When you bring in fun and play, your work may even be more meaningful.

A Gemini man recognizes the Virgo woman's mental depth. She is a no-nonsense soul with a sense of humor that comes forward when you point out life's ironies to her. He hopes he is a match for this earthy, spirited woman with an intense desire to excel at whatever she does. The Gemini man is attracted to her prim and proper ways, yet she has a passion that thrills him. He likes this feminine woman and hopes she will accept a few of his unpredictable whims. He responds to primal forces that bring out his sense of adventure. He may be perplexed that the Virgo woman understands this and that she fears and admires his wildness.

The Virgo woman perceives that the Gemini man is fair minded. She only wishes that he would say what he expects from her. "Maybe he doesn't expect anything," she muses to herself. She notices his words seem to dance around topics, yet she knows he has a deep, perceptive mind. She can't help but wonder if he is reliable. The word "commitment" seems to frighten him. It's not that this earthy Virgo woman wants to pin him down; she is as precise in business as in making love. She is entertained by his lively persona and his animated gestures. She wants him to be dependable because she doesn't want to be disappointed by his carefree behavior.

The Gemini woman is fond of the Virgo man's calm self-control. She wonders if a wild man lurks within. She is glad to meet someone who is conscientious. She wonders if her sudden meetings with friends and other social outings will irritate him. He listens with rapt attention to her words. He might even repeat them better than she could! Does she feel anything resembling passion? Maybe if they could stop talking about work or go on a trip together, it could happen. Anyway, she is eager to make it work.

The Virgo man is anything but bored with the Gemini woman. She is born under Mercury's influence just like Virgo but with a twist of the unusual. The Gemini woman doesn't reveal this easily, but she often sees herself as being different. There is always a part of her nobody will possess. He senses he isn't seeing the whole picture. If he likes this free-spirited woman, it doesn't matter if he ever really knows her hidden side. He thinks she must fly with Jonathan Livingston Seagull—now that was a free spirit!

Your romance isn't for others to judge. It's up to you to find the keys to unlock the secrets to each other's heart. You can write a whole new story together or revise the script that you had before you met. (You don't have to scrap the previous one.) Be sure to take the time to start the new story line because it pulls both of you in and lets you write parts of your own choosing. There is magic when you join forces as long as you don't hold each other to rules that would be better broken.

Gemini-Libra: The Live Wires

Gemini + Libra = Outgoingness

These two air signs share a mental curiosity about people. Your social group is probably large and diverse. It needs to be so you can match wits with as many individuals as possible. Gemini's powers of perception combine nicely with Libra's knack for strategies. Your romance endures through the desire to learn how to talk to each other with keen insight. Travel to beautiful places adds zest to your lives. Making decisive choices is challenging to your sign combination. That flair to constantly conceptualize can make it tough to choose one direction. The longer you are together, the easier you will find it to dance in step. There are few sudden turns in the road that Gemini-Libra can't handle. The twists along the way make life exhilarating for you two breezy souls.

Southpaw (Left Brain) Game

The games played in your Gemini-Libra relationship are associated with excessive thinking and not speaking your mind assertively. The *Southpaw (Left Brain)* game reflects a tendency for the two of you to get lost in the world of ideas but not to act on them. Inaction is always challenging for two air signs. Gemini and Libra have well-defined thought processes. To tell you not to think would be next to absurd. However, if you stay on the level of thought without taking action, you will become frustrated. This might be your way of procrastinating. If you continue to postpone following through on an idea, it can conveniently be put off until later. You may irritate each other if one or the other of you adopts this pattern. The left brain is the analytical portion of the mind.

It keeps you from bumping into the objects in front of you. Without it, life is chaos. On the other hand, too much use of the left brain tells our intuitive instincts to stay at home. You may have a habit of interfering with the initiating impulses of your partner. This is often not intentional. Your minds can be so conditioned to respond with another idea to each other that there is little thought of moving ahead.

Saying Yes When You Mean No Game

Have you ever agreed to do something with your partner that you don't have your heart in? Are the two of you too easily talked into obligations by others? If the answer is yes, you might be playing the *Saying Yes When You Mean No* game. It can make you downright angry if you realize later you allowed yourself to be dragged through something you didn't really want to do. Assertiveness should be easy for two articulate air signs, but that isn't always so! Gemini doesn't really like head-on conflict. The Twins get doubly nervous to even think about dealing with a potentially messy situation. Libra has an affinity for balance. Libra is a good mediator, but there is a catch here. Libra feels more comfortable resolving other people's problems than handling its own! So, masters of wit and tact that you are, you may not excel when it comes to simply saying no. It could be that you fall victim to the habit of feeling guilty if you don't say yes. You are not a happy couple if you give in to requests that are not really of your choice.

Parched Feelings Game

Air signs like yourselves don't always get down to brass tacks when it comes to feelings. You may go overboard in avoiding them as in the *Parched Feelings* game. Living in the land of thought twenty-four hours a day can become old. You may be good at keeping your partner away from your emotions. Your romance will lack caring and intimacy if you don't change your defensive posture. If you want to get to know each other on the deepest of levels, you must open up your emotional depths to one another. You don't have to bear your souls like Romeo and Juliet, but it helps to give your partner a clue or two about how to connect with your feelings. Communication in your relationship will not seem as real without a certain degree of emotional content. Dry words don't arouse a great deal of passion. It is difficult to receive needed support when you guard your tender heart too closely. Every garden needs water and so does your relationship. You don't have to be mushy, but you could use a genuine heart-to-heart discussion at least occasionally.

Strategies

How can you clear up these Gemini-Libra games? The *Southpaw (Left Brain)* game indicates that you need to bypass your left-brain tendencies and rely on your intuition. It might help to have friends outside of the relationship who know how to encourage you to move ahead with confidence. Eventually, with repetition, you can get better at doing this yourselves. The mind is a beautiful thing. Nobody is suggesting that you stop using it. It's more a matter of when and how to use your mental faculties. Balancing your strong logical tendencies with action and intuition will take you further than thought alone. If you regularly talk one another out of options because you can see other alternatives, you may need to restrain yourself. It will be better in many instances to go ahead with a decision. You can decide later how you really feel about the choice. This is better than procrastination. You both find power in acting on your mental impulses. Gemini and Libra are more dynamic when an idea takes form. It's like watching a movie you wrote by yourself or co-wrote with your partner. The creative process can sweep your relationship off its feet. Let it!

The *Saying Yes When You Mean No* game asks you to speak up. Don't hesitate to say no when you mean no. The two of you have a capacity to display creative insight faster than a cat's eyes adjust to the dark, and that's fast! You seal off that clarity in favor of confusion in this game. Assertiveness will be seen by you to be less painful than going along with decisions that are not in your best interest. There will be times you disagree with one another. You may decide to compromise to ensure you both get your way. That's plain, good old-fashioned negotiating. It isn't the same when one of you is doing all of the giving with very little taking. It takes courage and willpower to turn this behavior around. You need to adjust your assertive sails so they can catch the wind of opportunity. You want to stop wasting time put into endeavors that are not to your liking. Your creative drive might go up a notch or two with the empowering sense you achieve.

The *Parched Feelings* game only requires a small step in a new direction. You are trying to open the valve that leads to your feelings. Communicate from your heart rather than exclusively from your mind. It sounds corny to say the heart and mind can become one. In a way, that's what happens when you speak with feeling. It takes reeducating your mind. When trying to express an emotion to your partner, start with a sentence that leads with "I feel." Go ahead and try it: "I feel …" (fill in the blank). It might seem strange to even use the word feel. You may never cry at love stories. That's all right. You may not be the crying type. That's fine. Your partner may be shocked to see your softer side. Many couples are surprised to find that the romantic passion in their lives is sparked by simply being slightly more open about their feelings. You can still show a tough intellectual or breezy mental persona to the rest of the world, but give your partner a private showing of your more tender emotions. In the movies they call this a "sneak preview" of a new film. You may be surprised how much you like this dimension of yourselves. You can be amazed to learn that there are many frequencies within you if you take the time to tune in to them.

The Rainbow

Your Gemini-Libra relationship can rise to a level that shows the spectrum of happiness that two people can experience. The mental ingenuity of Gemini can flow gracefully with Libra's attraction to artistic thought. Libra's fondness for mental equilibrium certainly agrees with the delicate nervous system of Gemini. The objectivity of Gemini thought satisfies Libra's love of designing a well laid-out plan.

A Gemini man is quickly attuned to the Libra woman's eloquence. Her concepts are not flowery, but to the point with graceful tact. The Mercurian man loves to look at her face because her beauty shines through. The love she symbolizes stops him in his tracks, yet her voice and the touch of her hand prove that she is a real flesh-and-bones person. He hopes he can win her affection. This is one of the few times that he is tongue-tied, but somehow he manages a smile to assure her of his desire. He hopes his logic matches her needs.

Upon first meeting a Gemini man the Libra woman knows that she has found a fountain of information. She listens carefully to see if he has seriousness to go with his playfulness. This feminine Venusian woman is playful in her own right, but her play is attached to a plan. Her need for balance makes her look for a sensible partner. Her business sense tests his mind to find out just what type of material he might offer. It's not really money that matters as much as his capacity to live up to his commitments, especially if she ends up being one of them. Her heart is an interesting mix of fragility and strength. This Venusian lover doesn't want to open up her more delicate side to just anyone. She is in love with love, but is nobody's fool. Her mind tells her to take it slow with the eager man who is focused upon her.

A Gemini woman is in her element with the Libra man. He will wine and dine her. She wonders if he will adore her. She knows he expects this from her. She likes this Venusian man's voice. His voice is relaxing and reassuring; even when angry she imagines it to be pleasing. He is intense when talking about himself. His previous relationships don't interest her as much as current commitments. She doesn't want to compete though she certainly could. The female Gemini wants this Venusian man all to herself if she is going to go to the trouble to invest in him. She can let him into her life. This Mercurian woman, whose movements fascinate the Libra man, finds him to be deliciously attractive.

Out of curiosity, the Libra man wants to follow the Gemini woman for a day. He wonders what really interests this Mercurian being. Even if he hasn't yet ascertained it from conversations with her, he senses that her intellect is as deep as it is wide. He wonders if he can keep pace with her free-spirited mind. Her love of people matches her own. It's that insatiable seeking of knowledge that is a teensy bit threatening. It's not that he lacks mental prowess. He is concerned with keeping what he already knows in check so he can be decisive. He hopes he can handle adding to this the information that this intellectual woman brings to him. He wants to "go for it" because this woman has touched his heart in a way few others have ever imagined possible. Why is he so surprised? That's her gift!

Your life together can be a fun-filled expedition. Exposing each other to new places and ways of fulfillment is within your scope. It can be exciting to point your lover at the new horizons you have discovered, especially since you have found someone willing to walk with you to explore new horizons. You can walk into each other's worlds with passion and admiration. Don't lose sight of your unique, individual qualities. You can embrace with a feeling that rides out the ups and downs, taking you to more level ground. Those ups are certainly exhilarating, aren't they?!

Gemini-Scorpio: The Detectives

Gemini + Scorpio = Incisive Thinking

These are two signs that can penetrate through any challenge with a ruthless force. Gemini's inquisitiveness mixed with Scorpio's in-depth probing makes for interesting conversations. Small talk is Gemini's way of breaking the ice with those it meets. Scorpio is more subtle about getting to know someone. What goes on behind one's mind interests the Scorpion the most. Scorpio can't help but wonder what makes others tick even in the midst of lively conversations. You can consider subjects that many will avoid; the taboos of your society are not above discussion. Your romance is enlivened by new learning and business ideas.

Sarcastic Tongue Game

The games played in your Gemini-Scorpio relationship are linked to biting criticism of one another as well as hidden anger. The *Sarcastic Tongue* game is one in which the two of you overuse your wonderful sleuthing ability. You compulsively pick each other apart. Watch the criticism. It can interfere with just how close you will let each other get. You are never going to please one another all of the time. A mistake isn't the end of the world. After all, you are human. Sarcasm may be a reaction to being ignored. Now that's another whole story unto itself. One or both of you can become upset when your opinions are discounted. There is an inclination to respond with acerbity. This behavior can be a well-deserved plea for attention. Gemini finds it painful to have its ideas ignored—it's a real slap in the face. Scorpio doesn't fare much better in being treated with a lack of respect. It's like stepping on a Scorpion's tail. The expression of love hits a real low point if you can't cut off the lifeline of this game.

Sneak Attack Game

Rather than negotiate aboveboard, you could fall into the *Sneak Attack* game. Hidden agendas rule the day. This is a game in which angry behavior can manifest as unpleasant exchanges. You will not be admired for an onslaught that blindsides your partner. Gemini can take a round-about course to a point if sensing resistance. Scorpio can keep a secret until it sees the whites of your eyes. Secretiveness is something you can get by with to some extent. It's when things go ballistic that you need to be careful. You might actually be relieved if the battle gets out into the open. All of the moves and countermoves are what get nerve-wracking (and nerve wrecking!). It is impossible to work together if you aren't sure when the air raid siren is going to go off. When communication does not flow for long periods of time, this game waits in the wings. You miss out on too many good times when you fall prey to this trap.

Toxic Waste Game

Repressed emotions can turn sour in the *Toxic Waste* game. Gemini finds it difficult to hold back insights. This talkative sign must exercise free speech. Over the long haul, Scorpio feels a lack of power when not expressing passionate ideas. When you hold your peace for too long, your emotions feel strange. Your perceptions of one another turn gray as clouds of disorientation settle above you. The attempt to talk through emotional confusion is like swimming in a polluted river; it just doesn't feel right. Neither of you benefits from avoiding direct discussions. When you focus on what you don't like about one another to the exclusion of what you want to see happen, nothing is resolved. Somehow you don't seem to hear what each of you needs. Gemini's nervous system can be shot due to this game. Scorpio can grow just as exhausted. You don't produce a winner here. Your stubborn persistence to hold back is not the answer.

Strategies

How can you break away from the hold of these Gemini-Scorpio games? In the *Sarcastic Tongue* game, you both must learn not to focus excessively on each other's imperfections. Your criticism is hard to swallow, which is why you end up spitting it back at one another. You don't have to pretend to suddenly be sweet tongued. If there are some real issues to be ironed out, discuss them. Be harder on the problem than on your partner. Easier said than done, isn't it? You can't really change each other. However, a behavior that is seriously annoying could be adjusted if you try. If you start by responding to your lover's request, the impulse to talk sharply will lessen. You decrease the likelihood for biting remarks when you show you are paying attention. In a Gemini-Scorpio relationship, it is essential for each to prove through their actions that they can respond. Why? Because you both know that talk is dirt cheap! Communication with no action to back it up doesn't resolve anything in your eyes. So, if you want to lighten the frequency level of sarcasm, what do you do? Show through your actions that you have been listening.

The *Sneak Attack* requires a new strategy in discussing hot issues. If you are afraid to go near the fire, it's understandable. Nobody likes to be yelled at, and rejection is no fun either. Why don't you make a loose pact with one another? First, you will talk things out, even if it must be structured. One agrees to listen while the other is speaking. (Use a "talk" clock if needed. Why not? In basketball they use a shot clock!) Second, make sure you will not suffer from continuing harassment after your talk. Agree to drop the dispute right where you leave it in your discussion. You can find time to come back and talk again. It feels weird to take control of a situation that has been controlling you. You may find a better method than this to get you started. It is creative to learn how to communicate. Talking seems so easy, but it isn't when you don't watch your comments. Don't throw a lit match on gasoline. You want to bring sneak attacks out into the open. It's easier to fix a problem when you talk face to face.

The solution to *Toxic Waste* game involves flushing that poisonous material out to where you can deal with it. This is probably more difficult than other Gemini-Scorpio games. Gemini is not known for stubbornness, yet this air sign can grow quite aloof when it represses anger. Gemini conceals feelings behind a cool exterior. Scorpio can get downright headstrong. The power of the Scorpion is its ability to outwait others. Much to Scorpio's surprise, Gemini can outlast it! Gemini must snap out of its cold stare as chilling as that of Clint Eastwood in the film, *The Good, the Bad, and the Ugly*. Scorpio must conquer its hardheadedness. If you do, you have a chance to paddle through this swampland. Believe me, you want out quickly! The trick is that if you run away without really dealing with this game, you will return to play it over and over again while you are together. That's the shadow of this game. It can pull on you to play it. Don't play. It's better to be aware and to stay far from its clutches. Climb to safer ground.

The Rainbow

Your Gemini-Scorpio relationship is as insightful as they come. It takes quite a cool customer to put one over you. Heightened awareness can be the basis of your business savvy. To some you might appear to be an odd match. Quick-thinking Gemini romancing introspective Scorpio? Gemini simultaneously focuses on multiple directions. Scorpio concentrates its laser-like mind down to the depths of one subject at a time. Where is harmony anyway? It lies somewhere between your appreciation for authenticity and the courage to stand up for those you love. Both of you can do this quite well!

A Gemini man is intrigued by the Scorpio woman but isn't sure what has him locked on to her. Maybe it's her strong, clear eyes. Hopefully she can't burn a hole through his mind. He doesn't want her to know him too fast. The Plutonian woman seems possessive. Perhaps it's the way she pays such rapt attention to the job or task before her. He takes a deep breath because he doesn't like to get so engaged in any one thing unless it's his life work. He doesn't want to change for her. Will she expect him to do so? He is passionately drawn to her smile; it's like the Sun. He wants to frolic with her romantic and fun-loving side. He isn't really sure how to relate yet to the more serious side of this mysterious princess but, then again, he is anxious to know her.

The Scorpio woman is taken aback by the Gemini man's intellect as he sweeps into her life. She wonders at his sudden appearance and casts a bewildered gaze at this mercurial wanderer. Is he a ship passing by in the night or here for a long stay? She supposes it won't hurt much to humor him a bit. He seems harmless enough, or at least she convinces herself that he is. She notices that he comes with few strings attached. She looks in several directions to be sure of this. She is not so sure it is good to become dependent on him in case his ship suddenly departs for more adventurous waters. She loves the seafarer in him but would like to see an indication that he can be stationary. She isn't afraid of traveling in her own right. She just wants to be sure that she won't be the one who is always waiting for love to return.

The Gemini woman is willing to instantly approach a Scorpio man. Why? She can retreat as fast as she can advance! She wants to come into the grasp of this passionate being, but his bear-hug-like possessiveness worries her. She loves the way he seems to listen. Her words seem to arouse him. She hopes he listens to her mind because that leads to her feelings, which lead to every part of her. The Scorpio man seems to be interested in her whole sense of self; this intrigues her.

She wonders if he will grow weary of her wayward ways that take her to so many paths of knowledge. She wants this man to walk with her or at least not to stand in her way. She already knows that, eventually, the mischievous Mercurian calling to seek higher learning will come. Nobody can question this side of her. It is sacred.

The Scorpio man looks at the female Gemini and marvels at her refined communication of ideas. He is sure this relationship is for him. She attracts his passion by her direct, unintimidated gaze. He wishes she would at least blink. He is sure her appearance changes every time he looks away. Was there a subtle change in the arch of her eyebrow or the curve of her lips? Is it his imagination, or is she more than one woman? She isn't prepared to reveal her well-developed dual nature. Her duality is as natural to her as the tick of a clock keeping time. To the male Scorpio, she is unusually interesting perhaps because his probing questions don't shake her. Even the nervousness in her voice doesn't tell him much. He can't help but look for her secrets; it's in his bones to do so. He notices that she winces when he questions her and lets out a sigh of relief when he stops the interrogation. He thinks it's because he was too probing. She has been waiting for him to move on to something more interesting!

Gemini and Scorpio both have keen minds. Gemini displays this quality with an airy perceptive ease, flying high above the minds of others. Scorpio dives into the depths of research to find its answers. The Scorpion will work persistently until it masters a challenge. Your relationship does not like to take no for an answer. You may have found a companion who is a lover and ally wrapped in one package. Enjoy the discoveries you find in knowing one another. There will be many. That's easy to predict!

Gemini-Sagittarius: The Travelers

Gemini + Sagittarius = Galaxy of Ideas

You two are the most restless of spirits. You are opposite signs in the zodiac. Gemini is a bit more concerned with details than the expansive tendencies of Sagittarius. This isn't saying that Gemini can't open up to broad creative horizons. The Archer becomes more focused on details when its interest is captured (or you tie this fire sign to a chair!). Everyone else either loves your spontaneity or detests it. Let them be jealous or confused. You understand the inner dynamics that make each other tick from the beginning. If you missed something, it's no matter; you can catch up later while skipping merrily along together. You may wonder if the world is big enough to offer the information and knowledge you seek. Whether self-taught or through traditional schooling, education is a key to you both. You are insatiable students. Boredom isn't even a consideration. If it dares to rear its ugly head, it will feel your wrath in an instant.

Interpreter Game

The games played in your Gemini-Sagittarius relationship revolve around impatience, overly expansive tendencies, and a problem with stability. The *Interpreter* game occurs when you are unable to let each other finish your points. You fire back an opinion even before your partner finishes speaking. You often lose crucial information due to the hasty translation of what is heard through your speedy filters. Words or information may be taken out of context as well. How can two bright thinkers get caught in this scenario? Actually, it's your talent to use your intelligence to quickly influence a situation that may be to blame. This is a case of a good thing gone awry. The intensity of your individual mental processes is heightened in this romance. Hard to imagine, isn't it? Gemini's perceptions are translated to speech with lightning speed. Sagittarius is forceful with a rush of fiery enthusiasm when convinced that it is right. Slowing down is a must. You will need to work on this one because it contradicts your natural instincts. You need not give up your passion to respond and communicate quickly. You will turn your partner off if your responses show that you missed the whole point. Anger waits just around the corner in this scenario. You may even see a packed bag or two. Before one of you starts packing, find some patience—quickly! This is a frustrating scene to act out for two quick-on-the-draw individuals. If you refuse to change this behavior, your hearts grow cold.

Juggler Game

More than most others, your signs can travel on multiple paths without getting lost. If you grow too expansive in the heat of ambition, you may lose sight of one another. It's okay to let each other wander for periods of time. You prefer a long leash anyway or none at all. It's when you become too distracted by your divergent paths that the *Juggler* game appears. It may be hard to focus in any one direction together. Decisions are next to impossible for you two free spirits when everything looks inviting. It's that longing for adventure or for stimulation that leads you to pursue active lives. There may not be a single career, hobby, house, or anything that seems just right. It's not that you are so hard to please; you have a thirst for new areas of knowledge because this fits your romanticized image of the search for a fountain of youth. You may love the way your partner can quickly seize opportunities as long as you are not left behind feeling forgotten. Not getting the support you need for a goal is what is painful here. Neglect pains Gemini's and Sagittarius' hearts. Neither of you is very good at hiding it either!

Rolling Stone Game

Even though many of the other books rule against you, Gemini and Sagittarius can settle down together. So don't panic if the *Rolling Stone* game sounds all too familiar. Commitment can scare the h—oops—I mean, the daylights out of you. Rolling along to another relationship is tempting when the going gets tough. The dilemma in a Gemini-Sagittarius relationship is that it is hard to deny that you have found someone who understands you accurately. Your inner worlds are not so different though finding stability in the real world can be a challenge. If you are able to concentrate on each other long enough and like what you have, this game wanes quickly. You can give one another a bit of a jolt if your perceptions about your partner are right on the money over and over again. It can lead to the question: "How can somebody know me this thoroughly?" One or both of you may wonder if there is a way to define a clear enough commitment or some type of agreement. You must be willing to stay long enough to let the relationship deepen to the level of trust you need. The tendency to buck like a wild stallion could strike either of you quickly. Running away from addressing what you want from one another will not get the job done. It never does. If you can't decide if you have found a permanent or temporary soul mate in one another, it may be agonizing. If you grow impatient, the desire to fly away gets stronger.

Strategies

How can you fly above the confines of these Gemini-Sagittarius games? The *Interpreter* game requires a willingness to let each other talk. You might even need to practice repeating back to each other what you thought you heard. Remember the party game in which one person whispers to the next person what he or she thinks the previous person whispered and so on down the line until the message is repeated to the person who started the game? Usually the final rendition doesn't sound anything like the original and gets quite a laugh from everyone. We are only talking about two people in your relationship. Still, the message can get convoluted as you process what your partner has said. Gemini can put a unique spin on new information. Sagittarius has a way of enlarging whatever is said. It's that eagerness to communicate that can take the Archer by storm, getting this sign to lose sight of details. This is why it is urgent to slow down the rhythm of talking and listening. You may be only hearing a few out of every ten words said to each other when you two are in high gear. Gemini and Sagittarius can travel fast together on the physical or mental planes. Right now your interactions may involve a two-step: talk simultaneously, then try to beat your partner to the punch with a quick response. A new formula works better. Consider this: talk one at a time, then allow each to respond. Repeat as needed. Take your time. You need to resist reinterpreting what you hear.

The *Juggler* game isn't that hard to curb. You can keep running in multiple directions if you have the time and energy. Why stop? You will only get bored and want to do it all over again anyway. Somewhere between your travels, social engagements, meetings, and talking with friends, take a brief timeout together. Focus on one another. You can do whatever you want without losing your partner with a little effort. What you need is a romantic escape together and time to share your dreams. You excite each other to try greater challenges. If you didn't want to be stimulated, why did you choose this relationship or at least show an interest in it? Gemini sparks Sagittarius' mind like a tidal wave! Sagittarius incites a primitive, wild streak in Gemini. Face it, this is a romance that will be hard to outgrow as long as each of you is inspired. Focusing on each other's goals long enough is vital.

The *Rolling Stone* game won't be so bothersome if you both decide you really want to be part of the relationship. The old saying, "it takes two," applies here! Commitment can mean different things to Gemini and Sagittarius. Gemini sees commitment as a verbal agreement, sometimes in writing, that a relationship has been established. Sagittarius is hard to figure out on this subject. The Archer can be as loyal as a puppy, and no matter how far Sagittarius wanders, its loyalty brings it home. Then again, the Archer may never really be ready to settle down unless tied down. Sagittarius may still walk off strapped to the chair! The latter type is often romanticized because the Archer is an ardent lover who can be like a fairytale hero, but on a cold night you will find yourself snuggling with your cat or dog to stay warm. The Archer can be far away on a physical or spiritual adventure. Gemini and Sagittarius can commit to each other. Each must find its own reason for staying rather than leaving. Trying to talk one or the other into staying can make you tear your hair out. When you both plant roots, it can be for good! It is worth the turmoil when you finally do bond.

The Rainbow

Your Gemini-Sagittarius relationship covers the spectrum when it comes to self-exploration. As a couple you can respond quickly to the call of opportunity. Your enthusiasm is contagious. Life was never meant to move slowly for the two of you. You're not really highly driven type A personalities and don't fit those laid-back type B descriptions either. It's hard to label you, isn't it? Probably this is the way you like it. Commitment is attained as you live your relationship. That's the interesting thing about many Gemini-Sagittarius bonds: things happen as they happen.

A Gemini man is thrilled by a Sagittarius woman's personality. He likes her openly friendly and bubbly voice. Her energy revs his own to a high gear. He delights in seeing that this woman is as casual about being organized as he is. He likes to walk alongside this fiery sign. She has a heart as large as Jupiter and a mind that's as energetic as they come. The male Gemini is intrigued by the broad perspective of the female Sagittarius. He appreciates her openness to new ideas. He looks forward to traveling with her on many physical and mental paths. If only the two have a lifetime to get to the whole story!

A Sagittarius woman assumes that a Gemini man is as eager for new experiences as she is herself. She enjoys this lover of ideas who can speed along new mental highways. He can drive down the road while talking on the phone, reading a report, and listening to his favorite music, all at the same time. "He acts like he knows where he is going," she thinks to herself. She is fascinated that this mercurial person does not get overwhelmed by the life he creates. She is attracted to his way of letting her know she is important to him. He wants to impress her with fun activities. She wishes he would slow down for a moment because she needs to catch her breath. Then again, the exhilaration of this Mercurian man is exciting. He seems like a kindred spirit.

A Gemini woman notices out of the corner of her peripheral vision the steady gaze of the roving Sagittarius man. He checks her out kind of in a matter-of-fact way. She sees he is interested and wishes he would move closer. "It must be his mating behavior," she laughs to herself, wondering if he read her thoughts. When he does talk to her, she senses a youthful vitality much like her own. He certainly possesses a great sense of humor. She listens with great interest to his life story. The male Archer waits for the right moment to enter her space—when she doesn't look so preoccupied. He may introduce himself by stealing glances at her and directing his comments at her even before they speak. She may give him a look that lets him know that she is aware of his attention. They instantly recognize they are from the same inner country, and their outer sojourns could easily take them to the same destinations. It makes the Gemini woman happy to see his relaxed smile.

The male Sagittarius perceives the female Gemini can be a playmate for him. He would rather think about serious things later. He lives in the moment; at least he wants this feminine air sign to think so. He loves to hear her laugh. It resembles his own when he is truly happy. The intellect of the female Gemini soars right through his own. This laid-back man isn't often taken by surprise by anyone's conversational skills, yet her verbal volleys come at him like lightning bolts. He admires this woman. She is as arrogant (and even more polished) in making a point than he is—splendid! Now, what to do with this high-spirited soul? He wonders if he was reeled in by a very clever person who let him think he was the pursuer. He must see this imaginative and passionate woman again. This master of persuasion infrequently meets his match.

Gemini-Sagittarius is a fairytale liaison. You don't really belong to any century. You might make each other feel like you have been displaced by time travel from medieval days when chivalry was a household word. In the new millennium, you are a duo who defy being conveniently catalogued by one another or by any culture. You won't really tame the wildness in each other. You are better off accepting your mutual inner spirit of the teacher, advisor, traveler, and student. Don't force your knowledge on one another. You already know the way to each other's hearts, don't you? Be an open book to read for each other's delight. This is when and where you find all of the riches you seek.

Gemini-Capricorn: The Problem-Solvers

Gemini + Capricorn = Serious Ambition

Gemini's mental power stimulates Capricorn's get-down-to-business mentality. Together you can embark on great things—and finish them! Is "jumpin' jack flash" Gemini really a good match for the serious disposition of Capricorn? These signs do well together when seeing eye to eye on the big picture. Details are what can make for a tight squeeze through a small doorway. These two signs can figure out a way to wiggle through the tight spots with flexibility and a drop of ingenuity. You can be a productive combo indeed. Make sure you stop along life's way to notice sunsets, drink cappuccino, and enjoy candlelight dinners, or whatever else strikes your romantic fancy.

Cold As Ice Game

The games played in your Gemini-Capricorn relationship can be traced back to a lack of affection, self-imposed pressures, and a gloomy outlook. Stay away from these tendencies and life will be filled with more sunshine. The *Cold As Ice* game surfaces when you don't express warmth toward your partner. Frigid communication, which lacks emotion, will not open your hearts. Logic is dry when you don't reveal your feelings. It's as though your business dealings cross over to your love affairs. Even sex can lack passion. Gemini can be distant when it hides behind its intellect. Capricorn is sometimes guilty of being as guarded as its ruling planet, Saturn, which is guarded by its rings. You might be too insulated from one another. Fear can be the hidden component in this behavior. You need to thaw out. The resistance to coming out of the freezer can be tremendous if this is an old habitual pattern. Gemini likes to talk, and Capricorn enjoys reasoning. If you avoid talking reasonably, it only serves to keep you apart and to make you suffer where it hurts most.

Pressure Cooker Game

The two of you could become overly rushed by the schedules you keep. A time crunch can make you impatient with each other, which happens in the *Pressure Cooker* game. Gemini tends to spread many interests out on its insatiable plate of curiosity. Capricorn can take on additional responsibility in the blink of an eye. Put these instincts together and you may be in a relationship that is nonstop. You may prefer to stay busy, and nothing is really wrong with that. Things could get testy if you are pushed to the brink of your nerves. Gemini is not known for being as ambitious as Capricorn, yet you can't beat a Gemini teammate who has his or her heart set on learning and getting people to think differently. Gemini breathes ambition like a long-distance runner fighting for a second wind. So much for hasty generalizations. This warrior of the mind can move with determination. Capricorn is conditioned by its own fear of failure to try extra hard to prove its success potential. There is a constant awareness of getting ahead in your relationship. How do you move swiftly without forgetting one another in the process? You can feel like you are being tossed around in a pressure cooker. The conscientiousness you stimulate in each other to be thorough may make you go the extra mile to help others. Ignoring any sense of boundary lines will find you exhausted and confused. Stress might form a crack in your seamless union.

Down in the Dumps Game

Negative thinking can buy you tickets to play the *Down in the Dumps* game. If you feel disappointed because your expectations are not being met by your partner, you may begin to blame each other. Inflexible thinking may be an even greater problem. If one or the other of you is too attached to your own ideas, the other will be angry. A feeling of sadness is caused by your emotional distance. A career setback may lead to this game, especially if you can't flow with what life deals you. Your resistance to getting away from what is eating at your happiness can pull down your spirits. Gemini can't deal with extended sadness whether its own or someone else's. This light-spirited sign gets fidgety when an obstacle blocks its path. If Gemini can't find a way through, it will go under, around, or fly over it. Capricorn is different. This earth giant will push persistently. If this doesn't work, Capricorn will try to negotiate. Finally, this earth sign might just buy a bulldozer and push the encumbrance out of the way. The two signs have different approaches to dealing with problems. This is why you could become confused or impatient with how your partner deals with his or her own issues. What does this have to do with sadness? Plenty! Sadness is caused by your inability to allow each other to be supportive. You can be on such different wavelengths that you can't communicate when you are feeling down. This spells trouble if it goes on for long stretches of time. You will stay down if you don't reach out for help or take the initiative to move in a new positive direction.

Strategies

How can you rise above the Gemini-Capricorn games? The *Cold As Ice* game points to the necessity to show warmth rather than intellectual coolness. Gemini can come off the mountain plateau of the intellect. Capricorn can stop leading with a left jab of guardedness. You can retrain yourselves to get back on the highway of expressing feelings. Your passion will be stronger if you can touch the surface of one another's inner world. Gemini patrols the border of its feelings with a show of casual interest. Capricorn polices matters of the heart with a cautionary gaze. Meeting at a place where you both can relax and enjoy the intimacy awaiting you is essential. It is the key to a greater happiness. So often you can imprison yourself through limited thinking. It takes a dose of faith and a willingness to adopt flexible thinking to turn this game on its heels. Believe in what you can do, instead of focusing on what you can't. Options will then appear with greater frequency.

In the *Pressure Cooker* game, you need to determine the roles you are acting out that keep it a reality. You can then stop performing in a play in which you don't wish to participate. Your schedules might need to be more finely attuned to meet your needs. It doesn't take much for business and obligations to rule you. Very often it is possible to squeeze quality moments into a hectic daily routine. You will have to concentrate on inventing time that can be spent together that isn't undermined by everyday demands. Intimacy that is constantly bombarded by outside interruptions disrupts the flow of feelings. It doesn't mean you must throw away your career or other interests. You only have to create a respite for yourselves that will allow you to capture each other's romantic interest. It's probably easier than you think. If you talk it out with a serious desire to get the mission accomplished, you can do it.

The *Down in the Dumps* game presents a challenge. You can solve the puzzle but might have to look extra hard for the right pieces at the right time. Training your minds to think more positively is the first step. Without this ingredient, it will be difficult to rebuild the engine. In a sense, you are doing an overhaul of perceptions you have of yourselves as individuals and of one another. If your individual outlook is gloomy, you can't realistically expect your partner to always tow you out of the deep hole. Individually, you must assume the responsibility to adopt a positive mental attitude. You can be supportive of your partner in getting there. Help each other, but don't lean so heavily that the relationship can't hold you up. A career disappointment need not be the end of the world. Sadness is better than depression. The latter is what can take its toll over the long haul. It really helps to not put your whole attention on what isn't working as individuals or as a couple. The old saying, "Is the cup half full or half empty?" is good to remember. Success is often in the eyes and mind of the beholder. Changing an outdated way of thinking is at the root of this game. It is challenging to trade in old worn-out thought patterns even if they are not making you happy. It takes courage to accept new thinking. A small leap of faith is required, but to a fearful mind it appears to be a leap across the Grand Canyon. Reality is sobering. You measure yourselves by the amount of success you attain. When it comes to love, the intangibles are present. It is easy to measure everything as a success or a failure. There is a middle area that is pliable though the mind may see it as unmovable. This is where you can change your thinking. Reality isn't really black and white. Alter your reality. Find the way to break your attachment to what is bringing you down. Each of you might need to modify behavior that bothers your partner. Do what it takes to raise your awareness to a higher level where true happiness resides.

The Rainbow

Your Gemini-Capricorn relationship can think on its feet. You will look for a clear commitment from each other. This is a romance that seems to function better when the expectations are clearly defined. Some sign combinations would rather clarify objectives while in the middle of doing them. That line of thinking will not work so well for you. The care you put into maintaining your everyday feelings of closeness is a major component to being happy.

A Gemini man is impressed with the Capricorn woman's authority. Her every move is well conceived. With mercurial ingenuity, he figures out that this feminine, earthy woman has more stomach to deal with reality than he does. Part of him likes the fact that she can face down problems. The twin in him worries that she will find him too fickle. The Mercurian man can't help but notice the seriousness in her face. Even her laugh appears to come out of a healthy respect for life's realities. She seems more time-tested than he. Even if she is much younger than he is, this wise, feminine spirit can display a maturity that defies her age. The Gemini man likes the fact this woman can look into his mind and see a depth that many others miss.

The Capricorn woman wonders if the Gemini man will find her love of tradition silly. It's not that she is ruled by the past. It's only that so many people have expectations for her to meet. The Saturnian woman is not so impressed with the Mercurian man's knowledge. She is curious to learn how he reacts when the going gets tough. The female Capricorn wants to know if this fast talker can act in a crisis. She does love the beautiful, verbal pictures he creates of his experiences. "My passions are not so different from his," she thinks to herself. People with a grounded plan win her heart. She searches his face and words to make sure he is not so ruled by his ambition that he cannot be a true lover. She isn't looking for a knight in shining armor as much as a lover with his priorities in order. She would like to be no less than tied for first place. There is no desire to possess his free roaming mind. If only he will value her own ambitions. She hopes so!

The female Gemini meets a male Capricorn and wonders if he is always such a strong fortress unto himself. Where is his vulnerability? This man comes off as being as strong as a mountain. She is amused at his capability. He can do anything, yet his self-consciousness is endearing. His ambitions are interesting and possibly breathtaking to someone who cares about these things. Even his failures may seem to be limited successes in her eyes. She is not without serious aspirations of her own, but she has simultaneous paths to travel to find all the possible roads to fulfillment. Such is not the case with this incarnation of success in front of her. She loves his focus, but she hopes it will never be so directed at her that she feels hemmed in (though to be held by those steady hands could be reassuring). He seems to be solid relationship material. His goals appear to be a motivating force. There is the voice of experience in his words. He seems to possess a history that gives him a healthy respect for both the ups and downs of living. She likes that world that lives somewhere in between the highs and lows. She wants the challenge of exposing him to alternative insights even if this earthy man likes to keep his feet planted on the rungs of the ladder of success.

The Magic of Signmates

The male Capricorn is impressed with the mind of this restless Gemini woman. It takes a lot for someone to divert his attention when it is directed at his plan of action. This down-to-earth man wonders how this fleet-footed Gemini woman can reach her destinations so quickly with no apparent roadmap to follow. She must have eyes in the back of her head! He isn't all business; it just takes a minor explosion to get him off the work track. This feminine Mercurian spirit breaks through his mental plane and moves into his heart. "How did she do that?" he wonders. He can't remember handing her the key. He isn't sure where this relationship might be heading. It isn't like him to be loose, yet this feminine Gemini soul has an exciting way of distracting him. She is the master of perception. He wonders whether this mentally gifted woman will tire of his love of work. He soon sees she is nobody's fool. She keeps her ideas growing by placing them on diverse paths. He wonders why she won't put all her eggs in one basket as he is used to doing. Finally, he asks himself during a reflective moment: "Wouldn't it would be fun to be one of her baskets?"

Your relationship together is full of serious motives. Many projects will be completed. Money and even power could blow your way. The love you want to feel requires that you protect your vulnerable hearts. Passion is only a breath away though in your busy lives it could seem light years from you. Make the time for each other. Love is never really convenient, but it is comforting. Be there for each other. You can't protect one another from the rejections you will encounter. You can save each other from facing these times alone. Reaching out with creative imagination keeps your hearts beating—alive, romantic, and with a sense of shared purpose.

Gemini-Aquarius: The Brainy Ones

Gemini + Aquarius = Quick Mental Energies

Excitement is what you like. You are a couple who can enjoy changing directions. Experimenting with ideas is stimulating. You will encourage each other to lead active lives. You are freethinkers. Learning is a probable motivating influence. You are not above self-educating yourselves if there is not a teacher to be found. You empower yourselves through education, knowledge, and keeping abreast of progressive trends. Cutting-edge people attract your attention. You bring to one another a rich world of thought-provoking information. You may even grow overwhelmed by trying to take in too many facts. Communication is always right there at your disposal. Make it a good friend, and you will remain as close as two people can get.

Communication Breakdown Game

The games played in your Gemini-Aquarius relationship are linked to impatient thoughts, moving out of sync, and living too much in your heads. The *Communication Breakdown* game occurs probably when you least expect it. How can two airy talkers like yourselves not talk to each other? It happens when you stomp on your partner's favorite goals. "Ouch! That hurts!" you say. Gemini requires plenty of acrobatic air space. Stay out of its brainstorming sessions if you want to remain friends and lovers. This sign will let you know when it's okay to fly along with it. Aquarius has a unique flight path. You can't really join its squadron until you are admitted. Independence was invented by this airy daredevil. You don't really want to fly with Aquarius anyway—at least not until its mind is fully aligned to its destination. When that happens, the trip is more fun. Your two "air worlds" break apart when one suspects the other of not giving proper respect to his or her respective ideas. The breakup of your minds is faster than a level five hurricane, and that's fast! You two have the mental chutzpa to rearrange most of the world to fit your expectations. In the movie *Havana*, Robert Redford, who played an American adventurer visiting Cuba, said to Lena Olin, a Cuban political revolutionary: "I don't want you to change the world; I just want you to change my world." Gemini and Aquarius craftily ask each other to make a difference. The catch is each must do this with precision, not carelessly brushing aside the thoughts each holds near and dear. Both of your signs have certain goals that are placed on an altar in your mind for worship. Somehow you must stay clear of forcing your own opinions on your lover, though the active dialogue you awaken runs with animated imagination. It is tempting to break each other's rules for the heck of it. You never know when you might cross over into the other's sacred space—ouch again!

Stripping Your Gears Game

It must not come as a surprise to hear that you are a fast-thinking duo. It will take considerable care to make sure you don't run each other into the ground as seen in the *Stripping Your Gears* game. Gemini can get out of the gate as fast as an Olympic runner leaving the starting block. When the starting gun sounds, Gemini becomes one great storm of impulse. Aquarius isn't much different. The Water Bearer is *really* an air sign; make no mistake about it, please! The "water" poured from its jug is actually electricity, dating back to the earliest Aquarian ancestors, who probably worshiped lightning. Aquarius is an unpredictable thinker, only partially belonging to the culture that has tried to tame it. Who controls this hard-to-harness mind? Why, Aquarius does, of course! Gemini understands all about duality and being two-minded. The Twins recognize quickly that Aquarius expresses duality itself. It would then seem that these four minds will coexist peacefully. Maybe yes, maybe no. It is possible (more than likely, if you can stomach a grain of truth) that you will trip over each other's minds at times. You will get highly irritated if this happens frequently. When you and your partner run enthusiastically toward new intellectual adventures, you may hear an awful sound—the stripping of normally well-lubricated mental gears. You could get burned out from oversaturation. Two air signs who are nervous wrecks make awful company. Your nervous systems won't get a break because the excitement of plunging into all kinds of activity provides a high. You could come to a crashing halt together.

Talking Heads Game

You can live so much in the mental realm that you lose sight of your heart. The *Talking Heads* game is just that. Communications pass through a too-fine mental filter while you refuse to allow for further refinement through an emotional sieve. This is too bad because it takes the heart out of your connection. Romance needs an emotional charge. You can talk around issues of the heart. Notice how easy it is for you to dissect topics that are less personal. Intimacy could be scary or even awkward. Staying on the fringes of your feelings doesn't generate a sense of closeness. Sex could even feel like you are sleeping with a stranger. You are not touching the inner zones that bring you to trust each other. You want to know each other, but by speaking from a distant land that is miles from your heart, you can get the sensation that you live on different islands. When in your partner's company, you can perceive each other as strangers from a strange land. Love isn't really complicated; it's a feeling. The mind is what makes love complex. It is like a stone that is skipped across a calm lake, causing the water to ripple; the mind is the stone that creates waves in the sea of love. The mind enjoys labeling love but doesn't usually hit the nail right on center. You may get so caught up in your words that they lead you astray.

Strategies

How can you fly high enough to miss these Gemini-Aquarius games? The *Communication Breakdown* game requires you to honor your partner's independent thinking. You both have a right to your own ideas. Don't unrealistically believe that you will always agree because this is not going to happen. Gemini is not that hard to reach if you use reason. There is a sense of order in Gemini that few ever see. It seems that Gemini's thoughts have no pattern. Even Gemini may not perceive any pattern in its own thought processes. This air sign's thoughts travel lightning fast along mental pathways, almost as though Gemini has a speed chip implant. Gemini likes you to get to the point fast. Don't blame the Twins. This chip makes it urgent for Gemini to talk fast as its mind is already being prodded on to the next topic. Aquarius has a band of electrical circuits that jolts its mind if you are boring; at least it seems that this is true. This explains why this air sign wants you to make your point and then get out of its face. Gemini and Aquarius can deal with this side of each other. Now, you may need to run away for an escape and rendezvous later. Distance need not be threatening to you.

Trying to get too close too fast doesn't really work. You must be careful how you claim your space. To do so rudely is not wise because it makes your partner feel devalued. Use that great intellect to warn each other when a timeout is needed. Freedom means you can each have your own friends plus a few in common. You don't need to belong to the same group or the same anything. Carefully spell out the ground rules. Remember to forgive if you make a mistake and break one of the sacred taboos. It's inevitable that one of you will cross the line. Be respectful with an ounce of understanding. Respect and understanding tend to open the heart. There may be a breakdown in communication occasionally. It is important that you know how to fix it. Listen. Talk. Listen again. Focus on equal exchanges, back and forth. You *both* (note the emphasis) must participate. Two united minds lead to two romantic hearts.

The *Stripping Your Gears* game only requires your reasonable logic to turn this game around to your advantage. You might need to scrutinize the amount of information coming into your relationship. You can't always expect your partner to enthusiastically join in everything you try. It might be a good idea if one of you is on the sidelines objectively watching to make sure you don't go overboard. There still are plenty of activities or projects you can find in common. Experience working as a team. It encourages you to talk freely. Tension mounts when you stop paying attention to each other's goals. When your minds are racing and your lives are not following any sense of order, your sense of closeness could be disrupted. You are capable of getting away with a more unorthodox schedule than many lovers. You thrive on a wide variety of interests and friends. Be careful to manage your schedules to the degree that you feel like you are on the same page.

The *Talking Heads* game is going to ask for your willingness to explore your feelings. If you are more at home with logic, as it is customary for air signs, it is a stretch to break emotional ground. That doesn't mean you two champions of the mind need to be as limp as damp dish towels. A small dose of emotional expression opens up your feelings. At least acknowledge the feelings your partner communicates. Don't turn a cold shoulder, and don't make your relationship needlessly complicated. If you can talk straight about major issues, you are a good part of the way home. It's easy to forget that emotional sharing needs a regular tune-up. With regular maintenance, your relationship can run indefinitely, outlasting any warranty!

The Rainbow

Your Gemini-Aquarius relationship runs at an exhilarating mile-a-minute pace. You have a romance that can be full of fun surprises. Support each other's unique goals because this leads to being a hit with one another's heart. Boredom is something you likely detest. Refreshing new directions keep coming your way. Let feeling have a voice as much as the intellect, and you will reach the deepest recesses of your partner's mind. Trust comes when each of you knows that your opinions carry equal weight.

A Gemini man perceives an Aquarius woman to be a novelty. Her mind is quick. He isn't used to having someone be able to stay on his trail, as close as white on rice. He asks himself, "Who is this woman?" She seems to maintain a comfortable distance from the world so it can't hurt her. He wants to pursue her and searches through his list of favorite opening lines, but he sees this isn't going to do. It's time for new material. She makes him feel at ease, yet he is uneasy. This Uranian rebel is upbeat but can shift down to a sober traditional role when needed. She is predictable where she wants to be understood but very unpredictable in areas where she seeks freedom, flying high above the crowd. The more time he spends with her, the more the Mercurian man loves this free-spirited soul.

An Aquarius woman finds the Gemini man entertaining. She is not sure what he might want from her. He almost seems to be indifferent about whether she wishes to get to know him or not. Let's put it another way. Part of him wants to be intimate, but she has the distinct feeling that part of him is detached and observes her dispassionately. She would rather he come right out and say what he thinks of her. She enjoys how he talks about life as though it is a storybook. There is an element of fantasy in her too. His ambition is not so different from her own. She ponders him with a long and distant gaze (he senses she must be staring at the Milky Way), and her eyes seem to sincerely ask, "Will he fly with me into the unknown?"

The Gemini woman sees a hero in the Aquarius man. He symbolizes the revolutionary that she wishes she could be. She is surprised to detect vulnerability in him; he expresses the pain of not always being accepted by others. She uses her mind to fight for her rights. He has resisted authority figures with his soul. No matter, she realizes that the male Aquarius sitting before her has a similar mind. She wonders if he will be able to relate to her need to follow sudden instincts to take a course, travel, run to a movie, or get lost in a book. She wants him to be her friend as much as her lover. She is relieved to hear that he is looking for a companion to share the future. His eyes sparkle when he talks of tomorrow's promise. "He must be from there," she thinks to herself. He looks out of place in the present.

The Aquarius man isn't sure what to make of the quick-witted female Gemini. He loves the fact that he can't dominate the conversation. It seems like he is doing so until she comes back forcefully with ideas of her own. She is an avid listener. She reminds him of a foreign language translator who simultaneously translates with incredible speed. How does she hear and respond so accurately? Her mind interprets information, but a step above that is her amazing insight. It quiets him into a semi-trance. He is held spellbound by her words. Her passionate enunciation sends a chill through him. "Who is this woman?" "Who is this woman?" He isn't used to asking the same question twice in a row either!

Your close encounter together needs to be just that. Allow your hearts to warm to each other. Your minds generate incredible enthusiasm to experiment with new paths. The roads you travel as individuals and as a couple are lively. You make the best companions and lovers when open to each other's perceptions. The love you feel will depend on your willingness to open up to it. Create a vision that is big enough to carry you through whatever might come your way. When you talk to understand each other rather than to voice fixed opinions, your hearts grow fonder.

Let the Games Begin

Gemini-Pisces: The Wishers and Hopers

Gemini + Pisces = Anything Is Possible Outlook

These two signs are known for adaptability. Mentally adept Gemini can stimulate the strong emotional nature of Pisces to be more reflective. Inspired by its visions and strong feelings, watery Pisces lifts Gemini out of its mind and into the world of emotion. Pisces is not just any fish in the sea. This sign has a primordial intuition that doesn't know when to quit. Can a Mercurian sign live with a Neptunian sign? Sure! If they can both keep their feet on or above the ground at the same time. It's asking a lot, but it can be done. Gemini likes to think of options. Pisces would rather float through them. Oddly enough, both ways seem to work for this unusual sign combination.

Chameleon Game

The games played in your Gemini-Pisces relationship are associated with inaccurate perceptions of each other, diluted momentum, and confusion in communication. Gemini is a sign with a diverse set of ideas and interests. There is often a wide range of self-expression (like a man with rack upon rack of ties or a woman with a closet full of shoes). Each can enjoy having many possibilities from which to choose. Gemini can wear different personalities that suit every occasion: one for work, a different one for friends, another one for a lover, and so on. Pisces shares this attraction to different types of self-expression—at least one for every type of occasion. Put these two signs in the same room and you have more than two people. What's so bad about this? Nothing. However, if one or both chooses to hide behind roles, then it opens act one, scene one, of the *Chameleon* game. Determining to whom you are talking can be confusing. Direct communication is not happening, and honesty about what you want from each other is circumvented. Running away from closeness undermines loving feelings. Fear may cause this distancing behavior. It can be perplexing sorting out the "real" you from your personas.

Wishy-Washy Game

When the two of you feel indecisive or emotionally underwater, it might be due to playing the *Wishy-Washy* game. Gemini is lost or disoriented when it can't get its thoughts lined up in a row. This crafty airborne flyer can't stand to be on the ground for too long. Occasionally, Gemini's spark is doused by Pisces' worries. Instead of following its own ideas, Gemini talks itself out of moving ahead, and looks over its shoulder for approval that is not forthcoming. Pisces isn't necessarily even interfering; the Fish could be brooding over its own problems. Pisces can be thrown off course by Gemini's tendency to suddenly move into a vast assortment of directions. Pisces desires to tune into the right channel, following its imagination, often with no clear-cut direction. Restless Gemini would prefer to let an automatic scanner do the work. Your reasoning power contrasts fundamentally. One isn't better than the other; it is just different. You will feel like you are in a maze of missing logic when your plans disappear due to inaction. Your divergent ways of embarking on a course of action can become bewildering. If you are critical, it only makes matters worse. A tendency to blame one another can come out of this scenario. Divine discontentment is the atmosphere in which neither of you are easy to please. It may be hard to put your finger on what is wrong—like eating chicken soup with a fork!

Coloring the Truth Game

Talking clearly in your relationship is challenging, not because you don't know how but because you are unwilling to do so. The *Coloring the Truth* game has shades of denial embedded in it. The two of you draw entertaining pictures for each other but don't get to the point. Gemini can camouflage its needs behind a wonderful vocabulary. The conceptual framework of Gemini's mercurial mind can artistically talk around a subject without really committing to a position. Pisces has a flair for invisibility and ducking under the truth. This water sign has a talent in even making someone forget what the conversation was about in the first place! You can send out smoke screens that thoroughly get each other off the path. Trust is damaged because you aren't sure where each is coming from a lot of the time. You can stand a few feet from one another or in each other's arms but have the sensation of living on different latitudes. The intimacy you would like will be delayed as long as you are trapped in this kind of interaction.

Strategies

How can you get out from under these Gemini-Pisces games? In the *Chameleon* game, you can't really stop being yourselves. There is a theatrical dimension at work in your romance. It can be fun to reveal other sides of yourselves to each other. You must make sure that when you want your true selves to be seen that you don't hide them. Communication can be simple. To some extent, you are a bit more complicated in this relationship. Why? You tend to bring out a vast range of self-expressions in your partner. It is exhilarating to be stimulated in this manner. Use your inspiring creative energy to move closer. The way to engage in productive action is to talk honestly. You can have fun with your wonderful display of your multi-faceted personalities. Be sure to differentiate when you are serious from when you are playacting.

The *Wishy-Washy* game comes down to getting out of each other's way when you work together. It probably is simpler than it seems. If your shared goals are clear, you are about halfway there. Make sure you let one another pursue individual dreams. It really will help when it comes to working together. Your initiating energies are so uniquely different. It takes a lot to get used to blending Gemini, the thinker, with Pisces, the feeler. Thoughts and feelings, will the two ever meet? Take the time to tap into your partner's approaches to projects or tasks. Your way of finding solutions appears further apart than it truly is. Each of you likes to consider more than one method to solve a dilemma. You can space out each other's minds when impatient or show great dissatisfaction with one another's natural thought processes. All signs have a capacity to think and feel! It's the way you blend these processes that can be tricky. You may need to get away temporarily from discussing an emotionally disorienting issue. It might even take getting out of each other's presence to find objectivity. There are no hard and fast rules. Each situation will dictate the right answer in working together. Focus on unity and what you are trying to accomplish. Details can be revised as you proceed. Don't let the little things scramble your brains and emotions to the point that you give up. It takes practice to talk and work together. You come from different worlds. There is a meeting place you can discover that will show you how to best manage your energies when tackling something as a duo. Be patient. Show faith. Talk positively.

The *Coloring the Truth* game requires you to break a pattern of denial. You may not want to see what is wrong with your relationship. The temptation to sweep problems under the rug lengthens this game. You need to have faith in each other so that you can speak truthfully. The heart grows fonder when you communicate directly. It makes planning your future and handling everyday business affairs run more smoothly. You can choose to say what you think your partner wants to hear, but is this really what your partner *needs* to hear? Avoiding conflict can be a sure way to miss intimacy. It's true. Trust is broken when you sense someone can't handle the truth. Passion is a fiery thing; timidly skirting the heart of the matter won't warm your feelings. Choose faith over fear. Yes, it's scary if you aren't a frequent flyer on the path of faith. With more constant use of this travel lane, you will light a great fire of passion in one another. It takes more energy not to speak honestly. You have to keep worrying how to carry on the pretense. Will you be found out? Your relationship is strong enough to handle the heat. Are you?

The Rainbow

Your Gemini-Pisces relationship was never intended to make your lives uneasy. Whether consciously or unconsciously, you may challenge each other. You have the gift of seeing your way out of potential sticky circumstances before they bump into you. When you are willing to take control of your relationship as a confident pair, true magic manifests. The driving force to impress your gifts upon the world comes through with an awesome display of creativity. The alluring presence you represent for each other begins with that first glance.

A Gemini man looks upon a Pisces woman and sees a mirage. She looks real enough, but her words float hypnotically around the Mercurian man's head. Her beauty within matches that without. He wonders if she is always passive. He notices that she projects a carefree aura. Her gait flows and is almost surreal. He wants to walk in her world, but at the same time, worries that his world will evaporate. Will she be able to accept his peculiar life interests? What if his wit is too dry? This curious male soul wants to see if she really can speak the same language. She has a soft voice that stirs his feelings, and deep passion shines in her eyes.

A Pisces woman is indifferent to the male Gemini's personality. She wants to know what lies underneath his words. He talks a good game, but is he an honest player? This feminine Neptunian spirit is not a fool. She is idealistic but only to a point. She is not sure how to proceed with this mentally invigorating man. He is friendly enough, but will he be able to tolerate her perception of truth? Faith is her guide. The intangible forces at work know her by name. She can't talk to everybody about these things. This Mercurian man is cool and detached. Can he let her be? His passion for life awakens the spirit of love in her. She hopes he will be a soul mate, needing her as much as she will need him rather than just a passing fancy.

A Gemini woman is not sure how to read a Pisces man. She is perplexed because usually, without hesitation, she can read anything or anyone! This Neptunian man is intuitive yet seems to care about material things. He is a dreamer but has a master plan for success. She listens carefully to see if his world has room for her own ideas. She knows her own can accommodate his. He confesses to be a lover of life in pursuit of a cause. His devotion to a path is revealed in his face. The female Gemini perceives the Pisces man to be a romantic. She isn't sure what motivates him. Is it love, people, or his ambitions? She hopes it is all of the above!

A Pisces man is enthralled with a Gemini woman. She epitomizes the romantic myths he carries in his head. He wonders, whether consciously or subconsciously, if that idealized image can be maintained in everyday life. The Pisces man loves her speech patterns. Her perceptions can pierce through to his inner world. The Pisces man is anxious to know her better. He may be timid about his ability to match her fast mind. His intuition dances around her aura, but he is not sure he understands this feminine spirit. She seems to be talking to him and analyzing him all in the same breath. Wow! He dodges her sharp eye, hoping he has disguised himself enough. After all, he doesn't really know her yet. A contemplative question echoes through his head: "How does she already know me?"

You can be absolutely thrilled with being exposed to different worlds. There is much you can teach one another. Treat each other as equals. Define your relationship with clarity. Talk honestly and openly. This is the way to make your romance work for you rather than the other way around. You can come to see each other as the most loving of mates.

Cancer-Cancer: The Homebodies

Cancer + Cancer = Deep Diving into the Sea of Emotions

Cancer is a water sign, which means that feelings are a key theme in life. The Crab has strong opinions about home. "Home" may be defined as being at ease within and finding the right place to live in the outer world. A saying of the real estate industry applies here: "Location, location, location!" Cancer is emphatically trying to locate a sense of security. The Crab does this through sinking its claws into ownership. It isn't the possessions in themselves that please Cancer but the nurturing they might bring. The Crab can become quite attached to a lover, especially an attentive one. What about two Crabs in the same shell? There must be enough space for each to breathe freely. Cancer can thrust forward forcefully when excited by a new path. Two Cancers can influence each other to step past security zones, though it might take a strong nudge! Supporting one another's key ambitions goes far in winning mutual admiration.

Dark Side of the Moon Game

The games played in your Cancer-Cancer relationship relate to emotional disorientation, co-dependent behavior, and mood swings. When the two of you become emotionally distraught with one another or with life in general, the *Dark Side of the Moon* game is born. Two water signs can lock on to each other's emotions as precisely as a heat-seeking missile can find its target in the sky; that's great accuracy! It's easy to be so connected to each other that if one of you is moody or gloomy, the other can pick up on this energy. Within moments, you both can be ready to parachute for safety or to abandon a sinking boat. The more you worry about how to break free of this confusion the worse it gets. Communication can be strange. Often it resembles the sound of one hand clapping (i.e., silence). Usually this isn't silent, contemplative meditation. It is a type of quiet that leaves you confused and frustrated. Accusing each other of spacing out doesn't help. Closeness can disappear until you work out your feelings. Clinging to your partner desperately, thinking this is a way to make things better, won't work either. You may be able to cut the tension with a knife if this game persists.

Smothering Game

There is quality of closeness in every successful relationship. A clearly defined commitment will usually ensure the equality and freedom needed. The *Smothering* game takes caring too far. Dependency needs are not balanced. One or both of you may be so attached to the other that you won't let your partner out of your sight. You may be parenting each other too much. When blocking the autonomy each of you requires, growth is stunted. Trust issues are often at the bottom of this smothering behavior. It is possible that one or both of you brought old issues regarding trust into the current relationship. A Cancer-Cancer combination has a tendency to get both of you to face your most deep-seated fears. Why? The emotional power of your relationship asks you to rise above your issues. Old patterns that need to be confronted can come out. Maintaining your objectivity in the midst of emotional turmoil isn't happening. You could find that the harder you try to cling to your partner, the more firmly you are pushed away. Regulation of closeness and distance does not run smoothly; your relationship's engine is flooded with a sense of disorientation.

Tidal Wave Game

Cancer is ruled by the Moon, which regulates the ocean tides. The Moon is fast-moving, and Cancer gets into high gear faster than the Moon when its sense of security is threatened. During turbulent weather when one of you endures a career challenge or another major change, the *Tidal Wave* game can blow into your relationship, bringing the extreme mood swings that Cancer is sometimes known to exhibit. Cancer's anger is expressed through unusual means; Cancer's expression and words don't always match. A tense voice is a dead giveaway that the Crab is mad. You two can get angry when events do not go according to plan. Your sign is fairly adept at planning. It's the time it takes to devise a plan that bothers the Crab. You both become crabby if you can't depend on one another to follow through on promises. There are those unexplainable moments when nothing you can point to is out of place. Your life is good, yet you still may be subject to intense moods. Why? Your emotional antennae are your lifeline. Because your emotions are the great reservoir guiding your intuition and willpower, at times you may get explosive. It's your way of releasing your psychic intensity. No other sign does this in quite the same way, not even introspective Scorpio. What is actually a natural process can bother your partner. Even though you are both Cancers and would think you can handle this in each other, don't count on it. The fact that you can tune into this in each other may even make it more powerful! Moods can make it hard to trust each other or to talk.

Strategies

How do you stay clear of these Cancer-Cancer games? The *Dark Side of the Moon* game may require that the two of you talk when your emotions are calmer. You may find it essential to take a little space to get grounded again. Intuitive impulses are common in your Sun sign. Emotions can become larger than life itself. You may need to be determined to talk clearly. Don't assume that your partner can read your mind. Talking can clear up misconceptions. If you feel too emotionally exhausted, it is best to wait until you feel centered. It doesn't do any good to accuse your partner of ruining your day. If you overidentify with the worries of your partner, you both can be pulled into the problem. It is better that one of you stay mentally clear. You can be nurturing without merging with what your lover is going through. Cancer is a sensitive sign. Your caring attitude is going to make you feel the intensity of what each of you experiences. Somehow you must establish a boundary line that is a visible marker of your emotional space.

The *Smothering* game only requires a slight adjustment in how you show your concern. Don't squeeze so hard that neither of you can move. Allow personal goals to be pursued. It will make you find greater closeness that you can count on. In some respects you should adopt the old saying, "absence makes the heart grow fonder," as your meditation. It's okay to miss each other. Space can be threatening when you don't trust yourself or your lover. It takes practice and a little courage to let go and let your partner fly. Your partner's love for you will bring him or her back. Make your home a true castle—not with possessions but with an atmosphere of freedom and responsibility. You can desire a sense of closeness that is impossible for your lover to fulfill. Each of you has a unique drive to be happy in your own way. When you express your happiness, your relationship becomes richer and revitalized. Possessiveness backfires sooner or later.

It's okay if you feel deeply attached to one another. Breathing room gives each of you the space to reach your highest ambitions.

The *Tidal Wave* game could take an even greater awareness to neutralize its hold on you. Moods are not controllable. Channeling your intensity with greater spontaneity may be part of the answer. Bottled up self-expression can make you explosive. If you hold anger inside, it doesn't take much to release it. The two of you draw out each other's intensity, which is not a bad thing. You can anticipate strong outbursts in a passionate relationship. You only need to make this energy work for you rather than against you. Ignoring your partner's greatest needs can lead to an angry reaction. Moods can be your partner's way of getting attention. Nothing else works. It's how you talk after the fallout of a moody explosion that is a key ingredient in dealing with this game. Can you come back and talk through a disagreement? If you can, the healing process begins quickly. Running away from discussing a problem doesn't help. The intensity of the tidal wave can become even worse. Don't be timid. Talk—even if it means the words will get hot. Get your emotions out on the table. Look at what you both are feeling. There is an answer or way to get beyond these moods. They will never truly go away. Remember, moods are a part of your psyche that are tied to your perceptions. Moods are a good thing, but when they become extreme they rule you. Showing that you care after a heated exchange is a way back to clearer communication.

The Rainbow

Your Cancer-Cancer relationship is one in which you both can reach your dreams because the support you receive from one another can boost you to success. There isn't much you really can hide from your lover. Since you both were born under the nurturing, watchful eye of Cancer, you have the capacity to use a sixth sense—your refined intuition. The secrets you keep from yourselves may be exposed in this romance but not at the beginning when you first meet and are getting to know each other. Your secrets may come out while walking hand in hand on the beach or dancing the two-step or looking into each other's eyes with love. The secrets you keep are a connection to your power. When you reveal the dark side of your lunar nature, you form a bond that is engrossed in the light. The darkness itself is not bad or ugly, but your fears and feelings about intimacy are the problem. When you let one another into the parts of you that are the most guarded, you are a match greater than heaven. You are an interesting pair. You may become close during tough seasons or in the midst of a crisis.

The ability to appreciate abundance is a sign of wisdom. Times of plenty fill you with the courage and stamina needed to deal with leaner periods. You are a complex couple for others to comprehend. Your love of privacy may keep those outside of your immediate clan at a distance. You are attracted to the idea of an extended family. Your loyalty to those you care about is hard to rival by any other sign combo. It may be scary to realize you can break each other's heart. It is exhilarating to realize you can be the person the other has been to hell and back trying to find. You may sense that you know each other from some other time. A past-life familiarity may have set in quickly. "Don't I know you? You seem to know me!" The most urgent question is: "Do you want to do whatever it takes to understand each other now?"

A Cancer man is taken aback by a Cancer woman. She is comforting yet arouses his suspicion all at once. As a matter of fact, these two Crabs circle around each other to make sure it is okay not to be so protective. Your minds are in a "put up your dukes" mode though neither wants to admit it. A healthy respect begins to blossom as each comes to understand the other's demands. The nurturing qualities in both make the relationship hard to leave. Passion is released in one big explosion after another. This sign is noted for being quiet and reserved, which is not always the case in a Cancer-Cancer relationship. Both can release the warrior of feelings within. Fear may come after resting in each other's arms. Now, where do you go from here? The male Crab loves the appreciation of home shown by the female Crab. Whether she wants a home in suburbia or to be on the road like a dharma bum, she knows what "home" means in plain language. Her sensuality is reserved but far from dormant. She isn't pushy with her love. He has a feeling that this woman is from a part of the Moon that he doesn't know. Her radar can see under his skin. He likes this one instant but feels dreadfully insecure about it a moment later. "What does she want from me?" echoes in his mind. This feminine spirit, whose emotional power has blown people away since time immemorial, is at it again. The male Crab prays she will blow her breath of love his way. He is getting more attached to her by the second.

A Cancer woman is careful when meeting a male Crab. She knows that this emotional being has the magic to fool her into believing in him. She would prefer to believe in him after he proves his worth. This lunar man has a personality that can move a crater. He is talkative but careful not to cross into the sacred ground lying within each of them. She senses he is waiting for her to initiate deep talk. She is more comfortable in the shallow water with this fast swimming Crab. She doesn't want to give the impression that she can't outswim this lunar man. She holds back her nurturing side because she doesn't want him to see this just yet. She is fond of the warmth he expresses for friends and family. His voice is soothing, especially when he isn't so serious. She wants to play with this man who can be so entertaining. He is emotional but exercises great control. She wonders if he is always like this, or perhaps this is for show only. She listens carefully to his vision of home. It seems to align with her own view for the most part. She isn't so worried about him being good at making love. The lunar woman wishes from the deepest part of her heart that he is an honest lover.

You will cross many bridges together in this relationship. Build a strong foundation right from the start, and you will have no use for looking back with clouds of doubt. You are not the first people to travel to the Moon and reach out to a fellow Cancer. You could be two of the first to break every rule in the book and have a carefree life, throwing security to the wind. Your faith in each other is the barometer through which to measure your happiness. When it is low, you will wonder how you can make it. When it is high, you have only to look in your soul mate's face; your partner will be the lighthouse that guides you whether the weather is ominous or sunny.

Cancer-Leo: The Industrious Ones

Cancer + Leo = Pushing Steadily Ahead

The persistence of Cancer to put together something reliable combines smoothly with the "go for it" thinking of Leo. The two can turn dust into gold. The business instincts of each sign come to the forefront when becoming partners. Cancer and Leo can exhibit a lively display of emotions. The Crab intuitively knows how to massage the Lion's ego. Leo can heap praise on a lunar lover, making Cancer's heart glow with delight. Cooking up new enterprises makes life a gas! The two don't generally welcome unpredictable events. Cancer likes to prepare for changes well in advance. Leo would prefer to be the cause of change rather than reacting to it. A strong conviction to be true to each other instills deep commitment. The Crab gradually warms up to the Lion after growing comfortable with its roars. The Lion learns how to say the right things, maybe even purr, to get the Crab to come out of its shell.

Yo-Yo Game

The games played in your Cancer-Leo romance are connected to a confusion about how to stay close, competitiveness, and a lack of support. The two of you can feel like your romance stops and starts erratically. The *Yo-Yo* game can find you bewildered about what the relationship is. Cancer can pull back from the bold advances of Leo. The Lion can be intimidated by Cancer's need to know its innermost feelings. A hot and cold sensation can perpetually sweep over you both in trying to size up how to make this relationship run smoothly. You can feel pulled one way and then another by each other. Cancer doesn't usually approach decisions in the same way as Leo. The Crab will sometimes appear to move quickly. There is a restlessness to secure the present which doesn't translate into spontaneous actions. Cancer will take its time in really getting to know someone even if diving into a romantic encounter. The Crab retreats slowly in order to make sure this was the right decision. Then Cancer proceeds forward again only to step back. Progress is made according to the Crab's internal clockwork. Meanwhile, Leo acts in a different manner. The Lion is anxious to test the waters. When making an explosive and passionate entrance into someone's life, the Lion doesn't retreat—unless Cancer scares the roar out of it. It can take some getting used to in adjusting to this yo-yo-like movement. Sometimes Cancer's slow approach clashes with Leo's "let's get the show on the road" attitude. The Crab may end up chasing the Lion if it fears commitment, or the Lion may wind up running after a scared Crab. You both can lose interest if you can't read one another's needs. Each of you could feel rejected by the other's distant behavior. The lights go out of the romance if you can't define your relationship clearly.

Eclipsed Game

If the competitive side of your relationship goes to the extreme, the *Eclipsed* game can make an unwelcome entrance. Cancer will be assertive if Leo starts to step on its delicate emotions. Leo can become angry if its strong opinions are challenged. This game is more likely to occur when you are not sharing the spotlight. The passion you form together can propel both of you into creative high gear. Neither of you wants to take a back seat to the other. If you go too far to outshine one another, it dims your love. Angry outbursts are highly predictable. Being able to talk sensibly is difficult when you feel discounted. You will do better if you encourage equality rather than ask your partner to assume a supporting role. Cancer can nurture better than most but does not appreciate having its kindness taken for granted. Leo has great energy and can be quite good at sharing its wealth with those it loves. The Lion can get turned off if its generosity is exploited. Hurt feelings are at the heart of this game. When you face off over which of you is the most giving, this game keeps regenerating. It could become tiresome to fight over who is right or more benevolent. The feeling of not being appreciated probably hurts the most.

Vaporizing Game

When you set your goals into motion, they may disappear before your eyes. You may feel like you are vanishing as well. This is the *Vaporizing* game. You may have a tough time "walking the walk." Why? Perhaps you are not honestly communicating. Neither of you truly has your heart in what the other is planning.

Your best-laid blueprints can go up in smoke or steam due to a lack of faith. You are sensitive to each other's opinions, which you may as well get used to since it comes standard in a Cancer-Leo romance. Your words have either an empowering or a detrimental effect. In this game the latter is the more dominant. A passive-aggressive desire to sabotage your partner's goals is embedded in this interaction. You both are frustrated. Cancer loves to watch what it plants come to fruition. Leo takes great pride in proclaiming future plans. The disappearance of this drive to move forward produces resentment. You both want support from the other. When you hold back, it inhibits each other's progress. You may find it hard to believe that your partner's approval means that much to you. Cancer can be afraid to show its dependency, fearing rejection. Leo has too much pride to show vulnerability. Getting to a place where you are having true communication is fogged out. In a sense, you put each other's ambition to sleep.

Strategies

How can you get through these Cancer-Leo games? The *Yo-Yo* game asks you to become aware of your partner's emotional rhythms. Cancer and Leo trust intimacy differently. Don't force the issue. When you both relax into the relationship, it pays dividends. Each of you must feel the freedom to be yourselves. A fear of intimacy could be a real issue. Getting past this fear is essential to really trusting one another. Talking from your hearts instead of from your doubts is a surer path to closeness. You look for consistency. It causes confusion to feel little mental separation one day and then to suddenly slip into feeling like strangers the next. Pulling your partner close and then pushing away eats away at trust.

Cancer is usually slow to let anyone get too close. The Crab wants to know how many tomorrows someone will be around. When Cancer doesn't have to worry about this in a partner, the door to its heart is easily accessed. However, finding the entry to Cancer's heart is tricky; it is hidden in a maze that tries a fire sign's patience. Leo may blame Cancer for its emotional elusiveness. The path to Cancer's heart is clearly marked; it's just that fire signs can hurriedly rush right past it! With Leo, it's another story. The Lion will tell you that the door to its heart is always open. However, Leo doesn't broadcast its ground rules. The first is that effusive praise is the admission price. The second is that Leo is not going to readily admit how heavy the door can be to push open. You see, there is a mountain of pride resting against it. Cancer can get Leo to open up better than most. When Cancer pulls Leo's heartstrings, the Lion willingly opens up. If Leo will relinquish its powerful desire for control, Cancer will walk anywhere in the maze to meet its fiery lover. Meeting each other halfway is a good first step.

The *Eclipsed* game requires that you tone down your attempts to upstage each other. You need to get to the bottom of the matter. You probably are not talking *with* each other but *at* one another (or not talking at all). At some point, you must get your hurt feelings out in the open. If you are already in a shouting match, then you need to come back later when you are not so heated to be able to truly listen. Negotiate from the heart rather than engage in a clash of your wills. When the two of you rise to the top of your potential, the relationship flourishes. Feeling mutually empowered produces greater love and passion. Show that you really value your partner. Supporting each other's goals will make you both a hero in the other's eyes. Don't let anger bother you. Anger is often the first step toward reconciliation. Too much silence will cause a deafening roar of misery in your heads. Talking can extinguish the flames fanned by your differences. Blame only stokes the blaze. You would be wise to forgive each other in order to start fresh. Don't repeat the same mistakes. If you find yourselves regressing into old patterns, take a deep breath and head in a positive direction again. Stay conscious of your actions.

Learning how to work together will help to conquer the *Vaporizing* game. Honest communication is probably the main ingredient required in any formula you try. It isn't a crime if you can't participate in the same endeavors. In the projects you can do together, participate with your greatest concentration. It's wise to lend support and show your interest in each other's individual paths. You will both be less frustrated if you don't meet resistance from your partner. You will find that you engage in fewer skirmishes that are caused by not seeing eye to eye on what is important. You will need to compromise on jobs that require mutual commitment. Giving each other space to pursue individual interests need not threaten your stability. Don't criticize your lover's pet projects even if they aren't part of your own reality. Acceptance allows your love to work better than a Swiss watch!

The Rainbow

Your Cancer-Leo romance is alive with fiery emotions. Your dance through life can be filled with one celebration after another. You tend to feel the exhilaration of the highs and the agony of the lows more than most. Your creative punch is strong. You can achieve great milestones together. You are happiest when your partner has complete faith in you, aren't you?

A Cancer man is attracted to the air of confidence shown by the Leo woman. The lunar man finds this fiery feminine spirit energizing. He wants to be around such passion as much as possible because it adds zest to his life. He hopes the Leo woman will be impressed with his accomplishments or at least his ambitions. He isn't sure what matters most to her: his potential for wealth or his big heart. The Cancer man is self-conscious about his sensitivity. He doesn't want to be mistaken as someone who lacks willpower. If only he could read her expression. He feels that words are not as important as the conviction with which he speaks. The Cancer man hopes he can win the attention of this fiery spirit so that she will want to know him better. She doesn't exactly make him feel secure but doesn't make him feel insecure either. He gets the message that he had best stop doubting himself if he wants to keep up with this woman. After all, she seems to respond to self-confidence.

The Leo woman finds that the Cancer man borders on the mysterious. He can seem so sure of himself one instant yet can suddenly lapse into reserved contemplation the next. She appreciates his sensitivity but hopes he is not too moody. People who pout bother her. She wonders why people can't let go and just move forward. She likes his caring treatment of her. His ego seems more fragile than hers, but that is okay. She sees that he loves to be assured of his strength and of her support. The Leo woman wonders whether this lunar man will still see her as his sunny lover if she prowls along the paths that hold her dreams. You see, this spirited feminine lover can never be possessed. She might give the appearance that she belongs *with* him, but he should never act like she belongs *to* him; she wonders whether he can do this. The female Leo wants to explore life with the Cancer man, perhaps because his watery eyes seem to see her completely or maybe because the touch of his hands conveys his deep emotions for her.

Unlike so many others, the Cancer woman is not intimidated by the Leo man. She jumps at his first roar but then sees that he can be a big teddy bear. His strength is refreshing, but her sense of reality tells her he can't be tamed. She is annoyed if he throws childish temper tantrums. She expects that there is no way to stop this from happening because it is his way of saying, "I am important." She humors him but wants him to know in no uncertain terms that she expects to be treated with respect. He will listen to her and not monopolize the conversation. He will at least show through his actions that he cares even if he can't say that he does. The Cancer woman doesn't ask him for much—only that he respect her feelings and not laugh at her moods. These ground rules aren't due to her sensitivity but arise from her birthright to act upon her emotions. She has a sneaking suspicion that the Lion is a big-hearted soul. He can't afford to show this to everyone," she tells herself, "because it will be abused." She only hopes this Lion will show his heart to her!

The Leo man notices the Cancer woman's intense emotions. He isn't sure how to respond to her when she is upset or mad. Her emotions throw his mind into a panic. He wants to make her problems go away with one swish of his powerful tail. The Leo man faces a dilemma with a Cancer woman. He loves the way she makes him feel, but the Lion knows he has a lot to learn, or unlearn, about making this feminine woman feel secure. It isn't in Leo's nature to automatically lend support. The Leo man is inclined to protect those he loves by resolving situations. His protectiveness wins her heart. He soon sees that his sense of authority distances her. He rolls out the red carpet, hoping this woman will walk with him. He is drawn to her deep, inner clarity though it is a foreign world to him. She knows how to care deeply. He aspires to reach out to her with the same willingness. He hopes she will give him the time to get it right. What he doesn't know is that it's his conscientious effort to be a caring lover that means the most to her. If he takes the time to find this out, he will see her respond in ways he never imagined.

Your relationship is one in which you can discover deeper dimensions of yourselves. The big surprise is how you may see that you are more alike than you thought. Cancer will never be as ego driven as Leo. Leo will not show the same need for privacy as Cancer. However, each of you can confirm the need for closeness in the other. You can help pave the way for your partner's most abundant dreams.

Cancer-Virgo: The Thrifty Ones

Cancer + Virgo = Thorough Thinking

These are two signs that can blend together smoothly. Cancer's feelings of security depend upon a reliable future. Virgo will iron out any wrinkle to maintain a sense of order. There is a compulsive drive in each to make life respond as productively as possible. Neither likes to waste time, and both can save for a rainy day. Cancer's striving to put intuitive hunches to the test isn't unlike Virgo's restless work ethic. Both signs like to stay busy and become anxious if not hard at work. Cancer's desire for a comfortable home matches Virgo's need to have a haven in which to relax. On paper, these signs are clearly compatible. The raw ingredients are there to create a conducive atmosphere for getting along with each other. If you see from the beginning that pleasing each other constantly is impossible, so much the better!

Holding Back Game

The games played in your Cancer-Virgo relationship are associated with a reluctance to commit, indecisiveness, and too much criticism. The *Holding Back* game occurs when the two of you are reluctant to make a clear-cut commitment. You may feel that you have good reasons for not wanting to promise too much. Cancer, the Crab, moves slowly in order to make sure it is safe to come out of its shell. Virgo's watchful eye makes sure the relationship can fulfill certain pragmatic hopes. The problem comes in when neither of you takes action to reassure the other. Past emotional trauma may interfere with your ability to let go. This seems to happen with some regularity in new Cancer-

Virgo romances. Even Cancer-Virgo relationships that have existed for years tend not to forget old hurts quickly. Talking can help, but letting go of the past can't be rushed. Forgiveness can be tough to swallow but does open you to new possibilities. It isn't easy for Cancer and Virgo to approach each other because each is protective of its feelings. Cancer will conceal them while Virgo will intellectualize them. A fear of rejection is likely to be at the root of this game.

You Love Me, You Love Me Not Game

Decisiveness in matters of the heart isn't easy for anyone. A Cancer-Virgo relationship can alternate between clarity and confusion. Cancer's moods can stir up all kinds of thoughts. Virgo's analytical side can lead this sign to question the other's love. The feeling that you are continually being tested grows old and being subjected to another's scrutiny can make you mad. Trust issues swim under the surface of this game. Having to prove you love each other can get frustrating if not utterly exhausting. Distance will settle between your hearts if you don't get a handle on this one. Your expectations may be too high to attain. Be reasonable in what you think you need. A checklist that your partner must satisfy will not get the job done. Fragile feelings are part of your sign combination. You can be in a continuous process of reacting to each other's anger and disappointment without really doing anything constructive to fix the problems.

Critique Game

If you become extremely critical of your partner, the *Critique* game will come into play. Cancer can be dismayed when Virgo changes a schedule to better fit its own priorities. Virgo might become irritated with Cancer's sudden change of plans. There is a deeper potential problem in this game. Each of you has extremely personal routines in life. Virgo is especially careful to follow a daily ritual. Even if Virgo is carefree, this sign still has certain habits that are as predictable as the Sun rising in the East and setting in the West. Cancer is quite attached to maintaining control over its daily life. Control is this sign's self-nurturing mechanism. Few other signs understand this about Cancer. When either disturbs the other's schedule, hasty remarks can fly. The flexibility you need is nowhere to be found. Mutual acceptance seems to give way to demanding your own way. Silence can make matters worse. Cancer broods when it clams up while Virgo is no better and acts as though its world has been destroyed. Silence pushes you miles apart, and it can become harder to talk if you let too much time elapse. Criticism is impossible to avoid, and it's unrealistic to expect there to be none. It's important that you point out to each other what bothers you. By not saying how criticism makes you feel, you can't begin to put an end to the behavior.

Strategies

How do you stay away from playing these games? In the *Holding Back* game, you must define your commitment to each other clearly. Then you both will feel comfortable. It is tough to be at ease when you are not sure what kind of relationship you are in, and defining the relationship allows you to know how to put together a winner. Expectations are part of any solid partnership and give a barometer to measure how well you are getting along. If you are holding back old baggage from other relationships, try your best to not project unresolved issues onto each other. Cancer and Virgo don't like having to deal with messy emotional situations. You may have to give yourselves permission to allow for emotional messes. Fear of conflict will keep you from really dealing with deep issues. The two of you can handle going into deeper water together. You don't need to be each other's therapist. Get good at problem-solving. Your sign combination finds it easier to deal with impersonal circumstances. Handling business affairs individually or as a couple is a snap. You may lose your footing when you move into the emotional terrain. It takes practice to talk about feelings. Addressing why you watch each other from a distance is the way to move closer. You might feel that your partner wants you to take on too much responsibility; Cancer and Virgo attract their fair share. Make it clear you don't want to burden one another. Have some fun. Don't make everything work or a serious debate. It may sound too easy, but laughing together (and a foreign cruise) could do wonders for your intimacy—honest!

The *You Love Me, You Love Me Not* game requires a bit more soul searching. The Crab wants to test romantic waters carefully to make sure it is not eaten up by a shark. Virgo sticks a toe in the waters to see how much is at stake. You almost need to say to your partner, "I don't bite!" Self-doubt can cause missed opportunities. You may never get to be real players in the game of love if you don't trust yourselves. Nobody knows for sure if a relationship is going to last. How will you know though if you don't give your best effort? You can invent one hundred reasons to leave your lover. Find the right ones to make it work; you are closer than you think. You can at least say why you have doubts. It may not resolve your issues, but at least you know you gave it your best shot.

The *Critique* game asks you to be harder on problems than on one another. Remember, if you blast each other with negative energy, it is going to take that much more positive energy to counteract the damage. It is awkward to reprogram your mind. There is a tendency in a Cancer-Virgo romance to habitually repeat negative remarks. It can be hypnotic. You may be surprised at how you automatically negate one another. Train yourselves to talk without attacking or critiquing even though it is work—and more work! Imagine this, you are constructively learning how to communicate. Eliminating the "shoulds" and "oughts" from your remarks is a good start. Working together with a spirit of harmony doesn't happen in one day. It's a matter of small successes that accumulate into bigger ones. If you just show that you are trying to cut down on being critical, it will be a step in the right direction.

The Rainbow

Your Cancer-Virgo relationship can bring out your skill in making each other happy. The ability to learn from mistakes makes you both so strong. You need not try to be the perfect couple since perfection is an illusion. Go after the tremendous love and warmth awaiting you. Make your own rules as you proceed; cast away the ones that are too rigid. You are happier when you know that it is safe to trust your partner.

A Cancer man admires the exactness of a Virgo woman's thinking. She is precision in motion. Even her clothes fall into place with immaculate style. The Cancer man watches and listens carefully to see if this earthy woman is easily upset. He is surprised to learn that she can play as hard as she works. He appreciates the role models this woman has chosen; they are not so different from his own. The Cancer man wants to please the Virgo woman. He is drawn to her decisiveness but wonders if she is this way about romance. The male Cancer can relate to her need for a reliable partner. He hopes his fluctuating moods don't bother this high-strung, nervous woman. Her thoughts exhibit a mind that can run as fast as the fleetest of deer.

A Virgo woman is impressed with the Cancer man's intellectual thoroughness. She sees something in this lunar man that many miss: his eyes sparkle when he talks about his serious objectives. She detects a reservedness in him that pleases her. The female Virgo perceives this man to be a mix of extroversion and shyness. She hopes he can find the way to her heart. His practicality is comforting, and his imagination is inspiring. He expresses great loyalty to friends and family. She hopes her own connections with others will meet his approval. Her life is already packed with obligations. She doesn't want to feel this way toward him. The female Virgo delights to discover that her Cancer man is able to fend for himself.

A Cancer woman sees the Virgo man as a mirror image of herself in at least one respect: he is attentive to the little things about which he really cares. This attentiveness to small matters appeals to her. Her collectibles mean a lot to her. He acts like someone who will not laugh at this side of her. He seems responsible enough. She likes to hear him laugh because it reassures her that there is more to him than work. His readiness to face conflict makes her feel unusually secure. This lunar woman trusts the Virgo man instantly, which is unlike her. If only he won't find fault with her favorite escapes. She doesn't allow herself many, but no earthly soul had better mess with them!

A Virgo man treads softly on a Cancer woman's ideas. He senses immediately that this woman is easily hurt by his insights if they contradict her views too blatantly. This earthy man wants to be cared for by this nurturing woman. He wonders what she will demand in return. He thinks in terms of business when he should be thinking in terms of romance. He hopes she isn't as intuitive as he fears. There are certain thoughts he isn't prepared to share, including his life plans. His mind and heart begin to melt when she sends passionate love his way. This worker of workers is stopped in his tracks by the chance to romantically escape with this lunar woman. What he doesn't know is that she already has him pegged. Her plans can run circles around his any day of the week. He would be wise to look at her blueprint because it not only takes her where she needs to go but can take him further than his own plans.

You are in a relationship that spirals in beauty as it grows. You expose one another to greater worlds than you may see on your own. Each of you wants to experience the beauty of the other's world. Make the time for this to happen. Business will sometimes distract you from the happiness you could share. Your passion can explode and pull you into unpredictable directions. Hold on to each other's hand, and show your happiness when each of you reaches a new milestone. You can walk with an attitude that will never take no for an answer. You can accomplish great things when you feel united.

Cancer-Libra: The Plotters

Cancer + Libra = Hustle and Bustle

You bring out the doer in one another. On your own, you might be less energetic. Together you instill ambition in each other. The tendency to launch new projects is highlighted. You aren't going to back down from challenges when you believe in each other. Even your home may be a place where your creative drives are apparent. People like the way the two of you genuinely care about others. When mixed with the active perceptions of Libra, the emotional intensity of Cancer will leave few dull moments. As you share your wealth, your level of trust grows. You are probably at least a little possessive of your partner's attention.

Leaning Tower Game

The games played in your Cancer-Libra relationship center around unrealistic dependency needs, unresolved anger issues, and demanding attitudes. The *Leaning Tower* game will find one or the other of you off balance. You can't save your partner from every problem that comes along. Don't ask for so much that you totally drain each other. The tendency in this game is to try to either do too much or to ask for the impossible. Cancer will tire if people take more than it can give. The Crab's delicate emotions support a complicated psyche that needs a retreat to recharge its batteries. Libra's Achilles' heel is that its nervous system can burn out when this air sign exhausts itself by going far beyond the call of duty. When you forget your limits, you could get into trouble. Cancer is nurturing and may have trouble saying the magic word, "No."

Libra is so other-directed that it is easy to forget to monitor its energy reserves. Dependency needs are off center. You may avoid talking directly about how to achieve greater clarity.

Sweet and Sour Game

Cancer and Libra can cause quick mood changes in each other. In the *Sweet and Sour* game, you tend to go from a state of calmness to a condition of complete disruption without much notice. Why? If either one of you becomes angry, the other can quickly respond with the same emotion. This is the tricky thing about your relationship. You may become so tuned in to each other's thoughts and moods that it is easy to react long before anything is verbalized. Cancer can be protective but becomes upset if you don't follow its advice. Libra can offer wonderful wisdom but becomes miffed if you don't follow its prescriptions. In other words, you may be too attached to telling each other how to live. *Ouch!* This is not a good idea. You will rebel against control much like a cat that is told to stay off a favorite perch; it doesn't work! Your feelings will alter from sweetness to bitterness if you don't follow the old adage: "It is better to leave well enough alone."

Don't try to change your partner. Your demands would be like a lit match thrown at gasoline. You have a territorial agreement in your romance, but don't be surprised if it is still a secret. Cancer has an invisible dividing line between its world and that of Libra. The Crab can see this line. Libra can't! In contrast, Libra makes its boundaries fairly clear, but they are subject to change. Libra moves the boundaries to suit its needs. Libra can be driven by a compulsive need to be fair or to maintain equilibrium. If you combine invisible boundaries with changeable ones, it is downright mystical or confusing, isn't it? Blurry boundaries can create some strange feelings.

False Accusations Game

The *False Accusations* game comes your way if you resort to blame. Instead of really dealing with an issue, you blow off steam by defending your respective positions. This isn't so bad for short-term relationships, but if you go on and on like this, it doesn't bode well for the future. It takes a lot of power out of your passion to fight over who is right. If you don't compromise, you will battle into the fifteenth round. Even heavyweights eventually get tired. Fighting drains fun and romance from your relationship. It's not easy to take responsibility for a problem. There isn't anything wrong with getting angry to make a point, but it makes it harder to settle a dispute if you refuse to cool down. Your minds are locked into attack mode. If you refuse to compromise, you won't be able to talk through problems.

Strategies

How can you sail away from these Cancer-Libra games? The *Leaning Tower* game asks you to not go overboard in your demands. Even the strongest of people need a break. It's a good idea for your partner to receive as well as provide support. If one or both of you is going through a challenging time, create rewards to keep you both content. You may need to accept that your lover doesn't require you to be the saving grace in his or her life. Being supportive doesn't mean giving up all of your emotional and physical resources. Put your business sense to work to balance out your emotions. You can become too hooked on each other's dependency instincts. You may block each other's need for independence by coming to the rescue too quickly. Use your common sense when you come to each other's aid.

In the *Sweet and Sour* game, you need only be aware of boundaries. You will become less resentful if you don't try to change each other. The anger you feel arises from your desire to be left alone. You will find more sweetness when you communicate clearly. When you don't listen, moods are apt to intensify. The fact that you can read each other's temperaments is a good thing. It is a problem when you overidentify with what your partner feels. You lose the objectivity you need. An emotional roller coaster is less likely when you are able to stay mentally clear. Things sour when you become lost in each other's confusion. You need to be aware of when you enter each other's air space too deeply. Pulling out for breathing room helps to maintain perspective.

The *False Accusations* game is one in which you must learn how to negotiate. Grudges will keep coming back to haunt you. Blame is never constructive. You must somehow realize that winning an argument while losing each other might not be the best choice. Watery Cancer needs time to get over bruised feelings. Libra desires a chance to catch its breath before becoming calm and rational again. You may be better off going out socially and trying to work through this when you both are in the right mental space. Some hidden anger may have snuck up on you that needs to be expressed. An old issue from days ago may cause one or both of you to overreact to a present circumstance. The sooner you can talk about it, the better.

The Rainbow

Your Cancer-Libra relationship is lively. Neither of you enjoys being still for too long. You are inspired by an anxious spirit to grow. You bring out a "take charge" attitude in each other. Staying out of each other's leadership roles may be smart. Finding ways to support one another's key ambitions makes you strong allies.

A Cancer man is powerfully attracted to the Libra woman's smooth handling of human relations. She shows sensitivity with a remarkable sense of ease. She is hard to get out of his mind. He likes the way the Libra woman makes him feel. His confidence rises thanks to her wonderfully radiant attention. He thinks they make great music together. He hopes she shares the passion that he feels in his heart. He wants to be assertive but doesn't want to be too bold, yet being too reserved isn't getting the job done either. This Venusian woman smiles when he speaks of romance and places to go that enliven her spirit. He is getting the message!

A Libra woman explores the face of the Cancer man carefully; he looks as captivating as the man in the Moon. She is perplexed when he seems to disappear behind his moods. Perhaps he is taking an excursion into his introspective thoughts. When he returns, he seems refreshed. "Oh, well," she sighs to herself, "at least he is different from so many others I have known." She encourages him to be bold. She loves affection but needs a decisive partner. Her mind is already filled with opposites that press her for a decision. This lunar man may want a lot of emotional support from her. She will give it, but he had better be good at reciprocating. He is mysterious, but the security she feels when near him is endearing.

A Cancer woman finds the Libra man alluring. His voice is smooth and well cultured, and his speech has a flowing rhythm. Even when he acts indecisively, it is done with careful consideration of varying points of view. His opinions about justice and truth impress her. She hopes her strong feelings won't cause anxiety. She doesn't want to disturb his delicate balance. She wonders whether her need for a sensitive partner is now being realized. The female Cancer's emotions and caring reach out well beyond a partner. She hopes this will not bother her Libran lover. His mind is stimulating and awakens her own creative thoughts. She senses his inner restlessness, which is not so different from her own. She calls upon her intuition in the hope her clearest mind agrees with her emotions; her heart wants to race to this Venusian man.

Let the Games Begin

The Libra man is enthralled with the Cancer woman. She has emotions that penetrate his well-designed intellect. It gets dry to live so much in the head. He is reluctant to let go to his own feelings at first. She is a boost to his ego because she sees good in him even when he doesn't. She brings out his desire for unbridled passion. Maybe it's the way she challenges him to let go of his uncertainty. Perhaps it is because she steps beyond her own fears to open up her world to him. She cares about so many things, yet she still manages to see the real him. He knows that this can't always be reality but longs for the moments when this lunar woman casts her sea-like eyes upon him with waves of deep inner knowledge. He is delighted that she wants to taste the good life as much as he does.

Your relationship is one of abundance. When you trust your shared vision of abundant potential, you are on the right path. Don't give in to more limited perceptions that lead you to doubt your gifts. Cancer has the inner drive to make the best out of a situation that many would say is useless. Libra can show remarkable mental prowess when the going is tough. You make a formidable couple. Romance blossoms when you focus on the love you want to embrace in each other. Nothing can take away what you feel for each other when you truly take the time to understand each other's world.

Cancer-Scorpio: The Secretive Ones

Cancer + Scorpio = You Really Got a Hold on Me

These two signs can become quite attached to each other—like two peas in a pod. Two water signs can form deep, strong ties. Cancer has a need for family, roots, and deep emotional expression. Scorpio can create a strong bond with those whom it loves and admires. Each sign has a desire to protect loved ones. Together, the two can create a fortress of wealth and passion. When each allows the other to settle into the roles that work best, this is an awesome combination. A "stick together" ideology is at the forefront of your romance. You can intuitively know how to work together. It can seem as though your relationship is sealed with permanent glue.

Vindictive Venom Game

The games played in your Cancer-Scorpio relationship revolve around unexpressed anger, confusion about each other's emotions, and not giving each other enough space. The *Vindictive Venom* game plays off your tendency to hold on to your anger. Cancer is moody but not necessarily forthright in letting out its anger. Scorpio isn't much better. The Scorpion has a highly refined repression mechanism that can file anger deeply away in its subconscious. Two water signs can display a peculiar way of being angry at each other. It might even be a nonverbal war. This can go on for hours, days, and even weeks. The emotional intensity created by holding back can explode when you least expect it. It isn't easy to feel love when you hold on to this type of anger. Repressed anger tends to poison feelings of closeness. Communication is tainted with confusion. Anger is a strong emotion—as powerful as a bullet—and can tear a hole through your happiness. Your sex life is probably not as lively and can shut down until this is resolved. One or both of you may be frustrated with your own life goals or creative expression rather than upset with your partner. Discontentment with yourself can be turned on your lover. Whatever the reason, the bottom line is that this conduct deletes your love a little more every day.

Too Close for Comfort Game

Privacy is a key need for both of you. As a couple or as individuals, time alone is good for you. When you crowd each other too much, the *Too Close for Comfort* game becomes evident. How do you recognize it? When you feel resentful because you don't get any time to breathe on your own, you will know this game is cooking. Cancer and Scorpio become short-fused when getting little down time from everyone's demands. You each need a retreat. If you can't escape for short intervals, your moods kick in. If you don't get the space required, you are h—I mean, unpleasant, to live with. The patience a water sign can demonstrate is missing when there is not enough self-nurturing. Surrendering your personal goals to please your partner will backfire. You both need to strut your own talents. Passion is lessened when you don't test the deeper waters of your own intuitive hunches. Your attachment to one another can be so strong that it is challenging to wean one another away for even short intervals. Underlying insecurity could make you extra possessive.

Waterlogged Game

This one is just what it sounds like. In the *Waterlogged* game, you flood each other with feelings to the exclusion of grounded thinking. The result is that you float with no sense of direction. The problem-solving capacity of your two signs is probably watered down with worry. If you get your partner pulled into your own problems, you may both go under. It's a fine line between receiving a life preserver of help and pulling down the one trying to save you. Emotions can't help but be strong in a water-water relationship like this one. It is confusing when clear thinking eludes you. Panic makes matters worse. Usually this game is the trickiest when you don't take the time to think through your options. You will keep trying to force a path that is as impossible as moving through a glacier, and that's rough!

Strategies

How can you get through these Cancer-Scorpio games? In the *Vindictive Venom* game, you need to learn how to say what is on your mind. When your feelings are hurt, it's better for you to react in the moment or not too many minutes down the road. The confrontation you may fear is worth facing. Why? You will find that releasing your anger opens up avenues of communication. Attempting to talk while holding on to unspoken anger is like trying to trudge through a swamp. Neither of you is comfortable. The longer you delay getting your true feelings out in the open, the greater the chance for a big mess. With practice, you can talk more spontaneously. Expressing negative emotions can get easier. The main challenge is to move past the fear of doing so. Don't be so scared. To water signs like yourselves, coming out from your favorite hiding places is testy. Your partner will find it simpler to converse with you when hearing the truth. It may be unpleasant to listen to your partner's reaction to your actions. You will enjoy increased intimacy when you know you can get right to the point. Getting a water sign to talk can be harder than prying open a rusted old paint can. Loosen up. When you first try to converse more directly, it may be accompanied by a flood of tears, a few screams, and thrown dishes. It has to start somewhere, doesn't it?

The *Too Close for Comfort* game asks you to give each other the space to stay in touch with your own unique paths. Why is this important? It energizes the willingness to give generously to your relationship. A tired spirit can only show so much enthusiasm. Cancer and Scorpio both need time to process emotions. Cancer and Scorpio can benefit from a retreat. Each of you soaks up a lot of energy from people. It is a good idea to have your own sanctuary in which you can feel insulated from the woes of the world. Take turns as needed. If you feel really attached to your partner, that's fine. Love can be possessive. Love also needs to know when to let go and let be. You do wonders for each other when you show enough trust that your partner can follow the call to pursue a personal dream. Freedom can do odd things to your relationship. It makes you desire each other's company that much more. That's hard to believe, but try it. You will like it. Rather than having to sneak conspicuously to pursue your personal interests, encourage openness in sharing your aspirations. It enriches your ties to each other.

You may not even know that the *Waterlogged* game has you in its jaws until you are halfway down to its stomach. Water signs can get lost in denial. You can get so fogged by one another's emotional chutzpa that you lose sight of where you are going. If a major personal goal or a key shared one feels like it is sinking, you will then become aware that the boat is taking in too much water. This is an exercise in frustration, and you may feel that it is futile to try to formulate a plan. You may need to each work on your own part of the blueprint and then meet. Putting your heads together at this point might get you moving.

You can't change the fact that you are water signs, but you can alter the way you reach decisions. You might need to discipline your minds to stay on the topic you are discussing. You may have to take a step back to calm down in order to diffuse mental confusion. You could easily escalate the emotional intensity in a conversation. Try to stay detached enough to take care of business.

The Rainbow

Your Cancer-Scorpio relationship is enlivened by your vivid imagination. The two of you can stretch for the sky and actually reach it! The passion you bring to each other is immense. You may never have been loved like this before. Strong loyalty is at the root of your romance. When one suffers, the other can't help but identify with the pain. Your willingness to be there for each other whether the chips are up or down keeps you mutually devoted. Water signs can plunge into the deepest recesses of each other's thoughts and feelings. Your attachment can be the result of appreciating that someone knows you yet accepts the way you are—not an easy person to find in the world!

A Cancer man is drawn to the Scorpio woman's sensuality. She symbolizes the romantic myth of his imagination. His inner world is usually more liberated than his outer one. He likes the way this woman dazzles his wild side. It isn't that she is necessarily a wilder spirit than he is, but a primordial soul that fears no taboos lies in her subconscious. This lunar man would love for her to reveal the secrets she possesses. Then again, he wonders if he can deal with such a force. He quickly transfers his attention to more mundane matters. He likes the way this Plutonian woman manages money and time. His own sense of security jives with the common sense of this Scorpio woman. He wants to explore the potential to be free-spirited lovers. He senses with his own intuition that she shares his way of thinking.

When the Scorpio woman looks at the Cancer man, she sees a man whose feelings go right to the bone. It's not that he shows sensitivity. She reads these things like an avid book reader who hungrily skips ahead to the next chapter. Her radar detects a man with heartfelt ideas. She hopes he will not be possessive because she needs time to herself. Privacy is her birthright, and she values this more than many. Her love for him can grow if he isn't too demanding. She wonders if he can make her feel materially and emotionally secure. She doesn't want him to try to make her feel whole. This feminine woman has already turned away from those who want to own her. She knows that she borders on obsession with a man like this whose eyes are as bright as the full Moon. She doesn't see much harm in loving this Cancer man. After all, he seems as anxious as she to find a soul mate, and he needs to be held close but without too many strings attached.

A Scorpio man is awed by the Cancer woman. She listens to his sarcasm with emotion but glides softly away into the night of her innermost feelings. This Plutonian man wonders where her mind has drifted as he gazes into her expressive eyes. He is even more taken aback when he tries to overwhelm her with his powerful charisma. She digests the mind games and responds with darting quickness that cuts through to his solar plexus. Wow! He isn't used to this type of exchange. He loves mystery but usually prefers to be the object of someone else's curiosity. This Scorpio man has met his match in the Cancer woman. He isn't sure how to drop his guard with this seemingly harmless woman. Why is he so afraid? Fear in a strange way makes him want to come closer. This suspicious man with a good business head and a heart full of pleasure and pain is ready to go near the cliff's edge to seek out this lunar woman. He hopes she doesn't want to move too fast in matters of the heart. You see, he likes to slowly do a show-and-tell when it comes to feelings.

The Cancer woman approaches the Scorpio man with caution. The Crab won't come out of the safety of her shell for just anyone. She is not so much worried about the Pluto man's probing eyes as she is about her own desire to feel hidden. The lunar woman enjoys the invisibility of her feelings. She often lets her intuition be her guide in dealing with the past, present, and future. She can't help wondering if life might not be more fun with the likes of this Scorpio gent. He looks a little serious but has an aura of someone that isn't afraid to ask life for exactly what he wants. The Cancer woman muses that his willpower combined with her own would make them a feisty and passionate duo!

You have a relationship before you or surrounding you that speaks to your hearts as well as your minds. Cancer and Scorpio take each other into the deepest of the feeling waters. You can lift one another to the highest plateaus through your trust. You easily capture the imagination within your partner because it is so similar. Your differences will stir you to talk and negotiate. Use the wisdom in your heart as much as your head. The truth lies somewhere in between. You can be the greatest of friends and can figure out how to be the greatest of lovers.

Cancer-Sagittarius: The Restless Spirits

Cancer + Sagittarius = Love of Wide Open Spaces

The Crab and the Archer are a strange mix. The caution of watery Cancer sensitizes the blunt awareness of fiery Sagittarius. The Archer's self-confidence inspires the Crab to show some of its own. The two of you see rather quickly that the key to getting along is to put up with differences. At first glance, Cancer's need for a clear definition of home seems to conflict with the adventurous streak embedded deep in the soul of Sagittarius. Yet Cancer can tire of life on the home front! The Crab can enjoy packing its bags as much as the bohemian Archer. People can be surprised to learn that Sagittarius may grow weary of life on the road or of moving from one place to another. The Archer can seek a more stable place to hang its bow and arrows. Both signs often enjoy people. Cancer is more private though still good in dealing with the public. These two signs can learn to speak the same language.

Get Off My Cloud Game

The games played in your Cancer-Sagittarius relationship are associated with not honoring each other's right to make choices, jumping to erroneous conclusions, and not reasoning logically. The *Get Off My Cloud* game occurs because you may be annoyed with your partner's excessive criticism of your pet ideas. Cancer can react moodily. Sagittarius can throw up its arms in disgust. You each detest being discounted in this manner. You may not take the time to understand why your lover needs to pursue certain goals. If you don't communicate much about your personal ambitions, there may be a tendency in your partner to take them too lightly. Even if you feel you are following each other's plans, there is a temptation to evaluate in a Cancer-Sagittarius relationship. When you don't honor the freedom to determine your own paths, tension results. Criticism concerning your individual paths makes shared projects more difficult to perform.

You each need to feel you have a sacred domain that no one can enter uninvited. In this case, when you say the wrong thing, two is a crowd!

Hasty Judgment Game

Cancer can be quick to draw conclusions. Sagittarius does this in a matter-of-fact way. The two of you may tire of the other's not getting all of the facts before the jury has returned as in the *Hasty Judgment* game. Judgments are one thing. Holding on to them is another. The latter is worse because the same old problems keep coming between you. The love you want can be derailed by contempt. You tend to speed up each other's reactions in this game. The challenge is to realize when you are heading down the wrong highway. If you can't hear what your partner is saying, it is next to impossible to accurately perceive information and can lead to reaching erroneous conclusions. If you stubbornly hold on to your old perceptions even in light of new evidence, trouble is brewing. It can be hard for the Crab and the Archer to compromise because each wants the other to go first. You can sit in separate rooms endlessly. Time can be wasted by trying to wait this one out.

Magic Carpet Ride Game

You can be turned on by the imagination you ignite in one another. Imagination is a good thing, but when your minds influence each other to chase illusions, the *Magic Carpet Ride* game visits. Cancer's intuition, combined with the idealism of Sagittarius, can take you to far-reaching destinations. Be sure you do some reality testing as that is what is deficient in this game. You can talk each other into buying a swamp if you leave out logic. The excitement and enthusiasm that your signs can display, especially in combination, requires solid business sense to keep you in check. Twenty-twenty hindsight might find you feeling foolish. You can talk each other out of good decisions as well. An occasional inability to focus may reveal that you are not taking advantage of an opportunity. You might become disillusioned or angry with your partner if his or her reasoning spaces you out. Too much of a good thing could dilute your focusing ability so much that you can't get your main objectives accomplished.

The Magic of Signmates

Strategies

How can you get around these Cancer-Sagittarius games? To counteract the *Get Off My Cloud* game, you need to be aware of when you offer unsolicited advice. It is not endearing to hear negative input or other comments if you really don't want the information. You may need a ground rule or two regarding a "hands off" policy in certain areas. It is better to be supportive of your partner's goals. You want the same reception for your own ideas. Each of you is livelier anyway when you call your own shots in your favorite areas. It keeps you young at heart. You feel older than your years when fending off each other. With freedom comes responsibility. You will win each other's admiration when you show approval for unique thinking. It may be wise to let one another know just how much you need to follow a particular idea through to the end.

The *Hasty Judgment* game can find reconciliation through your willingness to be patient with one another. Listening is a great asset. As a water sign, Cancer usually makes a better natural listener than Sagittarius, though when the Crab is out of sorts, its hearing isn't as good. When Sagittarius' imagination is captured, it makes a better listener. It takes practice to get on the same page, and you have to pay attention. It takes discipline to slow down the mind's reaction time. The best policy is probably to say nothing when in doubt. Better yet, give your partner the benefit of the doubt! Talk things out before making assumptions. Jumping to the wrong conclusions only leads to the need for hasty fixes. Talking is simple, but taking the time to do so is challenging. Cancer can be in a hurry to finish a busy schedule. Sagittarius, the fiery, high-spirited adventurer, is just on the move.

The *Magic Carpet Ride* game reveals your propensity to get lost in an idealized version of the truth. You shouldn't knock imagination; after all, it can lead you to the discovery of new talents. When you wear this hat instead of the business one, you can get in over your head. Cancer can be convinced to try almost anything by a fast-talking Sagittarius. It's possible Sagittarius can be sold on an idea by the emotional pitch of Cancer. When you both are along for the same ride, look out! It had better be a reality-based strategy. You are not going to be thinking kind thoughts about one another if you go far out of your way for nothing. Adopting a sound plan may help you see through the illusion in front of you. Make sure you don't go way over budget to chase a false dream since it isn't going to fulfill your lives. You can pool your imaginative power together to do great things. Slow down and look with clear vision before taking a big leap.

The Rainbow

Your Cancer-Sagittarius relationship can take you to new vistas. There can be great joy in acting out your most energetic impulses. You are likely to lift each other right out of your comfort zones. Your hearts live in different time zones, but careful Cancer can be stimulated to dive into a lover's adventure as much as nomadic Sagittarius may be swayed to settle into a more predictable everyday existence. You can spur each other to express your greatest creative potential. When you help each other accent the positive, you blossom into the most passionate of lovers. The reliability you show to each other will keep you close. You will encourage each other not to worry about the rules of others. When you make fair rules for one another, life seems plentiful. If you keep an open mind to various translations of truth, you will be freer in spirit and more adaptable to each other's changes. You can delight in watching your love grow from a small seed to the tallest of trees with branches denoting your wealth on all levels.

A Cancer man sees many facets in the Sagittarius woman. She walks with a step that doesn't match conventional logic. Her appearance can change to fit many different social scenarios. Her humor shows a deep understanding of life's ironies. The male Cancer wants to let go to her vision but can't help thinking he may be too attached to his own past. (He has followed certain ideas in order not to lose his way.) He is comforted by the knowledge that she can understand his reality. She seems to process his comments as she talks and listens. His processing is on time delay. She doesn't seem to notice and goes right on talking. The lunar man loves this light-hearted woman. He observes that her thoughts can be as perceptive as a lawyer's and as deep as a philosopher's. In the next instant, she may dart out to meet friends at a museum. The Crab looks forward to seeing this woman with the inviting smile again. He needs to be around someone with such an upbeat attitude.

A Sagittarius woman finds the Cancer man to be worthy of study. He has an interesting way of expressing himself. She sees emotion in his face though he doesn't talk with much feeling. She perceives his awareness through his attentiveness. He truly *sees* her. Not many do. She isn't really sure what he wants from her. Maybe he craves her attention. He seems so lonely socially but at ease with his thoughts. This contradiction appeals to her curious mind even though she doesn't usually like complicated people. The lunar man possesses a secret deep within of which even he may not be aware. The Sagittarius woman perceives it; his secret is the power of his intuition to see the truth.

She wonders if he runs and hides from this side of himself. She wouldn't really blame him though she hopes he loves this side of himself because it is more beautiful than all of his possessions. His feelings come through to her even when he is determined to be coolly logical. She doesn't know why he is at ease with her but likes the way he can't hold back. She will explore love with him if he is up to it.

A Cancer woman is suspicious of the Archer's boldness. "He is certainly not from my planet," she muses. This wanderer makes her wonder if he is always so confident. Even when he is unsure of himself, he doesn't look timid. He talks a lot about himself. She observes that the Sagittarius man is more interested in her dreams and hopes than in her views about reality. This lunar woman's practical thinking questions whether she would grow tired of such a restless rogue. Even in a coat and tie, he seems ready to hitch a cross-country ride in a heartbeat or to jump a train just for the experience. She knows there is no way to tame this wild being, but this side of him interests her because he is an exciting lover. He is exhilarating not only in the physical realm but in the world of ideas as well, where he seems to have many connections. He is a creative freelancer who can undermine her intellectual comfort zones. Her emotions jump into high gear when he is near. The lunar woman wants to leave the safety of the shore and ride the high seas with this Sagittarius adventurer.

The Sagittarius man perceives the Cancer woman to be solid as a rock. She can be extremely pragmatic yet can roam with him to worlds that are only in storybooks. The Archer isn't sure if he understands this lunar woman's logic. He loves her penetrating emotional intensity that leads her to master anything she sets her mind to. He is startled by the thought of her really getting to know him. He laughs off this idea with a shrug of his shoulders. His own world is subject to change without any notice. He wonders if she can accept this or not. No matter. He wants to learn the secret of this feminine spirit's intuitive ways. He doesn't realize that this may take years rather than a mere matter of hours. Her feelings for him make her hard to get out of his mind. This haunting woman's face is more expressive than the Moon. He still can't figure out what he likes most about her. Is it her sensible outlook, the feelings that wrap around him, or the unpredictability that could be in their future? He concludes that all of the above are just fine.

Cancer and Sagittarius are cut from very different molds, but these signs meet in a quest for greater self-understanding. Cancer seeks understanding through emotional force. Sagittarius utilizes idealism to forge a path ahead. You are not so unlike one another when you see through the illusions that come between you. The way you go about respecting your lover's choices says much about your level of understanding. Your destinations are not necessarily the only matter of relevance. Enjoy the journey, which usually lasts longer than the time spent celebrating milestones. You become strong when you empower each other's dreams. You are a spontaneous couple who needs high energy outlets to keep you revitalized.

Cancer-Capricorn: The Protective Ones

Cancer + Capricorn = Reality-based Action

This is a great combination for putting ideas into a winning formula. These signs are opposites in the zodiac. Cancer supplies a force of feeling that Capricorn doesn't contact spontaneously. Capricorn offers down-to-earth pragmatism that Cancer doesn't have readily available. A little of each rubs off onto the other when involved romantically. When the two signs can get their roles in alignment, they are precision in motion. Each can accomplish much. Capricorn is usually born with at least one foot in the world of ambition. Cancer can fool people into thinking it lacks this same determination, but the Crab can race through a door of opportunity as fast as any sign. Defining the relationship in such a way that each feels appreciated is a way to ensure success.

Parent Game

The games played in your Cancer-Capricorn relationship are associated with controlling behavior, a lack of affection, and power struggles. The *Parent* game occurs if the two of you try to act like a mother or father toward the other. This is expressed as an "I know what's better for you" attitude. When one of you thinks you know more than the other, it can be a turnoff. Neither of you appreciates having your partner undermine your authority. Perhaps each of you likes to take care of others. Be sure you don't go too far with this regarding one another. Cancer is the nurturer or caretaker. Capricorn can be the provider. You may even appear to be the breadwinner to others. Trouble brews when you don't respect each other's leadership ability. The two of you become irritable when you doubt each other's capacity to take responsibility.

Conditional Love Game

When there is a motive behind your display of affection, you could be a half-step away from playing the *Conditional Love* game. An "if you will do this, I can love you" line of thinking governs your actions. Cancer and Capricorn can act like this as a result of fear. The Crab can be so afraid that its delicate feelings will be hurt that it is inclined to wait until someone shows his or her harmlessness beyond a shadow of a doubt. Capricorn can stay quite guarded behind a wait-and-see mentality. Neither of these tendencies is necessarily wrong. It could be that bad experiences with previous lovers prompts your caution. It may be due to an unresolved injury in your current relationship from which one or both of you need time to heal. This becomes a game when it is a deep-seated behavior that constantly comes up. It is difficult to establish trust when you keep each other at an arm's distance. Asking for proof that you are loved on a continuous basis will grow old. Cancer becomes numb if treated in this manner for extended time periods. Capricorn tends to become absorbed in other interests in the face of rejection. Defining your commitment is confusing if you are not always sure just when this shadow will slip in between the light you seek in your lover.

I Shall Not Be Ruled Game

Taking a rigid stand on issues might result in the *I Shall Not Be Ruled* game. You make a strong statement to each other, maybe even nonverbally, that sends the message: "Don't mess with me." The lack of respect for each other's power is the main cause of this game. You can only challenge your partner's ideas so much. If you overstep your bounds, a war of wills sets in. Cancer is assumed to be more adaptable than Capricorn, yet when romantically involved with the Goat, the Crab can be as hard to pry out of its shell as dry cement. A hurt Crab is definitely an angry Crab, which can turn into a stubborn Crab. Capricorn is certainly prone to stubbornness if its rules are questioned. The Goat follows well-defined thinking because this is what insulates its sense of security. Challenging Capricorn's authority brings out its huffiness eventually to the point of obstinacy. You both are strong in your own ways. Somehow your wills have become tangled. How you untangle yourselves can either be negotiated smoothly or filled with resentment and anger. A refusal to adopt a win-win solution keeps the game going. Is anybody having fun yet?

Strategies

How can you avoid playing the Cancer-Capricorn games? In the *Parent* game, you need to resist the urge to act as a mother or father toward your partner. When you treat your partner as an equal, it brings great rewards. Your dependency needs will be more in balance. If you act like a parent, it encourages too much dependence. You may be enabling actions that are not in the best interest of the relationship. You will both be happier when you assume a fair share of responsibility. You may be repeating your parents' patterns. It is better to see your relationship as a new playing field without having to play by a previous set of rules. Create an atmosphere that truly reflects who you are in the present. Encourage each other to exert your independence because this leads to greater passion and creative power. You will rejoice in the evolving beauty of your romance when you reject limiting roles.

The *Conditional Love* game takes courage and faith to leave behind. Fear makes anyone reluctant to trust openly. You need to eventually take the risk of loving without an "if" clause. Setting conditions blocks the spontaneity you want to express. The heart runs on only half of its cylinders, and engines in this condition have little power. The passion you could create together is lessened by this game. You will hold back your love if it takes bargaining to receive love. A more flowing interaction is what you need. You must talk about how this makes you feel. The two of you have to see the real rewards reaped when you act out of love rather than from fear. When you doubt your partner, you are not really ready to receive or give. Somehow, you must find faith in yourself and in each other. It probably won't happen in one night. If you make it a shared project, open to discussion, the chances are better that you will get there!

The *I Shall Not Be Ruled* game is one in which the two of you need to exert greater flexibility. Old habits are hard to change. Perhaps habitual behavior developed prior to the relationship or in the relationship has become deeply entrenched. If it has, you will need to be patient. The key thing is that you even try to reverse the game. If you can convince your partner that you are *trying* to grow, it helps. When you hold on to the old baggage, it hurts. It's that simple or complicated, depending on how you perceive your situation. The resistance you send toward each other is caused by convoluted power instincts. This great energy, if channeled away from the two of you and directed at creative pursuits, is awesome! Just think about how much more gusto you will have for individual or joint projects! You are carrying a weight of worry and disgust. Let go of it, and your romance will lighten up and kick into high gear. You will want to enjoy life together when you conquer this game.

The Rainbow

Your Cancer-Capricorn relationship promises happiness when you accept the commitment before you. You both are more at ease when you know you can relax with each other. The belief you show in one another is the catalyst for your love. Working together flows smoothly when you recognize the talent each of you possesses. The support you receive adds to your self-confidence. Cancer likes to know that it can depend on reliable Capricorn. Capricorn finds reassurance in knowing it can trust emotionally centered Cancer. Since you are opposite signs, you will mirror many fine qualities in each other and even a shortcoming or two. Cancer is fond of creating a stable home atmosphere that supports its work in the world. Capricorn puts a monumental focus on its ambitions but desires a stable home that offers some degree of escape from the world. You complement the inner and outer natures of each other rather well.

A Cancer man wants to see the Capricorn woman as someone strong and reliable. He needs stability in a partner to balance his intense emotional turmoil. His feelings, even when denied, still manage to make their presence known. The Capricorn woman appears to be stoic to the lunar man. Then again, she can smile with stress-free confidence. He wonders how she does this. She has a dry wit and speaks from experience, yet she can shift into a more fun-loving spirit. He likes this variable side of her since his own moods are as changeable as the phases of the Moon. She seems to be as reluctant as he is to rush into love. Will they ever really make a first move? He tries to muster up the courage to make it clear that he wants to know her better. His instincts tell him she can be demanding, but so can he. This is a woman that any matchmaker would recommend for him. The Cancer man wants to touch the heart of this stately woman.

The Capricorn woman perceives that the Cancer man has great insights into her outer world. She wonders if he will take the time to understand her feelings. The Saturnian woman's many emotions aren't always expressed in the midst of other people's demands on her. She knows her own strength but still can doubt her ability. She has proven her leadership ability over and over again, but not too many people acknowledge it. She wants this sensitive man to care about her, not out of need but for affirmation. She longs for an ambitious partner with a giving heart. Her beliefs don't seem so different from his. She hopes their values will overlap so they will get to know one another deeply. Few know about her idealism. She keeps much of this to herself. The lunar man seems to sense her dreams. She hopes he will fulfill at least one of them.

The Cancer woman is intrigued by what drives a Capricorn man. Is it ambition? Might it be a deep desire to prove that others are wrong about him? She wishes he would pursue her with such vigor. This Saturnian man seems so serious even when he is having fun. Time is his constant companion. He can't surrender his need for a schedule. The lunar woman's instincts warn her that she better stand her ground against this man's "tower of strength" persona, yet he has a look in his face that says to her: "Please find my vulnerability." She wishes he could relinquish control even for a minute. Wow! She believes she just saw an opening; he dropped his guard; his heart is passionate after all. The lunar woman has a way of opening up a Capricorn man that borders on magic. Her penetrating intuition breaks down the clouds that camouflage his feelings. He really feels strongly, that is, if you can help him refocus. She admires the capability and devotion to excellence this man displays. Her own enthusiasm for putting her best into what she loves is evident.

The Capricorn man is attracted to the Cancer woman's business sense. She is playful but with a similar instinct for the bottom line. She is a good judge of how to combine work and play. Her youthful laughter touches this reserved man. The Capricorn man loves to laugh wholeheartedly but doesn't always take the time to exhibit his sense of humor. The Cancer woman somehow makes him pause long enough to enjoy magical moments. The Saturnian man's identity is bound to his work. He takes great pride in acting responsibly. He hates to lose because it makes him feel inadequate. He carries a weight upon his shoulders that might crush others. He senses that the Cancer woman sees his seriousness and hopes she will not be turned off by it. She has touched the waters of his emotions that few ever reach. His heart is full of great passion and feeling, and she opens his heart as he falls hopelessly in love. He hates to lose control, but maybe, just this once, it's okay.

In a Cancer-Capricorn relationship, two people fall more deeply in love with the passage of time. The very reasons that brought you together are only the icing on the cake. A deep bond can develop. Your allegiance to certain shared beliefs may sustain you through whatever befalls you. Your business know-how will seldom betray you. Your hearts warm with the faith you stimulate in each other. You make your relationship a celebration when you give to each other freely. There is little separating you when you know that you have such a loving soul in your universe.

Cancer-Aquarius: The Hot-wired Ones

Cancer + Aquarius = Surprise, Surprise

These are two very different signs that get a kick out of playing with each other's minds. Cancer perceives reality through a myriad of emotions. Aquarius' thoughts are filtered through a kaleidoscope of impulses. Aquarius' emotions are conveniently pushed to the side so that feelings won't get in the way of its incredible brain power. Cancer doesn't have this luxury unless the Crab can deny its feelings. This is hard to do when airy Aquarius pokes around and jabs sensitive areas. The Crab enjoys taking an unexpected twist or two in front of Aquarius. Why? To make Aquarius think twice before mistaking the Crab's processing time as the lack of reasoning ability. Cancer and Aquarius reach the same conclusions through distinctly unique perspectives. Cancer spurs Aquarius to respond from the heart. Aquarius stimulates Cancer to think more objectively. Both can appreciate the home. Cancer wants warmth while Aquarius needs a place with walls to bounce off its ideas. This is a sign combination that can learn to appreciate differences and discover common ground.

Closeness Versus Distance Game

The games in your Cancer-Aquarius relationship center around inconsistent levels of intimacy, irresponsibility, and emotional turmoil. Cancer and Aquarius can dance around intimacy, vacillating between a romantic "head on the shoulder" slow dance and a wildly individualistic tango. When you erratically vacillate between emotional closeness and distance, you are indulging in the *Closeness Versus Distance* game. Cancer will resist closeness to preserve a sense of privacy. Aquarius emphatically desires breathing room. The trouble comes when one of you is ready for intimacy and the other wants space. You face a dilemma when fear keeps you from drawing into each other's feelings. Cancer retreats into its shell while Aquarius hides behind a cool and detached persona. It's okay to regulate closeness and freedom. Most couples do this to some extent, but you may have a problem in balancing the two. Emotional upheavals can throw you into a tailspin. Cyclones might come when least expected (they usually do). Intense emotional explosions result when you run away. If you stay away too long, you feel like distant strangers—like two tourists trading casual observations. If you remain too close for too long, either one of you may demand some time alone. The inability to talk logically about this game is why it comes like a thief in the night, upsetting your equilibrium.

Broken Promises Game

When you don't follow through on commitments, the *Broken Promises* game can result. It can be disturbing if one of you breaks an appointment at the last minute, and it's equally upsetting when the other doesn't show up for an event. Your sense of trust suffers if you keep disappointing one another. Cancer can be busy and overextended, causing this sign to miss appointments. Aquarius has been known to change its priorities at the last second. You are left with a frazzled partner, who wonders when you can be relied upon. It will be annoying if you don't put each other first some of the time. Your schedules may be such that the two of you can't ever catch your breath. When you lose sight of your partner, it isn't endearing.

Emotional Roller Coaster Ride Game

Cancer has strong emotions as surely as the sea has waves. Aquarius has a high-strung nervous system as certainly as electricity has voltage. Put these two facts together, and is it surprising that the *Emotional Roller Coaster* game exists? You can find it exhilarating to be together. On the other hand, it might be aggravating. Life isn't fun when you become drained by too much unpredictability. Your emotional highs and lows can reach such great extremes that it is nearly impossible to find a sense of balance. You may not know whether you are coming or going. You may have a nebulous sense of how to work together. Cancer can't put up with constant emotional upheaval. Aquarius becomes as mad as can be when led on a wild goose chase. Both grow weary of not seeing the results of actions. It will seem challenging to accomplish anything. You are working *against* rather than *with* one another.

Strategies

How can you fly above these Cancer-Aquarius games? The *Closeness Versus Distance* game requires you to learn how to talk more consistently. The more you do this, the less likely it is that you will run. Cooperation is needed for a couple to learn each other's requirements. Study your partner's patterns. You can make any rules you like. Some people even schedule time together and apart in order to train themselves how to do this more naturally. Cancer needs space to wring out the emotional energy picked up from the world; Aquarius is so overly stimulated by the environment that a retreat calms its mind, so you both could use time apart. It seems to make the time spent together more useful. Cancer and Aquarius do not adjust to each other's timetables easily. Growing accustomed to one another's schedules is challenging. Your tastes in certain areas will not be the same. Appreciation of each other's unique qualities eases tension. When you don't feel that you have to fight to preserve your own unique goals, you may experience greater closeness. Cancer warms up to Aquarius when insights are shared and interest is shown in joint goals. Aquarius is more likely to pull close when receiving the support requested.

The *Broken Promises* game doesn't take much to put it on the right path. Each of you only needs to concentrate a little extra on each other. Sometimes you tend to be led astray by other people or your own changing choices. Follow through on your promises because it builds trust. Be forgiving. There are times when it is impossible to make good on a promise. Giving a lot of advance notice regarding a change in plans is better than a last-second update. You want to make each other feel valuable rather than inconvenient. Treat your lover as a top priority!

The *Emotional Roller Coaster* game will become less of a nuisance if you don't drop bombshell surprises on each other. Sometimes picking the wrong time to discuss a touchy subject ignites an explosion. Neither of you are sharp when tired; Cancer is moody and Aquarius is grouchy. Not much difference, right? When you are impatient with each other, it might be like someone running a fingernail down a chalkboard (in other words, irritating). You may seem to be in a frantic hurry but without direction.

Blaming one another for wasted time doesn't bring you closer. Slow down and talk rationally.

The Rainbow

Your Cancer-Aquarius relationship is as experimental as it is inventive. The fun starts when you truly know one another and can talk freely. Moods are intense in your romance. You already know this, right? It was probably the electrifying effect you had on each other's hearts and minds that brought you together. When you give freely, your partner tends to do the same. Unlike Aquarius, Cancer isn't known for being rebellious, yet this water sign will buck the system if it fears that its identity is under attack. The Crab will fight to preserve its rights. The champion of the intellect, Aquarius, isn't known for expressing emotions, yet this carefree, high-flying air sign can be emotional. Aquarius' feelings awaken when someone isn't afraid to confront this bold thinker while still being supportive. Cancer can reach into the spirit of Aquarius with intuitive force. Aquarius can forcefully sweep Cancer away with a vision that is exciting and generous.

A Cancer man offers the Aquarius woman a mixed reception. He loves her individuality. The lunar man is enticed by this Uranian woman's offbeat perspective. Her insightful logic gives her powers of perception that can be a bit frightening. When he musters his courage, he finds that this woman is not so unusual after all. He senses that she is aware of his feelings but seems more at home with his mind. This feminine free spirit makes him think about changing his life, not to match her own but to welcome new opportunities. The Cancer man feels refreshed when he is with her, and he wants to see more of her. She is a passionate thinker who awakens his aggressive instincts. He wonders if this would be an everyday event. The Crab is not sure how fast to pursue this electrifying woman. An intuitive voice tells him he is in for the ride of his life.

An Aquarius woman finds the Cancer man pleasantly accessible. She bypasses his careful scrutiny by distracting him with her offbeat perspective. His puzzled expression suggests that he wonders how she did this. She offers interesting sound bites. She truly listens to his words when he talks. The emotion in his voice exposes his fiery passion. She wants to explore his emotional world but not to join it. She wants him to come into her own world but doesn't expect him to become a card-carrying member. He wants her to be close. She hopes he can deal with her need for distance. The Aquarius woman likes this man's touch, which is firm yet gentle. She hopes to discover what it is he is trying to show her. There is a chance that she has found a friend and a lover in this lunar man. Either would suit her, but to have both would be a dream come true. She will not be his Cinderella. She hopes this will be okay because she isn't looking for Prince Charming.

A Cancer woman is curious about the Aquarius man. The lunar woman approaches this mental warrior, who reminds her of Hans Solo in *Star Wars,* carefully. He can be traditional with a smattering of the unconventional. She isn't sure which she likes better, but whichever is more sensitive and consistent may be the answer. The lunar woman notices this man is a true individualist. His thinking is as eccentric as Uranus' orbit. He is a maverick, unpredictable, and sometimes self-centered. The sensitive Cancer woman asks herself, "What am I doing here?" She wishes her own conscience would allow a little reckless abandonment like his. She feels that perhaps she could then understand his perspective. Her heart is touched by his genuine beliefs. He can be fair but also totally unrealistic. She wants to see if he can live somewhere in the middle. His logic borders on anarchy, but somehow he plays by the rules he respects. She notices that he likes her cool, logical mind, which shines like the Sun setting in late fall. She intuitively senses that her emotions don't really scare him—at least not until she becomes possessive. Her genuine love for him haunts him. She doesn't want to make him feel uncomfortable, but she feels compelled to know his innermost thoughts and emotions. This feminine spirit can't help herself. She wants to see what's behind his formidable intellect. His sensuality isn't so different from her own. She wants to believe they are more alike than dissimilar. She notices that he seems to be getting attached to her. She isn't so sure she is ready to reveal how attached she is to him.

The Aquarius man sees that the Cancer woman is unique. She reveals her sensitivity yet can dazzle him with mental rockets if that's what it takes to impress him. The Uranian man (with electric spurs and a technicolor cowboy hat) wonders why he hasn't yet swept this woman off her feet. She must be waiting to see if he is a true lover. The Aquarius man is attracted to this female spirit whose eyes shine like moonlight. She seems to know him intuitively. Is she brilliant, mystical, or just taking the time to tune in to him? Whatever the reason, this unconventional Aquarian thinker "feels" delighted with this seemingly innocent woman. He wonders if he can make her see that he doesn't want to disrupt her life. He only wants to explore as many new experiences as possible with her. He finds that she is more prepared for this journey than he thought. She has sustaining power through her desire to see new horizons. If he is wise, he will let her show him a few new ones of her own!

The Magic of Signmates

You have the potential to reach dreams that others only talk about. You may walk individually at times in pursuit of your own goals. It seems to fuel your imaginations to do so. You don't like to admit that you need each other. The thought of losing your lover hurts too much. Then again, taking the risk of jumping off the edge into the unknown makes joining forces exhilarating. You dare one another to take chances. You know you are a sure bet; your path together is passionate and electrical. You were not drawn to each other out of boredom but through the hope that maybe you had found the answer to your questions, perhaps even to questions that you were unaware of or were afraid to ask.

Cancer-Pisces: The Intuitive Ones

Cancer + Pisces = Sensitivity Plus

These two signs have a capacity to know one another on the deepest of levels. Each can capture the other's imagination. Putting two water signs together means that feelings are stirred intensely on a regular basis. Cancer influences Pisces to reason through emotions. Pisces suggests that Cancer surrender its cautious ways and follow the path of faith. Neither will be right all the time. Life alternates between fantasy and making dreams come true for this intuitive pair. Decisiveness is a matter of floating into priorities until these two watery spirits become mentally focused. Love is inspired through a strong show of belief in each other's ability.

Mime Game

The games played in your Cancer-Pisces relationship are tied to escapism, emotional overload, and loss of focus. When you retreat into long periods of silence, you are probably playing the *Mime* game. The two of you may be as good as any actor, going through actions with various gestures and facial expressions but not saying a word. You can escape by acting this way, bringing confusion in place of getting things accomplished together. Water signs sometimes display timidity due to sensitive feelings. If you assume your partner can read your mind, you might be disappointed. It helps to speak a language you both can understand. Sometimes Cancer or Pisces will need a quiet moment to recuperate, which is perfectly fine. When you use silence to avoid dealing with issues, however, it is detrimental. Fear can cause you to think you ought to hide your real opinions. Cancer can withdraw into its shell rather than talk through a problem. Pisces can swim to the deepest part of the ocean to avoid facing conflict. By putting so much energy into escape, you have less vitality for love and romance.

Sinking Ship Game

Feelings are intensified when two water signs such as Cancer and Pisces are in a romance. The *Sinking Ship* game arises when you sweep over each other with endless emotional concerns. When one of you feels down, the other might be able to lend objectivity. If you both simultaneously experience high tides of emotional confusion, the ship can go under. It's easy for you to overidentify with your partner's pain. Your psyches can become fused. Be sure you aren't so united that the two of you lose sight of when the ship is sinking. Your intuitive strength is actually weakened in this game. You neutralize each other's clarity through shared confusion. Instead of stepping back from a problem, you are compulsively swept up in it. Dependency needs may be out of kilter. You can try so hard to save each other that it does more harm than good. If you attempt to shield your partner from a loss or setback, overprotectiveness can interfere with his or her growth.

Going in Circles Game

When you are lost in the woods, it is easy to wind up back at a starting point a few hours later (which means that you walked around in a circle and are just as lost as before). In the *Going in Circles* game, Cancer and Pisces can lead each other round and round with no real direction. The two of you can lose your focus by waiting too long to reach an agreement. Water signs may be tempted to wait for the perfect moment to embark on a course of action. The timing may never be to your liking. You can feel like you are adrift in a raft while you sit and wait for inspiration to move you. A lack of decisiveness is part of the picture. Unfounded idealism can cause you to lead each other in circles as well. You may get angry if you follow your partner in directions that lead nowhere. You are at your best when your instincts are grounded in reality. A lack of reality testing can waste a lot of time and energy. If you deny the need to be focused, disorienting consequences will follow.

Strategies

How can you sail around these Cancer-Pisces games? To turn the *Mime* game around, you two must talk. It's true that water signs need processing time, but you must balance talking with introspection. You can't expect clear communication without speaking in complete sentences. You might be able to read each other's moods. Great! This still doesn't replace a need to reveal your thoughts. If you want to end up in agreement when it is vital to do so, learn to speak up.

Language was invented for a reason. Guess what happens when you try to avoid dealing directly with issues? They either snowball or multiply. Neither of these possibilities sounds good, right? Cut to the chase and talk immediately at the point of disagreement. It is frustrating trying to discuss business when you don't get a response. Have you ever heard the Zen Buddhist saying, "What is the sound of one hand clapping?" Silence is the point of meditation, but in earthly reality it is not as wonderful. If you hide due to fear, then do your best to take a small step forward. Your partner probably doesn't bite, though maybe he or she barks! (Often the bark is worse than the bite.) Your sensitive, emotional nature, which your signs typify, shouldn't get in the way of talking with each other. Communication fuels your romance. Even sex will be more flowing when you take the time to say what's on your mind.

The *Sinking Ship* game is going to take clarity in order to avoid getting lost in each other's worries. You can awaken your partner's nurturing instincts with just a hint of anxiety in your expression. You must use your mental objectivity even if it takes stepping out of each other's presence to attain it. Your emotional nature can probe deeply beneath the surface to see what is really wrong. Be careful that you come back out and realistically assess a situation. Be supportive instead of trying to be each other's savior; this approach ensures that you both won't become part of the problem. There are instances when something may impact you both simultaneously. You can still calm down enough to get your bearings. Help each other to grasp reality. With practice this gets easier. Emotional clarity is what you seek. The intuitive power you produce together is awesome. The main message here is to make this resource work for you. You may care too much. Back up to the fifty-yard line, and don't try to carry your partner's burdens. Have faith that your partner is strong enough to get through a challenge. You can still be there with your loving support. Closeness requires insight to know just how to interact with one another.

The Magic of Signmates

The *Going in Circles* game is going to make you less dizzy when you stop spinning the wheel. How? First things first. The failure to make a decision is, in its own funny way, making a decision—just not the right one. The perfect moment seldom comes. Perfection is easier to picture in your mind than it is to find in the world. Let it get a little messy. A decision can be edited later. The creative process is more fun when you stop thinking about it. Taking the risk on making a choice comes when you get in the habit of doing so together. If you do, in fact, take each other on wild goose chases, then you need to become more reality oriented. As a couple, you can apply your vivid imagination to anything you do. Be sure you are not talking each other into decisions that, upon closer examination, you would not pursue. When you don't take on projects that are impractical on a whim, you will be less annoyed with each other. Focus clearly on what needs to be done. You may need to put your feelings aside long enough to establish mental clarity.

The Rainbow

Your relationship is inundated with creative imagination. As a couple your imaginative powers are off the scale. There is no limit to the heights you can envision together. When you define your roles adequately, you have less of a tendency to collide. A mutual love of escapes to serene places is probably something you have in common. Neither of you can deal with long-term stress without feeling drained. You make great lovers and allies because you are protective of one another. Life with each other will never lack for unusual learning opportunities. When you truly trust your partner, you make a winning combination.

A Cancer man doesn't exactly know what to make of the Pisces woman. She seems complacent yet shows glimmers of discontentment. The lunar man wonders how this Neptunian woman manages to function in the real world with such a vivid imagination. She seems more sensitive than he but shows great strength in believing in him. He is drawn to this dreamy woman who melts his heart. The male Cancer hopes he doesn't offend this woman's highly refined value system. She treads lightly upon his ideas, even the ones she dislikes. The Crab notices that her feistiness comes forward when he questions her idealism and those in whom she believes. Her ability to read his inner world puzzles him the most. How did she slip in through the guarded entrance? He quickly forgets this as she shows her concern. The moody Cancer man feels unusually calm and at ease in the presence of this Neptunian woman. He wants to answer his heart's longing to know her innermost being.

A Pisces woman sees a complex portrait when she looks at the Cancer man. Much as a bookworm loves to reread a favorite book, this Neptunian woman loves to study his face. The Pisces woman feels they are intuitively connected. He seems too embarrassed to admit that he senses something special in the air. She enjoys listening to his description of his home and his ambitions, and he responds positively when she talks about her own dreams. She likes the way he sees her as a whole person. She wonders if he will always see her in her totality or if this is a passing phenomenon. His laugh seems to come from deep in his solar plexus as does his self-confidence. He makes her feel accepted. If he only knew how much this really meant. She wants to tell him but thinks it would be better to let time bring them even closer in spirit. He knows how to come close to her heart. It almost takes the breath out of her.

A Cancer woman marvels at the way the Pisces man listens to an inner calling. He wants so much to meet the expectations of those he encounters but feels driven by a mystical force within. The lunar woman wonders whether this Neptunian man can possibly be true to both worlds. She really cares if he will be devoted to her because she needs someone who will take the time to discover all of her gifts. She doesn't want to be left behind. She either wants to come along on his journeys or pull him into one or two of her own. His poetic way of describing life's absurdities makes her laugh. She loves his smile because it reflects confidence that comes from self-knowledge. He doesn't seem to touch the ground when he talks about his highest ambitions. She is entertained and delighted when he speaks of the need for escape. She believes his visionary ways could get him into trouble but hopes he never stops dreaming. She realizes that his inspiration may lead him to bigger and greater things in reality. His "fountain of youth" attitude lights up her own imagination. She is happy when he focuses his attention on her and wants to capture that feeling for the rest of her life.

The Pisces man finds that the Cancer woman is hard to define. On first glance, she seems patient and domestic. On second glance, she is ambitious and sensual. He hopes she doesn't find him so overly sensitive that she thinks of him as a lightweight. For some reason he wants to be her hero. The Neptunian man wonders what it will take to win her heart. Riches and fame? Perhaps a show of creative talent? He is pleased to see that she is looking for someone who speaks from the heart. His heart is somewhat war-torn from losing his youthful idealism, but he believes he has enough love left for this captivating woman. She is his match in every way. He can't outsmart her nor can he run away from his emotions. His first impulse is fear at the thought of this sensitive soul wanting to

The Magic of Signmates

know the "real" him. He has portrayed so many roles for others, partly to entertain them, partly to amuse himself. Now he is supposed to play a real part. He summons his courage and decides to meet her halfway.

The love you seek in each other is there for the asking. Ask from your heart. You can mold life to be a reflection of your individual and shared selves. Make your way gently in order to avoid the confusion that comes when you try to be too forceful. Reach for the sword of courage and the fire of passion when life becomes too complacent. You know the way to each other's innermost being, so don't be strangers. You find the love you want in each other. There is a sense of familiarity when your eyes first meet. Lead each other into directions that don't betray your trust or faith. You have a chance to be the one the other has envisioned or perhaps has been too afraid to hope for.

Leo-Leo: The Directors

Leo + Leo = Engine That Could and Could and Could

This is a relationship that knows where it is going from the start. A Sun king and queen make things happen. You are able to promote each other to great creative heights, and your passionate romance blasts off into the stars. You may see each other as being stubborn occasionally. When you figure out how to negotiate effectively, working together runs like a well-maintained machine. You can be proud of each other's accomplishments. Sharing the spotlight helps to maintain your mutual admiration society. You probably like to play and work hard. Your self-confidence as a couple is hard to beat. You have a glow that is charismatic. People are attracted to the willpower you display. You like to call your own shots. Business enterprises can flourish.

I Plead the Fifth Game

The games played in your Leo-Leo relationship center around abuses of power and egocentric behavior. When the two of you refuse to talk to each other, you may be playing the *I Plead the Fifth* game. The fifth amendment can be invoked to protect yourself on the witness stand from self-incrimination. You don't want to use it against each other. There may be a standoff over disputed ideas. When you refuse to talk, it only makes matters worse and serves to reinforce the tendency to hold on to your separate positions. A clash of wills is expected between Leos such as yourselves. If you belittle your partner's stand on an issue, it pushes you further apart. Your egos can be sensitive in a dispute. When you don't communicate, it can feel like your opinions are rejected or undervalued. An unresponsive attitude can be perceived as a slap in the face. Even without talking, nonverbal signals are probably easy to read. Anger and hurt feelings fill the atmosphere. If one of you tries to force the other to talk, it may not work. You both like to have things on your own terms, don't you?

I Rule by Divine Right Game

You both like to run the show once in a while. There is nothing wrong with that, but when one or both of you becomes too bossy, the *I Rule by Divine Right* game manifests. Dictatorial behaviors can infuriate you. You aren't going to be happy in a kingdom where you have to always play by somebody else's rules. Why would it be any better to be forced into playing by those of your mate? It isn't! A sure way to start a war with each other is to try to overpower and bully your partner. Your sign is about the best at resisting the demands of others. When you forget to honor each other's rights, trouble is just around the bend. Freedom is a must in this relationship. One of you can't continually rule the other. Spontaneous passion disappears when you both lack emotional freedom to be yourselves.

Flamboyant Game

There can be a tendency to go overboard in trying to impress your partner or others, as in the *Flamboyant* game. You can have a compulsive urge to prove that bigger is better. Fire signs have an innate competitive streak. The two of you may try too hard to prove your success to others. You can go through a lot of money to make your point. A show of wealth could mask inner insecurity. The exhibitionist in you gets lost in seeking applause from those whose approval you desire. When you forget there are limits, you get into trouble. A constant craving for attention may be the root cause of this predicament. If your partner is ignoring you too much, it is tempting to seek love in other ways. Ownership and riches are not the issue; your happiness is.

Strategies

How can you respond appropriately to these Leo-Leo games? If you want to lessen the chances of getting caught in the snares of the *I Plead the Fifth* game, you will need to adopt changes. Express a willingness to talk. This is easier said than done if you already have a well-established pattern of withdrawing into silence. Issues are more quickly resolved between you when you put your differences on the table. You need to take a hard, honest look at your partner's point of view. It's so easy to become too attached to your own perceptions. If you can listen without responding to each other's perspective, it may help you to see a way out of this dilemma. When two people are tired of fighting, they usually can find a resolution to their conflict. It's vital that you don't escalate the war through impulsive accusations. Remember, blame only serves to hinder solutions. Try to see your negotiations as a process. You probably will find that you talk more when you make each other feel like winners. You will be happier when your mate sees you as a trusted lover rather than as a thorn in his or her side. Pride is a big deal in a Leo-Leo romance. Each of you needs to make the other feel important. Mutual admiration lights a fire in your leonine hearts and takes you across the moat of your separation.

The *I Rule by Divine Right* game occurs when Leo's power takes a wrong turn. When you both feel equally empowered, life will seem plentiful and full of good fortune. Getting there can seem like a great journey, but it may be shorter than you think if you can stay away from dominating center stage. You must walk side by side. One following the other only works if you alternate who is leading. It is essential that you promote one another. Each of you needs encouragement to fully use your talents. You thrive on the freedom to choose your own paths. This sense of liberation instills in you that much more passion for one another. Take this away and you are like a wilting flower. You both will be happier when occupying thrones of equal power. Relinquish those tendencies to exert control, and your love will flourish.

The *Flamboyant* game is symptomatic of too great of a desire for acceptance. You need to trust that it isn't necessary to be someone you are not. Let your partner feel accepted for being himself or herself. You are not happy when you assume roles that are not really you. Your true friends don't need a "show" to convince them of your value. Insecurity about love cannot be overcome through wealth and power. You still have to deal with the underlying issues. It may be easy to fool others through a display of self-confidence. You can't fool yourselves. When you express from your hearts, you are more at peace. The world will seem less hostile when you let go of a false show of power. You won't disappear just because you show a trace of vulnerability, and you might even tap into an inner strength that insulates you from your fears. It may sound corny, but the truth, in this case, sets you free.

The Rainbow

Your Leo-Leo relationship is going to propel you into robust activities. Life will roll out the red carpet when you exert your ferocious self-confidence. The two of you need plenty of creative outlets. You require adequate elbow room to keep from bumping into each other. Your romance can entertain all kinds of new ideas. Listen with an open heart, and you will find greater happiness. The road to intimacy requires a willingness to act as equal partners on the stage of life. You are at your best as co-directors. Pay attention to the details as well as the big plan. When you notice and act on particular ways to make your partner feel special, you will have a rewarding romance.

The Leo man sees a glimpse of himself in the Leo woman. She has a regal smile that resembles his own (especially after he has set the world on fire). This radiant woman certainly inspires him. Her willpower does not appear as forceful as his own, or could he be wrong? Is he seeing the "true" her or a dimension he wants to see? No matter. The Leo man knows he is game for whatever comes along. She is generous when he is giving. He thinks this is something best not forgotten. Her ambition is a match for his own. It's easy to love her passionate, bold self-expression; it is like looking into a mirror. The Lion is anxious to share his lair with this vivacious woman. He hopes he will be able to fulfill her dreams. She does dream big!

The Leo woman is attracted to the confidence projected by the Leo man. Though he masks it well, she detects his vulnerability. The Leo woman probably sees the subtler dimensions of the Lion because his roar does not frighten her. She humors him by acting like she doesn't notice his frailties. His creative drive is stimulating. He seems to believe in his own power. Her heart responds to his honesty rather than to what he thinks she wants to hear. His spirit is full of the same risk-taking impulses that guide her. The sunny Leo woman knows that this man's ego is in need of positive strokes. Her life seems brighter with him in it. She senses that they will share many celebrations. She suspects he will probably want to expand their kingdom. The Leo woman senses that she may need to watch his feet so he doesn't accidentally trample her own turf. She responds to the way he showers her with attention and doesn't mind returning the favor.

You have a relationship that can keep you happy. Once you find the way into each other's most intimate of worlds, you feel little separation. Make each other feel important, and you will never become strangers to each other's hearts. The commitment you want to make is easier when you are willing to be there for one another. Your romance has natural enthusiasm. Ride this lively spirit to the highest plateaus of happiness. Your staying power can sustain you through any challenge.

Leo-Virgo: The Broadcasters

Leo + Virgo = Lively Communication

The fiery enthusiasm of the Lion combines nicely with the energetic thoughts of Virgo. The two can enjoy meeting a wide range of people and discussing a large variety of subjects. Business enterprises can be profitable. Combined with Virgo's insights, Leo's hunches lead to opportunities. If there's a rub between the two, it probably is related to the decision-making process. Leo can act swiftly while Virgo prefers to analyze the best possible outcomes before moving forward (like using a simulated jury to test a case). Mercury can send its mental feelers east, west, north, and south in search of the odds while Leo is still eating breakfast. Leo's humor reminds Virgo to see the lighter side. Virgo convinces Leo of the importance of organization. Romantically, this is a better match than many think. Why? Leo can grow fond of Virgo's knack for knowing how to please a lover sexually and materially. Virgo is gratified with how Leo showers gifts and attention on those it loves (and sees as loyal!). The Lion's dramatic passion can ignite the same feeling in earthy Virgo.

Work City Game

The games played in your Leo-Virgo relationship feature compulsive drives and getting lost in negative thinking. When the two of you don't set any limits on your serious ambitions, you could fall into the *Work City* game. The type A personalities are lit! There's nothing wrong with the desire to be successful. It would be foolish to tell either of you to put your intense plans away for long, but when work overshadows play time, you become out of balance. Romance starts to dwindle. You don't look at each other with the same joy as you once did. Leo can get so swept up in the passion of a project that the Lion doesn't even realize its partner misses its presence. Virgo can be so overwhelmed by the details and feelings of responsibility in work that its attention is consumed. You are only going through the motions of being together. The quality of the time you spend with each other is being infringed upon. You may only have so much time due to frantic schedules. This could be a reality. There still is probably a way to cheat on your love of work, to steal greater romantic interludes for each other. When you forget to put yourselves as a couple first, you get into trouble.

Worry-itis Game

When you concentrate on what's wrong rather than right, the *Worry-itis* game is only a thought or two away. Virgo has a reputation as a worrier (some worry more than others). Leo can be a worrier too. The Lion hates to fail. When a long-term goal starts to wane, the Lion can go into a panic. Leo isn't usually as preoccupied with the little things as much as Virgo, but big problems often bother Leo more than patient Virgo. When you both are locked into high anxiety because things are not going according to plan, you grow more critical. First, you will berate yourself. Eventually, it will spill over to your lover. Excessive worrying brings on angry outbursts. The impact this has on communication is most telling. It can lead to talking only on a superficial level, and you may feel emotional distance. This pattern may go on for a long time before you are either aware of it or willing to discuss it honestly.

Not Now, Not Now Game

When you react stubbornly to each other, you can play the *Not Now, Not Now* game. Leo doesn't like to be told when and how to do something. Virgo can become obstinate as a way to irritate strong-willed Leo. This is your way of looking each other in the eye and saying flat-out, "No!" Usually unresolved anger brings this game out of the closet. It may disappear for quite some time, and then, suddenly, it's back in your face. What happens when you don't deal with unfinished business? It often resurfaces disguised as new business. It's really the same old baggage—a little older, more mildewed, and even heavier. You may find it harder to agree on ideas or plans. Frugal Virgo can perceive Leo as being too extravagant. Leo may see Virgo as not having enough fun. These perceptions may contribute to your problems with working as partners.

Strategies

How can you circumvent these Leo-Virgo games? In the *Work City* game, you need to catch yourselves before taking the work ethic too far. Leo's driving force, together with Virgo's relentless drive to finish a task, will lead you to push well beyond the call of duty. You need to be ready to set reasonable limits, that is, if you want to keep romance and passion alive. If you are tired from working excessively, your sex lives will pay the price. If you are exhausted, you won't converse clearly; a discussion can turn into a gripe session. Steal away to a tropical island, or at least find more leisure time. Take time from work to give to your relationship since usually it's the other way around. Try to balance the accounts. The payoff is greater intimacy and really feeling like you are rewarding yourselves.

You will need to be determined to get a lasso around the *Worry-itis* game. It's a tough one to corral. Leo will finally grow impatient with worry, as many fire signs do. How does Leo deal with anxiety? Leo will try to set dynamite to it! Leo is lost and miserable if sitting idly while uncertainty rules. This is so unlike Leo that it doesn't even sound right. The Lion needs to make things happen. Leo isn't known for speculation and creative power for nothing. The Lion wants to attack its problems energetically. Virgo isn't as ferocious as Leo but becomes restless enough to finally figure a way out. Virgo's tenacious problem-solving skills can make anxieties disappear, but nasty, nagging details can undermine Virgo's ability to relax. This meticulous earth sign can't stand to leave things undone. Leo isn't usually preoccupied with the minute particulars unless they get in the way of immediate gratification. Virgo can deal with delayed gratification better than Leo.

You seem to be a universe apart in how you perceive problems. How you deal with problems is the source of more dramatic differences. You need to comprehend each other's mental processes. Understanding may keep you from worrying each other to death. Take responsibility for your own problems. When you don't, you may be tempted to blame your partner for not making your problems go away. Don't panic. Leo can become hysterical if life is not going smoothly. Virgo can become a bit neurotic. Staying calm and collected doesn't hurt.

In the *Not Now, Not Now* game, you need to put old issues to rest and to ensure that new problems don't become old ones. Virgo can be timid when dealing with a heated issue. Leo may not be even remotely interested in dealing with old business.

How do you get around to talking? That's a good question. It takes courage and wisdom with a touch of patience. You are probably getting the message that it takes one heck of an effort! Leo, don't sell that courageous heart short. Talking cannot damage your ego. Virgo, don't underestimate your ability to withstand a little heat. You have a dynamic ability to resolve conflict. The two of you may be afraid of upsetting the other, so what do you do? You become quiet and disagreeable.

You can get past this game with an iota of willingness to change. When you act more openly to work through past differences, you raise your relationship to a higher level of trust and passion. If you try unsuccessfully to open one another up through criticism or force, consider another tactic. If you are willing to budge and be flexible, a miracle occurs. It will hit so fast you won't even realize when it happened. Let go of your fears a little at a time. Talk right through an issue. It makes confusion disappear!

The Rainbow

A Leo-Virgo relationship can achieve unusual success. Your feisty unwillingness to settle for anything less than what you want could make you the envy of others. You will egg each other on to be all you can be. There is a rich supply of valuable resources in your romance. The two of you can provide insightful ideas for each other. The Lion may not always ask for help, but Virgo can be a friend when Leo feels like the world is not its oyster. When Virgo begins to doubt its own capability, Leo can come forward with a strong show of confidence. You are at your best when dealing with a challenge. Tests seem to keep you near an edge that brings out your best. The two of you don't always thrive when the going is easy, which is not to say you don't enjoy peaceful moments, only that you are anxious to pursue goals and to put ideas into action.

A Leo man can move so fast that it takes him a moment to really see the Virgo woman. She seems to be humble yet at ease with her skills. He is delighted when she glances his way. The Lion questions whether he can be the answer to this woman's quest. He wants to be the one for her because this Mercurian woman seems to know him. His own sense of ambition is strong but not really any more potent than that of this intelligent woman. Perhaps it's her desire for perfection that intrigues him the most. This Leo man realizes fast he doesn't have her patience to do anything as precisely as she does—unless it's his favorite thing in life. This playful Lion wants to get to know the not-so-serious side of this insightful woman. She seems to always be a step or two ahead of him, like a great chess player. He thinks it would be interesting to see what it would be like to play for the same team.

A Virgo woman approaches a Leo man carefully. He is a picture of strength. She wonders if there is something hidden beneath the frame. The Mercurian woman can draw upon information and facts so quickly that it can befuddle a Leo's mind. The female Virgo is full of vigor for love as much as for work. She wants to be sure the Leo man is clear about that fact. The Lion's roar doesn't scare her, but his unwillingness to observe boundaries does. He is a hunter of new ambitions who needs to keep the fires of inspiration lit in his heart. She is attracted to his vision and inspiration. He doesn't strike her as always knowing where he is going, but it doesn't really matter much to this meticulous spirit. She reluctantly admits that this restless soul makes her heart skip a beat.

A Leo woman is amused by the Virgo man's ability to be at peace with his work despite his anger at the world's inefficiency. She notes that he usually believes his approach is the most effective. Some people wait an eternity for the insights that this Mercurian man has in one day! She is intrigued that he can live life with so much intensity, even though he knows how absurdly imperfect everything can truly be. His attention to the little things that light up her life wins her attention. This female Leo wonders if her intense desire to be free and spontaneous will bother this meticulous man. She likes to test those that love her anyway to make sure they are not going to try to limit her options. She appreciates the fact that he is not infuriated by her strong "me first" focus. Her success has come through incredible willpower and courage. It is gratifying that this inquisitive man can perceive her greatness. She is proud of her accomplishments and is loyal to those who have helped her along the way. She is relieved to see that this man is not jealous of those whom she considers friends and family.

The Virgo man is taken aback by the forwardness of the Leo woman. He loves her creative vitality. He is more in touch with his sensuality through his relationship with her. This incisive Mercurian man seems to strike a chord with this fast-paced being. His reasoning power captures the Lion's imagination. His ability to say the same thing in so many unusual ways delights her. Their sense of humor is similar, especially when talking about life's ironies. He likes her triumphant laughter because it doesn't seem to belong to this century; her laughter is a haunting echo of Leo's first victories. Leo is a sign that likes and expects to win. The Mercurian man senses he had better massage the sensitive side of this proud woman. He enjoys the way she makes him feel. He notices that his own vision of what he could ask of life mushrooms when he is with her.

Your romance is filled with an inner knowing that you are with someone who will back you at all times. You both need this from each other. Why? It keeps you from wasting time looking back when you propel each other's minds forward. You can reach great heights together. There is greater happiness when you see your partner attaining the same bountiful fruits as yourself. You are lovers who review your purpose on occasion. When you enjoy planning as much as the final results, you seem to take even greater delight in being together.

Leo-Libra: The Socialites

Leo + Libra = Big Plans

You probably recognized something special in each other at first glance. Leo's fiery zeal to dramatically impress others complements Libra's social flash. You two might feel you were made for each other. The romantic in each of you likes to perform for the other. Making your partner happy is a delightful experience. You both have a way with people. You could be successful together in the entertainment field, politics, or any endeavor dealing with the public. You truly find that the world is your stage from which to showcase your abilities. It is easier to define your relationship when each of you feels comfortable with your roles. There is a sincere desire to accomplish key goals that is intensified by being in this sign combination. The passion you feel for each other carries over into your creative self-expression.

Pleaser Game

The games in your Leo-Libra relationship are connected to trying too hard to gain acceptance and to losing awareness of limits. When you become overly accommodating, you can be caught in the *Pleaser* game. There is a tendency in Leo to seek applause in order to feel secure. It doesn't mean that the Lion has no identity, but without recognition or attention Leo can feel invisible. Libra can compulsively attempt to be all things to all people in order to be liked. This is a perplexing way to live. Put the Leo-Libra dilemma together and it spells *confusion*. You will struggle to move forward as individuals or as a couple if you get lost in this game. Your need to be accepted is out of control. The light in your usually bright romance is dimmed by giving away too much of your power. You lose focus on your partner when you perform for others. Signs such as Leo and Libra, which are so people-oriented, feel slighted when not at the center of attention.

When you shine your spotlight away from one another, it hurts. The very thing that made you feel so special to each other is missing.

Flattery Game

The two of you exaggerate your feelings about each other once in a while—no big deal. If you constantly feel you must lavish sugary praise on your partner, the stakes get higher. The *Flattery* game finds you withholding love or affection unless your partner gives you unconditional acceptance. You ask a lot from one another. Is it realistic? When you are honest about it, you know the answer is not really. A lack of boldness takes away from the impact you bring to each other's creativity. You can sense the fragile foundation that holds you together. The problem with this type of interaction is that the house of cards comes tumbling down as soon as one of you crosses the other. It's nice to have your ego stroked, but if it is something you always expect, there might be a feeling of being taken for granted. What's worse is that you aren't sure if the compliments are sincere. Your sense of trust certainly takes a dip, and the dipstick can register a few quarts low.

Overindulgence Game

Your two signs are not going to hold back in life. Why should you? Two big-hearted romantics want to live it up, but if you push a good thing too far, the result might be the *Overindulgence* game. Moderation is thrown out the window. Leo and Libra can talk each other into leaving reason behind when it comes to enjoying pleasure. At first glance, this looks harmless enough; it even appears good for such fast-lane lovers. But the second look, sometimes in the rear-view mirror when you backtrack, reveals trouble. You can overspend, overplay, or just plain overdo it! You will notice this game if you are distracted from getting things accomplished. Ignoring reality from time to time may lead you to be reckless or wasteful. The drive to take life as far as it can go may cause you to go down a wrong road. This is usually unconscious behavior. Good, old-fashioned denial is alive and well, cleverly hidden from your conscious mind.

Strategies

How can you handle these Leo-Libra games? In the *Pleaser* game, the two of you need to believe in yourselves. When you have faith that you don't need standing ovations from others, it puts you in touch with your own wholeness. Many people don't believe that Leo is ever insecure or really lonely. Leo feels strange when its creative power to influence others is in question. Applause is a confirmation that Leo hasn't lost its touch. Libra is an artful mediator, often feeling gratification in settling disputes between warring factions. Both of your signs love people. Without an audience to show your capabilities, it takes away from your life drama. You only need to stay away from getting lost in craving admiration. Having others say they like you can be addictive. Be centered in knowing that you are already complete. Others only add to what you already are. Your partner will love you that much more if you talk honestly. Stay away from being unreal with each other. It will be truly pleasing to focus your attention on one another without becoming distracted by looking in the wrong directions for love and attention.

The *Flattery* game can be transcended through the truth. It doesn't often feel wonderful to hear that you are not perfect or always right. Stepping around conflict with false praise sets up a troublesome situation. It's best to compliment each other when you mean it, not because you always expect it whether you deserve it or not. Trust is the sure way to your partner's heart. It instills your romance with even greater passion when you allow your differences to be voiced. A false show of affection only leads to shallow communication. If you want to know you can really count on one another, you are wise to only give compliments when you mean them. For people such as yourselves, who are as romantic as they come, you need to keep a genuine connection between you. Exaggeration of what you mean to each other is not as good as saying what you really feel to one another.

The *Overindulgence* game asks you to insert a dose of reality to catch yourselves before you go beyond what is reasonable with the pleasure principle. Leo doesn't instinctively set limits. Libra can do so but can just as easily throw itself overboard in the name of fun. You only need to watch out for this tendency when it can prove to be costly materially or emotionally to indulge yourselves. Your drive to express yourselves is the force behind this behavior. With practice, you can channel this potentially hard-to-harness energy into other activities or projects. Leo and Libra are not going to sit idly for long. Boredom might even be the cause of this game. Another possibility is that one of you feels ignored by the other. The main thing is, whatever the reason, to direct this expression more constructively. Neither of you may like the word "discipline" unless it comes to your work. The other areas of your life may need moderation. You can still play! The way you play might need an adjustment or two.

The Rainbow

Your Leo-Libra relationship can take you both to new creative elevations. You are both at your best when you show off your talents. People are moved by the self-confidence you generate. Enjoy your journey together; it can be delightful. Your relationship is filled with pleasure—from lovemaking to the joy of sharing a wealth of ideas. You can bring valuable resources to one another. You have a natural affinity to understand your partner. Leo's energy is vibrant and ardent while Libra has a scintillating, upbeat personality. The two of you make great music together. Libra can be indecisive but less so around "let's get going" Leo. The Lion may lack a strategy to make a plan work but not as often when it listens to Libra's savvy ideas. You influence each other to step past self-imposed limits. This could be your stairway to love and fulfillment.

A Leo man is attracted to the Libra woman's smooth way of dealing with him. He likes her cool grace combined with an unmistakably sensual smile. The Leo man needs a partner who will spoil him at times but not give in to all of his demands (though sometimes he forgets this when he falls in love with being spoiled!). The Leo man appreciates the Venusian woman's logical mind, but he thinks he had better brush up his romantic moves in case they are rusty. This Venusian woman wants to see what kind of a romantic the Lion truly is. He feels that life will be fun with her. When she talks about the importance of compromise, he wonders just what she might be getting at. It's not that she talks in circles but that she brilliantly presents opposite points of view. He senses she is testing him to see which side he favors though he notices that she is more interested in whether he is a true lover. His world of make-believe heroes and real success catches her attention. He wants to sweep her off of her feet with his passionate advances. The Lion knows this woman can keep up with his sense of adventure and maybe outrun him to the finish line when it comes to surprises.

A Libra woman enjoys looking at the world through the perspective of the Leo man. She doesn't want to live her life through him, but she finds it fascinating that someone could actually see reality in this way. She wonders if he ever tires of running after new ideas. This Venusian woman wants to be more than his fantasy. She would prefer to be the lover who inspires his dreams. The Libra woman knows this man has a wild side; he seems to live by the "survival of the fittest" rule. Whether he is a banker, artist, or truck driver, he seems to see the world as a competitive jungle. She doesn't fear this part of him but is rather intrigued by it. Then again, he can be quite civilized and romantic. There are times when he doesn't take as many risks and seems to be tamer (but not really tamed). She likes this reckless and sensitive man who has set out to achieve his ambitions in a most impressive way. The Libra woman doesn't mind being his audience if he will return the favor and be a most passionate admirer. She sees that they both feed off attention, and it is what brings them together. She likes the confidence of his embrace.

The Leo woman is careful not to be too blatantly direct with the sensitive Libra man. This suave man's feelings are just below the surface. The Leo woman notices that this Venusian man winks at her competitive spirit. His competitive soul only needs a slight push from her to bring it out into the open. The passion between them is almost embarrassing. She isn't self-conscious about what others will think, though she is interested in what he thinks. His mind is so full of colorful information; he can fire out facts about the stock market, world politics, or new fashions faster than she can comprehend them. It's the certainty in his voice that fascinates her. She is an in-the-moment woman who likes this in-the-mood-for-anything mindset. Her need to be loved appears to be similar to his. He seems indecisive when it comes to making big choices that affect them both. She wishes he would just step back and see that she wants to get on with the show. "If he doesn't make up his mind soon," she muses, "I will pull him along." After all, this flashy Lion doesn't want to miss out on any of the fun!

The Libra man is instantly attracted to the Leo woman's love of pleasure. He knows she is a doer with an incredible need to be playful. She can coax him to loosen his tie or to undo the top button of his shirt. He believes she is one of the most energetic people on earth. She can probably outwork and outplay him. The Venusian man is in love with her generous heart, which seems big enough to share not only with him but with whomever she loves. Her whole appearance can be a bold display of her power. The Libra man is fond of her smile because it takes away his blues in a flash. He hopes his own smile is filled with enough radiance to stop her in her tracks. He wants to be the center of her world, which is no easy task. If anyone can accomplish this feat, it's this fashionable man whose suave diplomatic air makes her want to get as "up close and personal" as possible.

Your relationship is like a gem in your hands. It becomes even more rare when you learn how to compete with the world instead of with each other. Love is always near but requires your willingness to let each other blossom as individuals. You can do amazing things. Tell the truth and keep an eye on each other's feelings. You may grow too attached to the attention you receive from your lover. Don't let it spoil you to the point of taking it for granted. Walk together with a healthy respect for each other's personal freedom. You will be happier when each of you retains that special spark that brought you here in the first place, remember?

Leo-Scorpio: The Negotiators

Leo + Scorpio = Passion and More Passion

These are two signs that can agree with deep sincerity and disagree with an intensity that makes the faint of heart uncomfortable. Leo and Scorpio really like to conduct business on their own terms. They possess a "don't mess with me" mentality. It's a good thing that each pays attention to the other's warnings. There are definite boundaries between these two powerhouses. Honoring each other's strengths is a lot smarter than thinking that one can really change the other. At the core, both are as hot as a nuclear reactor—fueled with passion and raw instinct. In a relationship together, the primitive instincts of these two signs awaken. Everyone born under these signs inherits this power. Your romance is intense. Anger might bounce off the walls, but it doesn't necessarily mean that anything is wrong. The Lion and the Scorpion can make war and peace and love in the same hour! Neither backs down from a dare. Leo is ready to take on any challenge while Scorpio is primed for any struggle. These two signs have incredible business savvy but are sometimes a quarter short on flexibility. With time, these signs can learn how to steer around each other's sore spots. A strong alliance can form that is sustained by deep levels of trust.

Under My Thumb Game

The games played in your Leo-Scorpio relationship reflect power struggles and blocked emotions. The *Under My Thumb* game is one in which one or both of you usurps too much power. It is very poisonous for Leo and Scorpio to try to control each other. This behavior translates into stubbornness and every kind of resistance imaginable. Leo must feel free to roam wherever it wants to express its enterprising spirit. The Lion enjoys breaking a rule now and then to show off that feistiness. Scorpio blossoms when there are few rules that it can't secretly circumvent.

The Scorpion will simply wait until the Lion tires of acting like a king or queen. When two signs with your power face off for a long war, disastrous consequences ensue. Short skirmishes are good for your communication skills, but those drawn-out conflicts can turn ugly. Clouds of resentment settle in if you don't talk it out. You probably will look at your partner and wonder why you are even together when this game gets out of hand. Both of you hate to be controlled or to receive orders. There is no winner here. Leo and Scorpio are a couple who must agree to be two winners. If not, "one is the loneliest number" may become your mantra.

Taking No Prisoners Game

When your anger swells like a typhoon, you may attack each other verbally as in the *Taking No Prisoners* game. This game is likely to occur in two distinct ways. First, you may undermine each other's drive for personal growth and self-expression. If this goes on for extended periods, look out! If you try to push each other off your unique paths, you could be setting a match to gasoline. Second, you may also try to convince your partner to do everything your way. This does not even sound plausible, but there are days and weeks when one of you is going to feel more "right" than the other. If you handle this with little foresight, you had better duck quickly to avoid flying objects. Anger is not a rational emotion. Actually, it was never invented to be used by the calm, the polite, and the passive. Anger allows you to get to the point in a hurry. When the Lion and the Scorpion step on each other's sensitive tails, expect an explosion. You sit on a ton of power in this relationship, so you must act with great awareness to enjoy the love, sex, and passion you could have. You will find that trying to conduct business through the debris caused by this game is a miserable experience. It's really tough to talk shop when you are ready to scalp someone alive. If you sit on your anger for months, it will be released with much more force than if it has been stuffed back for a matter of days. You pay a price for waiting to act or for refusing to listen. You miss out on a lot of fun and good times.

Desert Game

When you lose sight of your emotional link, it can bring on the *Desert* game. Leo isn't as creative or spontaneous when it loses touch with its feelings. The Lion becomes gloomy, even morose. Scorpio doesn't function any better when the creative waters dry up. Scorpio can look lost and dazed. You both feel parched when you shut down emotionally. You may not always want to admit that you affect each other's feelings tremendously. This is why you look so strange to each other when you hide emotions. Your romance is trapped in sand dunes when you shut your partner out of your feelings. The passion begins to fade first. The intensity you really feel for each other is held back. You don't show your anger and are not revealing any real feelings either. Your moods are apt to be unpredictable. Repressed material may take you into strange feelings. You may be starved for each other's warmth but seem determined to wait for the other to give in first. This is the one time when your patience may be used for the wrong reasons and may actually be based on negative motives.

Strategies

How can you get untangled from these Leo-Scorpio games? In the *Under My Thumb* game, you must relinquish the desire to control each other. You are powerful forces in your own right and need plenty of room to be yourselves. Leo must make constant contact with its fiery enthusiasm to create. The Lion is not happy when anyone tries to limit its options. Scorpio is ready in a second to go undercover to preserve its freedom. The Scorpion can claw its way through any obstacle to prove that it can walk on its own. Two immovable forces do better when they get out of each other's path. You have a combined willpower that is as strong as they come. Why even think about getting into power games? Let each other feel like the boss and you will get along. You are going to get on each other's case occasionally. That's human. Your compulsive tendencies jump out when you really don't trust your partner. Possessiveness can be part of this game. The attraction might be so intense you are insecure with each other's freedom. Opt for freedom. It isn't fun to be so worried when you are not in each other's company. You must wean yourselves away from controlling behavior. It takes courage to believe in each other. Forget about yesterday. Start anew each day until you break the spell of fear. Your sense of closeness will be awesome, but it probably will make you want some space!

The *Take No Prisoners* game whispers seductively in your ear, but you move further away from the one you love when you seek to inflict pain. The two of you need to release anger without smashing each other's faith in the relationship. You both can make this work for you if you can learn how to negotiate from a position of power rather than from confusion. When either of you feels that your own goals are being discounted, you want to launch a missile at your partner. You can't expect your passionate lover to stay quiet while you try to rearrange the world according to your own liking. This is asking for the impossible. If you aren't already getting an earful, you should be. If only you could listen to what your partner is thinking about you!

You benefit from not always being engaged in the same activities. Your intensity serves you better when channeled through various friends and other constructive outlets. Don't attempt to convince your lover to walk only on your own path. It will get too crowded in a hurry.

In the *Desert* game, you must return to the place that made you want to be together in the beginning. There must be a wellspring of feelings underlying your relationship, but it certainly feels parched when you deny your need for emotional support. You can be pathetic when you pout. Leo and Scorpio hold back feelings in order to make life uncomfortable for others. You don't want it to be yourselves! Forgiveness—it can irritate Leo's pride to even say the word, and it may bother brooding Scorpio to mutter the word. The two of you are probably more connected than you realize. Have you noticed that when one of you is down the other often feels the same way? When one of you is up, is the other as high as a kite as well? You mirror each other, especially in this game. You want to be able to read your partner's emotions. You want to see a reaction when you make a statement. A strange, polarized meeting results when neither of you will respond to the other. When you speak with feeling, your words are alive and send shock waves through each other. Otherwise, what you say is empty and devoid of meaning. You never intended to be a mirage for each other. You want to be the real thing!

The Rainbow

Your Leo-Scorpio relationship never promises more than it can deliver. You maintain a sense of realism even when you bolster each other's egos. You understand each other's thoughts more easily than most couples. You must learn to let go of your "survivor" instinct so you can feel safe in the knowledge that your partner cares about you deeply.

The Magic of Signmates

Your romance was never meant to make your lives simpler, but it wasn't thrown in front of you to constantly test you either. Your vision of the future is bright when you learn that you partner has unshakable faith in you. You want to erase any doubts about each other, which you can do by not hiding your true feelings and by courageously sharing your thoughts. The type of love that you experience is timeless; passion is not to be feared but welcomed. Give yourselves the freedom to trust your passion. Everyone dreams of sharing love with a soul mate; you are only footsteps away from discovering it.

The Leo man quickly falls in love with the mysterious forces guiding the Scorpio woman. He knows she is different, but how unusual she is he isn't sure. She can play with his mind and his heart. The Lion wants to follow this woman wherever she goes. He longs to escape with her. She can balance a checkbook faster than a blink of an eye. Her practicality is evident, yet she sometimes loses track of what is happening in her immediate surroundings because she is in deep thought. What drives this Plutonian woman to be so compulsively correct? Her intensity adds to her sexiness. The Lion wants to win her admiration. He wonders whether she will be attracted to him if he accomplishes a remarkable feat. When he says that he would like to build a world with her, he notices that she pays attention. Even so, her mind seems to go somewhere within. "She must have an inner sanctuary," he thinks. She is private yet so aware of him. He likes to touch her because she has a feeling of permanence that reassures him that she is not just here for one show. The Plutonian woman casts a spell on him. "This isn't strange," he tells himself, "It feels so refreshing." Her feelings cut right through his own because her emotions reflect his own.

The Scorpio woman loves and hates the Leo man. She loves that part of him that isn't afraid of the new. She isn't so fond of his suspicion of change. She can't stand his stubbornness. Then again, she finds his stick-to-it mentality comforting. The Scorpio woman hopes he won't become too bossy. He seems so young in spirit when he is soft and tender. He ages quickly when he tries to control what he fears. She doesn't want to scare him; his inner being is childlike and impressionable. She wonders if his ambition will allow him to express his more vulnerable side. The realist in her knows the world is not a Utopia, yet she wishes they could run off into a wilderness and be free from responsibilities. Leo and Scorpio have power and passion together. Only a blind person couldn't see it. The Plutonian woman is no fool. She believes this man is nobody's fool either. She can deal with his strength, and she hopes he can sometimes surrender to hers.

The Leo woman is fascinated by and weary of the Scorpio man. His different personalities reflect his passing moods. The Plutonian man is guided by primitive, survival instincts. What amazes her is that this intelligent man feels a connection with such primeval instincts regardless of whether he wears a suit or shorts with cool sunglasses. She is never sure of when his primitive instincts will come out, but she doesn't really care, just as long as he admires her. His sensitivity is visible even if hidden behind well-insulated padding. The Leo woman is relieved to find that he has some vulnerability and that his feelings can be gauged. She senses that his emotions only come out rarely though she is relieved to find that it happens more often than the return of Halley's comet! She can tell the Scorpio man is reserved; this reveals itself when he processes or calculates his options. He is as money conscious as she. They both want the power that money can provide. She would love to buy him something he dreams about owning. She hopes his generosity will be showered on her and craves attention from him. She loves the way he looks at her when he is interested. She wishes he would look away when he is distracted by his latest scheme for getting ahead of everybody else. She enjoys her ability to get through to him even when he is obsessed with thoughts about money and power. His passion is potent when he is confident. She likes to see his peaceful side, which is as soothing as a summer day that has been cooled by a rain shower. He doesn't relax into this often. She wants to know if he can let go of his doubts and just be a lover. This fiery woman wants an answer so she can see whether it's worthwhile to cast away her own doubts.

The Scorpio man is energized by the dynamic pace at which the Leo woman lives her life. He likes the influence she seems to be having on his spontaneity. He is more self-conscience than he likes to admit. She encourages him to cut right to the chase. He would like to be as ferocious in love as in his career. He has the intensity to be a great lover. He really wants to be loved but doesn't have a clue about how to get that message across. He has an unlimited vocabulary, so why can't he put what he feels into simple words? He believes that the Leo woman wants him to be strong. The passion they bring out in one another is clear, yet he stumbles over small talk. She is as playful as he is serious, but he likes the way she makes him feel. She has the determination to reach him even when he doesn't want to be reached. She angers and humors him all at once. That's a tall order for anyone in this man's world. She is too good to let go. He looks for the way to hold on to her. She moves back when he reaches out compulsively. He notices that she comes closer when he lets her make the first move. He loves the way she moves.

The Magic of Signmates

   Your relationship may have arrived in the nick of time. You may have met each other at an inopportune moment. You don't exactly make life convenient for one another, but you respond with intense love when your hearts are open. You will have to fight to hold on to what you have. There will be those who are envious. You need not be jealous of one another. Communicate with a real intention to make a difference in each other's life. You can't change who you are to better fit into each other's world. The drama begins when you adapt to your partner's unique qualities. You can't be something you are not. Be true to what you must fulfill, and you will never get lost.

Leo-Sagittarius: The Confident Ones

Leo + Sagittarius = Hearing and Seeing No Limits

These two signs are about as audacious as they come. Leo lights up the already optimistic Sagittarius with even more hope for positive outcomes. Sagittarius adds a love for new conquests to Leo's risk-taking instincts, which need little encouragement. Two fire signs can be constantly on the hunt for exciting activities. The Lion and the Archer can energize other individuals or couples with their dynamic, fun-loving ways. Each can lead the other to new trails. A playful competitiveness colors this romance, which has few dull moments. Boredom isn't even part of the vocabulary and is rarely an option. Leo's and Sagittarius' persuasive personalities launch this duo into more than is sometimes bargained for. It doesn't matter because more seems to be preferred over less. This is a dramatic pair who can be the life of any party.

Risky Gamble Game

The games played in your Leo-Sagittarius relationship are associated with taking impulsive chances and not following through on your ideas. The *Risky Gamble* game can lead the two of you to follow a whim rather than a thought-out plan. When you don't consider the repercussions of your actions, you get into trouble. The willingness to take a risk is what sets you apart from many. You may move on to better and bigger things by taking chances. The tendency to test the limits separates the two of you even further from others. When you don't really discuss options and instead leap quickly, a disaster could be waiting. In trying to hit the jackpot at lightning speed, you may lose money and time. Fire signs are impatient, and your natural rhythms pick up the pace when you become lovers. When you are excited by the potential of a risk, you can easily throw caution aside. One of you can grow frustrated with the other if you feel you are being misled by their bad judgment. Shouting matches over a partner's bad decisions are likely without foresight. Be careful with your tendency to keep raising the ante. A little bit of luck may tempt you to place much bigger bets that may not be in your best interest.

Me and More Me Game

Fire signs such as yourselves love to be the center of everything. You pull attention toward you. What might happen in a relationship with another fire sign? It does not take much imagination to see that a game like the *Me and More Me* game is possible. You both want to be seen as someone who is special. You may even do cartwheels to get one another's attention. A compulsive drive to receive all of the press is what is at the root of this game. You are not going to endear yourself if your partner feels ignored. It's never good in a fire sign relationship when focus becomes one-sided. Leo needs to have its ego massaged regularly. The Lion is proud of its accomplishments and wants them to be recognized. Sagittarius likes to be praised for its intellect and to be told that its ideas are special. When Leo and Sagittarius can't mutually give praise, all-out war can break out. Tempers add to your stress levels. You irritate each other when you do not share the limelight. Each of you pushes the other off the stage. There doesn't seem to be enough applause for you both, or so you think.

All Talk and No Action Game

Fire signs often like to talk about themselves or at least be the topic of conversation. When you discuss a course of action as a couple but don't ever move ahead with the idea, the *All Talk and No Action* game is in play. This game does not lead to mutual admiration. Fire signs can be notorious for igniting ideas but lacking the follow-through to get the job done. Although Leo can be great at tying up loose ends, it doesn't do so when involved with another fire sign. It's not all the Archer's fault though. The desire to proceed to other projects is an urgent feeling in this heated romance. Each of you contributes to a tendency to move in several directions with a resulting loss of focus on the current plan. You can be frustrated with each other and confused about why you have great ideas together but not much gets done. The road to results seems long and filled with distractions. You may distance yourself from each other, thinking that doing your own thing is easier. Working together seems like too much trouble.

Strategies

How can you move past these Leo-Sagittarius games? The *Risky Gambler* game suggests that you should slow down to assess what you are about to get yourselves into. Is it a wise decision? Is it going to cost you a lot more than you had bargained? If you take the time to talk things through you may save yourselves time and energy. There is an impulsive edge in your signs. The trick is to make this work for you rather than against you. If you focus this tendency at viable targets, you can accomplish much. You are a lucky pair. Don't tempt fate by thinking you will always win. Odds are you won't. Well-calculated hunches are better in the long run. Leo is great with speculation and making money through investments. Leo's business sense is sound. Sagittarius can tap into good fortune faster than a speeding bullet. The Archer can show sound judgment when it slows down enough to take careful aim. Often, the pace at which fire signs run leads to poor perception of risk. If you slow down your reaction time, it doesn't have to mean a missed opportunity. There are times when you will need to act quickly to take advantage of a situation. Your patience will turn out to be your best ally and will keep you from repeating the same mistakes. Reality testing is also a good policy. Step back from a hot and tempting gamble to see if it is as good as it seems.

The *Me and More Me* game is going to require insight about your place within the relationship. Remember that when you both feel valued you win. Your life together must be a team effort. Make sure you both get to the winner's circle by paying attention to each other's goals. You can be cheerleaders for one another. You will be happier together when you both reach your highest ambitions. One fire sign will anger another by trying to receive too much attention. Leo and Sagittarius like to be visible. You can't help it; it's in your natural sign chemistry as individuals and as a couple. You are lovers who are easier to live with when treated as equals. You will fight less if the spotlight is shared.

The *All Talk and No Action* game asks you to put a plan to work. You may disappoint one another if you make but don't fulfill promises. Leo and Sagittarius expect others to act upon assurances made to them, but you may not always reciprocate with the same enthusiasm. Leo and Sagittarius mean well. It's just that either of you can get hijacked by another interesting opportunity that intercepts a current plan. Talking is valuable because it keeps you on the same wavelength. You may think that "talk is cheap" if your partner doesn't follow through on a strategy. Learn how to live up to what you say you will do. Reliability builds trust. The passion is even greater when you light up each other's hearts by showing that you care through fulfilling your commitments.

The Rainbow

Your Leo-Sagittarius relationship is big on optimism. The self-confidence you generate is hard to rival. The Lion is stubbornly determined to achieve its aims. The Archer will travel to the farthest regions of the mind or the world to seek out new growth. Combined with the endless enthusiasm of Sagittarius, Leo's tenacity can stimulate the two of you to act out lively performances. You need a big enough stage to project your multifarious roles. You are big-hearted lovers who need the latitude to be yourselves.

A Leo man is enamored with the Sagittarius woman's charm. She has a fast mind that is philosophical in nature. The Lion sees that this woman is filled with merriment. She seems ready at a moment's notice to celebrate any noteworthy event. She is playful but at the same time assesses whether his intentions are sincere, or so it seems to him. He finds her to be mischievous and deeply perplexing; she appears to look out at the world with a sense of wonder and seems to be a carefree spirit. The Lion notices that she is sensitive about her freedom (she posts a "no trespassing on my right to freedom" sign). This Leo man wants to win her love. Even if it pains him to do so, he will talk from his heart if that's what it takes. The Sagittarius woman can slip into a serious mode in a flash. She is pleasantly adaptable. The Lion purrs when this jovial woman lavishes him with praise but is suddenly on the alert when she puts his principles to the test. He isn't too bothered by her inquisitive ways since he likes to talk about himself. He enjoys listening to her dramatic stories.

The Sagittarius woman perceives the Leo man to be self-centered and not so hard to understand. He has much to say since he is so intent on discovering himself through what he masters in life. She notices that he wants to hear about her desires and wishes. She hopes this Lion will want to help her realize a dream or two. She appreciates his boldness, and his passion captures her heart. He seems to have been through the blues more than once already. She has a sad tale or two of her own. His upbeat spirit catches her attention. She notices that this feisty fellow seems to be made from some of the same fiery stuff as herself. His appearance at times belies what he says. His expression is far more serious than his playful words suggest. She prefers his playfulness because it makes him more fun to love. His desire to love her had better not lead to an attempt to control her. She will escape any type of confinement. He believes that his heart leads to the deepest part of her own. Their minds are not so unalike. Each appears to seek the abundance that life has to offer and to make the best of the worst. His decisive intention to live with unwavering forcefulness sweeps her into his path. She may need to tell him to move over to make room for the both of them—at least every once in a while!

The Leo woman can see herself with the Sagittarius man. He is fair, even though he is definitely opinionated and attached to his ideas. This is not a big problem because the Leo woman is used to fighting for her rights. She wants to stand her ground because her ideas have the same power as his. The Leo woman imagines that theirs could be a deeply passionate love. She thinks they desire the same things even if both want their own way in getting them. The eloquent way in which he expresses his likes and dislikes amuses her. She wonders if he thinks the world was set up just for him. That thought has crossed her own mind more than once, though she has told few people. The fire in her is ignited by him just as she notices how she does this for him. Whether it is a short-term or long-term relationship, she wants to explore love with him. She believes there is nothing to lose and much more to gain.

The Sagittarius man falls in love quickly with the Leo woman. She is not easy to get out of his mind. The way she uplifts his confidence registers points instantaneously. The Archer wants to impress her. He knows he had better be careful if he tries too hard to please her. She will start to expect such treatment regularly. "Is that so bad?" he wonders to himself. Even the Archer must admit that he finds it intoxicating when she goes out of her way to please him. This robust, confident woman is looking for a hero or perhaps for someone worth believing in. This Sagittarius man hopes he will be the object of her faith. He thrives on the support of those who believe in him. He knows she does not care for frivolous things. He wants to give her wonderful things of the world as well as a few gems from his heart. She has stolen it already anyway!

The Magic of Signmates

Leo and Sagittarius can write a fascinating script for each other. Don't limit yourselves to roles that you outgrew yesterday. Live up to the legendary boldness of your signs. Follow your courageous impulses to love one another without hesitation. There are paths waiting for you now. Be true to your commitments because they sustain you in times of inclement weather. You are not exactly the most predictable duo. Unpredictability is what makes life together so enlivening. There are no rules that you must follow religiously. Be true to your partner because you have entrusted your hearts to each other. You are at your best when you believe in each other's potential. When you look at each other with generosity, you will know you belong with one another.

Leo-Capricorn: The Executives

Leo + Capricorn = Getting Tasks Accomplished

These are two signs that push each other to the limit. Fire-sign Leo is driven to express its creative potential. Earth-sign Capricorn is motivated by a finely tuned discipline that ignores all distractions. Wow! Even the playfulness of Leo is not as obvious when around serious Capricorn (though it should be said that the Goat can play hard after working hours). Capricorn must warm up to play while Leo must warm up to work. Somehow, when the two meet midstream, they can successfully steer their romance toward rewarding shores. This may be the most powerful combination of signs because it is created by two people who can will their way to the top. Each needs to watch the steps taken to climb those great heights. It's a long way down! This couple accumulates possessions and money like others collect stamps or antiques. Finding ways to share power makes or breaks this alliance. Even romance seems to follow carefully conceived guidelines. There appears to be a pre-relationship contract that spells out how each wants to be treated. The rules are subject to change but each must agree to the revisions. Wow again!

Creator of All Game

The games played in your Leo-Capricorn relationship have their roots in unclear power motives and a lack of emotion. The *Creator of All* game shows up when you are too attached to your own version of right and wrong. You need to move beyond the "black and white" moralism of your signs to acknowledge that gray areas exist. There are strong drives to lead and take control in both of your signs. If one of you wants to lead all of the time, there will be problems in a hurry. You are in the wrong relationship if you think you are the ultimate boss. You don't listen to each other when you are involved in this game. When you think your own game plan is far superior to that of your lover, you push each other away. You both have great ideas, but instead of sharing them in an empowering fashion, you force them down each other's throat. You will feel distant from each other when playing out this scenario. Neither of you can tolerate domination by others. You compulsively seek sole authorship when you fear relinquishing control. A very tense situation arises when you don't recognize your partner's ability to make decisions.

Stalemate Game

When your Leo-Capricorn power is at odds, you can fall into the *Stalemate* game. You are like two great chess players in a tight match that neither can win. Sooner or later a chess game is called a draw when there is no winner, but you don't get a tie in this game. What you end up with are two losing positions. Failure to see a reason to negotiate gets you into trouble. Resistance to compromise leads you to not want to give your partner a chance to state his or her point of view. You will have irreconcilable disagreements, which occur in a relationship with this much power. *Compromise* is the magic word that neither of you may want to hear. You lose out on love and intimacy by adhering to rigid ideas. You will eventually grow tired of waiting for someone to give in. Each of you can hold out indefinitely. Leo can demand things on its own terms. Capricorn can handle waiting by focusing on something else. You can keep each other from exploring more productive projects by acting out this behavior.

Brittle-Hearted Game

When inflexibility rules, you will find yourselves in the middle of the *Brittle-Hearted* game. When your hearts grow rigid, you become as cold as ice, and passion disappears. You may focus all of your intensity into work and leave nothing for romance. Leo looks and feels out of place when its partner doesn't show love. The Goat appears out of sorts when cut off from its partner's affections. When neither of you shows any affection, life together is miserable. You may feel like you live on separate icebergs. Where is the warm Sun of romance? Often anger underlies this game. Leo and Capricorn have their own ways of denying anger. The Lion will be angry at everything but show no feeling toward its lover while the Goat will become somberly quiet and act like nothing ever happened—quite a bluff on both of your parts. You are not having much fun. It's not easy to make love when you expend a tremendous effort not to disclose it. Even peanut brittle seems more pliable than your hearts when you are playing this game. You two are fragile when it comes to love but don't like the world to know. In some ways, you may not let each other in on this truth either.

Strategies

How can you fly above these Leo-Capricorn games? You must stop negating each other's viewpoints in the *Creator of All* game. You both are great lovers when you feel appreciated. Indifference kills Leo's spirit. Capricorn is greatly pained when its ideas are criticized. Even a nonverbal signal that you don't want any input is a turnoff. There are going to be times when you don't want each other's advice and don't need it! Yet it hurts when you never include your partner in major decisions. The consequences show up in your verbal and physical communication. If you want to really experience each other's best, you must allow yourselves the freedom to let go. You are co-pilots flying a jumbo jet in this romance. If only one engine works, you aren't going to fly smoothly. When you both run the relationship, you are dynamic. Creative forces were never reserved for only one of you. Creativity comes through each of you with great energy. You can be successful in business and love when you both feel the license to act spontaneously. You draw out much more love and passion when you encourage your partner to be an active participant in decisions.

You will beat the *Stalemate* game when you learn how to compromise. Leo and Capricorn are not good at standing on the sidelines while others call the shots for them. You will be happier when each of you is a winner. Long standoffs waste too much of your time, not to mention the fact that they are agonizing. Learn how to talk through the issues that make you the least flexible. Communicate even if it hurts or makes you scream. A small dose of sound collective bargaining will eradicate these long and tedious love strikes. Leo is known for its fiery and flamboyant ways, but Capricorn is not exactly a wallflower. Capricorn is a tower of strength, and this reserved earth sign can unleash a fury of passion. Capricorn tends to hold back its feelings when people challenge its power. Capricorn can't help itself because this sign wants to make sure the coast is clear before revealing its internal combustion system. When either of you chooses to control the other, you block the flow of love

The Magic of Signmates

and creative force. A small step to the left or right, out of each other's line of fire, opens up your emotional flow. Take it!

The *Brittle-Hearted* game points to a narrow perception of each other. Most problems start in the head and then work their way down to the heart, and so forth. Look at it this way. If you turn aside from your partner, you run the risk of misery and loneliness. If you approach your partner for understanding, you will find that your relationship is healthier and happier. Your defiance in the face of each other's willfulness may produce this game. You are making a statement when you rebel against your partner. Leo and Capricorn often withdraw into themselves when they meet resistance that is too emotional to handle. Remember, resistance means that your partner still has enough vitality and interest in you to react. It's worse when there is no rebellion; that means you are in deep trouble. Take advantage of your partner's defiant energy because it means you can still share a dialogue. You are probably a lot stronger than you realize. The fear of coming out into the open is what is so exhausting. Don't live in the confines of your fear. A frank discussion may lead to hurt feelings, but it also releases your fears. If you don't receive the love you want, you become icy and rigid. Communication generates the heat that melts the ice.

The Rainbow

Your Leo-Capricorn relationship is one in which you can have the best of all worlds. Material and romantic wealth are within your powerful grasp. When you let each other reach for the stars, you are prolific. The innate drive to determine your own ambitious paths must be realized. There is great staying power in your romance. Your commitment can be as bold as it is creative. When you conquer your fears, your hearts act as one. You are leaders by example. Others will admire what you accomplish as individuals or as a couple. Determining what rules to play by will take your mutual input, patience, and wisdom.

A Leo man admires how smoothly a Capricorn woman operates in the world. She doesn't really hesitate in business matters. He notices that this Saturnian woman acts more deliberately in matters of the heart. She respects the seriousness of commitment, or so it seems to the playful Lion. He feels his own way of diving into love and figuring out specifics later works for him. Will it work for this earthy woman? He likes her industriousness. She can work circles around him with her methodical schedule.

She and time are one. He likes to make time for work and pleasure. He is surprised to find that this woman plans her fun and work to ensure that both happen. She has deep feelings, which must be deep because she doesn't seem very emotional. He laughs to himself because he is usually not more emotional than the women he meets. He bets that this Saturnian woman doesn't show her feelings or love to just anyone. He wants to prove he can be the solid rock she seeks.

When a Capricorn woman looks at the Leo man, she isn't sure if he is only pretending to be strong or really is a mountain of determination. She is relieved to find that he can be ambitious and fun-loving. She isn't really longing to be with a serious man but with someone who can walk on his own two feet so she can pursue her own ambitions. This man beams with confidence in himself. He seems like an old-fashioned hero, and somehow she is amused by his traditional values. She doesn't need a hero as much as someone who can let her be one herself when she needs to shine. Her passion is well aligned with his. He seems to know how to knock on the door of her feelings. She usually responds when he taps firmly but gently. The need for love in his eyes draws her to him. She instinctively pulls back if he gets too pushy. This Saturnian spirit can't help herself when it comes to inquiring about his willingness to commit, but she questions her own readiness. "How will I really know when I am ready?" she often asks herself. The Capricorn woman looks over the edge of the cliff, then at the face of the Lion as he coaxes her to take that leap of faith.

The Leo woman has the Capricorn man pegged pretty fast. He has some of her spunky ambition but hides it from view. "Here's a well-guarded soul," she thinks. The Leo woman is brave and not so foolish when it comes to love. This is not a man with whom she is carefree unless he shows warmth towards her. When she sees that he can relax his stiff upper lip, she can be at ease with him. He has a serious disposition. She thinks perhaps this Saturnian man carries the weight of many on his shoulders, but she does not let him off the hook. The Leo woman has so much love to give. He may never have her emotion, but at least he shows a willingness to learn. She was worried about this because he talks in such a matter-of-fact tone about matters of the heart and delights in discussing his achievements. She is pleased to see that he understands the principle of give and take.

The Capricorn man knows that he is taking a risk with the Leo woman. She will stand up to his orders in a second. She not only displays a forceful personality but can lighten his spirit with her playfulness. He fears her and loves her at the same time thanks to her amazing willpower. Her presence in his life seems magical and almost destined. He wanted to meet someone who shares the same desire to make a difference in someone else's life. She is demanding but really no more so than he is himself. Unlike the Capricorn man, she is full of fun and affection; his sense of fun has to be teased out of him. He likes this woman because she perceives and understands his passion and feelings. Her presence bolsters him and makes him go from feeling insecure to self-assured in seconds. This is a true miracle!

You are two lovers who sense what you want. You can instill the momentum in your mate to climb the highest mountains. Hold on to each other in times of plenty as well as in lean times. There is nothing like the feeling you have for each other. When you surrender to the pleasure and acceptance that each of you can bring the other, amazing things happen. You are the greatest of lovers for your partner, not only because of your many accomplishments but because of those quiet moments when you are a patient listener.

Leo-Aquarius: The Spark Plugs

Leo + Aquarius = Bright and Exciting Thoughts about the Future

Yesterdays pass by quickly for this fleet-footed, fast-thinking sign pair. The sheer force of Leo's mind combined with Aquarius' lightning-speed intellect create a powerful match. These two can change reality with rugged determination and endless amounts of energy. Leo and Aquarius are quick to change course when a new opportunity captures their attention. These signs don't find it easy to concentrate on the present because the future beckons with tantalizing rewards. Both signs are fixed in nature, which does help in finishing what is started. Dramatic Leo and brainstorming Aquarius can lead each other into an exciting romance. Surprises seem to delight both signs. Each tends to spark new ideas in the other. Leo can inspire Aquarius to put its thoughts into action. Aquarius can help Leo to see a bigger picture.

Give Me Liberty or Give Me Death Game

The games played in your Leo-Aquarius relationship feature compulsive freedom drives and power struggles. The *Give Me Liberty or Give Me Death* game describes how the two of you might go overboard in declaring your own rights. There is a loss of perspective because your actions can be very one-sided. Leo makes no bones about the fact that its pet projects must be acknowledged (even worshiped!) by others. Aquarius may announce that its unique goals are off-limits unless someone is granted permission to see them. It does not take long to figure out that the two of you are hawks when it comes to your personal freedom. You may be doves on other issues but not this one! You have a tendency to take sudden rebellious action to make your point. The communication breakdowns that can become standard with this game are the real problem. You can grow distant in mind and heart. An aloof atmosphere surrounds you that makes life less satisfying. Equal freedom may be your goal but won't be achieved when you do not respect your partner's rights.

On Again Off Again Game

Fiery Leo and airy Aquarius can move at a fast pace. When your communication is erratic, you can be out of sync. The *On Again Off Again* game points to a disjointed type of relating. You can feel close one day and remote the next. Your individual goals may keep you from finding enough common ground. Each of you can be self-centered. Leo becomes quite attached to its creations. Aquarius can be pushy in asking others to promote its ideas. Independence is a must for you both. When you lose sight of each other due to the tremendous pull of personal goals, a feeling of separation can result. You may not make the effort to talk as much as you could. Becoming distracted by your own life can make it hard to concentrate on your partner. You lack the requisite focus to make your mutual ideas work. Somehow, you pull away from a team effort because of impulsive personal interests. Lacking mutual support for goals may be the problem. The two of you may feel there is no choice but to walk in your own directions.

Clash of Wills Game

Leo and Aquarius can be seriously at odds over decisions. When it reaches an extreme opposition, a *Clash of Wills* game is likely. When each of you makes up your mind about something, it may take an act of God to get you to change your position. The more you force your own will upon the other, the greater resistance you meet. An inability to adapt to your partner's needs can lead to scalding arguments. Each of you must feel that you can speak your mind. A strange silence can come between you. At this point you may be tired of fighting. A loss of interest in each other's goals is painful to swallow. Like a young child who so badly wants a parent to praise his or her talents, Leo craves attention. Aquarius wants its unique perceptions to be the center of conversation. This is a game that makes you intense adversaries rather than true partners.

Strategies

How can you steer clear of these Leo-Aquarius games? The *Give Me Liberty or Give Me Death* game describes a basic need in the heart and soul of each of you—freedom! Patrick Henry, who coined the name of this game, was not known to be a quiet and timid person. He was an American patriot and an outspoken revolutionary. So, you are assertive about demanding your freedom. Without it, you are lost. Can you have too much liberty? Probably not, according to you. Freedom requires that you act responsibly and with great awareness. You can find a way to coexist as equals. In this relationship, you will discover that cutting each other enough slack to pursue individual interests creates a winning formula. If you expect to always do what you want, the relationship loses balance in a hurry. You need to be conscious of how your actions affect your partner. If you communicate with a sense of doing what is in your *mutual* best interest, a miracle occurs. You do not feel a sudden urge to go off in a wildly reckless direction. Nobody can tell two such free-thinking souls to surrender their spontaneity. You may need to compromise on schedules once in a while; they do not have to be etched in stone. You will benefit as a couple if you have a means to keep track of one another. You can be outspoken people. This isn't bad *per se*. At least you know what is going on in each other's minds. Respect for each other's rights makes your relationship's work flow. It may be fun to shock your lover with a surprise, but be sure that you don't blow each other out of the water. You should also be sensitive about punctuality. You would be well advised to value each other's time.

The *On Again Off Again* game may be based on mutual fears. You may be frightened of getting too close. A sudden desire to push your partner away might be due to guarding your feelings. It simply may be that the two of you are changeable. You can't make up your mind about how much time you want to spend together. Interestingly, the one who feels this way could alternate. You are going to need more space than other couples. Be sure to regulate your desire for closeness and space through clear communication; doing so will prevent feelings of rejection. Sometimes it really helps to give in if your partner truly could use your support—even if it means you must change your schedule.

The *Clash of Wills* game tests your negotiation skills. Part of the success formula is your willingness to listen. When you are open to each other's point of view, a fair resolution to what appears to be an irreconcilable difference may present itself. You both have tremendous strength to forcefully push your ideas. Your adversaries would rather you fight with each other than direct your power at them. You have more fun when you are allies. Channel this energy toward your shared goals; it is more productive. Besides, much of your passion is lost due to the suction of this game. Turning this dilemma of opposing forces around does wonders for your love life and the realization of your dreams!

The Rainbow

Your Leo-Aquarius relationship is as unusual as it is creative. You can please one another with your attention. The directions you choose at times will be the same and at other times quite unique. You feel reassured when you sense your partner's blessings as you travel along your own distinct path. You can breathe confidence into your partner's spirit like few others can. When you take the time to learn the way to your partner's heart, you experience one great event after another. The love you seek in each other cannot be taken for granted. When you realize how much you have going for you, life seems more generous. You will never be able to walk in exactly the same shoes. Why would two such unique minds want to do so anyway? You are each guided by an imagination that can change reality with persistent effort. This is a romance that deepens when each lover dances to his or her own music yet can appreciate the music that inspires his or her partner.

The Leo man is quickly captivated by the Aquarius woman's innovative mind. He thinks she is quite a catch, that is, if he can catch up with her! She seems unpredictable yet can be predictable when she wants to see him. The Leo man finds the Aquarius woman's ideas exhilarating. He wonders if she ever really does half of the things she describes, yet he wouldn't be surprised if there were that many more directions her mind has already explored. The Lion is slightly intimidated by her ferociously independent streak. This Uranian woman is offbeat and has a rhythm that's all her own. The Lion wants to make music with her but isn't sure how to join her. The Leo man is not normally one for waiting for his cue, but this is one time that he tries to be on his best behavior. This seemingly cool woman flashes her warmest smile when he shows her that he is her greatest fan. He laughs to himself because she is a lot like him; being the center of attention feels wonderful. Her passion seems connected to her freedom.

Let the Games Begin

He knows he will never control the Aquarius woman. He isn't so sure he wants to because it's more fun to not know what she will do next!

The Aquarius woman enters the Leo man's life with some apprehension, not because she can't handle him but because his presence is so powerful. She likes the idea of a strong shoulder to lean on, but he is far too real for comfort. The Uranian woman notices that he appreciates her unique insights even if he does not follow her logic, which can be eccentric. She is pleased to see that he listens anyway. The Aquarius woman picks up the fact that he loves freedom too. She is not foolish enough to think they will ever be of like minds. If they are soul mates, their common bond is their passion to pursue their dreams. Mutual accomplishments are not the point of this relationship, even though some goals are shared. He has heart; so does she. He can be sensitive, huffy, passionate, demanding, tender, or royal. She can be warm, aloof, passionate, delicate, unconventional, and individualistic. She hopes his sensitive nature can connect with her softer side even while they relentlessly pursue one another, leaving all reason behind.

The Leo woman is not sure what to make of the Aquarius man. He lives in his own world yet invites her to join him. His mind is sharp when he talks about what excites him, and he has electric intensity when he describes his visions. He seems to be sensitive and has the air of someone who has been misunderstood. The Leo woman admires his boldness but wishes he could more readily express feelings. A well-defined intellect is his dominant feature, and his thoughts often seem to be far off in the universe. He loves his work. She hopes he will cherish her with the same intensity. She is excited by the thought of spending the future together. Her only concern is that their wills are as strong as they come. Her own feeling is that she can accept his aberrant ways if he will tolerate her own. She hopes this Uranian man can move beyond the intellect to connect with his feelings. He anticipates the thoughts of others with unusual accuracy. He is often one step ahead of even the fastest computer. She only hopes this unusual man can read her heart, especially when she holds it out to him.

The Aquarius man is moved by the vivacious spirit of the Leo woman. He detects a well-controlled wildness in her, or maybe he sees her like this in his imagination because it pleases him. He likes her laugh because it reminds him to do the same. He would like to let go and trust his feelings. When he is near her, matters of the heart seem surrealistic. He sees his feelings reflected in her. The Uranian man is a bit disarmed when he truly trusts a Leo woman. She loves his mind but doesn't worship it.

The Magic of Signmates

This is refreshing for someone so able to rule his world with his intellect. He loves her but is scared to feel so intensely about anyone—even himself. His world is as detached as the stars above the earth. The Leo woman reaches deep into the heart of the Aquarius man, that is, if he will let her in. The Aquarius man is a natural match for the Leo woman. It is his birthright to quickly take what he thinks will fulfill him. It is her birthright to seek out a partner who will passionately love her. These two signs enjoy mating when both fall in love with a partner of equal power.

If you're not two of a kind, you certainly are two with a similar plan. Even if your paths are not identical, you can follow your partner's lead. You may become disappointed that you can't always take each other's blues away. You will be glad you can incite each other to rebel against boredom and the things you shouldn't tolerate. Leo can make life respond to its heartfelt requests. Aquarius can direct the universe with its intellect. You are two lovers who need to be careful what you ask for because you are apt to find that someone, somewhere, is listening, and it might be each other!

Leo-Pisces: The Actors

Leo + Pisces = Intense Drama

At first glance, these two signs seem as different as night and day. What would a fiery, egocentric Lion and a watery, sensitive Fish have in common? Both have vivid imaginations. Leo may be known for acting on impulse, but Pisces can keep up with the Lion's pace when chasing its own dreams. The two can entertain each other with great theatrics. This imaginative duo will endure few dull moments. People will be convinced that this is a strikingly creative couple. These signs sometimes meet through unusual circumstances—like the hand of fate. Leo can excite Pisces to act on ideas. Pisces may influence Leo to reflect before exerting its dynamic will. Leo and Pisces find that watching each other perform is fulfilling and stimulating.

Back Draft Game

The games played in your Leo-Pisces relationship are connected to deflated energy drives and a loss of enthusiasm. The *Back Draft* game shows that the two of you can deny your anger for long periods of time and then suddenly be caught in an emotional explosion. When smoke pours from a fire-filled room, you must be careful when you open the door because flames could ride the air currents and rush right at you! Similarly, when Leo and Pisces hold back their true feelings, there is no telling what kind of response can be in store when this intensity is released. The fiery Lion bursts at the seams when it does not express its feelings. Pisces becomes disoriented and goes in circles. Each of you can experience great distance from the other. Instead of passion, you create confusion. The communication between you is probably unclear when caught in this game. The clarity you seek is overshadowed by the denial of your true feelings.

Love Is Blind Game

When the two of you don't want to see anything wrong, you may be playing the *Love Is Blind* game. Avoiding conflict is often the source of this behavior. Unfinished business can come back to haunt you later. Sometimes this game is due to idealizing one another. You do not see the true picture. Denial of problems may seem to make life more pleasant. In the long run, you only create issues that need to be dealt with later. Leo can want so much to be loved that the Lion will not want to see any flaws in others. Pisces can be so much in love with love that it is painful to do sound reality testing. It's not easy to make sound decisions in this atmosphere. Your commitment will seem vague and hard to define. Your love is too much on a surface level. You are probably resisting taking your relationship to a deeper emotional level. Infatuation only lasts so long. Eventually, the nuts and bolts of everyday interaction need your attention.

Disappearing Act Game

Leo makes a fine cheerleader for those it loves. Pisces can believe in others to the utmost level. When one of you notices that there is no support from the other, the *Disappearing Act* game can be in play. You seem invisible to each other. Leo can become so preoccupied with its own plan that it is totally self-absorbed. Pisces might put all of its energy into a cause. Hurt feelings could cause either of you to pull back. Usually, some form of running away is involved in this game. You may feel discounted if your partner has a pattern of not supporting your goals. Trust can be shattered. You both thrive on attention. The inspiration that comes from mutually believing in and supporting one another is absent.

Strategies

How can you prevent these games from interfering with the best of your love? In the *Back Draft* game, you must learn to talk honestly. Leo can show great courage when confronting adverse circumstances; however, Leo may back away to avoid potential fallout later. Pisces is not always passive, but the Fish prefers to contain its anger. Leo usually isn't as bothered by situations that become emotionally messy. Pisces likes to keep things neat, including angry outbursts. Both of you can be moody. Somehow, the real challenge is to understand the unique way each of you expresses anger. Leo would rather be direct and deal with conflict quickly. "The sooner the better" agrees with the Lion's way of thinking.

Pisces prefers to go slowly. The Fish is protective of its sensitive emotional nature. It doesn't necessarily matter how you get to the point as long as you get there! The explosion is less likely to occur if you two will keep the communication door at least cracked. Two passionate people such as yourselves can't tolerate the feeling that you are waiting for the bombshell to hit for long. Leo and Pisces intensify one another's emotional world. Let's face it, life isn't the same when you get together. Leo accelerates Pisces' drive to make dreams real. Pisces elevates Leo's consciousness and inspires the Lion to act with renewed creative passion. What happens when you hide your anger? Resentment and contempt take root. If you want to turn the page, the answer is simple. Talk with the purpose of bringing together your individual agendas; eventually, you will work as a couple.

In the *Love Is Blind* game, you both need to perceive each other more realistically. Your partner is not perfect, never was perfect, and never will be perfect. Don't try to change each other to fit an idealized myth about love. Pisces and Leo are both happier when accepting a lover's imperfections. It creates a relaxed and flowing atmosphere. Leo can be such a boost of energy for its partner. Pisces can show great faith in revealing its inner self to those it loves. When in a fantasy, the Fish can swim far out to the middle of the ocean, hiding its real ideas. The two of you will be more content when you can understand your partner's real needs. Denial isn't your friend. It takes courage to put your relationship under the spotlight. You may not like everything that you see in each other. Who does? What attracted you is only the beginning. With authentic communication, you can know your lover that much more. Intimacy and passion can reach all-time highs!

When you show faith in one another, you dispel the darkness of the *Disappearing Act* game. You are even a much more creative couple. Your individual talents rise to another level. You feel luckier! Two romantics who need to know that the other is solidly supportive—doesn't this sound like you? Leo can't stand to look over its shoulder for its partner or to wonder whether its lover is supportive. Pisces is disturbed when a lover takes a leave of absence when needed most. When you consistently show up for each other, your sense of trust blossoms. The lover you thought you had found can really prove to be real.

The Magic of Signmates

The Rainbow

Your Leo-Pisces relationship is filled with magic. You can lift each other's heart to new plateaus. You may be surprised because your ability to visualize and attain your greatest potential is enhanced through joining forces. When you make a solid commitment to each other, you feel free to show off your talents. Fiery Leo pushes watery Pisces to be bold in pursuing goals. Dreamy Pisces entices Leo to reach beyond doubt to affirm its strong sense of self-confidence. You thrive on each other's faith. When you communicate clearly, the happiness you desire is ever present. You were born under distinctly different signs in terms of finding love and success. Leo's energy is expressed through action. Pisces' energy is expressed through intuition. You have much to teach one another. When you are open-minded to each other's path to self-discovery, the doors to your hearts are never locked.

A Leo man looks in bewilderment at the Pisces woman. She weaves her magic right before his eyes. He is curious about how she manages to keep her dreams separate from reality. The two worlds seem to be merged, yet she handles both artistically. "Her idealism is somewhat like mine," he thinks. Yet, she holds out more hope in life than he ever dares to. She seems to be forever the romantic. He likes this side of her because it is similar to the romantic in him. She seems capable of acting out various roles, which appeals to this dramatic man. He can relate to this dreamy, Neptunian woman. He finds her thoughts more complex than his own, or perhaps she just approaches life with a more diaphanous sense of reality. The Lion hopes his directness will not offend this sensitive woman's heart. The Leo man tries to be on his best behavior, but this poetic spirit before him seems to enjoy it when he expresses his bold fiery self. He notices that she listens patiently to him and that she appreciates those times when he quietly focuses his attention on her.

A Pisces woman sees that the Leo man's faith mirrors her own, yet he acts upon his faith more readily. He bolts ahead without hesitation, which she can only do in her dreams. She wants the Leo man to see that she has a brave heart too. She does not want to reveal her sensitivity. He seems to truly listen to her, and she hopes he hears her cry for love. She senses that her feminine spirit has captivated this interesting, passionate man. She believes that he could be demanding and protective. Her concerns dissipate when she learns that he is as romantic as she is. The Pisces woman wants to take her time in getting to know this fiery Lion. She knows that going slow is not his natural inclination, and in this case it isn't her inclination either. She may rush toward him just as quickly as he does toward her if he will only treat her as the most special person he has met in quite some time.

A Leo woman may feel the need to take the lead in a romance with the Pisces man. He acts like time doesn't exist, but her heart doesn't like to wait forever. The Pisces man is as mystical as a Zen monk, yet can he as down-to-earth as a Wall Street trader. She is amazed at the depth of this man's feelings. He appears to have been looking for love for some time. She hopes her love is one that won't be passed over lightly. This fiery woman desires to be noticed by this intuitive man who seems to see distant horizons. He loves his causes; she sees this from their first meeting. When she looks into his eyes she recognizes a complex being. On one level, he is intensely private and does not want others to be able to read him. On another level, he seems to be an open book, but she soon learns that, in reality, he will only let you in so far. She takes heart when he appears to realize that he may never find anyone who will love him so passionately. The Leo woman is no idle dreamer. She wants to see if he can come out to play and become part of a shared drama. If he is, she will grab on, and he may never get her to let go.

The Pisces man is attracted to the lively spirit of the Leo woman. The Leo woman exercises a freedom he would like to more spontaneously allow himself. She makes him smile with her lively sense of humor. The Pisces man is hesitant to fall in love with such a fiery woman. Then again, the love she directs at him is so forceful and so delicious that he can't really resist. His ideals are energized when he tells her about them. Even when she is blunt, she exhibits refined sensitivity as though she knows the power of her time-tested words. The Pisces man is drawn to her self-confidence because it resembles his own when he rides the force of his own inspiration. He hates to admit how much she could eventually mean to him. There is a risk in falling for such a free spirit. Then again, this Neptunian man has already made many daring leaps into the unknown in the search for paradise, so what's one more jump?

You two can have a fabulous, exhilarating ride together. You greatly enrich each other's life, and you have an intense desire to show your love. Passion and romance will seldom fail to reach your receptive hearts. When you keep each other in mind as you pursue your own unique aspirations, the distance that separates you is never all that wide. You hold your partner's fate in your hands. From the very first embrace, you are lovers with a special flair for making one another feel special. You can be partners in business or love. Make sure to fulfill your promises to each other. When you are there for your lover in the good and the bad times, you become lovers for all seasons.

Virgo-Virgo: The Organizers

Virgo + Virgo = Powers of Analysis

This is a romance in which you are not afraid to do business. A pragmatic atmosphere governs this relationship. Your mercurial minds have a knack for details. As a couple, you can exercise great patience. You can go out of your way to please each other sexually. Virgo is not all business! A sixth sense for organization is a hallmark of this sign. Planning is usually a snap for this earth sign, which can make the most efficient arrangements on the face of the planet. Carrying a torch for work isn't much of a stretch here, but putting fun into the daily routine could be. It helps to see the lighter side and to recognize that life is more fun when you reward yourselves. Commitment is likely to be valued in this liaison. These signs take pride in being reliable. A dedication to excellence is likely a common trait.

Too Finely Sifted Game

The games played in your Virgo-Virgo relationship are associated with being overly critical and losing sight of the big picture. When the two of you find fault with each other, you could be in the *Too Finely Sifted* game. Telling Virgo not to be analytical is like asking a cat to never wash itself—impossible! The remarks you make regarding each other's imperfections may become aggravating. Virgo sees details that most miss. You will continue to be disappointed if you hope that your lover will become perfect. It doesn't work to try to change each other. You can really take the spontaneity out of life by getting lost in the details. Excessive reliance on the left brain may block your imagination; not enough of a "let it flow" mentality gets through your finely-honed perceptions.

Worry may cause you to be critical and make you unwilling to step back and cut each other some slack.

White Tornado Game

Guess what? The rest of the world knows that you are good workers. Your sign is a shoo-in to be a finalist for the hardest worker award (Capricorn is a strong rival in this category). The *White Tornado* game occurs when you take the work ethic too far. A failure to set limits can get you into trouble. It could deplete the romance account even to the point of bankruptcy. It's not easy for you to leave a job undone. What you start, you feel a compulsion to finish. Your schedules may be filled to the max with obligations. It doesn't take long to lose that old romantic feeling when you are exhausted. Burnout can haunt Virgo. Good intentions can somehow balloon in such a way that they exhaust you. Your sign loves to be of service. Once again, watch how caught up you get in causes and good works. There may be less and less time in your already filled schedules for romantic moments. Exhaustion doesn't do much for your love life. The balance between responsibility and leisure is out of alignment.

Not Seeing the Forest for the Trees Game

If you become too lost in the details, the *Not Seeing the Forest for the Trees* game can manifest. You may irritate each other by becoming overly preoccupied with nagging details. A broad perspective is missing. The powers of discrimination are so strong in your sign that they can keep you from gaining wider insight. Your distrust of intuition can be one of the causes. You may question each other's spontaneous impulses to the point that you don't even try them. Projects may go unfinished even though your instinct is to finish them. Disagreements over the way to fine tune the little things can keep you constantly bickering. You may disappoint each other if you can't stay focused on your primary objectives when you work together.

Strategies

How can you stay clear of these Virgo-Virgo games? In the *Too Finely Sifted* game, you need to somehow not become obsessed with each other's imperfections. Accepting the fact that you will make mistakes is a good start. Shutting off the analytical part of the brain takes practice. You have to show faith by not worrying. Stressing doesn't necessarily make a job go better. You can't really change your partner into someone who better fits your exacting standards. When you trust each other to the point that you are not scrutinizing one another's actions under a microscope, good things happen. There is more of a flow to your being together when you stay away from being overly critical. It is irritating to continuously have your life reviewed by someone. You will enjoy greater love when you free yourselves from your investigative tendencies.

In the *White Tornado* game, the two of you can refocus your work energies toward leisure or romantic activities. "All work and no play" numb passion. Virgo's imagination can be used to figure out ways to escape from responsibility. Virgo often is called upon to bail others out of jams. Don't make yourselves too available to serve the world. Let people learn to miss you so you don't miss out on exciting experiences together. You need to watch those busy schedules and get good at setting boundaries. It's easy to become addicted to routines. Learn to be open to unexpected opportunities that come your way.

The *Not Seeing the Forest for the Trees* game only asks you to stop getting so absorbed with details that you forget larger goals. Opening up your perceptions to encompass more far-reaching ideas can be stimulating. You have short-range planning down to a science. Virgo can write books on detail management. It's vital that you allow one another to embrace the future with intuitive imagination. Enjoying each step along the creative process is more fun when you have a vision of the whole journey, which makes the parts in the journey fit together. You both have minds that like to know all of the ifs, ands, and buts in problem-solving. You can adopt a more relaxed mental posture by trusting your intuition. Many people are so "right-brained" that they become spaced out. This isn't going to happen to you. Don't analyze when perhaps you could trust your intuition to allow you to see a broader perspective. Even when you try to share insights with your partner, it helps if you can tune in to your overall goals rather than merely looking for immediate solutions.

The Rainbow

Your Virgo-Virgo relationship can take you to paths that lead to great accomplishments. A no-nonsense approach guides you and allows you to see the ironies within the challenges before you. A sense of humor helps you to better digest your differences. A drive for perfection can't help but spill over into some areas of your life. Just be reasonable in your expectations of your lover; this is a key to your happiness. You delight in the way your partner remembers the little things that you like. There are few couples with your business savvy. You hate to waste time. Focus your critical eyes on what you want to solve together rather than worrying about how to change each other. You are both mercurial, so put that mental ingenuity to work so that your life together stays exciting. You will grow irritable when bored. Make sure that you throw an occasional monkey wrench into your routine. Travel may be an avenue of exploration that allows you to fall in love all over again.

A Virgo man sees some of himself in the Virgo woman. She likes exact answers. So does he. The male Virgo may try to act carefree, but underneath it all he doesn't care to be so spontaneous. He senses that the Virgo woman would prefer that he be slightly unpredictable just to keep her guessing. The Virgo man appreciates people with precise minds and is attracted to her earthy and sensual presence. The Mercurian man likes the way the Mercurian woman thinks. She is quick with her responses yet thoughtful about her feelings. He tries to conquer his reserved nature to approach this mentally acute female. She seems to anticipate his ideas. The Virgo man looks for a partner with a taste for business. He adores the down-to-earth logic of this woman. He is surprised to hear such a fun-loving laugh emanate from such a serious person. He is not usually at ease so quickly. He knows the search for a perfect lover is fraught with peril. He would like to cast aside caution and boldly show his true self, but the fear of rejection haunts him. Still, the thought of being in love with the Mercurian woman thrills him.

A Virgo woman knows she will need to be fast thinking when the Virgo man challenges her ideas. She sees that he doubts the validity of anyone else's thoughts. Not everyone can perceive this, but this Mercurian woman sees right through this man's logic. The Virgo woman isn't intimidated by his keen perceptions. She senses that humility guides his strong intellect. A river of passion runs through him; it's just a matter of getting him to stop long enough to tap into his feelings. She senses that their values are not so far apart and fit together logically. She appreciates his business savvy, and they share a strong rational streak. She would like to tickle his funny bone—if only to be sure he can laugh. He seems to be two men: one is all business while the other asks to be loved.

You are a couple who can realize goals faster than many. When you are committed to a project, it will be done with painstaking thoroughness. The joy you feel can multiply in the knowledge that you have such a thoughtful advocate in your corner. There isn't much you can put over on one another. You are of like minds. Allow for different paths that express your individuality because divergent avenues spice up your routine. Life can be enjoyable when you lift each other's perceptions to higher altitudes. Share your

Let the Games Begin

knowledge with your partner freely. You respond quite well when you give to each other without demanding that your partner plead for your generosity. You remain deeply in love when you don't forget to prioritize your hearts.

Virgo-Libra: The Allies

Virgo + Libra = Plenty of Ideas

Virgo and Libra give one another a lot to think about. The common-sense logic of Virgo mixes nicely with strategy-minded Libra. The two can find life together intriguing. Virgo's mental curiosity never really rests. Libra always compares and weighs options. Somehow, the two of you manage to put your minds toward the same purposes. Virgo will never be quite as ruled by pleasing others as Libra. Making peace with opposing forces fascinates Libra (which is symbolized by the scales). Perhaps Libra's sense of fairness makes it such a good mediator between right and wrong. Problem resolution is simpler for Virgo. This earth sign can cut right down to the precise answer. Virgo is not as attached to considering both sides of issues though trying to determine the "perfect" answer can be its own source of aggravation. Libra will eventually arrive at a choice after undergoing what seems like a mystical process. Libra really wants to have its decisions accepted and to be seen as fair. This sign pairing can be loyal lovers. Balancing feelings with logic comes with time. Each wants to have its ideas confirmed by the other. There are constant negotiations between the two. There seems to be more time for lovemaking and down-to-earth passion when both decide to keep life simple.

Second-Guessing Game

The games in your Virgo-Libra relationship are linked to doubting one another and not accepting your unique personal styles. Questioning each other too much gives birth to the *Second-Guessing* game. Libra has enough trouble making a decision without criticism of its decision-making process. It is a crushing blow to this fair-minded air sign to find its choices being undermined. Virgo can become quite irritable if its prerogatives are held under suspicion. What's worse is that both of you can be nervous wrecks if put under the microscope. You may have trouble accepting what you dish out, so watch those judgments. This may be a case of winning a battle but losing the war. You may feel miserable when you thwart one another's spontaneity because you learn to expect criticism. If you interrogate each other's ideas, you will not enjoy working through issues. Criticism makes it a real chore to have "fun" together.

Cramped Style Game

Let's face it, Mercurian Virgo and Venusian Libra are not always going to look at reality the same way. If you demand that the other adopt your way of seeing the world, look out! When Virgo is angry, it can come up with a few choice one-liners that send Libra's head spinning. If Libra feels pushed into a corner, it can respond with a fierce demeanor that would frighten Julius Caesar. You are not the same people when you do not pursue your unique goals. You are passionate lovers when nourished by individual ambitions. Crankiness takes over when you are not given adequate breathing room by your partner. You both have different thought processes; there's no getting around this. Your unique gifts seem to make you appreciate each other. Each of you will feel discounted if your personal autonomy is not recognized. Libra loves to have peers outside its primary relationships. Virgo needs multiple projects to stay stimulated. There are certain innate needs that must be tolerated. If not, you will sense that something is missing. Your romance isn't as passionate and fulfilling as you would like.

Skimming the Surface Game

When the two of you beat around the bush, you could be playing the *Skimming the Surface* game. Virgo may fear intimacy. Chitchatting is one way to stay away from the deep emotional waters. Libra can win "socialite of the year" awards. Libra can glide right over feelings in the guise of various roles. What is left in the aftermath of this game? Possibly a haze of confusion caused by not saying what really needed to be said. When you do not let each other into your inner world, it's hard to read who you really might be; you are just a figment of each other's imagination. In essence, you walk lightly around the borders of each other's feelings, and neither of you is willing to make the first move past the borders. The distance between you can be great. Fear is probably in the way of a meeting between your minds and hearts. You can be a busy duo. Spending time with each other's social circles and at favorite hangouts can be stimulating. When you sense that you don't really know each other on a deeper level, you hold back your sense of trust.

Strategies

How do you get untangled from these Virgo-Libra games? In the *Second-Guessing* game, you must have faith in each other's decisions. This is easier said than done, but think about it for a second. You are never going to trust your partner's ability to make decisions if you don't give his or her reasoning a chance. Neither of you has all of the answers. You are a much more dynamic team when each exercises his or her own powers of discrimination. Virgo doesn't have any greater claim to analytical abilities than Libra when it comes to the ability to resolve ambiguity. Each of you has powerful skills in the area of sound thinking. Putting your minds together works better when you show tolerance for individual opinions. You can both be creative thinkers. You can do great things for each other when you stay away from negative thinking. It might take practice to get good at responding positively toward your partner's perceptions, but the payoff is tremendous. The love you seek is easier to reach when you listen to one another's ideas. You don't have to agree! The main thing is that you are willing to consider the other's point of view.

Allowing each other to pursue individual goals lessens the likelihood that the *Cramped Style* game will show its face. You don't want to be accused of plundering each other's territory. Virgo resents infringements upon its routine. Libra has a love affair with its own personal style, which may be expressed in Libra's "look" or in the way this sign relates to a wide variety of people. If you tread these areas lightly, you are most of the way home to peaceful coexistence. Each of you needs a few creative outlets that allow you to prove that you are special. You owe it to yourselves to make sure there are multiple outlets for self-expression. You won't always fit neatly into each other's reality. It's tempting for Virgo, in its quest for order, to try to force another to fall in line with its reasoning. Libra has a special relationship to beauty or harmony that sometimes leads this sign to reinvent a partner in its own image. Neither of these approaches is wise. You will thoroughly enjoy each other if you embrace your unique qualities. Virgo's pragmatism seems to fit nicely with Libra's need for harmony. First, you must acknowledge each other's reality before you can expect the other to adopt your view of reality. Your minds are not all that far apart from the start. It may take some time to see that you both want your lover to be your friend.

The *Skimming the Surface* game asks you to let go of the fear of revealing your emotional side. Libra is naturally at home in the social world while Virgo is usually a bit more edgy in this arena. Since you both can pick up a lot to talk about through dealings with others, conversations with each other can be lively. You both still may hide behind factual information that isn't as threatening to discuss. When you open up your feelings, a deeper dimension of your relationship unfolds. It takes courage to let someone into your inner world and may even be scary. Once you take the plunge, it becomes easier to talk about your feelings. You may even find it empowering to keep fewer secrets. The trust that results will make you truly appreciate each other.

The Rainbow

Your Virgo-Libra relationship is one that offers both of you steady and reliable companionship. When you navigate toward exciting growth it opens your minds to vast potential. Your business sense is heightened, especially when the two of you feel free to participate in key decisions. It is essential that you pull back from the front lines of work. Romantic getaways calm your frayed nerves and allow you to focus on each other again. People will rely on your insights. You may find it rewarding to offer your advice to those in need. Be sure you don't go overboard in giving so much of yourselves to others that there is little time for each other. Common causes fire up your enthusiasm and add to the reasons you want to be together.

A Virgo man is quickly aware of the Libra woman. She handles herself with graceful ease, carefully balancing her mind and emotions. The Virgo man senses that this Venusian woman doesn't want someone to unexpectedly upset her sense of balance. He surmises that she likes the idea of surprises but not the disruption to her peace of mind that they entail. The earthy Mercurian man, who worships order, appreciates the Libra woman's organized mind. She is not as analytical as he is but has a keen awareness of what is directly in front of her. He feels that her heart is sensitive but not easily fooled. She seems to be more of a romantic than he. He wonders how he can convince her that he is a romantic at heart, though this side of him is often hidden in the real world. This Venusian woman encourages him to show more of his inner world than he likes for others to see. Maybe if he can give her things of value, she will love him. He suspects that she will want to at least catch a glimpse of his passion. This is a bit scary, but she doesn't seem intimidating or threatening. He wonders how she keeps her youthful looks.

A Libra woman looks right into the soul of the Virgo man and appreciates his love of ideas and well-conceived plans. He seems to be insulated against emotional trauma. She wonders how he manages to play the game of love without letting down his defenses. He is guarded by quick mental impulses that guide him as surely as a seeing-eye dog. The Venusian woman is moved by the details that this Mercurian man notices about her. He reads many of her thoughts clearly. He comforts her by listening. She senses that both of them know there is a great potential for real romance. The Libra woman finds his attentiveness to be an invitation to intimacy. She notices that when she shows interest in his accomplishments, he invites her to draw closer. She is not so afraid of the journey with the Virgo man when she observes that he doesn't criticize her choices. The Venusian woman has her indulgences. One indulgence is her many social connections. Another is her allegiance to beauty whether it is found in sunrises or stylish clothing. She will let go that much more when the Mercurian man tolerates the whims that sustain her.

A Virgo woman likes the way that the Libra man accepts responsibility. She needs to be assured of her partner's sense of responsibility before falling in love. She can't be blamed for feeling this way; it is a primordial instinct. The Virgo woman notices that the Libra man is bothered by choices almost as much as she. With her, it is caused by a relentless conscientiousness to be thorough. The Mercurian woman sees that decisions are hard for the Libra man because he tries to balance opposing factions. She senses that he has a past of ups and downs in relationships related to his desire to please others. He appears to be in search of a lover who will bring out his sense of adventure. The Virgo woman doesn't know what she likes the most about him. His voice is soothing—almost a meditation for her overworked mind. She is also fond of his beautiful smile. He draws out her sense of romanticism because he knows how to touch her love of beauty. The Mercurian woman wants to know how long their love could last. Once again, you can't blame her; she has an innate sense of reality that most lack in matters of the heart. If anyone can make her hopeful, it's this suave Venusian man.

A Libra man notices the adroit business perceptions of the Virgo woman. He likes her keen sense of how the world functions. She can keep up with the Libra man's many interests. He believes that she is a good match for him. He needs a partner who can point out when he takes too long to make up his mind. He notices that her face becomes animated when she talks about her dedication to a plan. She seems so serious one moment, but can display a lightheartedness that is refreshing. She doesn't seem to take herself as seriously as the demands others place on her. The Libra man is looking for romance and business in one package. This Mercurian woman almost seems too good to be true. He realizes that she isn't fond of those who take advantage of her resources. The Venusian man wants to please her with romance. He senses that she likes this but is more interested in his genuine feelings. The Libra man is warmed by the Mercurian woman's awareness of his sensitivity. She makes it easy for him to know her feelings. His only dilemma is deciding how fast to pursue this woman. He has a feeling that he better get a move on, or she will act on her own plan to take him by siege.

You are two lovers who fit together as smoothly as sky and earth. It's true that you probably use distinct reference points in judging your actions. You both feel freer when making choices based on your own prerogatives. Let each other have the leverage to make your own mistakes. That's better than having them made for you, don't you agree? Thinking things through together is where you set yourselves apart from many. You have a creative sign-mate chemistry. Let your love guide you to be fair and aware when deciding which courses to follow. You can offer one another new insights. Enjoy the world you can build together. It's big enough to fit all of your needs.

Virgo-Scorpio: The Thorough Ones

Virgo + Scorpio = In-depth Planning

These two signs can dissect any idea or thought down to its bare bones. An intense drive to be successful is part of this sign chemistry. There are few couples who can outthink or outwork this pair. Virgo can help Scorpio to stay focused on following through on decisions. Scorpio influences Virgo to remember that passion is required for one's best efforts to be successful. Both can be quite dedicated to excellence. These are two lovers who can fight and forgive in an instant. The emotional turmoil that brews regularly seems to fuel great creativity. Each prefers to maintain stability because it is easier on the mind and body. Virgo can encourage Scorpio not to miss important details. Scorpio reminds Virgo to be aware of the underlying reasons for actions. A winning formula is based on making each other feel confident in your chosen roles.

Introspection Game

The games played in your Virgo-Scorpio relationship are linked to becoming too contemplative and negating one another's greatest ideas. Both of your signs have a tendency at times to grow quiet in the midst of heavy-duty thinking. The *Introspection* game is one in which you both can disappear when you delve into possible solutions or choices. Watery Scorpio can withdraw completely when processing events. The Scorpion instinctively retreats to an internal cave, safely hidden from the outer world. Scorpio is emphatic about its privacy. Virgo can go into an apparent mental funk when reasoning through situations. This Mercury-ruled sign vacillates among options, trying to find a satisfying solution. Neither of these methods is wrong. Your signs have a tendency to sometimes cause the other to go even further within to figure out a problem. A lack of communication for extended periods may cause confusion. You may fear getting too close because you can be moody when you are thinking through things. Avoiding an open discussion usually leads to trouble. It's hard to know the right way to interact with one another. You may even give a signal to leave you alone. The dilemma is how to initiate a conversation when neither of you is approachable.

Constant Craving Game

If you get lost in compulsive desires, you may be in the middle of the *Constant Craving* game, which highlights a lack of awareness in setting limits. Work excesses can take over. Why? Virgo can lose sight of when to stop. The urge to achieve perfection can drive this earth sign to go on and on until it drops from exhaustion. Virgo can worry itself into nervous anxiety by obsessing over details. Scorpio can become consumed with control issues. How does this manifest? Possibly as an inability to know when enough is enough. The need for control can drive the Scorpion to forget limits. A deep, irrational desire to satisfy the hunger for success or love throws the relationship out of balance. The great perceptions and probing awareness that you share can be superseded by a strong drive to recklessly prove yourselves. Your relationship loses perspective if you make unreasonable demands on one another. The love you want to share is not as accessible if you are distracted by other concerns.

Sabotage Game

The Sabotage game is a case of positive thinking turned to negative thinking. This is often unconscious behavior, which doesn't make it any less unpleasant. You make it difficult for your partner to reach goals. This game may be caused by unresolved anger or jealousy. Virgo will be critical if its opinions are ignored. Scorpio is insulted when its feelings are trampled. Virgo seeks power through the implementation of its ideas. Scorpio finds it empowering to be supported in its decisions. The Scorpion will go forward regardless of the opinion of others but will resent being betrayed at the last minute. You both are sensitive about the acceptance of your key ambitions. You create minefields when you don't give the support each of you wants. The power you can create together is much less when you are two signs divided, not united.

Strategies

How can you get through these Virgo-Scorpio games? In the *Introspection* game, it helps to remember one main ingredient. Can you take a guess? Yes, you are right: communication! Silence isn't necessarily threatening to either of you nor should it be.

Virgo can use a calming period to get its thoughts in order. Scorpio likes time alone to process the past or to rehash present options. You can have the best of both worlds in this relationship. Just don't be too anxious about your partner's need for space. Then again, don't let too much distance settle in before someone breaks the ice. Your talent for going beneath the surface of things can be well utilized in business. You are two of the best-matched signs when it comes to negotiation skills. Don't let your lover's moods intimidate you, though you may need to pick the right time to discuss touchy subjects. Passion isn't passive. When you draw out each other's emotional intensity, expect strong reactions now and then. When one or both of you seek escape, it helps to let your partner know why you are withdrawing. It may be wise to let each other help with problem-solving. You may even get a boost in working through a problem. Privacy can be strengthening, but use it wisely; you can alienate your lover if you don't communicate. Encourage input from your partner because it will strengthen your bond.

The *Constant Craving* game takes discipline to curb its appetite. Set a few limits so you can have fun and romance in your lives. It's easy to innocently start a project and then allow enthusiasm to whip you into a frenzy. Success can make you want to work even harder. There is nothing at all wrong with this. The problem arises when your ambition or desire eats away at your time together. Anyone can succumb to the demands made by schedules. Sometimes, you will have to work more than you want to because that's reality. Be sure you don't needlessly contribute to a hectic lifestyle. Virgo and Scorpio stimulate thoroughness in one another. Keep an eye out that you don't become workaholics. Focus as much on romance as you do on business.

To shift beyond the *Sabotage* game, you need to be willing to refrain from negative, counterproductive comments. When you upset your partner, it actually hurts you. Getting anger out in the open is one way to defeat this game. Negativity has a way of holding you back. Your creative punch as a team is powerful. When you turn your energy against one another, it's like an airplane flying without all of its engines. It takes energy to think of ways to oppose each other. That energy is far more productively used to support each other. Love and passion are a lot more enjoyable when you rise above this game. You want to fly high with a positive regard for each other. Releasing the negative atmosphere reveals sunny skies with many possibilities.

The Rainbow

Your Virgo-Scorpio relationship can present numerous ways to find fulfillment. Life will test your perceptions to see if you can maintain a positive outlook. Stay clear on the values you have in common because this is a shared treasure. People probably see you as a serious couple. There is an intense quest to accomplish particular goals. You will likely challenge each other to live up to your own potential. A willingness to serve each other wins mutual admiration. When you are disciplined, there is little you cannot accomplish. When you make up your minds to take on a project, you can release a fury of energy to finish it. Finding the way into your lover's heart is easier if you make the effort to define a clear commitment. You both can differentiate fact from fiction in the business world in seconds. It is endearing when you know that you are receiving the best your lover has to offer.

A Virgo man is stopped in his tracks by the awesome presence of the Scorpio woman. She knows what she wants and how to get it, or so it appears to the Mercurian man. His mind can't seem to break through the mental frequencies of the Plutonian woman. She seems to know how to sidestep probing questions. This really gets the attention of the Virgo man. He likes her way of doing business. It reminds him of someone—himself! She has the tenacity to dig for information that most don't have the stomach for. The Mercurian man is thrilled by her passionate glance but is uncertain about his ability to connect with his emotions. He wants to let this woman into his life, though she may upset the order to which he is accustomed. "Oh, what the heck," he thinks, "life isn't going to be as much fun without her." The Virgo man's routines could use spicing up by this woman with deep, penetrating eyes. He only hopes he can keep her interest. She seems to already have figured out that he is hypnotized by her mysterious spirit. The Virgo man is delighted that this woman believes in him. "It must be true," he thinks. "What else explains how powerful and confident I feel?"

A Scorpio woman perceives the Virgo man as wise in many ways. He seems like he was born old. She enjoys his seasoned approach to life, but she wishes his view of passion wasn't so somber. He comforts her with his attentive listening. His eyes hint at a level of sensitivity that is not easily shown. Her persistence to know him wins his interest. She can't dedicate her life to him though he might want her to do so. The Scorpio woman feels allegiance to her own sense of self-mastery. Without it, she is lost at sea. She hopes this man with longing eyes will let her be. She maintains an inner reserve from which she draws her power; he must never infringe upon her space without explicit permission. When he demonstrates restraint and patience, she runs to him. When he shows impatience, she steps away. She, too, longs to be loved but not to be possessed. He looks like he wants to be claimed as her property, but she is not in the "lost and found" business. She is pleased that this Mercurian man's vision can see right into her heart. His courage to grasp the truth and to live according to his principles brings her into his life. She encourages him to see clearly.

A Virgo woman discerns right away that the Scorpio man has learned the ways of the world early in life. She responds to his heartfelt revelations rather than his penetrating intellect. "Intellectual coolness is his way to test me," she muses. The Mercurian woman can talk on the same level as the Plutonian man in business. She has been around the world in her own way. She may not have walked through his fires, but she knows all about heat. His vulnerability, which sneaks out when he doesn't even know that she sees it, captures her heart. The Scorpio man is strong. She hopes his strength was developed from standing up for his beliefs rather than fighting everybody else's. He is an ardent lover. She only hopes he knows about the deeper mysteries of love. His voice is sexy and cautiously guarded. He likes to evaluate her responses. She loves the way he reads her moods. She wants him to one day be as good at reading her heart. She has the time if he has the fortitude. His sincere desire to have someone understand him is intriguing. He is street smart and savvy about love. Why does this make her want him?

The Scorpio man recognizes that the Virgo woman is mentally alert. She has quick reflexes that guide her agile responses. The Plutonian man likes the way this Mercurian woman makes him think twice about what he says. He is usually reflective but not necessarily as a result of someone's remarks. The Scorpio man likes this woman's down-to-earth prognosis of life in general. It's not that she's negative—just that she is not overly optimistic. He tends to trust people who aren't too happy. The Plutonian man likes people who have real reason to be happy. He can't help this side of himself. He questions everything to see if it can pass the tests of time. The Scorpio man wants to explore love with the Virgo woman. Her powers of analysis haven't led her away from him, so he must have passed a test of her own device. She makes him feel love by responding to his feelings. He tries to resist his instinctual defenses because he really wants to feel her embrace. Not everyone can reach his inner sanctuary, which is invisible to most. She looks at him with curiosity and desire as if to say, "I will trust you, but I wish for once you will take me with you to that place within that makes your eyes sparkle."

You have a love that can take you anyplace in the world. There is sexual and creative power in your romance. You awaken desire and passion in each other that must be channeled carefully. Desire is nothing to fear but something to cherish. You can be the best of friends. Loyalty is something you expect and respond to in each other. You can't stand the thought of not trusting each other. As you talk during the times when life is testy, it brings you closer. Share your joy openly. Show your sorrows. Live your dreams visibly. Reveal your reasons for loving one another. It's all part of the package deal!

Virgo-Sagittarius: The Seekers

Virgo + Sagittarius = Yearning for Learning

In its own way, each of these signs has a sense of dedication. Virgo believes wholeheartedly in serving a cause or other worthy endeavors. Sagittarius wants to be the voice of idealism. The Archer loves to be a student and a teacher. Put these two signs together and you get power-packed philosophy combined with zeal and practicality. Neither wants to be preached to by the other. Virgo can become indifferent when its cherished beliefs are ridiculed. Sagittarius can turn a deaf ear when you question the truths that it finds self-evident. These two adaptable types like to travel to see what the world has to offer. Virgo and Sagittarius are at their best when sharing knowledge and self-taught expertise. This is a high-flying act when it comes to inspiration. Virgo helps Sagittarius to be aware of reality before taking a leap of faith. Sagittarius expands Virgo's perceptions. The two make lively lovers. Both want to make the other feel special.

The Glass Is Half Empty Game

The games in your Virgo-Sagittarius relationship are connected to a limiting attitude, changeable natures, and becoming too judgmental. In the *Glass Is Half Empty* game, you only see what you don't have and miss out on what you do possess. Virgo is careful to not neglect reality, and this inclination may go to an extreme and undermine an optimistic perspective. Usually happy-go-lucky Sagittarius can show signs of being extremely up or very down. If the Archer becomes disillusioned by circumstances, despondency can color and dominate its perceptions. It isn't much fun to perpetually see your life together as lacking opportunities. That's the antithesis of what you need in order to stay inspired. You will see fewer options if you don't embrace opportunities. When your mental attitude is negative, the impact you would ordinarily display on the world goes missing.

Mutable Game

The *Mutable* game is a case of creating too many options. The two of you can grow disoriented when your minds go in too many directions. Your hesitation to set limits can keep you from reaching decisions. Even the boundaries of your relationship may be vague. You can create so many possibilities that you don't move. Talking each other out of choices can be frustrating. Resentment can build if you start to blame one another for standing in your way. Virgo's desire to learn combined with Sagittarius' excitement for eclectic paths has gone awry in this game. Ignoring reality may cause you to take needlessly time-consuming turns in the road. You urge each other to reach for the sky but have no solid plan to get the job accomplished. Factor in a large dose of impatience and you have a daunting challenge. You may feel that your romance is like riding a wild bronco. It may be that you are both rebelling against having to answer to anybody. Your creative minds spill out suggestions faster than you can act upon them.

Judge and Jury Game

If the two of you become too opinionated, the *Judge and Jury* game can occur. Virgo can, in a one-sided way, run information through ultra-fine mental processors. Sagittarius can trade in a broad-minded outlook for a narrow vision that doesn't tolerate opposing points of view. If you get too caught up in this way of thinking, you feel judged. Judgmental attitudes block the flow of communication, causing hard feelings. Angry outbursts are predictable when you defend your positions. If you force each other to agree with your ideas, war breaks out. Rather than fostering a romantic atmosphere, you create a sterile environment. You will find that it isn't easy to win an argument with each other. Virgo is the master of factual analysis. Sagittarius can blow you away with its sharp analytical abilities. Neither will give in without a good fight if convinced their cause is just. Preconceived notions are not going to bring you closer. Communication is cold and distant when you indulge in this game.

Strategies

How can you steer clear of these Virgo-Sagittarius games? The *Glass Is Half Empty* game asks you to revise your mental attitude so that you view the glass as half full. Accent the positive if you want to break out to a more expansive vision. Virgo is happier when not thinking about what is lacking. Sagittarius becomes a beam of light in the darkness when its thoughts are positive. The momentum in your romance is upbeat when you change your perceptions. It may take practice to retrain yourselves to see life as a set of possibilities rather than setbacks. Your creativity intensifies when you are on the path of abundance. Even your wealth could increase because you are now able to attract what you need. Negativity is poisonous and brings little hope. The glass may be filled to the brim if you make the effort to look for a brighter future. You experience greater passion when the two of you have the faith to hope for the best.

The *Mutable* game need not keep you from the goals you have set for yourselves. You will likely find it better to go with a choice and worry about changing directions later. Eventually you can get better at limiting your possibilities to avoid making life aggravating. Too many options could produce doubt. You are two people who don't need to be limited by a narrow set of choices. At the same time, you are never going to set course if you worry about whether you chose the perfect destination. Your brainstorming capability is a talent. Why not set a given amount of time to compare notes? You might be wise to decide on a launch date or time and stick to it. You lack focus in this game. It takes courage and discipline to follow through on choices. With patience, you can achieve both.

The *Judge and Jury* game asks you both to accept each other's ideas with some openness. You limit your chances to resolve issues through this game. It helps if you can see that you both have valuable insights. The passion you use to disagree will serve you better if you can be supportive of each other. You are not going to be close if you judge your partner. Your adaptable minds love to explore options, so it won't be much of a stretch for you to get off this one-way street. If you can drop a dogmatic approach, you will be able to resolve your issues much faster. Neither of you will be right all of the time. Tolerating opposing opinions keeps you out of court. Besides, wouldn't you rather be romancing than fighting?

The Rainbow

Your Virgo-Sagittarius relationship is a never-ending story of searching for new directions. A restlessness to grow is at the core of your romance. When you adjust to the different ways by which you reach decisions, life has greater flow. Virgo's pragmatic perceptions temper Sagittarius' love of spontaneity. Then again, the Archer adds inventiveness to Virgo's repertoire. Your two signs can satisfy material needs and shoot for distant stars. When you can anticipate each other's thinking, you seem to communicate better. Following through on your promises increases your faith in one another. You can be a catalyst for your lover's dreams.

The Virgo man appreciates the lightness of the Sagittarius woman. She doesn't seem too bothered by anything that goes amiss. The Virgo man wishes he could be so carefree. He feels greater confidence in the presence of the Sagittarius woman. Her positive attitude appears to make her luck come alive. The Mercurian man notices that she understands his way of looking at the world. His ambition doesn't bother her. She appears to be well traveled and uniquely educated. Her eyes burn when she talks of her future aspirations. The Virgo man wonders how she will ever get so much accomplished. This free-spirited gypsy prompts him to toss out his time-worn routines; not just anyone can get him to do this. He is tempted to journey through life with her. He wonders if he can keep up with this fiery Archer. She changes direction faster than he can turn his head. Life is exhilarating when she is around. She inspires him to be slightly offbeat when he is with her. She seems to appreciate his insights. He quickly becomes attached to this philosophical, poetic woman. She suddenly shoots a "love" arrow into his heart; that wink of her eye should have warned him!

The Sagittarius woman cautiously wanders close to the Virgo man. She does not want to scare him off with her unorthodox opinions. (What she says is more unconventional than *how* she expresses herself.) She likes to listen to this Mercurian man. His precise logic focuses her mind. She grows tired of dreamers who have no intention of realizing their dreams. When he talks of his ideals, they seem to be substantial and tangible. This jovial woman will take a roller coaster ride now and then when life moves too slowly. She knows that her own love of adventure is not for everyone; sometimes it's not even good for her. This Virgo man is curious enough to at least try anything once. The adaptability of the Mercurian man wins her heart. She frees herself from his critical eyes like the Sun breaking free from the clouds. This humble man is wary of those who may take advantage of him. She notices his awareness of the little things. The Sagittarius woman knows she would drop so many details if she tried to carry them herself. Since childhood she has moved with a jump in her step. Nobody can take this out of her. The Mercurian man scores points by letting this woman sow her wild oats. They are better off this way. Why? She is more apt to come back to him. She sees that he pays attention!

The Virgo woman never really saw herself with such an untamed rogue as the Sagittarius man. He is too blunt for her liking. Why does she like him? He seems to act and say what she feels inside. Wow! He brings out her spontaneity, which is ever-present but resisted. This Archer can reach for an arrow faster than most can blink an eye. She loves his childlike yet ageless eyes. He reminds her of a displaced time traveler. She wants to lasso him with her charm. He is an easy mark for compliments because he craves attention. The Mercurian woman worries that he could leave on the next flight in search of excitement. She hopes he is ready to be with her. This Virgo woman needs a reliable partner. He does not have to be a knight in shining armor, just someone who is willing to cherish her heart. This quick-witted woman doesn't expect the impossible. She only hopes this jovial man will take her hand and be her man for all the coming seasons.

The Sagittarius man is attracted to the femininity of the Virgo woman. She doubts whether he is dependable. He would like to prove her wrong. He doesn't realize that this is exactly what she wants him to do. The Sagittarius man walks tall with a head full of ideas and plans. He notices the Virgo woman likes to exchange information with him. Their minds seem to encompass the mysteries of the galaxies when they really talk. The Archer is not really much for everyday routines but does his best to follow through on his commitments. He believes in truth but prefers his own version of it. He will tolerate differing views, but don't mess with his precious collection of well-preserved beliefs. The Virgo woman likes his honesty. He sees that she is wary of his reckless ways. The way she needs him makes her hard to leave. He finds it refreshing and confounding that this Mercurian woman feels she can trust him. He notices that she responds warmly to charm. She detests his impulsive judgments. She smiles at his humor and laughs at his sarcasm. The Sagittarius man is a wild spirit, but he knows a good thing when he sees it. The Virgo woman will expect him to make good on his promises. He gets a kick out of making people happy—as long as he is given a long leash!

Your relationship needs to stay open-ended. You will wind up breaking the rules anyway if they're too rigid. Keep your expectations attainable so that you will have fewer disappointments. You are people with great mental power. You are happier when free from too much responsibility. Travel helps you to remember your way back to each other's hearts. You will have to search far and wide to find such a great confidante. You are a bit of *yin* and *yang* when it comes to blending into each other's worlds. Maintain a positive outlook and life will bring you more rewards. When you allow each other to walk your own separate paths, you can come together as a duo with an empowering message.

Virgo-Capricorn: The Pragmatists

Virgo + Capricorn = Well-Defined Reality

Virgo and Capricorn are earth signs that like to know that their step-by-step movements rest on solid ground. This pairing is one of the best business combinations. Virgo's willingness to handle the dirty little details mixed with Capricorn's ability to focus on a strategy adds up to great accomplishments. Idealism does not turn these two on as much as dreams that can become reality. These signs can be true romantics. The trick is making the time for love. Work is a big demand, and both signs are quick to assume responsibility. People lean on the strength of this relationship. A healthy respect for tradition or the past is likely. A clear commitment makes both feel more at ease.

Working Harder Rather Than Smarter Game

The games played in your Virgo-Capricorn relationship are connected to taking the work ethic too far and falling into stale routines. Virgo and Capricorn can outwork most others. In a relationship you may wind up in the *Guinness Book of World Records* for outlasting everybody else. If you let your work drive go too far, you may be playing the *Working Harder Rather Than Smarter* game. Ambition probably is one of your greatest motivating forces. Earth signs like clear-cut goals. You will get into trouble when you don't know when enough is enough. You can be so focused on work that you lose awareness of romance. Sometimes this will happen because others ask a lot of you. If you continuously allow yourselves to be overly obligated, there may not be any time left solely for you. Another side of this game is that success can be contagious. Success makes you want that much more. An addiction to keeping busy can keep you from enjoying leisure time together.

Tunnel Vision

When you become absorbed with narrow perceptions, you can fall prey to the *Tunnel Vision* game. Virgo can be as mesmerized by the details of a plan as Capricorn can be obsessed with rigidly adhering to a strategy. You must exercise caution to avoid overlooking alternatives that might make your life more rewarding. The two of you may try too hard to force something to work. When you won't listen to each other's insights, you can be frustrated. Your partner may become angry if you refuse any input. You both could wind up stubbornly resisting helpful advice if you are too dedicated to your own ideas. This game depicts the tendency in your relationship to be so intent on accomplishing a task that you can't seem to adopt a flexible approach.

Play It Again Game

The *Play It Again* game is one in which you rely too much on routines and not enough on new ideas. Your relationship can lose passion if you don't energize yourselves with new material. The same old script with the same old lines can dull your minds. Earth signs can become attached to the familiar, but not branching out into new directions makes life boring. You may desperately want a more stimulating lifestyle but at the same time oppose any change. Your relationship could have such definite parameters that nothing unusual or new can get through the gates. You may feel uncomfortable if your partner desires to grow in other directions. Everything changes, especially people in a relationship. There could be a tendency for tension to increase if either of you wants to experiment with new approaches. The desire to stick with business as usual can cause friction.

Strategies

How can you rise above these Virgo-Capricorn games? Not working so much is the simplest way to handle the *Working Harder Rather Than Smarter* game. That's easier said than done, isn't it? You have to concentrate on restraining your tendencies because your natural inclination is not to stop. Virgo and Capricorn believe in doing a good job. You don't have to surrender your ambition; you just need to adjust your routines. You may even find that you enjoy work more if you take time away, and your creativity will improve if you allow yourself a break now and then. Your romance surely will benefit. You can be exhausted by putting so much energy into serious objectives. Creating rewards for jobs well done may be just the excuse needed to get you out of the work zone.

The *Tunnel Vision* game reveals that you would be wise to consider other ways to handle situations. Your minds can be so focused on goals that you may not see the whole picture. You will benefit from being open to each other's ideas. Flexibility is the key here. If you remain rigid, there is the chance you will miss out on opportunities. This game blocks spontaneous changes that could make your journey smoother. Considering all of your options is a good objective for you both. Virgo and Capricorn can influence each other to stay with the same plan whether it is getting the job done or not. Sometimes it's pride that blocks your reasoning. Make sure you are not holding on to a strategy only to defend a position you know is not a winner. If you don't listen to your partner's suggestions, it may bring distance and hurt feelings, so establishing clear lines of communication is not only wise but also essential!

The *Play It Again* game suggests that you should be more willing to explore new life directions. You don't have to revise every aspect of your lifestyle, but be open to new ideas and experiences. Even a minute change can sharpen your awareness. The familiar can provide stability and a reliable foundation for you both. Nobody is knocking your fondness for security. Earth signs are lost if they are not grounded. Regular reality tests come standard with your signs. Just be sure you don't allow your lives to be so insulated from change that you fail to grow. Let each other investigate new directions. If one of you expands your horizons, you both benefit. Don't feel insecure if your partner wants to try an alternative way of doing something. You both are better off when you have the energy and vigor to embrace new challenges.

The Rainbow

Your Virgo-Capricorn relationship has a persistence that can take you through doors that other lovers may never push open. You represent success and ambition at their very best. Your fearlessness of hard work elevates you to higher levels of happiness. When you adopt a certain degree of spontaneity to balance your caution, life seems full of rewards. You may not like surprises that are unsettling but can learn to appreciate the ones that stimulate your minds. Romance and business serve you better when you keep them separate from one another. You trust a future with a plan more than one left to chance. Let each other determine when it is time to move beyond comfort zones, and you will have a true ally. Trust makes your love come alive in this romance. Every once in a while, scrap your strategies when it comes to love. Let intuition show you how to make each other happy.

A Virgo man experiences abundance when he is with the Capricorn woman. She seems to plod along but can move with surprising speed when she realizes her goal is in sight. The Virgo man knows he has met a "solid as a rock" mind. He perceives that the Capricorn woman is a business yogi with a strategy ready to deal with any situation. He wonders if this Saturnian woman will resent his routines. The Virgo man has certain patterns that rise to the level of rituals. She doesn't appear to mind this dimension of him. She seems to learn through her experiences. She looks younger when she laughs and older when she talks about her past. Her feelings seem to be painfully deep, though no one would detect it at first glance. Her voice is cautious and her words a bit deliberate. The Mercurian man appreciates her definite likes and dislikes. He finds it easy to meet her halfway. Her heart seems to respond to his amorous advances. He longs for a commitment with such a stable force. The potential for love is in the air. He hopes she wants to be with a hard-working man like himself. Her own ambitions seem to blend with his own.

A Capricorn woman sees right through the Virgo man. He seems to think he is a complex, difficult to understand man, or so she has heard. The Capricorn woman won't promise him too much. She believes in earning everything the old-fashioned way. She will show her heart when he proves that he is committed to a long-term relationship. She can run in the romantic fast lane but has already been there and done that. This Saturnian spirit has learned better than most from the past. She is determined to avoid making the same mistakes. She figured out long ago that this is the source of wisdom. The Virgo man seems sincere. His dedication to his causes and work don't phase her. She has her own quirks, such as being committed to those who depend on her. She is a mountain of strength. She hopes this eager man will carry his own weight. That's what she likes in him. He is responsible and seems to share her viewpoint that love is romance and, in its own mysterious way, is serious, risky business!

The Virgo woman is slow to show herself to the Capricorn man. He appears to know how to play the game of love. She wants to be sure he will turn all of his cards up for her to see. The Virgo woman likes the Capricorn man's self-assurance. Her radar-like perceptions indicate that this is a man with something to prove. She doesn't want him to feel that way toward her. She would rather they enjoy being true lovers. She wants to share his emotions. He is so well versed in guarding his heart. When he relaxes and talks about his dreams, he seems almost childlike. Although his sense of dependability makes her trust him, it's the boy in him she adores. He is serious about commitment—almost too much so. She wonders if it's his fear of the unknown that makes him seek control or his love for new conquests. His passion is powerful but hidden because he fears betrayal. She coaxes him to let down his defenses. He exudes an aura of success whether or not he has achieved it yet. She can't shake the feeling that he can love her with a breathtaking force. Being with him is somewhat like playing *Wheel of Fortune*. You may need to spin the wheel again and again before you hit the jackpot. She hopes he won't make her wait so long!

The Capricorn man enjoys the way the Virgo woman handles herself. She is precise in conducting her worldly affairs. She seems to have him pegged as a driven, career-oriented man. He notices that this Virgo woman doesn't mind his serious demeanor though she relaxes when he smiles. The Saturnian man is driven by primitive, instinctual forces. He has to satisfy certain inner challenges that not everyone understands. The Virgo woman sees the pressure he puts himself through to climb the rungs of success. He senses she can ascend just as high as he. It's sobering to meet someone like her who can punch through to the core issues that hold up his world. This Mercurian woman has wit and a polished way with words. She lets him know that he doesn't have to prove himself to her. He wants to talk from his heart, but it is a stretch. He is not well versed in the language of love. He is a doer who prefers that his lover interprets his emotions through his actions. The Virgo woman is a good match for him. He senses that she wants to see whether he can be as good at love as he is at everything else. She longs for him to expose even a hint of those invisible feelings and to not worry so much about his performance.

You are lovers with a well-determined purpose. Make allowances for those moments when you can't agree. You can take separate paths and meet up later. Reliability is essential to both of you. A clear sense of direction makes you eager to greet each new day. Let life teach you how to revise the script at times. You can enjoy the best the world has to offer. When you don't take your love for granted, you are the truest of lovers.

Virgo-Aquarius: The Resourceful Ones

Virgo + Aquarius = Insightful Minds

This is a romance with a flair for making last-second decisions. Virgo tempers Aquarius' futuristic thinking with patience. Aquarius pushes Virgo to set aside caution and to act despite last-minute misgivings. These signs are good at making the best of whatever comes their way. The two seem to read each other's next move instantaneously when they work as a team. When each pulls blindly in its own direction, tension can build. Virgo and Aquarius will never operate in quite the same way. Virgo must consider the consequences of actions while Aquarius lets others be responsible for their own reactions. Earthy Virgo can't entirely shift its focus from the component parts while airy Aquarius can see the whole situation with a quick glance. Aquarius can miss details, mainly through boredom with minutia. Two lovers of these signs can delight in the nuances that each brings to the relationship. Acknowledging each other's mental ingenuity goes a long way toward maintaining stability.

Isolation Booth Game

The games in your Virgo-Aquarius relationship are related to intellectual distance and a loss of direction. Virgo and Aquarius possess strong minds. When the two of you don't acknowledge feelings, you may be hiding behind the *Isolation Booth* game. You live in the compartments of your own thinking to such an extent that you seem quite distant. Even if you spend time together, you can feel a million miles apart. This is a case of two people with finely developed minds who want breathing room. Aquarius is known for pushing people away when it needs space. Virgo will show a tendency to escape from everyone if it needs time to relax. Both of you can be aloof, which makes it difficult to talk. You go through the motions of speaking without really communicating. You pull away when one or both of you has hurt feelings. Not discussing issues tends to make them worse. The dialogues in your own heads can distort the facts. Your romantic moments will dwindle if you refuse to clean up old business.

Fried Wires Game

You both have an inclination to get worked up over sudden surprises that don't go in your favor. When you shock one another with the unexpected, you may be caught up in the *Fried Wires* game. Your relationship's circuitry becomes burned out due to last-second choices that are like bombshells for your partner. Business decisions that are made without your partner's input present another great source of aggravation. Virgo doesn't appreciate being worried to death by Aquarius' disregard for time. Aquarius can't stand Virgo's way of putting business ahead of spontaneous pleasure. You both are right in your own ways. You just need to take the time to listen. You are not that far apart, but it seems that way because of mental fatigue. When you push each other's buttons to the extent that you electrocute your nervous systems, it is annoying and destructive. Irritation sets in if you can't respect each other's rights. You both can show great impatience with the other. Unresolved tension doesn't make for romantic evenings. You may not use good judgment in timing discussions of heated topics. It's better to wait until you are not frazzled. Otherwise, it is hard to listen because your mind tends to jump to conclusions.

Flooded Engine Game

If you press the gas pedal too hard when your car is idling, you can easily flood the engine. The same thing happens in your relationship when you have a brainstorm of ideas but never move forward with them. Your sense of direction can be confused, which is the case in the *Flooded Engine* game. Virgo wants to take the time to consider all options. Aquarius would rather get going and worry about problems later. You can become annoyed with your individual preferences for initiating activities. There is another scenario to consider. Sometimes Virgo wants to take action after doing the homework required to make an intelligent decision, but Aquarius would rather try an alternative that has yet to be contemplated. This can keep you at the starting block, both feeling quite frustrated, angry, and you probably could add a few more descriptions of your own, couldn't you? It may seem like a waste of time to try to plan anything together.

Strategies

How can you get past these Virgo-Aquarius games? In the *Isolation Booth* game you will benefit greatly through expressing your feelings. You don't have to bare your soul, but it helps to let each other into your inner worlds. Intellectual electricity is lit easily in your romance, and you have great ideas. You may not be as emotional as many couples, but if you let each other know how you feel, you grow closer. Your support for each other's goals may even generate more passion. Running away from issues is not going to do much for intimacy. Talk through your problems. Remember, if you wait too long to speak up, issues have a way of multiplying. Nip differences of opinion in the bud by using your keen minds. Be assertive and get to the point. An ounce or two of patience doesn't hurt either. Give one another a chance to speak frankly. You are not the same couple when you avoid talking about serious issues. You are an awe-inspiring duo when you put your mental powers to work; they are potent enough to solve your problems in a hurry!

The *Fried Wires* game asks you to give your lover plenty of advance notice about your plans. You both will need to allow for some spontaneous changes since these are inevitable. Still, do your best to warn one another about changes. Surprises can be fun, but be careful about how you surprise each other. You can get to know what really blows each other out of the water. Be conscious of your actions; there may be repercussions that require significant repairs. Picking the right time to talk may be as important as the topic. You both can experience anxiety during hectic days when you are asked to resolve countless problems. You may not be ready to react positively or patiently to another dilemma. It would be wise to agree to sit down and discuss something when you both are in the right frame of mind.

The *Flooded Engine* game asks you not to interfere with each other's method of arriving at decisions. You both can be right. Your intellectual styles are a matter of personal taste. Try not to disrupt your partner's concentration. Virgo prefers to analyze facts while Aquarius has fast insights. You work together without friction if you avoid becoming too much of a proponent for your own side. You will tend to move forward smoothly when you take your time and let each other have input. There are times when you may need to exercise extreme patience. On other occasions, you will have to act quickly to take advantage of an opportunity. Try not to be too attached to any one method. Flexibility helps. Each of you may have to step back and cool down to see your next move clearly. With practice, you can learn how to work together as well as to make individual decisions—honest!

The Rainbow

Your Virgo-Aquarius relationship has some interesting twists. There is an unlimited potential for pleasure. Sexually speaking, you can be powerfully attracted. When you take the time to read what's on each other's minds, life is good. Virgo has a methodical rhythm to its thoughts that isn't so far apart from the unpredictable impulses of Aquarius. Both of you respect intelligence. Virgo is more comfortable with its conscious mind and thoroughly analyzes situations before setting sail. Aquarius is more impulsive and intuitive, though at times Aquarius moves with deliberate slowness. What prompts this final air sign to be so cautious? Aquarius is slow to warm up to unfamiliar situations and tests the waters before taking action. Virgo is not always so patient. This sign can hit the ground running when excited by a pragmatic goal. Both Virgo and Aquarius are eager to grow. When you provide plenty of latitude to be yourselves, your romance blossoms.

A Virgo man is fascinated by the Aquarius woman. She is an icon of freedom who acts to maintain her rights. The Mercurian man perceives that she is a radical thinker; her thoughts don't travel in a straight line like his. This Uranian woman's clarity sometimes turns his logic upside down. She can talk about virtually any subject. The Aquarius woman makes his pulse race, and he loves her sparkling, electric eyes. She seems to know where she is heading even when she skips from subject to subject. The Virgo man notices that she likes his openness to her ideas. He hopes they can join forces harmoniously. She shows a conservative dimension regarding ambition, though she can be unconventional in a split second. The Virgo man hopes he makes a good impression. His ideas almost seem too plain for this Uranian woman. He loves to hear her laugh, and she responds positively when he acts like himself. The Virgo man wants to pursue this elusive, free spirit. He isn't sure why but then decides it must be his desire to share her incredible ideas.

An Aquarius woman flies past the Virgo man but then does a U-turn to check him out. She could learn to love his stabilizing influence. He seems to understand the way she thinks. She longs for someone who is not put off by her instinctual need for freedom. The Uranian woman can't help but notice that he is a little intimidated by her wild ways. She can sense that he relaxes when she shows a sensitive side. The Aquarius woman hopes he won't expect to see this all of the time.

She is a free spirit for all seasons. This Mercurian man captures her attention when he talks about his blueprint for the future. She loves the future! His aspirations aren't too confining and confirm that she could squeeze into his life. He will need to keep his critical faculties under control if he wants her to be his lover. She answers to no one—unless she is treated as an equal and allowed to pursue her own path. The Aquarius woman appreciates the Virgo man's ability to test reality with his analytical mind, which is his compass to gauge if he is on target. She senses that they may even find a way to pursue special shared goals. This Uranian woman is not a loner. She only wants to walk freely whether alone or hand-in-hand with her lover.

The Virgo woman sees the Aquarius man as a real challenge. His directness can stretch her emotional and mental boundaries. She admits that he pushes her buttons. She hopes they will connect intellectually as well as emotionally. He appears youthful regardless of his age and seems to resist being a grown-up. This doesn't bother her because she has grown weary of being a grown-up too. "As long as he can take care of himself," she thinks, "he might fit the bill." The Virgo woman is not always ready to experiment, but she is thrilled with his offbeat personality. She wonders whether this enticing man with the electric smile is for real. Their relationship takes off like a roller coaster. The Mercurian woman knows the high stakes of love. She hopes he can see that, even though she is cautious, she is willing to take a chance with him, that is, if he will not try to overrule her decisions. The Virgo woman has well-seasoned ideas of her own. She finds that the Aquarius man follows her lead when she talks with experience and knowledge; he acts as though he has met an irresistible force. She is pleased by his response but asks, "Could it be this easy?"

The Aquarius man discovers that the Virgo woman really listens to him. She may not immediately understand his logic but listens so intensely that she figures him out. He is a bit worried she may not like what she sees. After all, he has his idiosyncrasies. He perceives that she is not as bothered by their differences as she is interested in what they have in common. She appears to know the ways of the world yet still seems to seek true love. The Aquarius man longs to be understood. He has been through romantic

The Magic of Signmates

adventures but wants to be in love. This Virgo woman presents a dilemma. He wonders if he has the seriousness to be her partner. She could easily be the right match for him because he wants someone he can count on. Her eyes are full of acceptance, but he knows he had better mind his manners. This is a woman who understands how to conduct business even if it concerns the heart. The Uranian man sees possibilities in the Mercurian woman. He hopes her vision will show her that their path together just might be wide enough for them both. They have the most interesting conversations. She can subtly switch over from the pragmatic to the romantic. As a matter of fact, he isn't always sure when that happens.

Your relationship offers many strengths. You share a wealth of ideas. When you truly communicate, whatever you must go through to stay together seems worth it. Your love grows when you accept each other's unique qualities. You will never be able to change each other. Don't even waste your time. It's more rewarding to recognize the strengths and weaknesses each of you embodies. Support your lover's goals and you will always want to stay close. You tend to grow fonder of one another when you realize how deeply and profoundly you affect each other. Your accomplishments symbolize the intensity of your mutual understanding.

Virgo-Pisces: The Perfectionists

Virgo + Pisces = Search for Meaning

These two signs are opposites. Virgo relies heavily on the conscious mind. Pisces swims freely in the streams of intuition. Causes usually appeal to this sign combination; they join in the quest to find outlets for their idealism. Being of service to others sometimes is a key theme. This is a romance with great sensitivity. It's not easy to be satisfied with the world because it often doesn't measure up to Virgo's and Pisces' expectations. Both yearn to be understood. Both inspire the other to seek fulfilling roles. This can be a caring relationship because each is profoundly aware of what the other goes through. Practical Virgo helps to keep emotional Pisces centered and grounded. Pisces shows Virgo the importance of trusting instincts. The two like to share their knowledge. The faith each has in the other is highly valued.

Expecting the Impossible Game

The games played in your Virgo-Pisces relationship have their roots in unclear dependency needs and emotional disorientation. When you make unreasonable requests of each other, you may be playing the *Expecting the Impossible* game. You could set your expectations far too high. There is a tendency in Virgo and Pisces to go too far to save others or to demand too much of others. Your dependency needs become out of balance when this happens. Either may respond to the other out of guilt. You can avoid dealing directly with issues, which compounds the problem. When you hurt your partner's feelings, you may think you are letting each other down. Resorting to blame only makes matters worse. No one is perfect, yet you may forget that perfection is illusory. There may be a seesaw effect where you alternate between being the savior and the victim. Refusal to accept responsibility for your own actions prolongs this game.

Lack of Faith Game

Virgo energizes others by offering practical advice. Pisces motivates people with unconditional belief. The two of you are devastated when you are in the *Lack of Faith* game. Why? You know what it feels like when you believe in each other. Your relationship is an empty void when you withhold support. You sometimes show that you disagree by withdrawing from each other. You may choose to express your opposition through silence, which distances you even further. Such behavior can be a crushing blow when you need your partner's support during a stressful endeavor. Negativity probably sweeps over you and makes it a challenge to care about each other. Too much criticism may be the real reason for this game. You may become sullen and can feel so rejected by the other that communicating is nearly impossible.

Virtual Reality Game

When the two of you feel like you are relating through a fog, you are probably in the grips of the *Virtual Reality* game. You may have trouble connecting because you see reality through unique filters. It may be hard to believe that you are discussing the same situation when you listen to each other's interpretations. The impatience you project toward each other is aggravating. Are you really hearing what your partner is saying? There doesn't seem to be enough room for shared perceptions. Virgo prefers to live without loose ends. At times, Virgo wants to pretend that all is well to avoid the need to worry. Pisces isn't as concerned with everything fitting exactly into place but is concerned with inner peace. Pisces can deny problems to avoid conflict. You view the world through dissimilar lenses, yet the strange thing is you may deny your inability to see things eye to eye. You want to keep up the appearance that you are in harmonious agreement. Unhappiness is usually at the core of this game. You go through the motions but are not really being honest. Perhaps you don't want to hurt your partner by talking frankly. You may not even know that all is not well because you repress negative feelings. This can be a confusing way to relate. A haze of doubt seems to linger over you. Inertia can result when you try to work together.

Strategies

How can you transcend these Virgo-Pisces games? The *Expecting the Impossible* game can be turned around if you do sound reality testing. Your partner cannot make your blues go away. Dependency needs must be clarified. You may provide a solid shoulder to cry on, but self-sufficiency is required from both of you. You put too much pressure on each other when you expect to be "saved" by your partner. Love can do a lot of things, but it can't make all of your problems disappear. Perfection is something that Virgo and Pisces seek to attain. Try to keep this tendency in perspective. Relationships can get messy and are not static or quiet. It's best to accept the inevitability of imperfection. You may find it more helpful to solve problems together rather than to wait for them to magically disappear.

In the *Lack of Faith* game, you need to determine what is eating at your willingness to give to each other. Do you feel too neglected? Discounted? It helps to know why you are responding in this manner. You won't understand by guessing. Somehow you need to talk it out. You are motivating forces in each other's lives. Mutual support for goals gives a real energy boost. Broken promises may be the source of diminished faith in each other. If this is the case, you must do better in making good on what you agree to do. One of you may give too much while the other takes too much. If you want to restore faith, you must offer good reasons for this to happen. Trust is what you seek. It makes your lives run like clockwork. Without it, you are out of touch with one another.

The *Virtual Reality* game can be handled by talking honestly. Hidden feelings are probably at the heart of this game. Possibly, anger has been repressed to avoid dealing with issues, which is how reality becomes warped. Don't pretend that everything is fine when you know something isn't right. You need to remove your doubts. The formula is simple but it takes a little courage. You need to come out of hiding and air your concerns. It may not make everything A-okay overnight. Remember, Virgo and Pisces are complementary opposites. Your hearts are not dissimilar, but your minds function differently. Virgo has a linear mind while Pisces utilizes intuition. Virgo's first tendency is to think. Pisces' first impulse is to feel. You both balance your intellect and emotions. It's just that instinctual responses to situations are divergent. How can you make these worlds come together? The shortest distance between the two points is to talk straight from your heart. If a rational discussion leads you in circles, trust your emotions. Converse with a conviction that you really want to enter each other's reality. It can be painful to listen to unpleasant things being said about you. There is no real shortcut. Don't blame, accuse, or criticize. Get to the source of your unhappiness. When you uncover and air those nasty old angry feelings, you will be on the right track. You can cause emotional reactions in one another. That's not a bad thing and is part of your chemistry. You never were meant to hurt each other, but you aren't supposed to live in an unreal world of perpetual harmony either!

The Rainbow

Your Virgo-Pisces relationship offers plenty of opportunities to expand your mental horizons. When you figure out how to work as a couple, your hearts seem to feel as one. Resolving conflicts comes with patience and practice. You are lovers who ask the world to fulfill big dreams. If you are willing to make the effort, you can reach your most cherished aspirations. The roles you choose symbolize your values. You will look to each other for inspiration. Share your material and emotional wealth freely with your lover. When you do, you are twice as wealthy. Perfection appeals to both of you; be reasonable in your pursuit of it. Remember, there are no perfect people, and it's okay to make a mistake. Forgive yourself and your lover. The journey is more enjoyable when you don't worry about each step along the way. Keep sight of your visions, and you will find less fault with life's harsh realities. You may feel a degree of discontentment, which arises from your urge to become one with your ideals.

The Virgo man is attracted to the Pisces woman. She is his emotional and intellectual alter ego. He longs to hold her because he believes that she will release his emotions. The Virgo man soon realizes life doesn't work that way. She can't speak for him; he must find the mysterious key to unlock his feelings himself. He worries that the Neptunian woman is an illusion and that he may become obsessed with her if he allows himself to become involved. His solid boundaries seem to disappear in her presence like sandcastles in high tide. Her love sweeps over him. He wonders if she will ever really be able to tolerate his suspicious, fact-driven mind. The laconic Mercurian man is drawn to this poetic woman who embodies idealism and high-minded values. The Virgo man is intrigued by how she manages to reach her goals with surreal, whirling dervish action. He wants to leave before he is in over his head but, before he knows it, it is too late. Her faith in him uplifts him. He feels pain when he hurts her. The Virgo man hopes he can put into words what this woman has already read in his face. She is a romantic, drawing out the romantic in him. He knows that she waits to see if he can trust his powerful emotions, which are beyond the reach of his intellect.

The Pisces woman knows she had better be careful with the Virgo man. He is worldly in business matters. She wants to see if he can share her feelings. The Pisces woman likes the solidity of the Virgo man. She may even be willing to stand with him if he is willing to explore the intuitive world with her—at least on occasion. The Pisces woman can change reality when she falls in love because she can look past many things. She wants to be sure that this perceptive man will not complain about her unusual perspective. She desires to show him that her logic can be just as sound as his own. Her thoughts don't need to be grounded but can soar to intuitive heights. Some consider her flighty. She sees herself as being quite reasonable and unafraid of heights. Her source of power comes from the intangible while Virgo's inspiration is derived from what he can see, touch, taste, hear, and feel in the physical world. The Pisces woman opens her heart to the Virgo man. She perceives that he struggles to understand her love. His tender caress tells her he can be a gentle lover. She wants to be sure he can let go to the magical power of that touch. His sense of obligation and responsibility comfort her. It's nice to know that he can figure out how life works with his persistent and probing mind.

The Virgo woman is amused by how the Pisces man thinks. He can get much accomplished but in a way that is foreign to her. He seems driven by a desire to conquer imperfection. The Virgo woman knows all about perfection. Keeping her life in order is a top priority. She wants to be sure this dreamy, Neptunian man will not disrupt her own sense of direction. He seems to understand her most deeply held ambitions. The Pisces man warms her heart with affection, yet he seems to be weary and wary of relationships. She notices that he is as suspicious as she is of things that sound too good to be true. The Mercurian woman thinks that perhaps he, too, has had his fill of mirages. She hopes he can see the gifts she offers. Her love is generous if it is not taken for granted. She has a soft spot for this gentle-voiced, romantic Pisces man. The Virgo woman doesn't bend easily until someone proves his or her worth. She doesn't know how the Pisces man manages to unlock feelings with just a touch. In her eyes, commitments are not to be taken lightly, yet she isn't sure just what she wants from this Pisces man. "Maybe," she ponders, "I should see if he can swim with me first and worry about the details later."

The Pisces man knows when he looks at the Virgo woman that they could be from the same ancient clan. They both share a longing to make life respond to their sincere desire for happiness. His ideals are steeped in emotion. Her dreams are as enduring as precious metal. The Pisces man wants this love to be real. The Virgo woman seems to accept his dreamy view of reality whether or not she understands it. The Neptunian man knows that he doesn't always talk in complete sentences. He leaves out bits of information, hoping this analytical woman can translate his thoughts for him. He is reluctant to fall in love because he needs to convince himself that this earthy woman will be there for him and that he will be there for her. The Pisces man wants the Virgo woman to see that his intentions can be well defined. He believes their worlds can be fused together. His ideals are fueled by a burning desire to rise above the doubts of the world. He senses that the Virgo woman has beliefs of her own that she would like to make real. The Pisces man takes a deep breath before casting away caution to sail with the Mercurian woman, whose eyes seem to ask, "What took you so long?"

Your romance will test your ability to talk clearly. Make sure you help each other understand your points of view. If you do, your shared reality grows brighter. You make each other happy with your effort to be an unconditional ally. Don't deny your feelings. Express your likes and dislikes. Be open to each other's dreams. One world is not better than the other, and be glad that you are unique individuals. Life will seem more generous when you inspire your lover and aren't afraid to show how much you value one another.

Libra-Libra: The Mixers

Libra + Libra = Lively Social Life

Two individuals from this sign are thrilled to relate with a wide variety of people. The outgoing nature of two Libras keeps life fun and exciting. A shared sense of values can be a strong compatibility point. The arts could be a popular subject. It's hard to think of two more romantic lovers than these two Venusians. The desire to indulge in the good things of life is a constant temptation. Each partner's contacts add an exhilarating touch to the romance. Others probably find this sign pair to be poised and able to respond quickly to all types of human encounters. A knack for knowing how to make people feel accepted is likely. The sign pairing highlights the ability to see both sides of issues. Wanting to please others is a natural tendency.

Other-Directed Game

The games played in your Libra-Libra relationship are associated with a lack of assertiveness and being too indecisive. The *Other-Directed* game occurs when you let other people determine your goals. You can try too hard to please one another or as a couple give in too easily to the demands of others. You both share a fine sense of what motivates people. That sharp social awareness sometimes plays tricks on your minds. It's easy to imagine that the ideas of others are sounder than your own. Usually a deep desire to be liked is at the root of this game. Self-doubt can cause either of you to want too much direction from your partner. Instead of listening to your own intuition, you become too tuned in to the needs of the individuals around you. An inability to detach your own reasoning from someone else's is the problem. It can be confusing if you keep giving in to each other's needs and sacrifice your own in the process. You may simply be too fair in the negotiation process. Conforming to what is expected of you may not always be in your best interest.

Sitting on the Fence Game

Indecision can be a haunting problem as is the case in the *Sitting on the Fence* game. Your sign has a propensity for considering the various sides of an issue with great dedication. It can become problematic if numerous options all seem equally desirable. Making a decision may seem next to impossible. You might even find yourselves constantly talking each other out of choices. Your talent for brainstorming becomes a source of torment in this instance. Your momentum is frozen, and a tendency to procrastinate may become your reality. You may find yourselves stubbornly resisting change. Sometimes the fear of making choices underlies this issue. Avoiding responsibility may be an offshoot of this game. It could be challenging to define your commitment clearly when you don't make definite decisions. The consistency you want to feel in working together remains evasive. It could be frustrating and disappointing not to be able to figure out how to make choices as a couple. The discipline to follow through on ideas may be in need of a tune-up.

Broken Scales Game

If you feel a lack of balance in your mind and emotions, you may be playing the *Broken Scales* game. Dealing with long-term, stressful situations throws peace-loving Libra into a tizzy. When the two of you go through drawn-out disputes with each other, it can make communication extremely difficult. When you don't discuss things clearly, neither of you is happy. If you let problems go on for too long before addressing them, you will feel great distance. There is another twist to this game. When you are too impatient with each other, your nervous systems are thrown off balance. Uncertainty about how to deal with an issue likely bothers you the most. When you panic, a dilemma occurs. Do you know what it might be? You forget your options. You may experience a compulsive drive to keep solving the same problem. Being able to switch gears to get over to another alternative is challenging. If you can't gain distance from a situation, guess what else happens? *You* become the problem! Libra enjoys a romantic atmosphere, but you are going to have less time for fun in the Sun if you don't learn to resolve issues expeditiously.

Strategies

How can you solve the challenges of these Libra-Libra games? In the *Other-Directed* game, you must learn to see that your own ideas are as valuable as those of others. Living out your own goals is more fulfilling than existing to please the wishes of someone else. Your true friends won't expect you to do all of the compromising. Your relationship will be more fun if you sense mutual support of goals. Help each other to become more confident. Learn to believe in your own instincts. Nobody can pave the road to happiness for you. Each of you will have to "walk your own talk." Your shared awareness of people is a talent. Let it work for you rather than against you. It takes courage not to overly accommodate others to get them to like you and requires great effort to turn around an entrenched habit. Don't expect this to change overnight. You might need to keep reminding each other to be true to your own ideals. As a couple, you may find it necessary to stay focused on what you need to accomplish. Putting other's priorities ahead of your own on every occasion is not in your best interest. You may need to err on the side of being self-focused at first in order to balance out the desire to compromise. The idea isn't to be selfish but to reclaim your own turf.

The *Sitting on the Fence* game requires your assertiveness to jump off and make decisions. Don't procrastinate. You will be pumped with more vitality when you get into the everyday flow without hesitation. There is nothing bad about reflecting or carefully evaluating a major decision. You just want to be sure that you don't procrastinate. Even many bad decisions are reversible. You may be too concerned about causing inconvenience for others by making the wrong choices. A lot more time will be available to you if you make quicker decisions. Communication may even grow clearer when you make spontaneous choices. Fear of making decisions will dissipate when you act upon your ideas. It's aggravating to wait in self-doubt. You can't really tell about the potential of a possibility until you give it a chance. You are so much livelier and happier when you are not stewing in indecision. Put those ideas to work. Leave the fence for someone else to sit on!

Prolonging the *Broken Scales* game exposes your two delicate nervous systems to unnecessary abuse. The idea is to treat each other as priceless merchandise. Every couple goes through times when they disagree about almost everything under the Sun. Disputes that go on and on like a world war get to all of us! Perhaps a bit of patience is important to consider. Are you panicking? Step back with that wonderful airy Libran sensibility, which allows you the objectivity to work together. There is likely to be an unexplored option or two. If you can relax mentally, you just might discover an acceptable solution. There is another way to look at this. Even if you make war, why not call a truce? Smoke the peace pipe and listen to each other's opinion on the matter. There are two sides to the scales; they may need to tip toward one side this week and over to the other side next week. Catch my drift?

Rainbow

Your Libra-Libra relationship has an artistic flair. The actor in each of you enjoys performing. The two of you probably have few lonely moments with the many social circles you frequent. You are two lovers with never-ending imaginations. Your upbeat, outgoing personalities open doors of opportunity and make people believe in you. When you encourage each other to go after those enticing dreams, life is wonderful. You share a love of beauty in all of its forms. When you treat your lover with fairness, you are seen as special. The two of you have a better-than-average awareness of others. Your perceptions are usually on the mark.

A Libra man finds much of himself in the Libra woman. She shares his fondness for fine food and romantic getaways. He perceives that his Libra lover is a woman for all occasions. He hopes she won't be upset when he suddenly changes his mind, which he often does. She seems to adjust better to change when he can point out that it is a win-win situation. The Venusian woman is easy for the Venusian man to relax around. He admires her sensitivity and common sense. The Libra man enjoys the business world. He needs a partner who can hold her own in conducting affairs of the heart and mind. The Libra man is aware that he better talk from his heart as much as his mind if he wants to keep the Libra woman close. She seems to be a true romantic's romantic. Her eyes hint that she has tried to find love along many paths. The Venusian man hopes he can keep this sensual woman interested. He is delighted to see that she can translate his words into feelings. He sometimes stumbles to find the right way to express his affection. This woman, whose face tells a thousand stories, is certainly exciting.

A Libra woman perceives something unique in the Libra man. He has an understanding of intimacy whether he can put it into words or not. He knows how to make her feel special. She hopes his gallantry won't lapse due to familiarity. The Libra woman sees that he can talk vivaciously about worldly affairs but slips into a contemplative tone when he discusses himself. He enunciates each syllable so carefully, even beautifully, to be pleasing to her ear. The Venusian woman listens from within while he talks emphatically about his life. She likes the ring of heartfelt emotion in what he says, which shines with the same love of beauty she possesses. He does not talk so much about his feelings, but she doesn't care—as long as he will continue to adore her. Their hearts may well become as one. He seems like a soul who is searching for an understanding mate. She hopes he can be her true lover. This Venusian woman can make it clear how much she cares. She waits to see if his love will last only for the moment or will still be there at the end of the winding road.

You have a romance that can become rich in mutual adoration. It only takes the desire to make it so. The depth of emotion you share will come after the initial sparks of passion. You light such a fire in each other's heart that it takes your minds and feelings a while to catch up. There is no rush, but don't tarry in making one another feel highly valued. You might want to be careful in pursuing one another because this could be a relationship that is tough to leave, that is, if you let yourself get caught. You are lovers who arouse a sense of deep purpose in each other. There will be fun times interspersed with serious and thought-provoking ones. Satisfying your goals will be followed by many toasts of champagne to celebrate your milestones!

Libra-Scorpio: The Calculators

Libra + Scorpio = Perceptiveness That Spots a Good Deal in a Heartbeat

Socially minded Libra encourages Scorpio to be more forthcoming. Emotional Scorpio influences Libra to feel as well as to think. Leave it to Libra to know how to knock on the door of Scorpio's privacy with a diplomatic touch and be invited in. This is no easy accomplishment (ask the many who have tried and given up). The quiet contemplative nature of Scorpio can cause Libra to become aware of intuitive instincts that have never been deeply explored. There is passion in this relationship from the first conversation. The attracting power these signs have on one another is awesome! A magnetic current seems to link their minds and bodies. Each looks for a soul mate who can handle life's ups and downs. That search to find a partner who mirrors a similar longing for love and understanding pushes these signs together. Emotional extremes seem to be balanced through honest discussions. A blowout or two over differences of opinions may serve to pull the two closer. These two don't scare each other away easily.

Topsy-Turvy Game

The games played in your Libra-Scorpio relationship are associated with emotional explosions and a tendency not to always see each other's point of view. When you completely upset each other's emotional equilibrium, you are likely to be involved in the *Topsy-Turvy* game. Libra has specific plans that aid in staying centered. These strategies are really a polite way of saying "Don't mess with my thinking." Like any air sign, a sense of direction is godly to these people. Take that away, and confusion results. Scorpio has hidden agendas, which, when broken down into simple language, translate into covert strategies. Libra's strategies can be called visible agendas while Scorpio's schemes are really invisible strategies. When these two worlds collide, the outcome is explosive. More often than not, it causes pure disorientation when Libra's highly visible world, which is characterized by brilliant insight, meets Scorpio's invisible world, which is typified by intense emotions. You may at times feel you can't be completely within the relationship for fear of losing your footing. Communication could be fraught with missed details. You have to figure out what the other is thinking. The business side of your romance may be frustrating because an inability to make decisions could keep you from clearly defining the results you want. The love you seek to trust isn't as reliable when you are not sure of what each honestly expects.

Taken for Granted Game

Libra is sensitive about receiving attention. Scorpio can grow resentful if pushed over to the side to fit someone else's priorities. The *Taken for Granted* game drives a wedge between your hearts. Angry outbursts are inevitable as a means to get attention. This doesn't mean that things will get better through emotional eruptions. The two of you may become quiet if ignored for too long, and silence seems to do the most damage. Air signs like Libra must talk or problems likely will be blown out of proportion. It does Scorpio good to speak up. When the Scorpion goes into its sacred inner space, it can take a minor miracle to pry it back out. When you don't include one another in major decisions, major issues surface. It isn't as much fun to watch each other brood as it is to sit by the warmth of a fire. The Berlin Wall may seem inconsequential when compared to the separation you experience when your feelings are discounted.

Breaking the Bank Game

The two of you don't like to do anything halfway. The urge to make things happen brings out your intensity and creativity. The *Breaking the Bank* game could come into play when you find it impossible to set limits. Compulsive drives to succeed or to acquire possessions may cause you to lose perspective. Tension may arise if you grow disenchanted with each other's wasteful habits. Denial of the problem doesn't help.

Instead of utilizing the fine common-sense perspective your sign combination can show, you are ruled by obsessive drives. Disputes over money seem to go hand in hand with this game. It all relates back to pulling in opposite directions over how to use your resources.

Strategies

How can you steer clear of these Libra-Scorpio games? In the *Topsy-Turvy* game, you must find a way to talk in a common language. It's easy for each of you to become attached to your plans. Figuring out how to allow for individual expression is important. You will need to integrate some of your ideas in order to feel like a couple, yet you will be happier when you both feel free to explore unique, personal goals. The freedom to pursue your own goals will make it easier to focus on a shared agenda. Commitment is tough if you feel a need to protect your own agenda. Turf wars will lessen if you don't feel forced into compromises. Foster a flexible atmosphere that accommodates your individual hopes and wishes. Creating strategies with mutual benefits wins mutual trust. You will trust your partner that much more if you see that you can have your cake and eat it too. The saying "make love, not war," will be profoundly true in this romance when you let each other into your private goals. When you discuss matters with the intention of producing clarity, you will land on your feet instead of on your head.

The winning recipe for the *Taken for Granted* game is simple. Revise behavior that makes your partner feel devalued. Libra is swept off its feet when given the respect that its ideas deserve. Scorpio doesn't appreciate having its mind undervalued and its emotional support ignored. If you can identify the area that hurts the most when you don't receive support, then by all means now is the time to do something about it. The nice thing about this game is that as soon as you change the pattern, you feel immediate gratification. Share center stage. Don't compete. There is plenty of room for both of you in this relationship. You bring out greater passion and intimacy when showing you make each other feel special. Sometimes being a friend is the quickest way to become a lover.

The *Breaking the Bank* game can occur for a few reasons. Sometimes people are just bored. If you work too much without any celebration, a tendency to binge is greater.

People who are too strict on themselves, such as being too thrifty, may impulsively overindulge. Reward yourselves. Libra and Scorpio can be quite ambitious. There is nothing wrong with that. You want to be sure that your life together doesn't become all business. Rebellious behavior in the form of outrageous purchases or uncontrolled appetites is possible. Pacing yourselves and setting limits might be wise. You don't want to find yourselves gravitating to extremes when moderation will make you happier. If you both feel the freedom to have your say regarding major purchases, it may alleviate the necessity to make flamboyant individualistic statements. Acknowledgment of each other's power certainly helps in maintaining your emotional and material stability.

The Rainbow

Your Libra-Scorpio relationship delivers spectacular gifts. You both can delight in the love you find. There is a strong loyalty to preserve each other's happiness. Wealth in both the material and emotional sense can be realized. Libra's fondness for companionship blends well with Scorpio's search for a trustworthy lover. You fuel one another's passion. Your relationship possesses a unique sensuality. When you solidify your commitment to each other, deeper love awaits you. Life rewards your most inventive visions. Pay attention to what each of you needs, and you will never be disappointed.

A Libra man falls instantly for the mysterious Scorpio woman. She holds sway over his unusually even-keeled mind. The Venusian man perceives a sense of self-mastery in the Plutonian woman. She seems to be extremely perceptive and intelligent. Her laugh strikes the Libra man as being a mixture of sarcasm and pragmatic amusement. She appears to understand life's ironies. The Libra man believes that the Scorpio woman is an icon of realism in a world of make-believe. She may pretend to be naive, but somehow the shoe just doesn't fit. Her love of mystery delights the Venusian man's quest for an interesting soul mate. The Libra man notices that this Plutonian woman has a quiet countenance though she can be delightfully charming when she is out with him and his friends. She seems to force herself to be sociable, or does she really possess such an adaptable personality after all? The Libra man likes to be near her because she understands real passion. The Venusian man's refined sensuality seems to deepen when in the embrace of this intuitive, forceful woman. He wants to be loved by her because she knows the way to his heart. Sometimes she is sweet, but she can suddenly become saucy. He is attracted to her unpredictable, volcanic emotions. Although he is tempted to run for cover, if he finds his wits he will realize that he is witnessing an incredible display of fireworks.

A Scorpio woman is comfortable with the Libra man's gentleness though she wishes he would occasionally get mad or show a little emotion. She taps into his heart with her passion. The Plutonian woman perceives that the Libra man can handle her many moods. She needs a coolheaded man if she feels the call to explore society's taboos. The Libra man's mental ingenuity and diplomacy please her. She admires him for not running from her temper, and he even shows that he has a temper himself. This Plutonian woman is careful not to be too intense with the Libra man. She evaluates his sincerity even as she listens to him talk about his ambitions. The Scorpio woman doesn't like to waste her time on frivolity. She wants a lover who can let go to the moment and who looks to the future eagerly. The insecurity that change causes in this strong, spirited woman sometimes embarrasses her. She likes the fact that this man does not laugh at her weaknesses and appreciates her strengths.

A Libra woman longs for the true love of the Scorpio man. Sex with him is only the beginning. She wants to enter his deeply private world, but he doesn't share himself so readily. The Libra woman is reluctant to trust the Plutonian man until she sees a few of his hidden cards. The Venusian woman senses a potentially deep bond between them. She is aware that he is dangerous, intriguing, and attractive all in one package. Her instincts tell her to walk slowly, but her treacherous heart urges her to run. It isn't that she must have him, but it's not easy to get him out of her mind once she meets him. The Libra woman is insightful enough to know that love can have a high price tag. She senses that this Plutonian man has already paid the price many times. She wants to be special in his eyes. Her wisdom tells her life might be easier without him, but her adventurous streak can't help but bet on this outrageous chance at love for the ages. His gaze is captivating, but sometimes she ducks so he won't see the "real" her. She hopes a time will come when they are the happiest of mates.

A Scorpio man sees a path to immense pleasure in pursuing the Libra woman. The Scorpio man is quick to fall in love with the Venusian woman. She makes him feel appreciated. Her affection melts his reserved nature. He senses that his love makes her feel special. She seems to instinctively know when to be patient with him and when to impatiently shake him to see if she can get a response. He doesn't enjoy being social but is coaxed out of hiding by this feminine explorer of humanity. She seems to be demanding, but in a way that appeals to him. He feels even stronger when he is with this woman but not because she is no match for his mental prowess. On the contrary, she is quite aware of who he really is. He is scared by her perception of him yet peculiarly comforted at the same time. He cultivates an aura of mystique by hiding behind social "masks." He is puzzled by her ability to see behind all of his veneers. She wins his heart by not revealing this secret to even her closest friends. The Plutonian man is tempted to shake this Venusian woman off his tracks. Then again, will he ever find someone who so persistently follows him to where it is he truly resides?

You can climb to the greatest of fulfilling heights together. Don't look down while you seek the highest plateaus. Your commitment is strengthened when you aren't afraid of closeness. You don't need to rush each other. It's more important to enjoy each step of the journey. There are some who will envy your faith in one another. They probably won't be aware of the growth you have brought about in each other, and the tests you have endured. The love in this romance is as powerful as an ocean. When you find a mutually comforting level of trust, the gentle, loving breezes that embrace your relationship are impressive.

Libra-Sagittarius: The Gregarious Ones

Libra + Sagittarius = Two Fun-Loving Minds

Libra can hold its own in any social gathering. Sagittarius has an affable nature. Both signs discover opportunities through meeting the right people. Romance is apt to be full of drama. Each elicits assertiveness in the other. As a couple, Libra and Sagittarius are able to generate support for projects. Neither really wants to face direct confrontations. The diplomacy of Libra and the statesmanship of Sagittarius can circumvent much friction. Both seek pleasure in many different forms. These signs can share a strong desire to escape together to exotic locales. Airy Libra encourages Sagittarius to slow down before acting on sudden impulses. The Archer may need to consider the potential consequences of its actions. Sagittarius' enthusiasm may push Libra off the fence to take action. Libra benefits from the Archer's love for immediate gratification. The love of companionship these signs share is a source of strong compatibility.

Sugarcoated Game

The games played in your Libra-Sagittarius relationship are linked to avoiding adversity and grandiose hopes and wishes. When the two of you refuse to deal directly with issues, you may be in the middle of the *Sugarcoated* game. A tendency to keep your interactions light might lead you to run away from serious problems. The romantic in Libra can detest the need to confront a problem. The idealist in Sagittarius may refuse to even perceive that anything is wrong. The situation sours eventually when you realize that distance has developed through not addressing differences adequately. Passion diminishes because you only scratch the surface of real communication. You may sense that you are both holding back your natural intensity.

Great Expectations Game

As lovers you instill in each other the desire for a lot from life. A tendency to make each other feel that anything is possible opens your mind to many possibilities, so what can go wrong? The *Great Expectations* game arises when you think that your partner can magically deliver happiness. Unrealistic promises might get you into trouble with each other. Libra has an innate instinct to be liked by others. Similarly, Sagittarius pleases others to receive attention or compliments. When the two of you hit full stride in this game, you might spoil each other to such an extent that you start to expect too much. Feelings of rejection or disappointment arise when you don't receive the support you feel you are entitled to and can lead to confusion within the relationship. You drift apart if you do not perceive one another clearly.

Bittersweet Game

When outside observers view you together, they probably see a happy and energetic couple. You can spark each other's passion. The forceful energy in a Libra-Sagittarius relationship can get things accomplished in a hurry, yet there can be a shadow in your relationship that is hidden from plain sight as seen in the *Bittersweet* game. This game is caused by feelings of sadness. Often the core cause is the lack of support for your goals. When Libra suspects that a lover is opposed to its cherished plans, indecision manifests itself. Libra can't stand the onset of self-doubt brought on by a partner's lack of enthusiasm. Sagittarius seems to lose its soul when a lover isn't behind its burning desires. Angry resentment can build to the point that it makes you feel like strangers. Neither of your signs does well with drawn-out, angry disputes. You become irritable. The happiness you bring to each other is weighed down by a ton of worries. You aren't good companions when unresolved business makes you nervous. The intimacy you have grown to adore can be dissolved by the emotional hurt. Talking with each other can become a routine in which you go through the motions. That spontaneous passion you appreciate is held back by a lack of trust.

Strategies

How can you conquer these Libra-Sagittarius games? In the *Sugarcoated* game, it helps to roll up your sleeves and decide to work together to solve your issues. It takes a lot more energy to avoid a problem than it does to deal with it! Your commitment will become more clearly defined through frank communication, which deepens your trust in each other. Libra and Sagittarius are not signs that benefit from being unassertive. You both are more fun to be around when you say what is on your mind. When you tiptoe around issues, you are just not the same lively individuals. The romantic in you blossoms brightly when you speak honestly. Don't fear the intensity you share. Passion isn't necessarily passive. Your sign chemistry will lead you to have strong opinions. You don't have to agree on everything. Become comfortable with honest verbal exchanges because it is your gateway to intimacy.

The *Great Expectations* game asks you not to exaggerate what you can do for one another and to be realistic in what you ask of your lover. You can't help but think big in this relationship. Libra and Sagittarius can be good for each other's self-confidence. The positive attitudes you instill in one another ignite larger-than-life dreams. Cultivate patience, which will keep your expectations in perspective. No one could ever convince you to stop trying to change the world. You can put a plan together while on the run. A restless urge to make life come to you is at the heart of your romance. When you each are willing to go the distance required to make your relationship work, you are most of the way home. Your lover can't dispel the blues from your life entirely but can be a positive force in your corner. Utilize each other's gifts without relying too heavily upon them. You will be happier if you keep dependency needs balanced.

The *Bittersweet* game requires your mutual support of each other's highest dreams. If you do so, you will be a hero in each other's eyes. Anger will evaporate quickly with a little attention. There can be a tendency to become self-involved when your lives are busy. This is a subtle game. You may not really be aware you are in this one until long after it starts. You may feel sadness but wonder about its source. For you, positive regard can become a craving and may even feel like love. Be reasonable about your demands for praise. Your willingness to share your partner's goals adds closeness to your romance! Showing that you care greatly increases the love you share.

The Rainbow

Your Libra-Sagittarius relationship can be filled with many joyful experiences. The two of you don't like to look back. New adventures keep you both mentally alert. You can show a special flair for taking advantage of opportunities. The inspiration you awaken in each other is readily apparent. Even when you disagree, it isn't that far to common ground. Generously sharing your resources makes your hearts grow fonder. You can become attached to the passionate highs of this romance. Celebrating your successes is a favorite pastime. Your friends are likely to be from many walks of life. The two of you seek stimulation from a wide variety of people. When you give each other the latitude to branch out to your natural callings, a special sense of intimacy develops. You can be the best of friends and lovers. You embrace progressive ideas. It is a thrill to travel through life with such an invigorating lover.

The Sagittarius man is instantly in trouble when he meets the Libra woman. She knows how to hook this man with her attentiveness. The Sagittarius man soon realizes when he pursues the Venusian woman that at any moment she may do a quick U-turn and pursue him. The Archer probably promises more than he can deliver, but he notices that, as long as he is sincere, she will cut him some slack. He needs to watch his manners because this woman will let him know in no uncertain terms when he has overstepped his bounds. He hopes she will understand when he feels the need to go on spontaneous journeys (though he thinks it could be fun to have a travel companion, and perhaps he won't go away as much if she becomes a central player in his life). The Sagittarius man longs for a soul mate who can match his love for knowledge and passion. This mentally adept Venusian woman seems to have both bases covered. He admires her way of moving ahead while balancing opposite forces. She appears to calmly take life matter-of-factly, yet she seems to be sensual and passionate. He would like to let her further into his inner world because it is lonely to be an explorer with no one waiting for him at home.

The Libra woman is suspicious yet hopeful when she meets the Sagittarius man. He seems to be too good to be true. The optimistic Sagittarius treats his ideals as though they all are easily attainable. The Venusian woman wonders if he really believes this himself. In some ways, she doesn't care. It's refreshing to be around such a positive spirit. He can clown around one moment and then suddenly tell a sensitive and serious story. The Libra woman enjoys listening to him. His ideas show what reality could be if people

The Magic of Signmates

had faith. She wonders if her own solid logic will jive with this eclectic man of many cultures. The Venusian woman finds him to be fun-loving. He is a romantic in his mind as she is in her heart. He isn't mushy about love and proves the depth of his feelings with action. She is careful to shelter her most sensitive feelings from his sarcasm. He has a smile, which slowly sweeps across his face, that penetrates her heart. He seems to see into the deepest recesses of her mind. She asks herself, "What does that look mean?" Perhaps this is his way of saying she has no real secrets she can hide from him, or maybe it's his way of paying attention to her. The Libra woman likes the strong embrace of this free-spirited man. She wants to show him her free-spirited side too. She hopes he is up for the ride of his life—after all, she is!

The Sagittarius woman likes the charm of the Libra man. It resonates with the beauty she looks for in love. The spontaneous Sagittarius woman notices that the Libra man is frozen by indecision if confused by opposing viewpoints, but he seems adroit in finding a way out of tight jams. The Sagittarius woman is intrigued by his mind because he is logical and his reasoning is sound. She hopes he does not mind surprises. What she does today is not necessarily based on what she did yesterday. Her "let's live for today" attitude is a secret to her happiness. She still is willing to save for a rainy day, but she doesn't like to put off an adventure until tomorrow if it can be experienced today. She wants to show this Venusian man her romantic side. She doesn't know exactly why. Maybe it's because he listens with interest, or perhaps he knows how to reach her sentimental side. This Venusian man combines sensitivity and detachment; she suspects that he weighs these opposing forces before he acts. She can accept the good and the bad in him as long as he can learn to live with her outrageous and spontaneous tendencies.

The Libra man perceives that the Sagittarius woman is unique. She doesn't exactly fit his idealized image of a lover. He wonders whether this is why he is attracted to her. She comes into his life like a comet and blasts away boredom and complacency. The Venusian man is not boring; he just isn't as fast to plunge into emotional matters as she is. Her humor lightens his worries. He wonders how she can appear to be so lighthearted yet show such intense ambition. Her passion attracts him (not everyone can entice him). He wonders if this woman must always lead. He soon sees she is as adaptable as they come—to a point. Her spirit guides her to follow no one. She seems to let her heart dictate the pace of her love. The Libra man enjoys how the Sagittarius woman strokes his ego. She is attentive and vibrant. He also knows that he had better reciprocate or this fair-minded, brilliantly aware woman might just start keeping score.

Your romance can be the source of many reasons to celebrate. Your expectations don't keep you together, but the surprises and new spurts of growth that replenish you as a couple do. You can rejoice in putting together a plan that includes all of your greatest dreams. As long as you are not reluctant to hope for the best and to use your full potential, you will never stray far from each other's loving embrace.

Libra-Capricorn: The Reliable Ones

Libra + Capricorn = Ambition with a Well-Conceived Plan

Ideas with sound reality behind them can be a hallmark of this Sun sign combination. Libra's ability to think through various alternatives to a situation satisfies Capricorn's need for thoroughness. Capricorn's fondness for structure blends nicely with Libra's tendency to build from a clear mental blueprint. Capricorn can show old-fashioned values regarding romance but will not be out of its element because Libra can display a respect for tradition. These two signs don't always fall in love with each other as much as they carefully prepare a foundation that can sustain a relationship. Intimacy seems to come slowly after these signs become comfortable with the idea of being lovers. Then there can be spontaneity. Both can instinctually act on impulses that excite the imagination.

Chilly Forecast Game

The games played in your Libra-Capricorn relationship are associated with a too reserved nature and fixed opinions. If you notice that affection isn't easy to show or that warmth is slow in coming from your partner, you may be in the *Chilly Forecast* game. A lack of trust causes this game. At the beginning of a relationship, fear could be the distancing factor. Breaking the ice may be a slow process. Libra can back off from someone through cool intellectualism. Capricorn can bring everything down to a business level to create distance from emotions. You can feel like you are left out in the cold when you try to determine why you can't communicate. Your romance may seem to have little warmth. You go through the motions but something is missing—a bit of denial is at work. Libra can ignore discontentment by pursuing other interests. Capricorn often will bury emotional woes in work. Breaking through your resistance to talking doesn't become any easier if you wait. Getting at the causes of this game can be frustrating.

When Does the Fun Start Game

There could be times when you wonder why you work more than you play. You could be in the *When Does the Fun Start* game. Libra has a romantic streak that never really goes away. Even in the midst of a great dilemma, the love of romance is in Libra's heart. Capricorn can be a passionate lover when it can forget its responsibilities. People are sometimes surprised to see that this earth sign can play with almost the same dedication as it works. When your relationship is lost in the business side of life, playfulness may disappear. Fun and romance may be sacrificed to a demanding schedule. A life in the fast lane is likely in your relationship. When you forget to park in Lover's Lane, life isn't as rewarding. You may even sense that you do not receive the same attention from each other that you once did.

Power Ploy Game

When you are at odds over differing points of view the *Power Ploy* game can surface. Libra won't easily compromise over certain strategies. Capricorn could become so attached to an idea that it is unwilling to change course to please anyone else. You may show a stubborn streak when it comes to getting your own way. A desire to outmaneuver each other can become compulsive. Winning can develop into a strong drive. A power struggle might create considerable distance between you. When you refuse to listen to each other, the going gets tough. This is probably the game that brings out the most anger. It's worse if you don't show any hostility. Hurt feelings can cause you not to support your partner's key ambitions. Intimacy suffers from a lack of communication. To give is not easy when you don't receive.

Strategies

How can you get through these Libra-Capricorn games? The *Chilly Forecast* asks the two of you to loosen up. You will find yourselves talking *at* instead of *to* each other if you can't let go. Fear requires a dose of courage to loosen its hold. Imagine taking a small step. Abandon your favorite defense mechanisms. It isn't all that scary once you honestly communicate. It's more awkward to hold back your true feelings. With practice, you will find that it becomes easier to share your real thoughts. Libra likes to establish intimacy through talking. Once Capricorn gets past its self-consciousness, it gravitates toward comfortable intimacy. It doesn't matter how you get there. The main thing is that you begin to trust one another. It's possible that you aren't as affectionate toward each other due to a lack of focus. Too many distractions can be the problem. You may need to escape together in order to regain the warmth you lack.

In the *When Does the Fun Start* game, it's easy for you to get so caught up in responsibilities that you forget how to relax together. You may need to make sure that you don't trade away all of the fun for the love of work. You both could be so obligated to others that you don't even realize that you are sacrificing pleasure. The romance you want as a couple can come back if you take time away from the workaday world. Concentrate on creating quality time even if your schedules are loaded. There is usually a way to fit in a romantic rendezvous when you really want to do it. Love takes foresight. Your signs are two of the best in designing a successful plan. Some refocusing away from one area to energize another may be required. You can have the best of both worlds when you put your mind to it.

The *Power Ploy* game derives from a competitive part of your relationship. You both probably prefer to lead in your chosen areas of expertise. Relinquishing power doesn't come easily when you both are determined to win an argument or to pursue a life path. Learning how to negotiate in such a way that you don't undermine each other's self-esteem is wise. Flexibility can help to resolve issues faster. You can't expect one of you to make all of the compromises. When you make each other feel like winners, it really helps your attitude. If you harbor anger, letting it out is better than sulking. Listening to each other's point of view surely helps you feel like you are on the same team. You are happier when you do not hold back support for one another. When your joint power is pointed directly at your goals, life is a wonderful thing!

The Rainbow

Your Libra-Capricorn relationship has a promise of great longevity. The two of you can enjoy greeting each year with your best creative drives. The love you feel deepens with time. Helping one another realize your serious ambitions makes you strong allies. Showing that you can be trusted brings your lover closer. You both express love more spontaneously when you are in a stable commitment. You need definite plans, but be sure to allow for surprises as this seems to revitalize your passion. A healthy respect for the past, a realistic assessment of the present, and a sober anticipation of the future define your relationship. Yet, there may still be a wildcard of unexpected opportunity that makes your lives exciting and full of exotic pleasure.

The Libra man finds the Capricorn woman to be comforting. She does not rush to come close but certainly shows that she has "been there and done that" previously. Her eyes reflect her knowledge and experience. The Libra man notices that this Saturnian woman has a clear sense of commitment. She appears to have well-defined boundaries that rival the Venusian man's own. Her face lights up when she talks about her ambitions. She relishes the idea of people needing her. He hopes she will see him as being reliable. Her ideas are as solid as an oak tree. This woman's practicality masks passionate sensuality. The Venusian man wonders if she is self-conscious about her feelings. He is not forthcoming about his ideas or how to win his love. He sees a strength in her that would be wonderful to count on. The Libra man appreciates her willingness to take the lead. The Venusian man needs this in a partner at times when he juggles his options. He notices that she is interested in his ability to hold his own in the business world. This earthy woman certainly knows her way along the busy atmosphere of Main Street.

The Capricorn woman perceives gentleness in the Libra man. It's not that she thinks he is weak, but he seems to understand that a heart without love withers. The Saturnian woman is careful. She doesn't show her love openly until her lover displays his willingness to hold up his end of the bargain. This Venusian man appears to know how to negotiate. She needs this in a partner since her own tendency is to test her lover's sincerity. His sense of fairness pleases her. The Capricorn woman enjoys his attention. He certainly knows how to treat a lover. She hopes her desire to go slow won't bother this romantic man; she can't help it that she has a reality-testing mind. This earthy spirit loves that which is durable. She isn't so foolish to think that love lasts forever but feels this way when the Venusian man looks into her heart with his sensuous eyes. Her desire for lasting love is at the core of her idealism. She hopes he doesn't lack ambition for material success and that he will share his wealth of emotions.

The Libra woman views the Capricorn man as being in control. He seems to enjoy knowing where everything in his life belongs. She likes to be out of place in order to get his attention. The Libra woman quickly notices that the Saturnian man can take for granted whatever he has under his control. She is attracted to the determination that comes through when he speaks about his goals. His desire to impress her with his accomplishments is obvious. He has a résumé that could impress many. She listens to find out if he can be kind and generous. The Libra woman likes the fact that he seems reliable. He seems burdened with responsibility. She feels the same way herself when she tries too hard to please others. She hopes he doesn't expect too much. She is good at making others feel needed. The Venusian woman hopes he will be a lover whom she can trust. She thinks perhaps his commitment to work could easily be transferred to his romantic interests. His serious expression is softened when she charms him. She seems to say, "Don't be afraid of me." He appears to be steeped in tradition. She doesn't mind as long as he treats her like a newly discovered treasure!

The Capricorn man isn't sure what to make of the Libra woman. She glides through business with the ease of a figure skater. She is a polished speaker. He discovers that she cuts through to his heart and his feelings. She isn't easy to back into a corner. In some ways he likes her better from the distance because he isn't quick to show his true intentions. He is intrigued by how she tries to figure out his innermost thoughts. She seems to think he hasn't given her the full story. He becomes attached to her soft touch. She is a smooth operator who subtly takes the lead to see how he feels. He knows he had better not resist if he doesn't want to lose her. He senses that she may be the answer to his longing for love. He gets the unspoken message that if he wants the pleasure of her company, he needs to show a bit of vulnerability. The Venusian woman wins his love and respect when she is unafraid of his stiff-armed approach to take what he wants. She sees that the road is big enough for the two to walk side by side.

Your romance can prove to have great endurance. Even if you go through ups and downs, as all loves do, you stay afloat through holding on to the truths that keep you strong. Your decisions can reflect a wisdom that comes from working through business and emotional matters. Neither of you is impressed with what comes easily. You like to make your luck through relentless effort. Don't forget to forgive. It's a sure way back to the "good old days" in case you lose the way. Remember the spark that brought you to each other. It's still aglow if you make the time to keep that fire of love lit!

Let the Games Begin

Libra-Aquarius: The Surprisers

Libra + Aquarius = Premium Insightful Thinking

These are two air signs that can view issues with objectivity. Your vision stays clear as long as emotions don't create a fog. The ideas that circulate through your romance are as lively as honeybees swarming in the hive. Your minds can meet through a range of subjects. Love is energized through a steady diet of new experiences. "Boredom" is not in the vocabulary of this sign duo. The two of you may not always agree on everything and can enjoy an occasional good-old-fashioned debate. The road to each other's heart requires equality and acceptance. When you champion your partner's causes, love becomes that much stronger.

Copy or Original Game

The games played in your Libra-Aquarius relationship are connected to a lack of assertiveness and an inclination to exclude feelings in favor of the intellect. The *Copy or Original* game shows the two of you are not sure how to be yourselves. If you try too hard to please others, you will become confused. Libra can compulsively seek acceptance as much as Aquarius can force its unique ideas to fit the expectations of others. You are not at your best when you follow what people want you to be. When you leave your own plans behind, your sense of direction is muddled. Even when relating to each other, there could be a tendency not to exert your own will enough. The vast intellectual domain you share is so strong that you may live in the world of ideas to the point of not acting out your real needs. You are not the same empowered individuals when you look for outside direction too much.

Communication Blahs Game

When you do not talk with any feeling, you may sense that you are experiencing strange encounters. The *Communication Blahs* game depicts how you might intellectualize all of your exchanges. An aloofness settles across your relationship and leads to feelings of distance. You may not make the effort to break through defenses that keep you emotionally apart. There is a coolness inherent in two air signs that won't bring as much emotion into your romance as may be found in other relationships. That's okay. You do need to be aware when you purposely lead each other away from intimacy. Your sexual relationship may not be enough to bridge the emotional gap between you. This is a case in which your ability to talk clearly, a real asset, is not fully utilized. Fear or a reluctance to let someone get very close may lead you to be players in this game.

Lovers and Strangers Game

You can seem like the closest of soul mates, can't you? Do you suddenly find yourselves feeling as though you live on separate planets? The *Lovers and Strangers* game is one in which your sense of intimacy vacillates between extremes. You will do anything for each other one day, but the next may find you pulling back your support. One reason for this game may be unresolved anger. Air signs such as yourselves don't always like to deal with anger. Gliding around intense issues is the path of least resistance, but it doesn't make you feel better. The same old "now you see me, now you don't" behavior can show its unwelcome face. There's another fact about air signs worth mentioning. You like to hang out in your own airspace—like a solo pilot in a cockpit. You have your own "no fly" zones. What you need to determine is how to let each other know about this sacred space. Sudden withdrawal to your personal retreat can break your lover's heart. The heart may or may not grow fonder with absence. Sometimes the heart hardens and becomes unforgiving and resentful if you exhibit a pattern of unpredictable flight.

Strategies

How can you fly above these Libra-Aquarius games? In the *Copy or Original* game, you need to stand your ground and act on individual impulses. Libra naturally considers opposing points of view. The trick for Libra is not to be ruled by the expectations of others. Aquarius has an innate drive to express its individuality and never feels quite at home when not listening to its own voice.

The two of you must speak up with each other. Be assertive. You will be happier when you receive the best each has to offer. You were meant to make your own news—bring those ideas to life with creative action. Put your concepts to work. There is so much original material flying around in your romance that you don't have to look far to find a great script. Encourage your lover to act out his or her dreams. You two are a high-flying act when you trust your instincts!

What can you do about the *Communication Blahs* game? One or both of you may be so bored with your current lifestyle that it dulls your mind. Your interactions will lack the passion you want if you don't show some feelings. If you have a fear of intimacy, you need to find a way to trick your mind into letting you drop your defenses. Neither of you probably bites—even if you do growl! Many of your fears have power over you because you don't deal with them. The best way to get past this game is to face your fears. You may even find what you are anxious about is a figment of your imagination. When you break the habit of hiding your emotions with intellectual sound bites, you are well on the way to reaching your partner's heart. You don't have to be mushy, but you could at least reveal a glimmer of emotion. The expression of emotions makes your mental brilliance that much easier to understand anyway!

The *Lovers or Strangers* game is a test to see if you can handle emotional heat. This game shows that you share passion and deep emotions. When you take a closer look, there may be a tendency to beat a hasty retreat; air signs approach each other in this strange way. At least you are both air signs, so your behavior may be more alike than you think. Let each other come along on one of your flights. Show each other your unique ideas and inner desire to maintain your freedom. Libra is known for a love of companionship but doesn't want its independence to be taken away. This particular sign needs to know there is enough elbow room to hang out with friends and to avidly pursue subjects of interest. By nature, Aquarius is independent and loves to shake up everybody else's reality. Life can become lonely for the rebel. You both have something valuable to offer. Simple, honest discourse is the shortest distance between your minds. You don't need to feel like strangers in a strange land. It's a short skip and jump into each other's embrace, which certainly promises to be more enjoyable than a solitary journey. The trips to your own airspace bring greater joy when you both know you are coming home to a lover, not a stranger.

The Magic of Signmates

The Rainbow

Your Libra-Aquarius relationship has a touch of genuine originality. Acceptance awaits you if you are willing to allow it into your life. Your minds have a common attraction to people with imagination. The love you share stimulates the expression of inventive ideas. The stars will seem like they brought you together when you find your way into the deepest part of each other's being. You enjoy taking excursions to romantic locations. The journeys you take together can fill you with a sense of wonder that replenishes you.

A Libra man feasts his eyes upon the Aquarius woman. She appears to move to internal music, which he would like to share. The Venusian man is drawn to the freedom-loving ways of the Uranian woman. She listens to him with an awareness rarely found. She seems to see right through him. That doesn't bother him so much because she makes him feel exhilarated. Her mind ignites his to think about new horizons. The Libra man can't help but think this woman's mind is unique; her words are scintillating. He is moved by her dedication to her goals. The Aquarius woman is a symbol of freedom, which fascinates him. He feels better when he sees that she knows how to conform to custom though he must admit he hopes her unorthodox views never fade far into the background.

The Aquarius woman realizes that the Libra man is as attached to his ideas as she is to her own. He certainly is careful not to offend her beliefs, though she detects that he can go on the offensive if someone puts down his pet theories. She appreciates his duality. On one hand, he is concerned with justice and fairness almost as though he is on a mission to right the world of its wrongs. On the other hand, he is a romantic who would look at home on a tropical island, sipping piña coladas. He seems to be more predictable than she, but the Aquarius woman must admit that a stabilizing factor may be a blessing in disguise. The Venusian man seems to be the personification of her romantic myth—a lover who creates an amorous atmosphere as well as he makes love. She thinks this mentally quick man can keep up with her lightning flash impulses. The Aquarius woman can't really be blamed for being changeable; she was born under the influence of unpredictable Uranus. To many, she seems irresponsible. To many more, she is a remarkable spirit with a mind of her own yet with a sensitive connection with those who know her. The Aquarius woman is hard to label. She likes this Venusian man because he weighs their relationship in his mind and somehow the balance comes out just right.

Let the Games Begin

The Libra woman meets the Aquarius man with the brunt of her intellect. She hasn't bumped into such a formidable mind in some time. The Libra woman likes his refreshing insights. He doesn't mince words and prefers to get right to the point though sometimes he has a near miss regarding her feelings. She fires back at him and notices that he likes her spunk. He seems to be unpredictable, apt to suddenly "shoot from the hip." She appreciates his sensitivity when she broaches matters of the heart. He does not express much feeling, but it is evident that his feelings are intense. The Venusian woman isn't looking for a sure thing as much as the exciting promise for love that he offers. She perceives that he does not take friendship lightly. The Libra woman wants a partner who can be a loving mate and not run at the first sight of friction. It's not that she is so brave; she simply understands that love is risky business. He talks gingerly about his past—at least the part he has enjoyed. The mystery is what he doesn't like in personal relationships. He has much to say about the state of the world. He seems to be a revolutionary, not really fitting into the rules of any culture. She only hopes he will become a citizen of her world, where he will be most welcome. If he plays his cards right, he may get the key to the city.

The Aquarius man knows when he is under the steady gaze of the extremely perceptive Libra woman. Even from her first probe, he realizes he had best stay alert. He doesn't fear her; rather, he wants to understand as quickly as possible how to show that he cares. The Venusian woman can easily lead in matters of love. It doesn't take the Uranian man long to see that. She likes it when he makes the first move because she then knows for certain that he is interested. The Aquarius man doesn't really know if this love is a short-term or long-term affair. He likes to think of himself as an "in the moment" lover whether or not this is true. The Libra woman seems to know his number. He likes the way she can read his ideas. Electricity is in the air when she is near. The Aquarius man likes to talk with the even-tempered Venusian woman. He needs a lover who is able to hold her ground and won't be blown away by his sudden changes of direction. He wants to give her what she needs. The way she makes him feel accepted even when they disagree is like magic. The Uranian man wants to make a good impression on the Venusian woman. He sees that he may have the "right stuff." It may not hurt to take a few cues from her since she walks in the world of love much more gracefully than he. The Aquarius man gets the feeling that he may already be wrapped around her finger. Anyway, he likes the way she anticipates his next move.

The Magic of Signmates

Your romance contains the missing ingredients to happiness that you can't supply on your own. Each of you can offer the other a fulfilling glimpse of what real love can be like. There is no sense in looking back at the loves you have already missed. There is enough here to erase any sad or bad memories. The love you share is cause for happy celebration. When you really let go to each other, the payoff is enormous. The joy you seek is as close as your commitment to being together.

Libra-Pisces: The Romantics

Libra + Pisces = Plunge into Love and Romance

Both signs are strongly driven to find a soul mate. Each of you hopes the other can fulfill your greatest wishes. Libra can help Pisces to be more mentally clear in defining goals. Pisces influences Libra to trust intuition instead of constantly favoring the mind. Both signs share a love for the arts. A common bond might be a never-ending desire to create a large circle of acquaintances. The two like to bounce their ideas and ideals off others to ensure that plans will hit the mark. Each is other-directed to some extent. Libra cannot help but seek approval from people regarding its talents. Confirmation bolsters Libra's self-confidence. Pisces may not show its need for acceptance as readily. Underneath an outer appearance of contentment is a longing for recognition. Life can be a magical journey filled with inspiring paths when these two get together.

Waffling Game

The games played in your Libra-Pisces relationship center around unclear choices and fantasies that test living in reality. When the two of you feel it takes forever to arrive at a decision, the *Waffling* game may be in play. Each of you can take pains to make perfect decisions. Libra must weigh all the issues carefully to bring the odds to its favor. Pisces would just as soon ignore the details and leave the outcome to chance. This clash in strategies makes it hard to see where you might be heading. Figuring out how to understand each other's reasoning could be irritating. Libra will show anger if someone refuses to consider a sound plan. Pisces can brood with the best of them when tired of thinking too much. Flipping back and forth in an effort to please each other could become exhausting if you aren't sure what each wants in the first place.

The underlying issue here is often not visible. Denial is another dimension of your interactions. Denial keeps you in this game long after you hope to run out the clock and get on to better things.

Idealized Images Game

When you only see what you want to see in your partner, you are in the *Idealized Images* game. Libra and Pisces both want a relationship to work out so badly that each sometimes will choose to ignore the unpleasant. You are born romantics. A tendency to not do a little reality testing could make your perceptions of each other miss the target. In working together, you may convince one another to go in directions that waste time and money. Communication probably goes around issues rather than getting to the heart of matters. If you relate to your partner as the *image* created in your mind, you may find it difficult to talk to the real person. You do not respond to your partner's *real* needs. You paint pictures of the relationship that could be illusory. It's not that you don't have the raw materials to put together a winning romance, but there is a tendency to run away from the truth.

Lost Horizon Game

Two people who need to be inspired to reach goals—does this sound familiar? In the *Lost Horizon* game, you dilute each other's key aims with doubts or a lack of faith. You have the ability to sway your partner to take other directions. When you constantly keep each other from moving forward, your long-term objectives may fizzle. Seeing the big picture becomes challenging if you can't work together with any sense of consistent unity. Dependency needs may be the main problem. You may have lost perspective in knowing when and how to lean on each other. When the boat sinks, you lose sight of the destination. Libra becomes agitated while Pisces goes into peculiar mood swings. The end result is a couple without a reliable compass who frantically sends out an SOS. The situation deteriorates if you deny the need for help out of this jam.

Strategies

How can you deal with these Libra-Pisces games? In the *Waffling* game, the two of you need to trust your decision-making power. If you interfere too much with one another's choices, it may be better to back off. When you try to make joint decisions, a little time apart might help you to see clearly. You may space each other out. How does this happen? You could be too sensitive about your lover's needs. You may have to train yourselves to allow for more personal autonomy. It is tempting to count on one another as part of your decisions. Learn not to doubt your partner's choices if you want the same treatment in return. Libra and Pisces can be so connected mentally and emotionally that it might seem you are Siamese twins. A show of faith gets you both to move forward. You can read doubt in each other's faces as fast as a mother can tune in to her baby's cries. You have the ability to tap into what your lover is feeling. This gift can actually turn into a liability if you hinder each other's actions. If you want to discover honest communication and deeper passion, encourage your lover to come forward. Getting out of each other's way is as vital as being an active participant!

The *Idealized Images* game asks you to leave behind the fantasy "script" of your imagination and to step into real-life drama. You will turn this game around by not projecting personas upon each other and by seeing the actual person. You are romantics from the get-go. Your relationship perhaps began under unusual circumstances. It may have seemed like the stars moved into a magical alignment to bring you together. Everyday living with its many ups and downs is what you may fear. Surrendering illusion doesn't mean letting go of love. It's more likely that your closeness will become more genuine when you talk honestly. Defining your commitment becomes easier when you step down from the pedestal of love onto a level playing field. In this setting you stand a greater chance of achieving the outcomes you desire. You will never be able to live up to all of your lover's expectations. No perfect people exist, but when you play by a set of rules that allows you to engage in intimate conversation and to make sound plans, your relationship can blossom. You can "dance the night away" as two lovers with realistic dreams.

The *Lost Horizon* game can become a paradise found when you help each other steer toward goals that empower you both. The winning ingredient is belief in your individual ambitions and roles. Faith seems to ignite shared goals. When you sail off together with the hopes of finding real love, be patient in your expectations. The boat takes in water

The Magic of Signmates

when you depend too heavily on your partner. Also, if you stay too focused on the little things, the greater purpose for your being together may be lost. You instill great idealism in each other. You easily try to live out your dreams through one another. Why? Perhaps it's because Libra and Pisces spin dreams from a sense of hope. Libra uses its keen intellect to seek peace and cosmic meaning. Pisces' powerful emotions almost compel the heavens to hear its appeal for unity. Put these two together, and it adds up to a powerful force. When you don't trust your own visions, the horizon disappears right before your eyes. When you will not believe in your shared outlooks, the skies seem to be full of ominous clouds. When you get to those thoughts and insights that restore peace and fulfillment, you know where you are heading. The love and acceptance you want from each other is a constant need. The better you get at acknowledging your needs, the faster your two hearts feel as one. You have the power to maintain a steady course. Awareness of major objectives seems to help you stay happily afloat.

The Rainbow

Your Libra-Pisces relationship has endless imagination. You probably see many different people in each other. There is a theatrical quality to your romance that brings out your humor and self-expression. When you stay focused on the gifts you each have rather than the shortcomings, you travel to amazing heights together. You share a love that many others will not understand. The two of you may sometimes wonder if you knew each other in past centuries. The chemistry you live out together doesn't always feel like it belongs in the present. You may symbolize romance to others. Your way of relating needs time to reveal its style to you. Don't assume that you have figured each other out too soon. There is a subtle mystery in your being together that may be obvious at a much later time. You can eventually read your lover's mind as accurately as a master reader can interpret a tarot card spread. When you can separate reality from fiction and illusion from insight, your ride together is as high as the sky.

A Libra man glides into the life of the Pisces woman. She seems to ride the waves of emotion. The Venusian man is amused by the way the Neptunian woman interacts in the world. Her face reflects wisdom derived from past experiences, both happy and sad. She has a breadth of vision that sets everything—past, present, and future. The Libra man notices how this feminine spirit searches for faith. She seems to see that life has the possibility to deliver endless beauty or infinite imperfection. The Libra man observes that she doesn't readily show her heart even though he feels he already knows her from somewhere. She is not really familiar but is like a memory of something pleasant. He wants so badly to taste this love again. If only he could figure out how to talk to her. His clever mind devises scenarios that reveal his emotions, but this Neptunian lover doesn't seem as impressed by his wit as by his inner qualities. He wants to move her with his ambition. She is a funny character and hard to predict, but she seems to appreciate his common sense. Her floaty logic is stabilized by the solid reasoning of the Libra man.

A Pisces woman finds the Libra man to be a lively thinker. He seems to generate intellectual enthusiasm in her. The Neptunian woman likes the fact that this Venusian man is an outspoken romantic. He excites her mind and heart. The Pisces woman perceives that he tiptoes around her because of her sensitivity. She wishes he would simply be himself so she would not feel guilty about her sensitive, dreamy nature. It's not that she can't be bubbly and theatrical, but there are moments when her consciousness drifts to process memories in order to put them where they belong, and this can happen in the middle of a sentence or even in her sleep. She doesn't want to be known as a dreamer though her ideals show through like a beacon in the night. The intuitive forces that guide this feminine spirit are foreign to Libra, yet the Neptunian woman notices that the Venusian man follows her thoughts. She is self-conscious because her ideas are steeped in emotion. This woman responds to primordial forces. She is in love with the intimacy that quickly arose with the Libra man. She thinks he is a good catch, that is, if he doesn't just see her as another fish in the sea. He seems to have had many experiences in the arena of love, but she believes that her powers of attraction can lead him to stay with her.

A Libra woman finds the Pisces man to be an enigma. Her mind identifies him as part of the present, but her intuition can't classify him as belonging to any particular time or place. The Libra woman is so intrigued that her instincts lead her to chase after him. He is like a phantom, easily slipping through her hands. She sees that he is devoted to his beliefs. Can he believe in her? She hopes so because she is attracted to his sensitive eyes and mysterious smile. Romance is not so difficult to feel when she is with him. His intuitive mind splashes all over her logic. She likes the way he can see so many potential options in front of him. A divine discontentment appears to guide him to question the lasting value of everything. She hopes he can see that her affection promises a permanent connection. His feelings seem to reach down to the core of the earth. He is easy to know on the one hand and complex on the other. The Venusian woman wants to nail down a commitment with him because this seems to be the best way to define him. He has a peculiar yet loving personality; separating these two aspects is the challenge. She is up to the match if he can be a true player. The Libra woman can't deny that this man is worth the trouble.

The Pisces man never counted on the Libra woman being such a persistent lover. He reads her passion clearly. His heart can betray him as much as her own when it comes to falling in love with the wrong people. The Neptunian man's imagination runs along the same frequencies as that of the Libra woman in romance. He senses that they both need to prevent past loves from guiding their thinking. The Pisces man is drawn to her frank gaze, which says to him, "We could make a fine duo." He realizes his hesitation about her contributes to her indecision about him. He wants to take a leap of faith and dispel his fears. They could make a wonderful team. The Pisces man is dazzled by her eloquence and her sensual touch. The love he longs for could be his if he learns to trust her. The Venusian woman is no fool. He knows she won't wait forever. His heart says yes, but his mind questions his actions. That first step to love can be shaky. He finally convinces himself that this Venusian woman is worth the gamble. Once the decision is made, he cares little about the past. He looks forward to the future that the Libra woman can enjoy with him.

Communicate in order to spread clarity throughout your romance. In those moments when you don't understand one another, try to seek the eye in the hurricane. You will test each other's patience; that is a given. Can you learn how to listen and respond to the needs that only time will reveal? You have a love that can carry you over any hurdle. The understanding you want from your lover will come when you return the favor. Visible results alone will not fulfill you; intangible connections that nourish your inner dreams are what make this relationship special.

Scorpio-Scorpio: The Researchers

Scorpio + Scorpio = Intense Feelings

Two Scorpios can form a deep bond of loyalty. Incisive instincts to make money are highly possible. This is a romance with strong opinions and feelings. Neither can force the other to change his or her mind. It's better to negotiate and recognize one another's strengths. Power is a major issue. When both feel equally empowered, the relationship functions more smoothly. This is a water sign with a love of privacy. Each can perceive the other as a challenge to understand. Open conversations contribute greatly to the success of this duo. It is inevitable that disputes over possessions may arise. Scorpio can become extremely attached to belongings. The establishment of clear boundaries regarding what each owns is another wise policy. Protectiveness of one another is a likelihood. Passionate mutual interests seem to keep the two close.

Guerrilla Warfare Game

The games played in your Scorpio-Scorpio relationship center around hidden anger and power standoffs. The *Guerrilla Warfare* game is one in which the two of you will do anything to avoid a direct confrontation. Even if there are strong feelings, little emotion is displayed. You may choose to strategically sabotage each other's plans. This doesn't do much for trust. Explosive outbursts are predictable when you sit on your emotions. Privacy comes naturally to you both. This takes the space principle too far. Okay, so you both like to retreat to a favorite sanctuary to shake off your worries. There is nothing wrong with that, but when your lover can't get through your defense mechanisms, troubles multiply. When you don't deal with matters, you may constantly react to each other with little objectivity. Getting a job done together is a misery. You can't bond when you don't know when the next attack is coming. Life with high anxiety is no fun.

Money Woes Game

Two Scorpios like yourselves are happier when money is split evenly. You don't feel secure when there is tension over ownership. The bottom line is that you can get into real power struggles when fighting over material resources. Trust is the underlying issue. You have chosen a partner with a similar need to manage his or her own wealth. Neither of you likes to be told how to spend your money. Sometimes this game involves secrecy regarding each partner's wealth. It can make communication sticky if you sense your lover is not being totally honest about his or her financial situation. Pulling in separate directions regarding how each of you wants to put your money to work can be another hot spot. Suspicion about each other's ability to share the wealth keeps you at arm's length.

Stinging Moods Game

It is not a big surprise to hear that you can be moody, is it? The Scorpion's stinger can lash out if you push each other into decisions. Negotiating from your own power bases makes you easier to live with. You may find your lover unwilling to move another foot if you try to force your own will. Two water signs are not always going to be direct in dealing with unpleasant circumstances. If you completely deny your feelings, your moods can be as turbulent as a storm at sea. Emotional turmoil can generate waves of fury that spray over your partner. You may be hit by your partner's outburst in return. Emotional exhaustion and mental confusion are not a passionate formula. The more you run from discourse, the worse things become.

Strategies

How can you get through these Scorpio-Scorpio games? You can neutralize the *Guerrilla Warfare* game by coming out into the open and dealing with differences. This won't happen overnight if you have been in the habit of avoiding confrontation. There will be less infringement on each other's lives if you can learn to talk more directly. It might feel awkward at first to discuss things openly—even downright strange! It won't work if only one of you is up front about your opinions; you both must play. The payoff is big. You won't worry about the next onslaught. The ability to relax around your lover is vital to your peace of mind. Intimacy increases by leaps and bounds when you stop the surprise attacks. Adopting tactics with a constructive quality will do wonders for your passion. Working together will become pleasurable rather than agonizing.

If you can work through issues with a win-win philosophy, you have gained wisdom. This is truly how to take care of the *Money Woes* game. There are two things to consider. First, be sure to demonstrate that you value your lover's ideas. Nothing feels worse to Scorpio than to find that its insights about money and its proper use are discounted. Sensitivity to your lover's desire to feel mutually empowered deepens your connection on every level. Second, you will get further if you allow each other a chance to call the shots. Each of you needs to be involved in the decision-making process. Power issues do not need to come between you. When you rise to the level of self-mastery you seek, great things happen. You will even become wealthier! Yes, you attract bigger and better things because you extend that creative force out into the world. A lack of trust in your partner is counterproductive. Channel this potent expression positively, and you will accumulate more than you thought possible.

The *Stinging Moods* game asks you to talk more frequently. Moods are as natural to Scorpio as crying is to a newborn. You need quiet time when you do your "processing." You can make it clear when you must be left alone, but don't get carried away. There is such a thing as staying in the cave too long! Introspection is okay to a point, but don't use it to run away. Make yourselves discuss issues thoroughly. Yell and scream if you must, but do get it out. Don't expect your partner to be a mind reader even if he or she is a psychic. Your minds can go as deep as a submarine on the ocean floor to stay out of sonar range. Your moods will not be as unpredictable when you communicate. Don't mumble. Talk.

The Rainbow

Your Scorpio-Scorpio relationship can deliver. Let your partner have a voice, and you will be pleasantly surprised. The love you share is deep and expressive. You were never meant to take a back seat to your partner. Your cry to be heard can find a willing listener in your lover. When you are patient with each other, your business decisions carry the kind of weight that yields winning results. The odds are in your favor to find mutual success when you take the time to create successful paths for one another. Nothing can break your bond once you explore the depths that your relationship truly contains. A fierce loyalty binds this relationship. Your hearts are joined in a merry dance when you trust the intentions each has for the other.

A Scorpio man has his eyes wide open when he encounters the Scorpio woman. He knows instantly that their minds could either powerfully attract or strangely repel each other. The force with which they meet blows him off his feet. Unspoken signals are as potent as what is said. The Plutonian woman's chemistry creates an intense reaction in his mind. The Scorpio man knows he has met an immovable spirit who cannot be won by sheer force. The female Scorpio appears to be in the starting position to meet any challenge. He wonders if she even sees him as one of those challenges. The Plutonian man hopes she wants to break through the mystery in him that he doesn't always understand himself. There is an air of the unusual about her that captures his interest. He longs to share her well-protected feelings. This woman seems to know all about business. Whether wealthy or poor, she seems to have mastered the art of survival. The Scorpio man is a survivor in his own right. She strikes him as having traveled some of those same back roads in search of sanctuary and meaning. He is in love with the way she powerfully carries herself. Whether she is feeling up or down, a passionate atmosphere envelops her. He isn't sure what her moods are like when her spirits are low, but he sure would like to be near her when she is on a high.

The Scorpio woman perceives that the Scorpio man relishes a good bargain. She is interested to see if he can negotiate from the heart as well as with his powerful mind. He doesn't miss much when he looks at her. She sometimes feels consumed by his presence. She wonders if he feels the same way toward her. He seems to be possessive, but the Plutonian woman loves his intensity. It reminds her of her own when she pushes herself to the utmost. He acts like he can read her innermost thoughts. She knows this isn't possible when she hides her feelings from sight. His indirect way of inquiring if she is available intrigues her. He seems shy and forceful all at once. He warms up to a risky situation just as she does. She senses that he, too, can't stand rejection. She isn't worried about his demands because they can't be any worse than her own. This mysterious woman isn't afraid to pursue or to be pursued by the Plutonian man. He had better be ready, for if she decides to be caught, she will watch him closely for signs that he is ready to commit to a relationship. She will be inviting if he can recognize her need to be heard.

Let the Games Begin

You can capture each other's heart through being advocates for one another. Others may be jealous of your love and success. Don't be distracted by how you are viewed. Pay attention to special needs that are easily seen as well as to the subtle ones that come through knowing each other's hidden dimensions. You can be passionate lovers and move with intensity on the road of ambition. Be sure to pack enough awareness and sensitivity for the great journey so you don't lose each other along the way. You are lovers who will sometimes play it safe but on occasion will tempt fate by blazing a trail off the beaten path. Whichever highway you take, the trip will bear greater fruit when you take the time to listen to each other's visions.

Scorpio-Sagittarius: The Motivators

Scorpio + Sagittarius = In-depth Curiosity

This sign duo can sift through new learning material as eagerly as a reporter looking for an earthshaking story. Scorpio leads Sagittarius into emotional waters that the Archer might not investigate if left to its own devices. Fiery Sagittarius points Scorpio into spontaneous directions that the Scorpion could shrug off as being too risky if not persuaded to take a leap of faith. Both signs have an inclination to test fate. Sagittarius will do so by ignoring the odds against success, thanks to this sign's supreme self-confidence. Scorpio's reasons for taking chances are connected to a desire to improve its sense of security. The end results may be equivalent, but the Archer and the Scorpion don't look at life the same way. Sagittarius has idealistic tendencies that propel it to new vistas. Scorpio views the world soberly, trying to gauge just how much effort it will take to get the job done. The two signs seem to work well together if each learns when and where to reveal true intentions.

Here Comes the Judge Game

The games played in your Scorpio-Sagittarius relationship are associated with too much criticism and a lack of enthusiasm for joint projects. The *Here Comes the Judge* game shows how you may direct unwarranted disapproval each other's way. This is one of those "I told you so" episodes in which each may hurt the other's feelings. Narrow judgments don't endear you to each other. You can be in a struggle to prove who is "right." There is a cantankerousness in this game that can find you refusing to agree to disagree. Emotional coldness is what really rubs you both the wrong way. It isn't easy to feel close if your minds are far apart. When you refuse to let go of rigid opinions, a warm and cozy retreat is out of your reach.

Deflated Faith Game

When the two of you don't show faith in each other's abilities, you are in the *Deflated Faith* game. Sagittarius becomes angry when people don't believe in its abilities. The Archer is emphatic that a lover must have implicit faith in its goals. Scorpio can feel stabbed in the back if a lover withdraws encouragement. Your sense of a direction as a couple will be lost if you can't get behind each other. It may be that anger undermines your show of support; a grudge is probably more on target. The refusal to let go of an issue may be the behind-the-scenes culprit. An unwillingness to work through a problem can be like carrying a lot of extra baggage. You may simply have trouble accepting what the other sets as a top priority. The way in which you deal with your differences may be a bigger problem than what you are fighting over.

Quagmire Game

When you lock into your own separate ideologies, you could find yourselves in the *Quagmire* game. When you fail to move as a couple in making decisions, the footing under your feet is as soggy as a wet marsh, and a solid foundation is sorely needed. Scorpio can be determined to have things fit according to its own plans. Sagittarius can slip into a dogmatic philosophy about its own vision. Put these two frames of reference together, and the end result is blurred and muddy. It is tricky to determine how to reason with one another. A tendency to hide or to be cunning can interfere with your sense of trust. Your discussion becomes a guessing game rather than a clear dialogue. You may feel like your individual needs exclude shared dreams because it seems to be easier to do your own thing than to figure out how to work together.

Strategies

How can you circumvent these Scorpio-Sagittarius games? In the *Here Comes the Judge* game, the two of you must find a way to let each other have the freedom to stretch your mental horizons. You will never fit conveniently into one another's concept of right or wrong. Establishing open communication will bring you the closeness you want. Scorpio retreats behind a huffy wall of silence when under attack. Sagittarius grows

The Magic of Signmates

belligerent when someone tries to pigeonhole its thinking. The sooner you trade this game in for a more refreshing way of perceiving each other, the happier you will be. Extreme criticism only keeps you apart. Accentuate the positive. Better yet, let each other feel free to have independent ideas because it stimulates your minds.

The *Deflated Faith* game requires that you both make a pact to show greater interest in what the other is doing. A bit of positive energy directed at each other quickly multiplies your options. Scorpio is more generous when a lover believes in its ability. Support seems to bring out its passion. Sagittarius displays greater energy when fueled by a lover's faith. You are a couple with clearer individual and shared goals when you encourage each other to go for it! You simply are able to build stable plans with strong foundations when you are willing to show visible support. Your lover's light will come out when you are interested in his or her future. You can affect each other's self-confidence in a big way. The key is to err on the side of offering too much support rather than offering too little.

In the *Quagmire* game, you both need to show greater assertion in bringing out the best in one another. You could be too timid in approaching your lover. Both Scorpio and Sagittarius will postpone dealing with conflict resolution. Doing your own thing definitely is the right answer on occasion, but it doesn't come through all of the time. You need to address the "why" of this game. Why don't you allow yourself to trust shared directions? It's better to be up front than to hide your feelings. You will find the ground better suited for walking together when you clear up your differences. You want to trust each other, don't you? Scorpio persists in doing things on its own terms as much as Sagittarius insists on getting in the last word. Finding that elusive middle ground where you respect each other's insights is the key. Be problem-solvers. This is certainly a dilemma well within the reach of your energetic minds. It only takes a willingness to connect with each other's hopes and wishes to get the show on the road.

The Rainbow

Your Scorpio-Sagittarius relationship leads you to explore creative realms you may not investigate on your own. Each of you can push the other to take on new challenges. A boost of confidence comes through your love for one another. Scorpio challenges Sagittarius to put those ideals into practice. Sagittarius eggs Scorpio on to make those hidden aspirations more visible. The trust you attain is the ingredient that brings you close in mind, body, and spirit. Your willingness to be advocates for one another makes you feel you are part of something special. The commitment you would like to maintain rests on the effort you make to have your relationship fly in any type of weather.

A Scorpio man sees the Sagittarius woman as a gem in the rough. He isn't sure how to size up her ideas. Her mind is fast and vast with an instinctual ability to change directions in a snap. The Scorpio man likes her enthusiasm for adventure. The Plutonian man knows he will need to stay abreast of current trends if he is to understand her. He perceives that she is not as shrewd as he is with money though she can spot a good deal as quickly as he can. The Scorpio man admires the frankness of this in-the-moment woman. His own speech has a deliberate quality. He notices that she enjoys sharing her knowledge and stories about her travels. Her humor lightens his worries. The passion he feels for her ignites his creative drives. The Plutonian man's patience leads him to take his time to launch a plan, which can be a torment for others. This carefree Sagittarius either hides her own worries well or is just not as ruled by them. He wants to make the first move but notices that she beats him to the draw.

The Sagittarius woman recognizes that the Scorpio man is strong in business matters but a little short in the feelings department. She isn't so bothered by this since he seems comfortable with his world. She hopes he will understand her need to entertain all sorts of new ideas. It's not that she sees the Scorpio man as lacking mental ingenuity, but his reasoning differs radically from her own. She wants to break down the wall of mystery surrounding him. He doesn't seem so hard to know when he lives in the present and stops thinking about the past. She is fascinated by how this self-assured man makes the world respond to him. She wonders why he seems to feel guilty about his emotions. The love she seeks does not pay great allegiance to a governing set of rules. She likes to make at least one or two rules as she restlessly moves along. The Sagittarius woman likes to see that he can tolerate her need for freedom. She will be loyal to the lover who brings her to the dance but wants him to know he can trust her if she decides to share a tune with a friend now and then. This fun-loving woman likes to soothe the Scorpio man's edgy moods. She quickly sees where he is a bit too time-tested. She feels up to the task of loosening his reserved feelings.

The Scorpio woman experiences a sense of familiarity with the Sagittarius man. She realizes later that it was his way of acting like they were old friends that suddenly made her go with him onto the romantic superhighway. The Scorpio woman is not taken anywhere unless she is willing to go. This adept man, who can juggle many ideas at once, entertains the Plutonian woman. She is warmed by his attention. Even when he starts to direct conversations solely toward himself, she is not disturbed. She believes it is the adventurous little boy in him who is speaking; he wants to be young forever just like Peter Pan. He awakens her own childlike curiosity and wonder. Her practicality runs circles around that of the Sagittarius man, yet somehow he lands on his feet. She realizes that he is enthusiastic about his plans for the future, and his confident idealism shines through. Her feelings for him come forward more spontaneously than usual. This woman, whose emotions are carefully protected, can't help but let down her guard for this court jester whose philosophical mind is uniquely refreshing. She worries when he acts outrageously sure of himself. She feels more at ease when he is his usual fair-minded self with the good sense to see there are many avenues to the truth. The Plutonian woman sends an invitation of love to this highly spirited man. She hopes he will take her on an adventurous rendezvous in which they both can fulfill their deepest needs.

The Sagittarius man is captured by the penetrating eyes of the Scorpio woman. This wanderer doesn't stop in his tracks for just anybody. The Sagittarius man admires the Plutonian woman's commitment to keep her feet planted in the demands of the present. He also lives in the present but is ready to set off on a new adventure at a moment's notice. He is aware that their views of reality agree to a point but then take a fork in the road. The Sagittarius man isn't alarmed by this; it's business as usual in his changeable world. His understanding is that commitment is open to ongoing interpretation. The Scorpio woman seems to prefer to stick to a plan. This fun-loving man can adapt. He senses that the Scorpio woman wants to see if he can fit into her life. The passion that runs through him in the presence of this intensely emotional woman is enough to make him learn any new trick. The Sagittarius man has to admit that the reasoning savvy of this capable woman spurs him to refocus on the essence of his own ambition. "We will make a great team," he thinks. He appreciates the way she challenges him and still encourages him to rise above his doubts to chase a dream. He quickly realizes that he needs to have faith in this sensitive lover if he wants to receive her support in return!

Your romance was never meant to be really predictable. The paths you explore together grow bigger and wider when you rest securely in each other's arms. Erase the doubts by a spontaneous show of faith. There is little need to look back. Keep your eyes focused on the potential of the present. There isn't anything the two of you can't figure out. You can be a tenacious couple in making something work. The art of patience is an ally. You may sometimes be angry when you don't get your way. Don't blame your lover when life doesn't fulfill all of your dreams. You can enjoy being confidantes for each other when nobody else is willing to listen. The depth of your love grows by leaps and bounds when you pay attention to what brought you both here in the first place.

Scorpio-Capricorn: The Power Brokers

Scorpio + Capricorn = Relentless Drive to Succeed

This sign combination is one of the best in finishing what it starts. This relationship wears a "management" persona. These two ambitious lovers always have a plan circulating through their minds. Knowing when to break away from stress is something both must learn. Balancing power keeps love flowing. Neither of these two wants to feel totally in service to the other's demanding lifestyle. Grabbing hold of a hectic pace maintains happiness. Both often take commitments seriously. Each expects the other to back up his or her words with actions. A well-defined alliance can make both feel secure. Trust has to be earned in this business-like atmosphere. Sound instincts about how to make money are found within the framework of this liaison.

Deadlock Game

The games played in your Scorpio-Capricorn relationship are linked to getting caught in irreconcilable outlooks and addiction to work. The *Deadlock* game is found when you can't talk through a power struggle. Scorpio will fight to the death to protect its most cherished ideas. The Scorpion can't afford to surrender its impulse to be in control of its own destiny. What about Capricorn? The Goat is determined to control its life to the point of emphatically fighting off outside influences. So where does this leave you? Scorpio's tendency to call its own plays combines with Capricorn's leaning toward leading its own way. The dilemma is how to approach each other's favorite way of making life rewarding. Your discussions are so quiet you can hear a pin drop. It feels downright weird (or odd if you prefer that word) for two forceful people to lack the initiative to negotiate a favorable win-win situation. It is lonely to be apart. Passion truly suffers as does the level of contentment. A lack of communication takes the firepower out of your lovemaking. An unwillingness to forgive can be at the heart of this one.

Below Zero Game

Scorpio likes hot passion. Capricorn is not as cold as people like to believe, so how can you fall into the *Below Zero* game? If your relationship is brand new, the answer is simple: fear! It isn't uncommon for Scorpio to test the waters carefully before showing a small dose of feelings. Capricorn is reserved when first encountering a potential lover. An outer show of success is often at the forefront of the Goat's presentation. After moving well into a relationship together, if you still don't reveal much emotional warmth, perhaps the fear is as vast as the Pacific Ocean. Relax! You can still turn this one around. There is another possible cause for this cold emotional display. A hurt person can become an angry person and eventually turn into an emotionally withdrawn person. Scorpio may not show hostility openly if the issue is very old business. Hostility is buried under layers of repressed hurt. Capricorn puts up a defensive shield to conceal its anger. Battle scars still may exist from previous relationships for each of you. When filtered through this kind of debris, verbal exchanges can be as frigid as ice. Your relationship lacks the inviting warmth that makes you both feel appreciated.

Work-itis Game

In work, you both still may be energetic while others already feel tired to the bone. In the *Work-itis* game, you can leave rational reasoning behind in the wake of long working hours. The desire to get ahead or to assume responsibility isn't the problem. Forgetting how to relax together is the main issue. If you follow compulsive work drives, it might leave little time to feel like lovers. An "all business with no play" mentality keeps your hearts divided. This is a case in which a talent to follow through on obligations has gotten off target. Either of you could resist hearing that a time out would be a smart thing to do. Romance is work in itself in that it requires regular maintenance. Somehow you have become focused on the realization of serious goals to the exclusion of the relationship. You feel rejected if you always play second fiddle to the other's untiring ambitions.

Strategies

How can you sail around the impeding predicament of these Scorpio-Capricorn games? In the *Deadlock* game, the two of you must somehow be able to hear each other's position. What often happens in this game is that a tendency not to listen makes it impossible to reach a resolution. When you see that your lover doesn't pose a threat to your control of individual choices, you are most of the way home. You must reassure your partner that you don't want to rule his or her life. If you respect one another's power, there is less chance of getting stuck. If you work through past issues, it can unlock a closed door. Forgiveness doesn't hurt as much as your imagination may suggest, but be sure not to repeat the same mistakes that you forgive in the first place! You have a powerful alliance. Your lover is not someone you want to cross recklessly. You can erase the hurt that was caused by not acknowledging your partner's rights by more carefully regarding his or her needs. Use your power to achieve great successes. Victory starts by aligning your immensely strong individual desires to be the master of your own destiny in such a way that you can stay clear of collisions. Be patient if you don't get this right the first or second time. Practice will show you how to dance in step.

The *Below Zero* game can melt when you let go of your fear. A shot of courage may not be too hard to swallow. Healing begins with that first painful, agonizing step from your hiding place. You may find, as many do, that once you show warmth toward your lover, the process becomes natural. A regular expression of feeling or at least showing that you care goes far in developing the kind of closeness that wins the heart. You don't have to be Romeo and Juliet. This is not a contest; this is about your happiness. If old hurts are at the root of this game, then you probably need to start talking about them. You can't uproot longstanding issues if you won't face them. Scorpio and Capricorn can do just about anything they set their minds to do. Resolving this game takes some of that same focus and determination that you likely pour into your serious projects. Open your lines of communication. You will be surprised at how fast those lines can be reactivated. The warmth you share is the backbone for the intimacy you desire.

The *Work-itis* game needs you to slow down and reassess your priorities. Your passion for work is not being questioned, but when you do not dedicate enough time to your relationship things are out of balance. Scorpio resents taking a back seat to Capricorn's whirlwind of activity. Likewise, Capricorn feels slighted when forgotten in the midst of Scorpio's ambition. Lassoing those busy schedules might be more challenging than roping a wild bronco. You can have the best of both worlds. Successful careers and a delightful romance can be combined. Be careful not to give so much of your time to others that your leisure moments are few and far between. You must be alert guardians over your schedules so that your romance isn't squelched. Don't keep each other waiting until the next job is completed. Surprise your lover once in a while with a spontaneous move into a fun and romantic adventure.

The Rainbow

Your Scorpio-Capricorn relationship can be as pragmatic as they come. When you openly show affection to the point that a pair of binoculars isn't needed to detect it, your romance picks up trust. Love intensifies when you go out of your way to share your resources with your lover. A clear definition of mutual expectations makes you both feel more at ease. It's okay to leave some gray areas that you can fill in when the spirit moves you. Well-calculated investments can add to your wealth. You are at your all-out best when each of you is happy with the roles you have chosen. Neither of you can stand being told when and how to perform. You are both capable of reaching high levels of self-confidence. You enjoy watching each other live out your most cherished goals.

The Scorpio man likes the way the Capricorn woman handles business. She has a solid grasp of reality that pleases the Plutonian man. The Scorpio man shrewdly looks into the eyes of the Saturnian woman, probing to see where her logic and passion meet. This man of extremes observes that this woman likes a level playing field. He notices that she is more open when she senses that he has no hidden cards. He likes the fact that she isn't probing his feelings too quickly. It's not that he is not emotional, but he prefers a long warm-up before getting into such personal matters. The Scorpio man is eager to show that he can be true to tradition if that is what she wants to hear. He has no real allegiance to the past but shares her healthy respect for it. He detects a trace of ambition in her voice but not an all-consuming drive to succeed. The Scorpio man hopes he can match this woman's strength of commitment. He can form a deep bond. For him, commitment flows out of the trust that develops. She doesn't seem so different from him. Her dependability is awesome and might be refreshing for a man who has been there and done the relationships that promised little permanency. He might be willing to show that deeply private side of himself down the road after they both see that this romance will stay awhile.

The Magic of Signmates

The Capricorn woman is not so sure how to approach the Scorpio man. He seems to scare easily. She detects reluctance in his voice when deeply personal matters are raised. She is careful to stay on topics that are comfortable for him.

She notices that small talk doesn't do much for either of them. The world of politics and business turn him on. She is no stranger to these topics either but would like to know more about his personal likes and dislikes. She doesn't want to pry. The Capricorn woman tries to catch a glimpse inside this complicated Plutonian man. He prefers to keep life simple, or so it seems to her—maybe so he can maintain control. She knows all about control and could write a book on it. Control is not all it's cracked up to be. She hopes this Scorpio man has learned a lesson or two about love—that it can be more fun when spontaneous even if emotions are protected with a few safety nets. She thinks his mind can hone in on her feelings. She is intrigued by his personality. He is an interesting mix of introspection and extroversion. He seems to vacillate between the two as predictably as the night eventually turns to day. She finds him a mystery worth investigating, that is, if he will take the time to see what makes her tick. This Saturnian woman isn't going to waste time on a lover who will not hold up his end of the bargain. She likes the way he stimulates her most taboo thoughts, which could get her into trouble but make her heart beat faster. The Scorpio woman is quickly aware of a success drive in the Capricorn man. He has some of the same innate instincts to control his world as she. The Plutonian woman likes to know as much about a lover, from head to toe, as possible. After all, she doesn't want to invest in someone who is not serious about creating stability. The Scorpio woman has an intense desire to reach a high level of self-mastery. This Saturnian man is sensitive to this heartfelt need. She wonders if he can talk from his heart as well as he appears to read her own. He has the look of someone who knows how to get what he wants. The Scorpio woman is tempted to see how far he will go to pursue her. She isn't yet sure what it would be like to be caught by him. The Plutonian woman could easily take the lead but doesn't want to scare him off. This shrewd, business-oriented man seems to have faced down his fears, yet he also seems to be sensitive, which he tries to conceal. He seems embarrassed to act with feeling. This Plutonian spirit knows she has the power to make him connect with his own feelings. Right now she is more interested in taking it slow. He seems to be in no hurry. She likes a patient lover though she doesn't want him to wait so long that their passion evaporates. He has strong hands; she likes to hold them because they seem durable and permanent. She doesn't mind terribly that he is reserved, but if a wild urge overtakes him that suits her as well.

The Capricorn man makes a slow entry into the Scorpio woman's mind. He isn't exactly sure how to begin the conversation. She looks like someone who has heard every story in the book. He had better have some original material. He is surprised to discover that she responds warmly when he is natural and authentic. The Saturnian man feels as weakened by rejection as Superman is by kryptonite. The Capricorn man will do almost anything to avoid a losing proposition. He knows this truth about himself but never will openly admit it. What drives this man from the moment of his birth is the need to stay in control. He delights in creating winning outcomes. For some reason he doesn't feel a need to prove anything to this Plutonian woman. Maybe it's because he feels she has seen it all before. She seems ready for a romance that is real and reliable. He likes the fact this woman can take care of herself. He gets the message that he better not expect her to be the power behind his imaginary throne. She is quite capable of ruling her own world. He wouldn't mind exploring a love with her that can define a new reality with greater opportunities for them both.

Love can endlessly fulfill the two of you. You have a potential to determine a future based on a carefully laid-out blueprint that makes you both happy. The two of you are a rare sign combination when it comes to putting ideas into motion and having the stamina to push them all the way to completion. Know when to be flexible. A change of direction will replenish your minds when you are tired. Take a break now and then to recharge. Be good to yourselves. Create rewards that keep reminding you how wonderful it is to be soul mates as you greet the challenges of each new day.

Scorpio-Aquarius: The Determined Ones

Scorpio + Aquarius = Awesome Display of Willpower

These two signs can persistently move forward until they get what they want. This is a romance with passion and extreme resourcefulness. Turning the odds in your favor is a matter of luck and daring. This relationship is not always big on moderation. Usually there are a few things that each must own that stretch the budget. Each of you must have your own territory clearly marked. It's best when both are happy with your own chosen fields of expertise. Having things on your own terms is a theme in common. Neither will budge if suspicious of where the next step may lead. A degree of ruthless telling it like it is makes for intense encounters. Both of you enjoy taking your time in making decisions. If an opportunity manifests that is too good to pass up, each is capable of mobilizing forces in a hurry.

Squatter Game

The games played in your Scorpio-Aquarius relationship are associated with infringing on each other's turf and not being able to compromise. The *Squatter* game occurs when the two of you act as though the other's territory is up for grabs. The Scorpion will strike with its stinger to clear people away from its terrain. Aquarius will shout and scream if someone trespasses. You both are sensitive about your freedom. This game presents a problem in that it probably arouses as much anger as you can handle. A regular pattern of not respecting one another's rights is bound to create great distance. You won't be able to trust each other if you don't acknowledge one another's personal autonomy. Scorpio needs to mark the boundaries that are established to secure its privacy. Scorpio's power is derived from the knowledge that its "personal space" is well understood by a lover. Aquarius needs to know that the lines of demarcation are observed by its partner. Aquarius' freedom ignites its mental energies. When you do not observe the "no fly" zones, it can get you into trouble. If you don't honor each other's need for space, communication is tricky.

Cat and Mouse Game

Sometimes Scorpio and Aquarius aren't sure if they want to be caught, which is the case in the *Cat and Mouse* game. If one gets close, the other pulls away. The indecision over just how close you want to be makes life confusing. You will find it difficult to establish commitment if you can't find a consistent sense of stability. Scorpio can feel smothered by closeness. Aquarius might see it as the end of life. It's a question of being ready to identify what makes you run away. Neither of you is too keen on surrendering the private worlds you have come to adore. If you perceive the other as threatening the individual goals you cherish, settling into a relationship isn't likely. You can continue to ebb and flow like this indefinitely.

Pulling in Opposite Directions Game

The two of you can find it a test to move toward the same goals as in the *Pulling in Opposite Directions* game. Sometimes this is a tactic to throw each other off guard. Both of you can rebel in this way. You say an emphatic "No!" to get each other's attention. You might even remain tightlipped and let your actions do your talking. Scorpio can do the silent treatment better than anyone. Aquarius can be aloof and disinterested better than most. You will observe that intimacy falters. There is not a lot of romance when you do not connect on any level. Compromise seems far from your minds. Finding the way back to intimacy seems extremely far removed.

Strategies

How can you get through these Scorpio-Aquarius games? In the *Squatter* game, the two of you must observe certain guidelines about personal space. Scorpio must be careful not to hide behind the desire for privacy in the same way that Aquarius must be conscious of not becoming too protective of its freedom. The idea is not to keep each other at a distance by compulsively protecting your privacy. Trust plays a role in growing comfortable with the territory each of you needs. When you both relax in the relationship, your individual and shared decisions have more flow. Doing your own thing should not upset your partner. The tendency to invade one another's worlds is less likely when you make a conscious effort to see your lover as a unique person.

The *Cat and Mouse* game can be handled by seeing that your lover has some of the same fears you have. You don't need to pressure yourselves into rushing things. If this is a new relationship, agree to go at a pace that is acceptable for each of you. If you have a romance that has already been in operation, specific decisions may cause this game. Usually, if one of you feels like a deal is a losing proposition, the tendency could be to split the scene. It comes down to being able to talk openly about your fears or dislikes. Scorpio might choose to quietly or moodily pull back to show disapproval. Aquarius can act either mentally distant or display a bit of sarcasm. The idea is to stick around and address concerns. You will find it less frustrating when you get the truth from each other. You are a stronger couple when you face your differences of opinion directly.

You are strongly opinionated lovers who are never going to see eye to eye on everything. It's not in your sign chemistry to give in that easily to one another's will. So what can you do about the *Pulling in Opposite Directions* game? For starters, you might try to accept that on occasion you are better off acting separately. It makes you both more cheerful when you hang out by yourself at times. Give each other permission to take a break and to stop worrying about your being at odds. The more pressure you feel to comply with each other's wishes, the more stuck you feel. Your unique traits are an asset but may be perceived by you as liabilities. It wasn't sameness that attracted you in the first place. You have to be aware that you are people with individualistic urges to control your own lives. The trick is to join forces so that you feel like a couple. You have to cut each other a little slack. If your partner attempts to rein you in, you will react with anger or resentment. Passion and intimacy are restored when you let each other walk tall. You need to redirect power clashes. Instead of fighting to lead the wagon train in the direction that best serves either one of you, find the route that favors you both. The path is definitely there if you take the time to see it.

The Rainbow

Your Scorpio-Aquarius relationship is a gift that reveals greater treasures as you explore being together. The creative power you share is immense. You enjoy the support

Let the Games Begin

of someone who is able to fill you with his or her belief. Don't be possessive of one another. Each of you likes to establish your own way of doing things. It's your birth right to answer first to yourself and then to each other! You have the power to make things happen. With your clear vision, watch for unfolding directions that best serve your individual and shared purposes. Be willing to adjust your choices to be better prepared for a changing future. Your tenacity to accomplish goals is impressive. Don't let stubbornness come between you. Learn to work together with a spirit of unity, and you will be happier than you can imagine.

A Scorpio man's first thought when meeting an Aquarius woman is that her mind appears to be in overdrive. The Plutonian man likes to think things through. He isn't really prepared to bare his soul all that quickly. He soon sees that the Aquarius woman may be talkative but does not exactly expose her feelings. The Scorpio man is entertained by this woman's mental symphony. At first glance, her sense of direction seems scattered, yet he notices it is crystal clear to her. His own plans develop slowly. He hopes she won't be bothered if he doesn't pick up the pace until later. The Scorpio man likes the way she speaks her mind. It's refreshing to meet someone who, like himself, is inclined to weigh words carefully. Even when he talks fast it isn't anywhere near the speed of this cyclone. Their passions seem to run along similar veins. They both ask life to deliver whether they get it or not. The Plutonian man would like to get to know her better. They circle around each other like two unfamiliar cats. He hopes this Uranian woman will make a move just in case he becomes so hypnotized that he continues to orbit and forgets to cross her path.

The Aquarius woman feels from her first encounter with the Scorpio man that something unusual has happened. He seems to be as solid as a rock, though she notices that her willpower can move him as much as his does her. "His power comes from experience," she reasons. She hopes he will not hold her to the standards of his previous lovers and find her wanting. This Uranian woman believes in the freedom to be herself. She wants her lover to see her as refreshing and unique, as someone who can bring innovative meaning into his life. After all, she isn't thinking about her own past as she tests his romantic aptitude. The Aquarius woman enjoys the peculiar way this man makes her feel secure. Even when he appears to be jealous, his passionate gaze seems to say, "You need to be with me." This doesn't worry this free-spirited woman. Well, maybe not too much. She knows how to slide out of any hold on her autonomy (she has practiced this for years). She senses that if the two can learn how to dance without stepping on each other's sacred space, life might be beautiful. She is up for the risk if he is. The Uranian woman has grown attached to the emotional depth of the Scorpio man. He finds it difficult to share his feelings, but there is a never-ending well of feeling that glimmers in his eyes. This passionate, insightful woman doesn't like sentimentality anyway.

The conversation—both verbal and intuitive—begins when the Scorpio woman meets the Aquarius man. Each tries to read the other's mind. These lovers offer acceptance from the start. Tolerance is necessary because both have well-defined worlds. The element of surprise is that you understand each other. The big question is: Do you like what you see? The Scorpio woman has already proven to herself that she can go it alone. The survival instincts in her are as strong as the Sun at noon. She senses this Uranian man feels that it's easier to "walk your talk" alone without someone breathing over your shoulder. She likes his arrogance but doesn't want to be the sole recipient of it. She feels it is too much for any one person to deal with this man's mind when it flies off on a tangent. The Plutonian woman would prefer to keep her private thoughts to herself. It is a relief to see that this is more than he wants to know anyway. She can't talk about what isn't yet clear even to herself. It is pleasing to see that this man with the Wild Bill Hickok demeanor can act responsibly. He has a rebellious mind that seems to know the limits while he stays out of the reach of conventional expectations. She doesn't want to curtail his freedom any more than she would choose to give up her power. The Scorpio woman looks with watchful eyes to see whether he wants to be the reliable lover she seeks.

The Aquarius man sees a tower of strength in the Scorpio woman. She appears to have the stamina to stand up for herself. He needs this in a partner because sometimes his mind will go on the offensive. It doesn't mean he is trying to hurt anybody; his feistiness drives him to express his right to freedom. The Plutonian woman captures his attention because she doesn't seem fazed by his ideas. He needs a lover who can think for herself. The Aquarius man isn't always ready to show he needs help. He senses that she can tap into his weaknesses while she artfully disguises her knowledge. Ordinarily, this might bother him. Her power doesn't intimidate him, but he is concerned about what she might think of his unpredictable nature. The Scorpio woman seems to light up when he is carefree. He perceives that she trusts him more when he follows through on his promises. She is a woman who may hold him to his word but seems to be able to forgive lapses. The Uranian man hopes she can relate to his longing to run to the future.

He can't help being this way; the stars always call to him to look around the corner of the present. The Aquarius man realizes sooner or later that he must satisfy the obligations of the here and now before exploring other whimsical paths. He senses that her love will flow more generously his way if he can prove that he can keep her in his thoughts as much as he does those inventive ideas.

The love you seek in each other will deliver the rewards you desire. It only takes a clear commitment from you both. Becoming accustomed to your lover's own way of doing things can be tricky. You have a chance to make each other feel like you are on top of the world. There are few couples with your fixed determination to push forward. When you are able to define the purposes you have in common, it erases your doubts. The support you extend to each other comes back to you tenfold. Be generous in sharing your resources. When you do, you greet each other with open arms.

Scorpio-Pisces: The Mysterious Ones

Scorpio + Pisces = Feelings and More Feelings

This is a sign combo with intense emotional exchanges. Mysterious forces pervade this romance. Perhaps you met under unusual circumstances. Two water signs can form the deepest of psychological bonds. Neediness forms early in the relationship whether you admit it or not. Both grow dependent on the other for support. Scorpio helps Pisces to get over self-consciousness in order to move toward goals. Pisces reminds Scorpio that faith is a great tool for overcoming self-doubt. Each can develop a deep attachment to the caring atmosphere fostered by this relationship. Romance blossoms when each gives equally. Love is an intuitive feeling for these two in particular. Both are quickly attuned to each other's moods.

Hypnotized Game

The games played in your Scorpio-Pisces relationship are connected to a lack of communication and confusing emotional exchanges. When the two of you act as though you are in a trance-like state, the *Hypnotized* game is on. Scorpio can become mesmerized by its projects. Pisces can get lost in causes. This adds up to going in separate directions and very often doing this unconsciously. You need to snap out of it. Communication can lack clarity. You may talk without really hearing each other. Short attention spans dominate this game. It may seem like you are in a waking sleep; you lack awareness of your partner's needs. Drifting apart can be painful. To make a long story short, you do not experience much passion or fulfillment. The fact that your partner is constantly off on wild goose chases or is unavailable leaves you feeling empty. You can really miss the love you once enjoyed.

Possum Game

The *Possum* game is based on denial and occurs when each of you "plays dead." You want to show that your lover can't get to you. Anger is another theme in this game. Resentment that perhaps needed to be expressed yesterday or years ago gets in the way of the present. Eventually, you grow tired of waiting for your lover to show the vitality and passion that brought you together in the first place. A refusal to talk makes matters worse. Scorpio can go into the labyrinth within to show that nothing can elicit emotion. Pisces can disappear into an inner world of silence. You both may be content to wait in your favorite hangouts until the coast is clear to come out again. When you both seek sanctuary, there is no guarantee that either one of you will take the initiative to open peace talks. Water signs can show sensitivity to the point that they would rather escape than deal with unpleasant circumstances. The dilemma here is that you are lonely when you withdraw from your partner.

Convoluted Game

Extreme emotional confusion might turn into the *Convoluted* game. Your minds and feelings become so intertwined that you aren't sure where one begins and the other ends. Defining the relationship can be an exercise in futility. You might anxiously crowd each other's space when you try to fix the problem. This usually makes things worse because you can't step back far enough to be objective. Your mind can become fixated on worry rather than on sensible solutions. It is easy to project things onto one another that aren't true. Your perceptions can be governed by what you think is wrong to the exclusion of how to make things right. Talking would help greatly. Unfortunately, you might not trust that you can reach the clarity in each other (or yourself) that is needed. It is tempting to throw in the towel if you lose faith in your ability to mend areas of your romance that need repair.

Strategies

How can you sail through the challenges presented by these Scorpio-Pisces games? In the *Hypnotized* game, you need to refocus on your lover. Whatever has been a distraction might either need to be eliminated or at least given less time. It can be tempting to cast discipline away when Scorpio is passionately taken by an idea. Working long hours is quite possible. Pisces can get into a timeless consciousness when floating into creative endeavors. Watching your limits is wise. Every relationship needs to be nurtured with attention. You don't have to give up your most important dreams. You do need to balance your ambitions and time together. Perhaps it's true that absence makes the heart grow fonder, but continuous disappearing acts make the heart grow discouraged. Don't take advantage of each other's generosity. Someone can wait only so long before becoming disillusioned with being held in limbo.

The *Possum* game can be turned into a winner by being more assertive about your feelings. Don't run away. Stick around and get to the bottom of issues, that is, if you want to have a wonderfully close relationship. Hiding doesn't get the job done. You will always enjoy your privacy. You both like to get away from stress to rest. A retreat to get centered is a smart thing to do. If you use a need for space as a convenient way to duck issues, the problems mount. Unpaid bills accumulate interest. Not dealing with anger increases its intensity. Talking regularly is the best policy. Denial that anything is wrong takes away from a greater intimacy you can have. Take a risk and speak up. You don't have much to lose when there is so much to gain!

In the *Convoluted* game, you must figure out how to get your thoughts and feelings untangled from one another. It may take a few remedies. First, be willing to calm down and let each of you have your say. This means you must listen and refrain from quickly firing back an emotional reaction. Second, a little break from one another may help you to see clearly. Decide on how long feels right. If you talk about it, time apart seems less threatening. It's part of getting to the road of mutual understanding. If you can't get clear in each other's presence, then take a little time to gather yourselves. Doing so could make it easier to work through to a solution. If you keep overreacting to one another, a bit of downtime doesn't hurt. Finally, it is a good idea to show you really believe in one another. Faith seems to remind water signs like yourselves that you can forgive and forget as long as an effort is being made to improve the way you treat one another.

The Rainbow

Your Scorpio-Pisces relationship can exhibit creative passion. The romance you share can fill you with exuberant energy. There is no way that you can make all of your partner's problems disappear, but you can be a source of magnificent inspiration. The sensitive way in which you show you care about one another gives you a feeling of security. It is entirely possible that you will help each other heal wounds from the past. You can become trusted allies with a remarkable way of elevating your lover's self-confidence. Business investments can prove profitable by following your hunches. Romantic getaways keep you close in mind and spirit.

A Scorpio man can't help but notice the dreamy presence of the Pisces woman. Her way of handling herself is in stark contrast to his suspicious, cautious stance. The Pisces woman is a sensitive being in his eyes. She wears her feelings almost as openly as clothing. The Plutonian man likes the way this Neptunian woman reads his moods. She doesn't seem disturbed by his quiet, contemplative ways. As a matter of fact, she appears to appreciate them. Her intuitive spirit arouses his laid-back emotions. She seems to hope for the best and reality tests everything after the fact. He wishes that trust came so readily for him. The Scorpio man is mindful that he should speak from his heart to this emotive woman. This is a tall order because he doesn't always know how to interpret his own feelings. He has deep and intense moods that seem to be alchemized with his thoughts in ways he doesn't totally understand. All that he knows is that he enjoys the way she makes him feel. She seems to look for his idealism. He measures people by their earning power as much as by their sex appeal. This fair-spirited woman seems to know how to move him over so their worlds fit together. She seems quite able to handle herself. After all, she can handle him.

The Pisces woman sees different things in the Scorpio man. Her heart senses a great lover. Her mind perceives him to be capable of giving and receiving with the best of them if he trusts himself to do so. Her intuition believes he might be the mate she has dreamed about. The love she seeks is well understood by the Scorpio man. He has traveled many roads in search of security. The Neptunian woman wants him to feel welcome. She wonders if she can play that bargaining game he seems to like. She believes that it must be his way to test if the risk is worthwhile. She hopes he knows the difference between business and love. His charisma is apparent when he smiles, and she admires his confidence. He warms her with attentiveness. She is attracted to the passion he pours into his ambition. The Pisces woman wants to become part of what he avidly will go after. The formula to win his heart may be to play hard to get. She would rather not waste the time and would prefer to get on with the romance. She will send him clear messages. She wants to say to him, "Please show your authentic feelings and honest intentions." She counts on finding these attributes in him and longs to see his true self emerge.

The Scorpio woman is drawn to the creative passion of the Pisces man. He pours so much into his causes and beliefs. She wonders if he will ever care about reality in the same way she does. It isn't that he lacks ambition; he seems to like the things money can buy. The Plutonian woman wishes he would not be so distracted by the scenery of the side roads. His time could be frittered away in the attempt to accomplish too many things at once. She doesn't want to stop him from chasing the dreams that haunt him. She desires to have him near and within reach. The Scorpio woman is fond of her privacy, and she sees the same need in this man whose eyes remind her of a fine mist rising from ocean waves on a sunny afternoon. The Plutonian woman wants him to believe in her as much as he asks this of her. She becomes fond of the way he understands her spoken and unspoken communication. He seems to be someone who could glide in and out of her life. She hopes his stays are long and that his sojourns are short.

The Pisces man is a little intimidated by the power of the Scorpio woman. Her willpower can make reality stand at attention. He wonders how she performs this miracle. Maybe it's his imagination that causes him to think that she is intense. The Neptunian man wonders if it's better to tiptoe around this emotional being. He soon realizes that she is interested in making peace and love. The Pisces man is drawn to the way this woman stimulates his courage. He wants to show her he can be just as powerful. It's his unconditional faith in her that seems to make her laugh and smile. She has seen the best and worst in others. He tries to stand out as someone who is special. He recognizes that the effort he makes means a lot to her. The Plutonian woman acts like she knows about the nature of love. This sensitive man has learned a trick or two himself. The Pisces man can't wait to be with this woman with the air of mystery. She seems to change his world in a way that fills him with surprise and that renews his ever-expanding ideals.

You can write a script that suits you both. Each of you likes to play parts that allow your thoughts plenty of room to grow. You have a shared imagination that all may not be able to follow. The key thing is whether you can stay on the same wavelength to the point that you appreciate the wonderful companionship you have in your journey through life. Whether this is a short trip or long journey together, enjoy the moment. The enthusiasm you awaken in each other keeps you as close as two can be!

Sagittarius-Sagittarius: The Gypsies

Sagittarius + Sagittarius = Leaps of Inspiration and Enthusiasm

This is a romance filled with a fiery zeal to pursue endless paths to self-discovery. These are two people with a tendency to forge ahead and a lack of interest in what is left behind. A Sagittarius-Sagittarius relationship is driven by multiple purposes. Single-minded directions don't appeal to these two. An awareness of other possibilities keeps both of these energetic souls in constant pursuit of new directions. Goals manifest in the blink of an eye. The students, teachers, and philosophers of the world can admire these two. Learning and the search for knowledge pierce directly through the heart of the Archer. The love these two share instills the faith to soar over obstacles. Physical and mental travels together are common themes.

All Roads Lead to Rome Game

The games played in your Sagittarius-Sagittarius relationship are associated with an untiring restless spirit and a too-narrow perspective. The *All Roads Lead to Rome* game finds you both becoming too scattered. It can be next to impossible to finish what you start when you are pulled in numerous directions. You lack discipline and focus. The impatience to move on to the next exciting thing produces this behavior. You can become annoyed with one another if you never get key goals accomplished. There is a tendency to leave things undone even if you are more than halfway through them. Disappointments can cause tension between you.

Grass Is Greener Game

The *Grass Is Greener* game can make settling into a commitment challenging. One or both of you may believe that happiness lies elsewhere. You don't find the level of trust you seek if you only have one foot in the relationship. Defining the relationship is tricky if you sense that your lover is planning to escape. When you keep your bags packed (whether literally or figuratively), it hinders your ability to be intimate. Freedom is a big requirement for your sign. You might say that this game takes independence to the extreme. How you communicate in this game is not the source of difficulty, but the extent to which you share your plans could be a problem. If you start to think life would be better elsewhere, it may sway you away from productive ideas. The bottom line is that your work together can be hijacked by alternative temptations that deter you from productive action. You pay a steep price if you are swayed to go after an illusion that isn't as good as it seems.

My Way Is the Only Way Game

You don't win each other's hearts when you express dogmatic points of view, as in the *My Way Is the Only Way* game. Sagittarius is at its best when it shows tolerance for opposing opinions. The Archer is at its worst when it is too judgmental. Self-righteous ideas will not make you feel close. You will argue until you are blue in the face if you try to change each other's mind over certain issues. You can be like two litigators fighting it out in court. There is no winner here. Your sign can be long-winded when it comes to defending your principles. If you are fighting for a cause, no one can talk you out of your ideas. Arguments over your ideals can cause some heated scraps. It's not endearing when either of you chooses to adopt a narrow perceptive rather than a broad-based approach that includes more than just your own perceptions.

Strategies

How can you solve these Sagittarius-Sagittarius games? In the *All Roads Lead to Rome* game, you must practice the art of concentration. Patience doesn't come easily to fire signs such as yourselves. You will need to train yourselves to commit to following through on a plan. You will feel better when you learn how to master the restlessness that propels you through life. Harnessing this incredible energy takes fortitude. Challenge yourselves to channel that raw force into productive outlets. The eclectic nature you share will naturally lead you to more than one way of looking at situations. Even in problem-solving, you tend to consider various solutions. It may be true that more than one path will make a job more fun. Be sure you don't get so lost in spicing up the journey with extra sightseeing that you forget where you are heading.

The *Grass Is Greener* game can be turned around by becoming more committed to each other. Escapist tendencies must be curbed. You won't know what you have in each other if you don't give it a real chance. When you sense that your lover is eying other options, it doesn't give a sense of permanency to your relationship. Dropping your defenses with each other can be freeing; withholding emotions can actually take more energy. Your relationship will seem more intimate and relaxed when you perceive yourselves as a stable couple. No one is suggesting that you should ignore your adventurous instincts. The two of you will always have the innate urge to hop a freight train to adventure. Be the rogues and adventurers you were meant to be, but it's more fun to know you are truly on the same team. You might need to watch out for an inclination to pull away from goals when there may be greater riches elsewhere. You are a highly energetic pair that runs circles around most people. Learn to stick with your current projects. When you both can show that you are there for each other, there is magic in your romance.

The *My Way Is the Only Way* game is not the way to go. The two of you have expansive intellects, but when you become too attached to your own version of the truth this game enters the scene. The intellectual capacity of your sign is awesome. There aren't many people who can outdebate you on your favorite subjects. You become feisty when your ideas are challenged. You will find that your lover draws closer when you don't need to have the last word. The passion you share to be right can lead to two wrongs. Direct this dynamic part of yourselves at your creative projects. You both have too much belief in your own ideas to ever really be talked into accepting another's perspective. Share your knowledge. Let go of trying to convert one another. Dogma only causes friction that you don't need. Show the openness that is the trademark of your sign. You will like the passionate response of love you receive.

The Rainbow

Your Sagittarius-Sagittarius relationship takes you to exhilarating places. A "live for adventure" motto is probably never too far from your thoughts. You can convince others to believe in themselves. Your undying faith burns a path in front of you while fanning out in several directions satisfies your thirst for knowledge. Your pace can accelerate at the first sight of a new opportunity. A lively stride through life seems to be typical of your sign. You will fight for your ideals and show a strong allegiance to honesty.

A Sagittarius man perceives that the Sagittarius woman shares his enthusiasm for life. Her quick, light stride catches the eye of the Archer. This Sagittarius woman is eager to explore all corners of the earth. Her laughter touches his heart. He loves that which is jovial whether it be people, places, or things. The Sagittarius man is thrilled to exchange philosophies with this fiery woman. She talks with a conviction that he rarely sees in others. She really thinks her dedication to her ideals guarantees their success. The Sagittarius man doesn't dare to point out flaws in her thinking because this soft-voiced woman can counter with a jab at his own lofty ideas. He senses that this is a fundamental truth. The Archer is puzzled by the emotions he feels when he is with her. He doesn't always like to feel so strongly because it gets in the way of spontaneous action. "She must really arouse my passion," he thinks, "or why would I feel like I'm sinking into watery ground?" He enjoys how their chemistry can magically transform them from thoughtful introspection to "full steam ahead" action. The ideas they share ignite great creative imagination in the Sagittarius man. He notices that she is happiest when they talk less about what is possible and act on in-the-moment impulses. He can go for this!

A Sagittarius woman sees a bright reflection of herself in the Sagittarius man. He seems to possess the same disregard for playing it safe. His propensity for risk-taking is no greater than her own and his light-heartedness may equal her own. She likes his sense of humor because there is nothing that is taboo or off limits. He appears to be on his best behavior but seems embarrassed when he unwittingly puts his foot in his mouth. (She has done this once or twice herself.) She wonders if the two of them could learn to agree to disagree. It's obvious from her vantage point that they may strongly disagree on their favorite interests. She's not afraid of the fiery man's temper. In fact, she likes to trip him up on occasion to see how he will react. He gets over his tantrums, especially when he sees that it's all in jest anyway. The Sagittarius man has an air of playfulness, but she sees that underneath the mask is a determined soul. He is almost tormented in pursuing his dreams. How does she recognize this? Her own world is filled with ideals and altruistic beliefs. She thinks it's exciting when they walk in each other's terrain. She notices that he isn't concerned about putting everything back so he can find it again. "Oh, well, just as long as he doesn't tread over sensitive issues," she thinks. He may be "mate" material, after all.

You may have seen from the start that you can walk proudly together. There is no reason you can't make your lover happy. You both share a love for the future. Even if you are impatient with the present, you find a way to satisfy its demands. Schedules don't impress you. Planning entices you only when there is a need to accomplish your highest aspirations. Commitments are foreign to your mind. You tend to surrender to time when you are captured by the magical allure of opportunity. When you show patience with one another, you move into a deeper sense of why you are together. The exchange of ideas along with a tromp or two into unchartered lands keep you close in heart and mind.

Sagittarius-Capricorn: The Ambassadors

Sagittarius + Capricorn = Quest for Excellence

The inspiring, elevated vision of Sagittarius can cajole normally reserved Capricorn to embrace the uncertain future. The down-to-earth wisdom of Capricorn levels Sagittarius' playing field to a more sober atmosphere. The two can plot a course that is wide enough to accommodate the idealism of the Archer and the hardcore, realistic thinking of the Goat. Both can handle being in the public eye. Affable Sagittarius enjoys performing for others. Pragmatic Capricorn offers well-crafted expertise to the business sector of the world. This is a winning "know-how" combination that can bowl others over. You awaken an ability in each other to pinpoint opportunity as accurately as a hunting dog can track its prey. This is a romance with a propensity for common sense as well as having a good time. Combining work and pleasure is a talent.

Touch-and-Go Game

The games played in your Sagittarius-Capricorn relationship are connected to a fear of closeness and not flowing with life's ups and downs. In the *Touch-and-Go* game, the two of you aren't sure what to do with each other. You like spending time together but suddenly pull away. Sagittarius can panic if feeling constricted and can get cold feet if not ready to commit. Capricorn can become antsy when someone wants to get too close. This tendency in both of your signs to become fearful makes establishing a commitment challenging. If one of you tries to force the issue, the other may choose to flee. You may alternate between one of you wanting to get closer and the other choosing distance. It might become confusing to get a fix on where you stand in each other's life, making it hard to get a hold on the romance you want.

Paddling Against the Current Game

Sagittarius can act first and worry about the consequences later. Capricorn may exhibit a forceful nature that will fight the carefully calculated odds, not wanting to alter its course. If these tendencies are taken to the nth degree, the *Paddling Against the Current* game manifests. The two of you can show remarkable resilience and continue to work through all types of obstacles. When you don't listen to reason, you may fight the flow more than necessary. You could become angry at each other for not heeding ominous warnings about your plans. You may influence each other to keep going when logic says to stop. Time and energy wasted, plus the stress of running an endurance test, add up to aggravation. This is a case of not choosing the right time and place to make a strategy work. This game can become particularly irritating when you don't listen to each other's advice, *especially* when one of you suggested a better alternative direction. You may find a regular habit of playing this game keeps you from working effectively together.

Sad Sack Game

There are times when the two of you seem to see life as limiting or as not offering opportunities. If your faith and happiness take a real dip, you are probably playing the *Sad Sack* game, which is contrary to Sagittarius' positive philosophy. Capricorn is known for getting heavy, but the Goat often can see the way out of a low period by refocusing the mind. When you both lose perspective and become negative, life isn't fun and romance isn't as spontaneous. You may even dig yourselves deeper into this game by putting too much emphasis on work and not enough on play. The balance between ambition and leisure may be absent. Sagittarius wants success in a hurry and may be disappointed when it does not happen overnight. Capricorn deals with delayed gratification better but may worry that life won't come through. You may find it easy to tap into each other's anxiety, which can make matters worse. Rather than flying above the demands of life, you both are grounded.

Strategies

How can you get past these Sagittarius-Capricorn games? In the *Touch-and-Go* game, it helps to talk about how to make each other feel comfortable. Sagittarius eases into a relationship when the rules aren't too rigid. Capricorn needs structure to know what is going on. Finding a happy medium is wise. Flexibility is a good thing. Fear may lessen if you get some of those expectations out on the table. At least you will know what the score is. If you can find a way to loosen up, do it! The idea is to take most of the worry out of this closeness-distance dilemma. If you are too afraid to say what you need, you won't get what you want. If the two of you really can see a future together, then make sure you find alternative ways to handle your fears. When you let your partner know what you need to hear in order to feel trust, you will be able to develop a "touch-and-stay" style of communication.

The *Paddling Upstream* game requires that you reconsider your plan of action if it isn't taking you where you want to be. Many strategies need to be redesigned in midstream to better respond to current circumstances. Sagittarius can be so convinced of its vision that it takes a miracle to get this sign to slow down and listen. Capricorn seems to find it painful to inch away from a preconceived idea. Use those enterprising minds to make your journey smoother. You have one of the best sign chemistries to make dreams become real. *Flexibility* is the magic word. Embrace it. Adaptability will save you from embarrassing results. Your successes will come with less blood, sweat, and tears when you mix in flexibility. When you don't force things to happen, you will probably have even greater creative energy.

The *Sad Sack* game will not be as prevalent if you don't set yourselves up for it. If you find it easy to overidentify with each other's worries, learn how to stand back far enough not to get pulled into the problem. You can't be part of the solution by merging with your lover's worries. You are great allies when you establish a solid, supportive stance. Sagittarius can use the determination and grounding power of Capricorn. The Goat benefits from the positive mental force of Sagittarius. You can deliver good fortune to each other in your own unique ways. Focus on the good at least as much as that which is troublesome. Worry relinquishes its hold on you when you help one another climb to a higher altitude. Deal with your problems, but don't be enslaved by them. Preoccupation with your difficulties postpones the love you could enjoy. The darkness may not go away immediately, so learn to not obsess about what you can't control.

By taking a break from your obstacles, you may build up objectivity and muster the steam to get past them.

The Rainbow

Your Sagittarius-Capricorn relationship can take you along routes that feature solid growth and lasting memories. There is the promise of fulfilling both of your greatest wishes. The action-ready Archer and the cautious Goat can figure out how best to work together. You will certainly follow unique paths. Sagittarius responds to the calls of distant shores and must have the freedom to explore impulses. Capricorn can suddenly bulldoze a path where few will tread. The Goat may not wait for approval when convinced it is time to make a move. There will be many shared roads to walk. It will take time to discover when to move in unison or to do a solo act. You can delight in the way you expose each other to new insights.

A Sagittarius man is both suspicious and curious about the Capricorn woman. He wants to be sure she won't be so demanding that his wings are clipped. Her experienced gaze tells him she has seen the best and the worst the world has to offer. He hopes she perceives him as a positive force in her life. The Archer is often surer of his ideas and adventurous streak than he is about reality. He wants this Capricorn woman to recognize his reliable side. He goes to great pains to summon it for her. He discerns that this Saturnian woman has seen this act before. Her face and demeanor show she is not impressed with words. Actions convince her that his heart is in the right place. The Sagittarius man finds her ability to view the world in "black and white" terms refreshing because he sees the world in shades of gray. He wants to pursue this ambitious, fast-paced woman and thinks that maybe she won't mind if he takes a back road once in a while and meets up with her later. She even seems to like the fact that he isn't absolutely guided by a sense of right and wrong. You can't blame the Sagittarius man for his free-spirited ways; these are instincts that have been honed from time immemorial.

The Capricorn woman's dreams are awakened when she meets the Sagittarius man. He looks younger than his years. Maybe it's because of that smile or his far-off look. She wishes he would pay more attention to her; competing with the universe just isn't fair. This Saturnian woman has the power to bring his focus back to earth though she knows it had better not be rushed or this fiery man will show his anger. He seems flighty, but his ideas are soothing to her. She can join him if he will only give her a chance to warm up. The Capricorn woman does not want the Archer to get the idea that she wants to corral him. She isn't always so eager to commit because then she has to be responsible. She doesn't want to scare the passion out of this potential lover. She is only trying to get him to pick up the cue that it's time for him to come closer. The Saturnian woman can enjoy solitude. It would be her luck to run into a man who is able to break through the ice protecting her heart. He makes the thought of being alone dreadfully boring.

This ambitious woman wants to connect with this imaginative, bohemian man. She wonders if this man is only interested in the chase and whether he will stick around once she is caught. He makes irresistible promises that no one ever fulfills, yet for some silly reason she is convinced this high-energy man can cover all of the bases. There he goes again with that peculiar, daydreaming gaze. She mutters to herself, "Where does he go?" She doesn't want to ask him; it's more fun to guess.

The Sagittarius woman isn't sure what to make of the Capricorn man. He is so sure of his place in the world. The Sagittarius woman thinks he epitomizes worldly success. His self-assurance is part of his attraction. The Sagittarius woman can relate to his hopes because her faith in her ideals motivates her. "He is so practical that he could squash my dreams in an instant," she muses. The generosity in his voice keeps the door to her heart open. She admires his drive. She has goals of her own that are near and dear. He seems so much more serious about where he is heading. The Sagittarius woman wonders whether he could enjoy the journey with her as much as the destination. It's in her spirit to be a seeker. He seems to be governed by a reality that doesn't allow for much play. This lighthearted woman thinks she could teach him that life is not all work. Maybe some of his pragmatism could rub off on her. She seems to think they could make a fine couple, especially if he can abide by her need to satisfy her thirst for imagination and learning.

The Capricorn man is fascinated by the gypsy-like ways of the Sagittarius woman. She can go from being helplessly dependent to ruggedly independent right before his eyes. Even her ideas can instantaneously shift from the traditional to the radical. Her own version of the truth isn't that hard to swallow because it is so persuasive. The Capricorn man likes his lovers to be predictable. He doesn't have the time to worry about their likes and dislikes. It's not the same with this woman. She disrupts his thinking and seems to enjoy it—like a mischievous child. What's interesting to him is that he likes the fact she can get him to leave the serious world behind. The Saturnian man isn't quick to change, yet he could for the right person. If he sees a good thing, he may try to adapt to the needs of a lover. He isn't opposed to learning new tricks, especially if taught by someone who has captured his heart. This is no easy task. Few really get there. This captivating, passionate woman knows how to convince him to change. Do you know what else is interesting? He knows it!

Your romance can blossom into a creative explosion. The success you experience can be fun to share. When you go through a low, it will be soothing to have your partner to lean on. Your strength grows when you talk from your hearts. Don't hold back from the truth because honesty is your secret agent for staying close. The world can be a fun place to try out your self-expression and to test your ideas. Don't be too disappointed if one of your dreams doesn't get airborne. Simply rally around the positive forces that can bring you back to try it again. You two are top-of-the-chart lovers when you worry less about yesterday's shortcomings and look to the possibilities of today.

Sagittarius-Aquarius: The Freedom Seekers

Sagittarius + Aquarius = Thrill a Minute

These are two signs that seldom lose sight of future goals. Each is inclined to enjoy a fast pace. Sagittarius instills action into Aquarius' mental flashes. The Archer can't help but move on the restless impulses that swirl in its head. Aquarius' cool, detached insights influence Sagittarius to look out for the pitfalls ahead of time. It's good for the Archer to listen to the input from such a thought-provoking sign. The two are about as independent as they come. Neither is going to follow the rules of the other. In fact, they prefer none! Making up the script as they go suits them. Romance is an adventure in the hands of this duo. Going around fast curves satisfies their love of surprise. If life becomes too predictable, both can panic. They will put up with a certain degree of routine to meet conventional standards. It's the attraction to what lies beyond the ordinary that is a motivating force. Each of them can show a strong dedication to their most valued beliefs.

Maxing the Sound Barrier Game

The games played in your Sagittarius-Aquarius relationship revolve around not taking the time to understand each other's needs and an extreme desire for freedom that destabilizes harmony. The *Maxing the Sound Barrier* game exemplifies what can happen when you move so fast that you do not hear one another. Your excitement about individual aims can lead you to blast off with the power of a takeoff from Cape Canaveral. Sagittarius is easily self-absorbed in the pursuit of its interests. Aquarius can become self-centered when lost in special goals. You may be unaware that you are drifting apart. Your signs feel greater security when you are in the hunt for new opportunities. If you lose yourself in an array of tantalizing options, you may become distant. Communication can be less intimate. Most of your passion may be directed away from one another toward outside interests.

Wobble Game

It surely must come as no surprise that you detest boredom. Your sign combination will sometimes pull in opposite directions to express your own unique creativity. The *Wobble* game personifies how you could experience friction when disagreeing about certain shared goals. You might not give enough support to each other's plans if disgruntled about joint efforts. You may make one another anxious with sudden changes of direction. Your ability to move ahead with key strategies may be undermined due to the unevenness of your communication. An inability to integrate your need for personal autonomy so that you both can feel liberated is at the heart of the problem. Your propensity to instantaneously latch onto exciting new ideas may sometimes derail the blueprint (if there is one!) you carefully constructed. You may feel hurt if it appears that your lover does not care about your causes at all. Refusing to listen usually causes the greatest disappointment in this game.

Heavy Metal Freedom Game

What's that noise? It sounds like a drum and an electric guitar. No, it's not a heavy metal band but the heartfelt and sometimes compulsive beat of your own thinking. The *Heavy Metal Freedom* game occurs when you can't help but express your freedom to be an individual. Sagittarius responds to an inner calling to travel to the far corners of the earth to satisfy an insatiable hunger for knowledge. Aquarius must follow its electric impulses as well. You may rebel against each other's ideas out of impatience. Your exchanges may become as impersonal as e-mail. Intimacy may be transfigured into an atmosphere of indifference. The closeness you desire seems to be as far off as the Milky Way.

Strategies

How can you fly above these Sagittarius-Aquarius games? You must pay attention to your lover in the *Maxing the Sound Barrier* game. Try to remember what drew you together in the first place. A show of mutual interest regarding important aspirations must have been a key ingredient. It's all too easy for each of your signs to stimulate speedy movement. There's nothing wrong with life in the fast lane. A too-slow flow of traffic will not keep you interested for long. It is not good for your mental or physical well-being to follow those who lack imagination. It might be helpful to get away together so you can focus on each other. Disciplining yourselves to make time for one another is wise. In today's world, schedules are overloaded with so many demands. Add to this the extra-curriculum activities you want to investigate, and it means that you need to budget time for each other. Spontaneous lovers like you may choose not to plan your romantic moments. If you notice that your intimacy and lovemaking are disappearing before your very eyes, then consider getting control of the situation. If you don't, it controls you. Cluing each other in on any last-second changes will make you happier. If you at least allow a fragment of predictability into your relationship, it makes the in-the-moment adventures more palatable.

The *Wobble* game can be brought back to better balance through negotiating. Two freelancers like yourselves can't expect to always agree. Alternating which of you chooses the lineup for a day or week is a way to stop wobbling. Otherwise, you may completely fall apart as you fight for the lead. Forget about asking one or the other to make all of the compromises. The sparks are less likely to fly if you can work together. You can't help but instinctively think as individuals. There is less likelihood that you will try to talk your partner out of good choices when you support each other's goals.

The *Heavy Metal Freedom* game first requires awareness that you are two feisty individualists. That's fine! Thinking for yourself is natural for you both. How do you make a good attribute an asset instead of a liability? It will take commitment to get this done. It's imperative that each of you knows there is enough latitude to experiment with creative ideas. Next, you must build a stable intellectual platform as a couple. Two opinionated lovers can learn how to talk *and* listen. Responding to each other's needs is crucial. You must show that you care. The best way to accomplish this is to become people who tangibly support one another. It's that simple (or, to your line of thinking, it's that complicated)! You might not be as far apart as it sometimes seems. Two fast-paced people like yourselves can become as adept as figure skaters in moving together. The balance you seek is only a conversation away.

The Rainbow

Your Sagittarius-Aquarius relationship can machete its way through uncovered trails that others want to follow. Make sure you leave tracks. The independent eddies in your minds lead to fascinating moments together. It must have been the way you startled each other out of complacency that got your attention. Your romance burgeons with excitement when you anticipate new adventures. Even when one of you wants to hold on to comfort zones, the other can't help but pull you toward the unknown. Your similarities did not lead you to be lovers. Rather, you feel an attraction as a result of the unique qualities that rule you. The stars in the distant sky speak to you and lead you along individualistic paths. When you reach a meeting of your minds, you feel comfort. Reassuring your partner that you have found an "in" with one another magically captures your heart and may win your love. You both share a drive to take risks on a hunch. You can be the inspiring partner you both eagerly seek.

A Sagittarius man wants to share the world of the Aquarius woman. She is mentally alert and as quick as a cat to pounce on opportunities. The Archer notices that it will be a challenge to keep pace with her. She is a constantly moving target. The Sagittarius man recognizes that the Aquarius woman slows down when he offers up-to-the-minute information. She likes news hot off the press. There is something youthful yet strangely ancient in her gaze. Like him, she seems to look ahead with longing and the hope that the future will be quite different from today. Yet, he sees she is also nostalgic for the past, which fills her with inspiration. She seems to vacillate between the past, future, and present. The Sagittarius man finds that she is an exhilarating thinker who is passionate about the mind. The Archer is a man of many tastes. He has to admit that she is as about as free-spirited as anyone he has ever met. She comprehends his ideas with lightning speed. She flirts with him in a delightful way with a suggestion of friendship perhaps masking deeper feelings. Whatever her intent, it's enough to arouse the serious advances of this normally lighthearted jokester.

The Aquarius woman isn't sure how to impress the Sagittarius man. He loves to talk about his own life as much as she. They both could write multiple versions of their own autobiographies to cover the diverse roles they have played. It's not solely stories of adventure that capture her fancy. She likes his "straight as you see" talk. His sense of humor tickles her funny bone like few can. She wonders how he can get a "pass go" card every day with his roundabout philosophy of life; however, he can move with incredible speed, hardly breaking into a sweat, when he is inspired to accomplish a lofty dream. She imagines he is a wild and passionate lover, which is not so far from her own reality. His nomadic ways make her wonder if he will wander off in search of a Holy Grail of truth. She is no stranger to being a trendsetter. The Uranian woman would like to know if he wants to be a temporary or more permanent lover. She understands this man probably better than he knows. The Aquarius woman is relieved to see he understands that romance is not just an ideal but takes real effort. His principles are almost from another century. She is touched by his honesty but wishes he didn't always feel it his duty to blurt out the truth. She is drawn to his openness. She likes the fact that their inner and outer worlds seem to each be equally in need of new material.

The Sagittarius woman is not sure if she has ever met anyone like the Aquarius man. He appears to be so sure of the value of his ideas. His emotions seem well hidden under a carefully planned mental framework. His feelings are as entombed as a mummy, yet emotions flash across his face when he laughs or is caught by surprise. The Sagittarius woman likes to hear him talk about progressive issues. Her own mind enjoys entertaining ideas that are beyond the norm. This feminine spirit sees that he speaks with a voice of experience. "He could pull the wool over my eyes," she observes, "if I fall for this rebel." She is glad to see that he can be playful when he drops his guard. The Sagittarius woman is thrilled with the lively spirit in him, the inner dimension that reveals that he cares. Her sense of adventure doesn't lose its intensity in his company. Her barometer for love sometimes is measured by her lover's commitment to higher beliefs. She needs to know that this Uranian man won't stand in the way of her development. She believes he understands that to be her partner he needs to recognize and accept her inner calling to follow her own path.

The Aquarius man is refreshed by the Sagittarius woman. She has the spunk to tell him right to his face that he doesn't have all the answers. Her feisty way of walking through life isn't so different from his own. The Aquarius man is attracted to her optimistic mind. She wears her ideals like he displays his ideas. She incites original insights in subjects that he had not previously considered. The Uranian man sees that his inventiveness takes this woman to some other galaxy within her. He wonders what it would be like to talk to her every day. Surely they would run out of things to discuss, or would they? He likes the way she elicits his passion. It sneaks up on him when he least expects it. Amazingly, his mind starts to slow down like a helicopter suspended in midair while his heart pounds loudly (he hopes no one can hear). This Aquarius man is rarely emotional. He is a rational person who can't afford to be distracted by foolish feelings, or so he thinks. The Sagittarius woman can make him forget himself even if it is just for a minute. He is beginning to like that!

You don't have a relationship that stops and waits for you. You enter this relationship as though you were sprinting with bags in hand, trying to jump on a moving train. Maybe it's more like hitting the ground running when you put your energetic ideas together. You can't wait too long for a strategy because you long for tomorrow to hurry up and get here. Why? So you can start looking anxiously ahead to the next horizon.

Sagittarius-Pisces: The Ideal Weavers

Sagittarius + Pisces = Shoot for the Moon

There aren't many other sign combinations as idealistic as this pair. Neither Sagittarius nor Pisces is too keen on accepting limits on ideals. The two are kindred spirits when it comes to ignoring the odds. Romantic imagination abounds in either one of these signs. Put them together and you have a potential Camelot. Inspiration drives the fiery Archer and the watery Fish. Without it, the Archer's arrows miss their mark while the Fish is swept away by strong, resisting currents. An "anything is possible" belief system keeps these two hoping for the best even during lean seasons. Each looks to the other for faith and support of their aspirations. Sensitive feelings permeate this romance; neither likes to experience emotional distance. Sagittarius and Pisces may form a strong attachment to unconditional regard. Realistic expectations keep the relationship on even keel. These are signs that stir each other to tap into deep creative instincts that lead to new horizons.

Somewhere over the Rainbow Game

The games played in your Sagittarius-Pisces relationship involve unfounded idealism and a failure to make decisive plans. The *Somewhere over the Rainbow* game can illustrate how your lack of reality testing may lead to trouble in perceiving your partner accurately. Sagittarius can be quick to jump to conclusions that don't always prove to be correct. Pisces has incredible intuitive powers that may not be grounded in precise analysis. You can set impossibly high standards for one another. You will be disappointed if you expect your lover to become someone he or she cannot be. Your goals may be so unearthly that it is virtually impossible to bring them down to earth, and you may not be willing to put in the effort required to turn your inspirations into reality. In other words, your thoughts never seem to become sufficiently concrete to enact a goal. When it comes to getting down to the job, your mind seems to wander off to other ideas. Frustration and a lack of faith in each other can result. It hurts to lose the faith of your lover.

Round and Round We Go Game

Adaptability is a fine quality, and you two are at the top of the scale in this category. Can it be a potential problem? Yes! How is this possible? In the *Round and Round We Go* game, you may find that you never really resolve anything. You try to define your relationship, but you refuse to state your needs or expectations. It could be that what you want from each other keeps changing. Consistency is lacking. When you try to make a decision, you skirt the issue at hand. Sagittarius tends to talk a lot without making a point. Pisces can dreamily ramble without finishing a single thought. You don't want to hurt each other's feelings, so what do you do? You avoid dealing with issues, hoping they will fade into the sunset. This tactic doesn't work. You lack the assertiveness needed to grab this game by the scruff of its neck. You get tired of procrastinating, don't you? Hiding behind excuses doesn't get you to the destination you seek. The ability to take direct action is thwarted by your tendency to walk in circles. Feeling dizzy yet?

Looking the Other Way Game

"Denial isn't a river in Egypt"—have you ever heard that one? The *Looking the Other Way* game allows you to conveniently not deal with issues. You both can fear the anger that may come your way when you confront each other, yet the fallout from a skirmish is better than the anxiety and confusion that result when you run away from a problem. Your problems become magnified when you pretend they do not exist. Every relationship has to deal with something. There are no perfect romances. Don't be disturbed by getting down and dirty. You may be making the situation much worse by refusing to confront it. The love of peace in a Sagittarius-Pisces relationship will sometimes translate into a willingness to do anything to avoid a fight. Ducking confrontations reflects a lack of trust in yourselves. You do not believe enough in your abilities to work through challenges.

The Magic of Signmates

Strategies

How can you go beyond these Sagittarius-Pisces games? In the *Somewhere over the Rainbow* game, the idea is to focus on reality. If you make a commitment to follow through on an idea, do so. Getting things done in real time is the best way to get through this one. When you really make the effort to carry out a plan, it does wonders for your relationship. Keep those expectations in check. No one should ever try to convince you to throw out your ideals. You probably won't buy into that kind of reasoning anyway. The trick is to balance your idealism with action. Reaching for the stars is what drives you. Completing a mission together confirms your faith in one another. You are your own best confidantes. Learn to encourage each other to put your best effort forward. Don't look back; inspiration kicks into high gear when you are on the move. Be sure to consider some of the risks so you don't bite off too much. Sagittarius can overestimate its resources. Pisces may forget what it does or does not have at its disposal. Make sure your feet at least touch the ground. Then take charge and move ahead. You connect with an expansive creativity when you adopt at least a minimum of structure.

In the *Round and Round We Go* game, you will know where to land if you trust your decision-making potential. Your signs hate to be confined to concrete reality. You can rival Houdini when it comes to escapes. You will find that passion and sex may be more enjoyable when you stop holding back. Stop circling and get to the point. If you can't state clearly what you seek in your relationship, you will remain uncertain about how to feel close. Talk with the intention of promoting clarity rather than confusion. Faith in yourself and your lover will get you through this dilemma. When you clarify your commitment, the solidity of the relationship is rewarding. You will enjoy the intimacy that encircles your hearts.

The *Looking the Other Way* game asks you to direct your attention to your lover's mind and heart. You are running from the very thing you came here to find. Everyone feels apprehension about wanting to be loved and accepted. Taking bold and courageous steps to address what has been denied releases a flood of energy. Your fears impede the flow of energy you could experience in many other life arenas. So you aren't perfect people. Find it out sooner, not later. Dealing with each other's anger actually fuels your passion. You can become moody and brood if you don't release those feelings. Let go of repressed fears. The way you deal with heated arguments is possibly the key to revealing your emotions. You will care that much more about each other when you show the faith to uncover your issues. You will spend more time as a fun-loving couple rather than as two anxious, lonely individuals.

The Rainbow

Your Sagittarius-Pisces relationship makes you reexamine all you thought you knew about love. The romance you share is a never-ending story of ageless wonder. You can find a mate in one another who speaks the same language even if your perspectives differ. Your desire to strive for your dreams is enhanced by being together. The chemistry of your relationship is like an alchemical reaction that spurs you to greater creative heights. The climb may not always be pleasant, but the view from the top is beautiful. When you share your personal vision, you awaken a new understanding that sees fertile possibilities where you had previously experienced sterile futility. Your relationship is enveloped in a rich, emotional atmosphere. In seeking your dreams, be supportive of your partner's ideals as well. Your faith can fulfill your partner's needs as long as you remain pragmatically optimistic. You are defined by the choices you make. Be clear in your intent so your relationship contains all the ingredients you need. Your thirst for love could be quenched in this romance.

The Sagittarius man is enthusiastic when he meets the Pisces woman. This Neptunian goddess seems to be a dreamer, which is something he can relate to. She feeds him ideals in small doses to see how he reacts. No matter, the Archer sees that a relationship with the Pisces woman is worth testing. The Sagittarius man is attracted to foreign territories. In his opinion, they both seem to have a shared fondness for experiences with few strings attached. The Sagittarius man treads upon her sensitive feelings carefully. She seems to possess an inner strength as though she knows something no one else does. The Archer wants to swim after this elusive Fish. She is unlike anyone he has ever met. Her sense of reality is many-sided and seems to go far beyond the tangible world he knows. Her mind and heart appear to be attuned to another, spiritual dimension that can't be mapped. This seeker of new frontiers never bargained on meeting someone whose stories are as awe-inspiring as his own. He tells tales to feel important and to attract attention. She shares the mysteries of life through her stories. The Neptunian woman seems to be shy, but she is part actress, part mystic. She is also just trying to find the right niche in life. The Archer's heart beats fast when he is near her because she seems to reach the depths of his mind. He hopes they can determine a course that will be expansive enough to keep them interested in each other for a long, long time.

The Pisces woman perceives the Sagittarius man to be rough and ready yet gentle. He seems battle weary from trying to make life comfortable. He still has a sense of humor no matter how many ups or downs he has encountered. He certainly has been through one or two testy bouts with love. His broad philosophy appeals to the Neptunian woman, and his enthusiasm spreads through her like wildfire. She is not uncomfortable with his energy. Her soul is enlivened by his rapid, spirited concepts. She believes they are not entirely dissimilar; they seem to have been destined to be together by the stars even if they live thousands of miles apart. The carefree, bohemian Sagittarius responds favorably when the poetic Pisces woman speaks strongly from the mind and heart. They understand each other easily from the very beginning. She wants to take a chance on this gypsy, who somehow seems to know how to get others to like him even when he behaves outlandishly. He seems to be the kind of man whom she has been warned to avoid. He could steal her heart and run off with the faith she has placed in him. It's just like him to attract her attention and entice her to place a bet on him to be *the one* even if her mind says it can't be. Maybe it's that devilish smile with the innocent face. No, it's probably the way he teases her. Better yet, it must be the way he asks her to pick her favorite dream and imagine him as part of it. She wonders to herself, "Why can't I listen to those warnings?"

The Sagittarius woman likes the way her world becomes romanticized when she meets the Pisces man. The Neptunian man seems to be part artist, part idealist, and, somehow, part entrepreneur. He doesn't like her to see his sensitivity, so the Sagittarius woman pretends to view him as an all-out macho man. His attentiveness sparks her interest and leads her to believe that this man might fit all seasons. The Archer would like to test his resolve to be with such a free-thinking spirit. This Neptunian man seems to know how to adjust to new situations. The adaptable nature they share goes over well with this option-oriented woman. The Sagittarius woman will not chase someone who does not want to be chased nor does she want to be pursued by someone with false intentions. This man who speaks from his imagination can't really hide his heart, that is, when this woman decides she will get to the bottom of his feelings. He is strangely intuitive yet seems to be uncomfortable with his intuitive abilities. The Sagittarius woman gets the idea that she reminds him that it's good to feel. She waits as patiently as one can to see if he will make his move. The Fish can swim close to the shore where she awaits him and suddenly retreat to deeper water. This doesn't bother her; she is reeling him in slowly whether he comes willingly or not!

The Pisces man never dreamed of meeting a woman as hard to peg as the Sagittarius woman. Her ideas are presented forcefully as though she has defended her principles many times before. He appreciates the way she can fleetingly move one way and then another toward what is inspiring her in the moment. The Sagittarius woman has long-range vision. The Pisces man has to listen to her for a while before catching on that she means business. He has heard so many people talk about such visions and goals, but it was idle chatter. The Neptunian man realizes this woman actually intends to accomplish these missions. The dreamer in him is in love with her courage. The realist isn't sure how to relate. He has a feeling that it's time to live under her terms and to stop trying to interpret her world. He notices that she is more inclined to react to him positively when he is active. "She likes a man with emotions," he thinks, "but not if he is so waterlogged that he can't run with her." The Pisces man is moved by the Sagittarius woman's frankness. She is more to the point than he is, but she can be sensitive if he steps too hard on her ideals. He likes the fact that they both have a strong dedication to their values. He finds that she is growing on him. It must be the way she encourages him to act on a hunch. No, it's probably her enthusiasm as a lover, or maybe it's knowing he may have found someone who reads his unspoken language and still wants to be close.

You may recognize that your relationship would not be easy to replace. The way you communicate can be deep and meaningful. If you don't take advantage of each other's faith, your romance will be durable. You have found a lover who can match you thought for thought and vision for vision. It's not that you are an exact mirror for one another. You have your own unique way of performing in the world. Even in the same drama, you can play multiple characters in each act. Adaptability is strong. Your dedication to principles and making your greatest dreams come true may be what brought you together. The effort you make to iron out the wrinkles goes far in maintaining your mutual admiration. Remember the reasons you settled on this lover. There is magic in your romance that you may find with another partner, but you would need to look far and wide to repeat this good fortune.

Capricorn-Capricorn: The Strategists

Capricorn + Capricorn = Two People with a Firm Grasp of Reality

This might be the most driven of all sign combinations. Two Goats can patiently plod along to get a job done, but there can be a swift move to make a dream come true. Delayed gratification doesn't scare them. Patience is what earmarks their power of endurance. Romance isn't necessarily all business for these two. The more secure they feel, the greater the passion that is expressed. The two naturally excel at managing time. Capricorn likes to give clear definition to most things. Doing so offers a feeling of being in control. Finding roles that express the talents of each is a must. Both seem happier when each becomes a leader. This is a relationship that attracts responsibility. Balancing work and play is a constant necessity.

Stiff Joints Game

The games played in your Capricorn-Capricorn relationship revolve around inflexibility and pushing too hard to rise to prominence. The *Stiff Joints* game typifies how you might not loosen up enough in negotiating. Your sign is known for being a great finisher. It takes the force of a gale wind to knock you off course. When the two of you head in the wrong direction or at least one that needs a slight change in coordinates, this game can be troublesome. You might feel discounted if your lover won't listen to your concerns about the need to seek a new course. Inflexibility is a sure way to waste time and money. There are instances where a refusal to listen to each other or to the insights of outside observers can lead to disappointing results.

Climbing the Ladder of Success Game

Ambition is a good thing, but if you become consumed by the drive to get ahead, the *Climbing the Ladder of Success* game might become your reality. The two of you have an innate competitive drive to make great strides in your chosen fields. It doesn't matter what roles you take on, you tend to excel at whatever you undertake. Fame and power are not bad things in their own right. They become problematic if you forget each other as you strive for reputation and success. Taking your lover for granted is going to make intimacy a stranger. Putting most or all of your energy into work could take its toll on your private moments together. You may experience the relationship slipping away due to a momentum to make it to the top. The balance between your high-profile public life and private life is upset. You will experience tension if you feel neglected by your lover. Loneliness can be all too present.

Time Crazed Game

Have you noticed that you magnetically attract responsibilities? When your day planners are crammed to capacity, you could enter into the *Time Crazed* game. Be careful about becoming so constrained by the needs of others that you stop paying attention to each other. You tend to take commitments seriously, don't you? It's easy to forget to make yourselves a top priority. You have the potential to get burned out by stress and may not always realize you have pushed past your endurance level hours (or days!) ago. Your romance can be exhausted. Passion can't get aroused due to low energy levels. Mental or physical lows don't make for romantic highs. Communication is probably fragmented. You are not talking enough to be aware that your relationship is not rejuvenated the way it was in the past (or you are afraid to acknowledge it). You are overdue for a tune-up!

Strategies

How can you circumvent these Capricorn-Capricorn games? Adopting greater flexibility helps to alleviate the *Stiff Joint* game. It may feel worse than getting a tooth pulled to change a plan. Don't resist so much. It is wise to hear out your partner. Your lover may be able to sense problems in the midst of acting out a strategy. The world isn't going to end if you alter an agenda. You might even get a job done less painfully by being open to alternatives. Diversity is good to preach to yourselves. You do have the strength to honor your commitments. The end result can still be accomplished if you make the journey less taxing. Including each other in decisions allows for additional flexibility.

The tendency to get trapped in the *Climbing the Ladder of Success* game is lessened through reassessing what's important to you both. Success is a wonderful thing. It is good for your self-esteem to achieve milestones and honors. Be careful with ambition; don't forget the people who are there for you. You may find that you fall into the habit of putting off your partner's needs until you have accomplished the next feat. Success is contagious, especially for you. You may be excited about rising in status and seeing your hard work paying off in financial gain. Keep a watchdog eye on how driven you become. There is a tendency to neglect your romance if you don't carefully weigh your priorities. Stay true to each other. If you are in a high-energy career, be that much more aware of the need to focus on each other. Be as determined to increase the value of your relationship as you are to improve your skills. You can have the best of both worlds. Life will seem even to be more magical as you come into your own with a special someone sharing in your good fortune.

The *Time Crazed* game does not have to torment you. You may need to weed out unnecessary tasks from your agenda to make more time for yourselves. It becomes tiresome to feel that you are squeezed into your partner's schedule at the last second. You need to control your calendar to allow for increased time together. Delegating responsibility is something to consider. Your sign tends to do everything by itself. Trusting individuals to assist frees you to do other things. You don't want burnout to get in the way of appreciating the good times. You will tend to enjoy talking if you are not so mentally and physically tired. If you have major duties to fulfill, it takes your commitment to make time for each other.

The Rainbow

Your Capricorn-Capricorn relationship can bring you great satisfaction. Each of you may come to realize that you have found someone equally conscientious. You enjoy a commitment bathed in genuine effort. When you talk with a purpose to create clarity, your romance is easier to appreciate. The two of you can excel in business. Your determination to succeed is hard to rival. When you pay attention to the needs of your lover, there are few moments that won't be delightful. Pushing one another to new heights is a given. Learn to enjoy the processes of life as much as the results. It will allow you to appreciate the little things as much as those time-consuming accomplishments. The idea of work likely appeals to you. When each of you finds the roles that allow you to perform at the peak of your talents, life is extra special. If you remember to reward yourselves for the efforts you make, a spirit of happiness is pervasive throughout your lives.

The Capricorn man quickly sees that the Capricorn woman is every bit as ambitious and capable as he himself is. She is dependable—maybe even more than he is. In matters of the heart, he wants to prove himself worthy of love. The Capricorn woman is a solid player in whatever she takes on. The Saturnian man perceives that the Saturnian woman has the same respect for tradition. It's not that either of them necessarily bows to cultural expectations, but each has a sense of obligation to preserve what they deem worthwhile. The two are not going to change something just for the sake of modernization. The Capricorn man notices that she is weary of untested theories. He has a bit of this in him as well. He senses that each has learned lessons from the past. She seems wise and memories appear to color her expression. She definitely can think for herself. The two can either fear the confining ties of commitment or rejoice in being part of a similar plan. The Capricorn man notices that his strategies resemble those of this clear-thinking woman. She has intense feelings and seems more forward in showing them. The Saturnian man can't help but try to define everything as compartmentalized bits of reality. He is a master planner with an eye for a deal. His strength has greater power when he sees the virtue in giving as much as receiving. This earthy woman knows the rules of the game as well as he does. The Capricorn man wants to embrace her before the moment passes because he does not want to fail to seize the beauty of a loving moment.

The Capricorn woman wonders how the male Goat stays so focused on his ambitions without getting distracted. Yet, in her experience, this is not that rare of a phenomenon. As a matter of fact, she is adept at making time fit into her schedule as masterfully as this Saturnian man. The point is that she doesn't always see this dedication in other people. This man's face tells so many stories. Surely he has been a leader or has carried a heavy burden of responsibility. His shoulders look strong but slightly worn by life's heavy realities. He has a look that suggests that he is weary of supporting others through their times of sorrow. She wants the two of them to make up for the past with future pleasures. Deep within the heart of these two self-driven souls is a hunger to celebrate.

The Magic of Signmates

The Saturnian woman and man understand that each has a need to be successful. The Capricorn woman senses that this man shudders at the thought of rejection or failure as much as she. How can she get him to show those well-hidden feelings? He obviously has passion, which is revealed in his voice when he speaks of his work and serious interests. She aches to grab on to those elusive feelings because she sorely wants to touch his heart. The Saturnian woman has no doubt that each wants to control destiny. Neither is fond of fate unless it's on their payroll. She longs to get away with him to a retreat where work and responsibility are dirty little words. She is trying to muster up the courage to give him a look—the one that always gets him to stop working, the one that says, "Let's escape to a place where we can truly see what we have."

You are lovers with a purpose. You may not be trying to change the world. Perhaps adding something to each other's life will suffice. It can feel good to have a dependable ally to help see you through the good and hard times. Although you share the same Sun sign, you have unique tales to tell. You each have a desire to see what can survive the test of time. Your romance can endure when you treat it as a special entity. The mountains you climb will surely leave you with lasting memories. Don't forget about the low country where you probably spend most of your time. These are the lands where you grow your trust and closeness. Cherishing the love you have together is perhaps the ultimate secret of your wisdom.

Capricorn-Aquarius: The Anticipators

Capricorn + Aquarius = Tons of Know-How

These two can sniff out a good deal with the best of them. Capricorn and Aquarius are an interesting combination. The pragmatism of Capricorn influences Aquarius to slow down and shrewdly consider all the options. Aquarius stimulates Capricorn to go beyond its sense of obligation and to even go against the norm. The two are quite different when it comes to love. In matters of the heart, Capricorn is businesslike. Relationships are taken seriously. Aquarius' strong fondness for the future makes Capricorn uncomfortable and enlivened all at once. Capricorn instinctively wants to carefully structure the present. Aquarius usually tries to maintain spontaneous movement through life endeavors. The two can find a way to coexist. It is a prerequisite that each of you do your own thing. The Goat needs to know the bills will get paid. Aquarius wants to make ends meet without sacrificing personal autonomy. Both signs definitely have one thing for common: you both will work hard to reach your goals. Capricorn can inch ahead, grinding out a plan. Delayed gratification does not discourage this earth sign. Aquarius wants to throw a long pass and move on to the next goal. When you learn what makes each other tick, you can be happy together.

Square Peg in a Round Hole Game

The games played in your Capricorn-Aquarius relationship involve reasoning powers that are in conflict and a lack of intimacy. The down-to-earth philosophy of Capricorn could be at odds with the futuristic perceptions of Aquarius. The *Square Peg in a Round Hole* game describes how you may not be able to fit into each other's way of seeing things. The interesting thing about this dilemma is that you both may be aware of the problem. Solving the issue is what seems to be out of reach. If you panic and try to force your lover to see life from your view, tension results. Capricorn can show an unwillingness to adapt. Aquarius can stubbornly want to negotiate on its own terms. An inability to talk makes this a tough game to resolve. Capricorn can retreat behind a wall of resistance. Aquarius can take a defiant stance. The bottom line here is that there isn't much romance under the stars. Capricorn may decide to make all of the decisions while Aquarius rebels and refuses to go along with anything. You can't seem to find the road to compromise.

Too Cold for Comfort Game

There can be times when the two of you may have trouble showing any feeling as is the case in the *Too Cold for Comfort* game. This game could be caused by a fear of closeness. Capricorn can hide emotions behind a business persona. Aquarius can bury feelings behind the intellect. Passion can be hard to find. Unresolved anger is another possible instigator of your relationship's frigid atmosphere. Past issues can have a hold on you both. The inability to work through old business can make it next to impossible to feel affection. Neither of you makes the first move to solve the crisis. If one of you tries to break the ice, the other could stubbornly resist working it out. You are left with two unhappy hearts. You need to step back for a minute to find the best path to reaching an attainable deal.

Power Outage Game

Your signs seek empowerment in divergent ways. Capricorn finds power and confidence through focused activities. Commitment seems to bring out the Goat's stamina. Personal power comes to Aquarius through autonomy. This sign also can display great follow-through. The *Power Outage* game occurs when your circuits are overloaded with leadership struggles. Neither of you likes to play "follow the leader" often. Clashing interests may lead to debates. Fighting for your own preferences could cause real stress if you can't find any middle ground. A determination to win your point does not help the team. There are some things on which you won't be able to agree.

When you are so worked up about being right, you may detract from each other's momentum to move forward. The power you can generate to do great things is extinguished by incongruous outlooks.

Strategies

How can you sail around these Capricorn-Aquarius games? In the *Square Peg in a Round Hole* game, the two of you must let each other be. Capricorn needs to know that some things in the relationship are etched in stone. Aquarius may shudder at the thought. To keep the peace, a few rules must be followed by you both. "Freedom!" is a rallying cry in the Aquarian mind. Aquarius must be assured that certain rules can be broken or at least amended as needed. Anarchy drives Capricorn mad, but it should be said Aquarius can lose its focus without structure. Somehow, you have to live out this play of form versus freedom. Each of you will feel that you fit together when your approach is incorporated. You can't be like your partner. Don't try! Capricorn is meant to be sober about planning; the Goat shows the rest of us that it's possible! Aquarius must buck the norm to be a role model for those who follow the crowd. When you learn to appreciate your respective roles, your life together is wondrous. You don't step on each other's feet when you promote the unique qualities each of you possesses. Your commitment is unified when you both see that you are accepted at face value. A compromise or two is inevitable, and conciliation doesn't mean you have to be someone you aren't.

The *Too Cold for Comfort* game can thaw if you avoid indulging in fear. Capricorn sometimes needs to see that it hurts worse to run from a situation than to face it. Aquarius must realize that emotion won't drown its mind. It takes some faith in yourself and each other to get past the hurdles to intimacy. Don't pressure each other. Take it slow if you must. Even after a passionate beginning, day-to-day interactions can reveal where you hide your fears. Expressing even a small amount of feeling helps to make greater intimacy a reality. If anger keeps you in colder emotional climates, then you both need to find a way to talk. The anxiety you go through when you don't communicate is worse than anything you could say. You can't release anger if you won't address the issues behind it. Don't be scared of the anger that may come out. After your real opinions are expressed, objective ideas may result. Don't blame each other for what you don't have. Start anew to prevent long delays in communicating. It takes lots of practice and effort!

The Magic of Signmates

The *Power Outage* game isn't impossible to turn around. You must have your own leadership abilities recognized. Individual pursuits probably are the way to make you feel better about working together. When the two of you feel you have clout in your individual spheres, power struggles are less likely. You can't work together if you try to force each other to adopt your plans. You aren't meant to emulate one another. Cry out an emphatic "No!" if your partner seeks empowerment through imitation of your style. Be true to your own hearts. Your shared goals will flow when you are convinced that your lover respects your rights.

The Rainbow

Your Capricorn-Aquarius relationship can surprise you by leading you toward illuminating directions. Even if you don't always agree on what is worthy of your time, there can still be plenty of fun in store. Your passion ignites when you least expect it. This is what makes life together enticing. Recognizing experiences that lift you out of the humdrum of everyday life picks up the pace of this partnership. You need to be focused on the present. The effort and time that you commit to understanding each other's thinking pays great dividends. You are an interesting mix of traditional and unconventional values. Respecting one another's goals goes far in establishing a strong foundation. Don't take each other for granted. You win your lover's trust by showing you are paying attention. Loyalty is in the "skin and bones" of your liaison.

The Capricorn man is struck by a sense of familiarity when he meets the Aquarius woman. Perhaps he responds to her firm intention to make life respond to her wishes. He has a little of this in his own blood. The Uranian woman follows her own path. The Capricorn man detects that she is true to those who acknowledge her independence. He knows this free-spirited woman will not stand for attempts to control her. Sometimes she shows a hint of respect for the past. Those things she doesn't openly rebel against might win her allegiance. The Saturnian man watches his step so he doesn't get on the wrong side of this fast-thinking woman. He observes that she will let him lead when he doesn't make a big deal out of it. The Capricorn man wonders if she has an internal clock set ahead of everyone else. He likes the way she makes him think in new directions. He learns that it's best not to squeeze her too tightly; she likes to know that he cares but prefers to be free to go in search of what interests her. He sees that she expects him to accept her many friends; they make a fine traveling caravan. She is that much more loving when he accepts her whole world, not only the part that makes sense to him. The Capricorn man wants to know the Aquarius woman. He wonders if it might take a lifetime to do so.

The Aquarius woman recognizes that the Capricorn man is a serious soul. She wonders if he does anything but work. Even when he plays, he may be looking for an income tax break. The Uranian woman can't help but admit that he is inspiring. She doesn't always focus on work for hours on end as he does. Her philosophy is to make that effort when the spirit moves her. She can surprise others (and even herself) by accomplishing major projects even when her mind desperately wants to get on to something else. She hopes this Saturnian man knows how to be a lover and friend. She doesn't really want to be protected as much as equally valued. The Aquarius woman sees that this man has acquired wisdom through good and bad experiences. Reality is a fine teacher. She hopes he can be open to his imagination and fly with her to romantic getaways. "We make a fine pair," she thinks. "We are not afraid to bring dreams to earth." Her feelings are sometimes camouflaged by a fine network of ideas. She wonders whether he will ever show *any* emotion. He responds passionately once he casts off his preoccupation with material success. She is impressed with what he has done and what he plans for the future. Their connection is a rhapsody of harmony when neither worries about where the relationship is going. She hears the message, "Enjoy the moment." Does he hear it too?

The Capricorn woman is moved by the Aquarius man's vision. Even when it seems limited to him, it still often outdistances that of many people. The Uranian man has a uniquely laid-back attitude, even if it is a pretense, and seems to believe the show will go on one way or the other. She isn't always as calm and cool but will roll up her sleeves and put some order into chaos. Romance seems to be a mental game to him. His ideas are wonderfully entertaining. The Saturnian woman can display a remarkable sense of new trends when she tires of the old ones. The Aquarius man seems to have an inner connection that keeps him abreast of innovative changes. She wonders why he sometimes seems to go against his forward-thinking nature by resisting change. Perhaps it's his way of rebelling. The Capricorn woman likes that he values friendship. Every once in a while his unique insights send a thrill through her. He talks clearly when he wants to be understood but can weave around the point when he is afraid of enemy fire. She wants him to see her as a lover who can write a new agenda if that is what it takes to be his companion. It's not that she can't live without him. She can even survive solitude better than most, but he is fun to have near because she never knows what he will say or do next.

The Magic of Signmates

The Aquarius man isn't sure how to make himself appealing to the Capricorn woman. She talks and acts as though her life were as solid as a rock. Even her loose ends are tightly bound. Her commitment to responsibility is remarkable. She pushes herself to be seen as dependable. The Uranian man is delighted to realize that she is a different person when removed from duty. He can be serious himself, so he hopes they can learn to play as much as work. Their thinking can be at odds. He likes to be spontaneous at times. This does not seem to bother her as long as he doesn't become too eccentric. The Aquarius man notices that she loves to surprise him. It makes her laugh when he is caught off guard. Her passion is intense—when there is time to be a lover—but they both can be in a hurry. He sees that she is entertained by his perspective about life. There are few things they can't talk about. Her ambition is well defined. It makes him uneasy to watch her put a plan in motion and carefully navigate it to completion. He has a free-flowing way of carrying out a strategy. To the outside observer, it might even appear to zigzag. Their communication is stimulating. He likes the fact that she isn't put off by his unconventional side. She seems reluctant to trust him unless he shows some vulnerability. He tries to learn how to talk more openly since this is apparently the road to her heart. The warmth in her eyes breaks down his tendency to filter his emotions through his mind.

Being together can further your claim to happiness and success. This is a relationship built upon mutual support. Without it, your relationship has a start-and-stop movement. With it, you never doubt the reason you are together. The love you seek only needs your willingness to rediscover it. You are a passionate pair when you take the time to really concentrate on one another. There is little you cannot accomplish. Life without challenges will bore you to tears. This is an alliance that hits the ground running because you are not afraid to take risks. Your courage to stand by one another keeps proving that you have made a wise choice!

Let the Games Begin

Capricorn-Pisces: The Conscientious Ones

Capricorn + Pisces = Wondrous and Thought-Provoking Journey

Can the Goat and the Fish achieve harmony? Yes, but you will need to stretch beyond your ordinary ways of doing business to capture each other's heart. These are two signs that can have an affinity for seeking causes. Capricorn is attracted to ambitious roles. Pisces is attuned to self-expression. While the Goat can focus most of its energy through a single goal, the Fish would rather seek fulfillment through several outlets. Capricorn helps Pisces see how to make its ideals take root. Pisces inspires Capricorn to be less confined by a narrow vision of success. The two can be hopelessly in love when they respond to one another's deepest needs. Mutual devotion may make others envious. The earthy Goat likes to know that it is walking on stable ground. The watery Fish prefers unpredictable currents. When the two of you are aware of your partner's style, you can be happier lovers.

Disillusionment Game

The games played in your Capricorn-Pisces relationship are connected to disappointed expectations and confused emotions. The *Disillusionment* game occurs when the two of you see that your worlds do not fit together. Capricorn may hope that Pisces will become less dreamy. The Goat can push the Fish to be more linear and logical. Pisces can plead with Capricorn to reach out with imagination instead of always looking for rational explanations. Pisces wishes that Capricorn could see the value of intuition rather than relying solely on logic. This is a tall order! You might want to change each other in ways that are impossible. A judgmental tone in your voices could be a turnoff. Your romance may not have the inspiring force it once had. When Capricorn views the future, it's often colored by the demands of the past. The Goat pushes forward out of fear of losing ground on the road to success; not so with the Fish. Pisces sees the future with a colorful, romantic vision. This sign more or less floats along and is not intimidated by what may not come to fruition. The knowledge that many possibilities abound motivates Pisces. Each of you may not be able to relate to the other's life choices. By not energizing each other's goals, you may drift apart.

Sleepwalking Game

The two of you could feel like you move aimlessly together as in the *Sleepwalking* game. You may find it easier to make choices as individuals. When you try to put your heads together, you may feel disoriented. A tendency to skirt around serious issues comes with this game. Capricorn and Pisces can get lost in work or causes. Denial dilutes your mental and emotional connection. You can sense that your lover goes through the motions but that sincerity is lacking. You want to feel some intensity but tend to alienate each other when you try to figure out what is wrong. Capricorn likes to be in control and can become irritable when it loses focus. Pisces doesn't like to be pinned down to a single possibility. The Fish may become moody if backed into a corner. Neither of you is comfortable with confusion in your relationship. If you don't talk, the feeling of separation becomes stronger. The way back to feeling close isn't out of reach, but to your aching hearts it seems to be an insurmountable distance.

Shallow Water Game

When your communication seems to be overshadowed by doubts, the *Shallow Water* game manifests. Fear can make intimacy a rare event. You want to show that you care about your lover but have a hard time acting upon your desire. You rarely express emotions. Self-consciousness or your reserved nature may hold the two of you back. Sometimes this game is caused by unresolved anger. Hidden resentments certainly block the expression of feelings. It's difficult to reach the deeper emotional waters if you cling to unresolved issues. When you don't make an effort to solve problems with enthusiasm, it can be hurtful. Your commitment can lack definition because you cannot gauge how dedicated you are to making the relationship work. You could give in to anxiety and worry. The faith you need in one another is nowhere in sight.

Strategies

How can you rise above these Capricorn-Pisces games? To stay away from the *Disillusionment* game, the two of you must accept each other. It's not likely that you are going to share each other's approach to making decisions. Capricorn is as ruthlessly realistic as Pisces is extremely idealistic. The mistake you don't want to make is to assume the other will always show the same tendency. Yes, it's possible that the Goat can dream and the Fish could develop remarkably grounded ideas. It might not be the first or second instinct but might come in third. Tolerate your lover's own way of getting through life. Criticism doesn't win admiration nor should it! When you can get past the other's thought patterns—whether they be practical or dreamy—you feel more in love. You can be united in many endeavors. Finding the patience to let each set your own pace makes you a happy duo. If you believe in each other, anything is possible—anything! Inspiration is something you both need. Capricorn will enjoy the journey if it knows that it need not be lonely. Pisces is driven when someone cheers on its aspirations. You are a radiant couple when you bask in each other's support.

The *Sleepwalking* game ceases to be as damaging when you both realize that you need to refocus your attention on each other. You may not be entirely conscious of this game when it starts. You may be so caught up in your personal ambitions and dreams that you forget about each other. You may need to get away together to reprioritize the relationship. Worry doesn't help. Capricorn wants a quick solution while Pisces would like the problem to go away. First, you need to accept where you are. When passion is missing, distractions are usually the culprit. The time for intimacy may be lacking. It requires effort to turn this one around. Taking each other for granted must be transformed into valuing one another. Tangible actions (not promises) lead you out of the darkness into the light.

In the *Shallow Water* game, you need to trust your lover. Expressing feelings takes courage. You can't get into one another's inner world without revealing a glimpse of your own. If anger stands in the way, it's imperative that you break through the obstacles. Anger and passion go hand in hand. If you can learn how to say what you feel in the moment, you won't have to worry about the past overshadowing the present. The anxiety you could put yourselves through by not talking is probably worse than dealing with issues. Your commitment is more strongly defined when you learn how to negotiate with each other. Capricorn sometimes can view everything as business. Pisces may be too flowery in its definition of love. Each of you needs to walk halfway toward the other to find the meeting place of your hearts. It's a magical feeling when your minds connect. To form a deeper bond, you will need to exercise patience. Let go of excessive control. Surrender your doubts. Be sensible. Don't be afraid to go beyond your comfort zones to tune in to the channels that are most frequented by your lover.

The Rainbow

Your Capricorn-Pisces relationship can bring you both into fields of happiness. Capricorn can feel refreshed by the intuitive gifts of Pisces. The rugged determination of Capricorn instills ambitious drive in the ideals of Pisces. You can whet one another's appetite for success and love. When you are able to reach out to each other with understanding, the road to the heart is never far. Your shared vision can be profitable on both the business and romantic fronts. Be open to learning from your lover. You may grow attached to the confidence your lover has in you.

The Capricorn man is bewildered by the Pisces woman. He is dazzled by the glitter in her thoughts and the flow in her voice. The Saturnian man's definite boundaries are turned upside-down by the Neptunian woman. She defies labels. The Capricorn man finds this both exciting and confusing. The part of him that loves a challenge is attracted to her. The side that fears the unknown is a bit terrified of her. He notices that she admires his ambition. Her face seems to light up when he exhibits his sense of playfulness. It can be awkward for the Capricorn man to be spontaneous. She makes him lose all sense of time, which is quite a feat because he is ruled by the mythological god of time, Chronos (i.e., Saturn). Her nonlinear approach achieves results that do not fit his conception of earthly reality. Yet, the Pisces woman feels her way along like a blind person—with one exception—her unshakable inner faith is her guide. "What in the world is that wavy look in her eyes?" he wonders. She captures his heart and mind with her diaphanous presence. The cautious man with a pragmatic streak wants to get to know this woman. Why? He plans to answer that question later, after he has figured out the way she sees her reality. He thinks this could take a lifetime! She has a delightful way of switching the tracks of his mind to less business-oriented pleasures. He believes he could get used to this, especially after she gives him a private screening of the inner world that inspires her.

The Pisces woman perceives the Capricorn man to be as grounded as she is attuned to the invisible forces of life. His grasp of reality is impressive. The Neptunian woman searches carefully for clues to his heart. He is not an easy man to read, but she is a master of interpretation. His voice undeniably contains the wisdom of lessons learned from the past. She hopes his heart isn't so tired that her dreams bounce off with no resounding impact. The Pisces woman sees that he is inspired by her dreams. She doesn't want this man to think she can't walk on firm ground. The Neptunian woman likes the way she feels when leaning on this strong, dependable man. It would be so easy to be needy, yet she knows the way to happiness is to be his equal in all endeavors. She wants him to express his own feelings because it is tiring to be a channel for the feelings of others. That's a role she doesn't need. The love she feels is probably partly motivated by the potential she sees. This Neptunian woman has an instinct to idealize what love with someone could potentially be like. She hopes this realistic man can step into her spiritual world, where the sky and stars talk to each other. She doesn't care if he understands as long as he won't interfere with the inner world that sustains her. She needs some make-believe to make reality palatable. His regular diet consists of ambition and business. Life with him is refreshing because he reminds her that a dream is even greater when brought down from the clouds to a place in time.

The Capricorn woman doesn't really see the Pisces man at first. He seems to be invisible because he appears like a mirage, but suddenly a real person stands in front of her. The Saturnian woman appreciates the sensitive perceptions of the Pisces man. She can feel him tune in to her feelings. His inner world appears to guide him. She wonders how he can put one foot in front of the other. The Capricorn woman senses a romantic atmosphere when near him. He makes her think of natural panoramas—bubbling brooks and scenic waterfalls. The Saturnian woman is relieved to hear that he is ambitious. She can't help but be focused on the material world. People always depend on her to be there for them, and she doesn't want a needy man. She prefers a partner who can stand on his own. He seems like an interesting person. His mind doesn't make it easy to label him. His causes and hobbies outnumber her own at least two to one. Her need to focus is important to her. She can't have someone enter her life and want her to rewrite the script. If he can accept her as she is, she certainly could cut him some slack. She knows the score at most of the turns in her life. She is at a crossroads with the Neptunian man, whose mischievous smile touches her. He makes tempting suggestions for romantic escapes. She thinks his vivid imagination is nicely aligned with her own. Make no mistake about it, she has a playful spirit, which is reserved for the right loving person.

The Pisces man is taken aback by the Capricorn woman. His invisibility has run right up against the visible. This earthy Saturnian woman knows how to play the game of love *and* work. She is serious until you get through to her playful heart. Time pressures her more than most. The Pisces man sees that he had better not be just another demand in her already demanding life. She handles responsibility magnificently. The Pisces man wonders how comfortable she is with love. Her face is strong and shows that she has been through all of the ups and downs of love. He wants to be the part of her life that is elevated. He thinks they make a good pair. The Capricorn woman reminds him that dreams take effort. He hopes he instills in her the thought that love takes risk. She comes closer to him when he is not asking the unreasonable. He has fallen for her clear way of making him feel he is part of her world. He knows she is waiting for him to do the same.

Your romance is a mystery that is apt to make you both stronger when you least expect it. You are the strongest when you feel the most vulnerable. Don't hold on to each other so tightly that you can't walk as individuals. Don't lean so heavily that you both topple. Look for the real person inside your lover. It isn't so hard to do when you are determined to talk from the heart. Trust your intuition when you want to find greater faith. Reality testing will keep you on the balanced path. Be honest with your lover, and you will have a great rendezvous with love.

Aquarius-Aquarius: The Rebels

Aquarius + Aquarius = Jet Propulsion into the Future

Two people of this sign in a relationship are locked in fast forward. This romance features a love of surprises and new gadgetry. The mental realm is exhilarating for both. Freedom must ring resoundingly for both of you to feel welcome. Equality is a must. Both are apt to lead lives that are nourished by unique interests. Group involvement could be important. You don't get any more independent than these two. You must watch out for aloofness. A tendency to live life on separate terms is in the background. Sharing blossoms when each exercises personal autonomy. Insights leap out at any moment. The past and present are appreciated when both of you express your key goals. The romance can begin in unusual ways. Friendship is a strong need for both of these mentally active people. Inventive instincts can make life together exciting.

Scrambled Frequencies Game

The games played in your Aquarius-Aquarius relationship are linked to confusion in communication and living too much in separate realities. The connection between you could blur as it does in the *Scrambled Frequencies* game. Your minds may race ahead so quickly that your perceptions of each other become unclear. A hectic pace can distract your concentration. Your futuristic impulses may keep you from really knowing each other in the present. This is probably not intentional. The chemistry between you promotes speed. The two of you like to get to the point quickly. Nervousness could affect the way you perceive one another. Impatience with your lover could result in angry responses. Your ability to work on the same projects is lessened by an unwillingness to slow down and focus. Frustration could occur because you feel that it is useless to pursue shared goals. You may feel that your commitment is on shaky ground because you are not able to read each other's next move.

Light Years Away Game

In the *Light Years Away* game, you may send unclear messages as a way to not be perceived accurately. This is a way to hide your agendas. Communication can become as distant as the stars. Aloof exchanges are a barometer that the intimacy is not what it could be. Fear can be at the root of this game. Intellectual defenses cover your anxieties. Extreme independence is another way this game manifests. A desire to have little or no structure can create chaos. Anarchy sets in that makes it tough to define your relationship. Emotional distance doesn't do much for trust. A sense of alienation from one another is disappointing. That "old loving feeling" seems to be out of reach.

Herky-Jerky Game

You could become upset with each other's unpredictable actions. The *Herky-Jerky* game describes the way you can feel yanked around by your lover's sudden agenda changes. When you perceive that your rights are abused, it can be explosive. Your sign doesn't enjoy getting angry because it throws off your mental equilibrium. Being subjected to unsuspected changes can anger you. When you lose out on some of your own plans due to your partner's spasmodic ways, resentment can build. You might cause each other to be nervous wrecks if you don't become good planners. Irresponsible actions can lead to serious contentions.

Strategies

How can you get through these Aquarius-Aquarius games? In the *Scrambled Frequencies* game, you might need to slow down and pay attention to each other's needs. When you take the time to listen, great things can occur. It would be foolish for anyone to tell you to slow down. That's not going to happen! Your minds are lightning fast, which can speed up action. You must learn to talk clearly. There could be a tendency to speak in shorthand. Quick blips of information may leave out too many key details. Air signs like yourselves have extra amounts of nervous energy. It means you must be that much

Let the Games Begin

more careful to focus when working together. Patience comes when you experience a small amount of success in pulling off a project. Two Aquarians naturally resist one another's leadership. Let's face it: you have a rebellious streak. It's what makes the rest of us admire you! Your perceptions sometimes fight through your own resistance to each other's opinions. Learn that giving and receiving are vital to your romance. Support your partner's paths, and harmony is likely.

The *Light Years Away* game asks the two of you not to be stingy with your feelings. Aquarius is an intellectual giant, but its emotions are sometimes stunted. Sharing an ounce of emotion is better than none. One of you may be better at expressing emotions. Your relationship will benefit if you make the effort to share what you feel. You don't have to be maudlin. That's not likely to happen anyway. You would rather think and act than reflect. If you experience distance, you may need to conquer your fear of closeness. You can still do your own thing if that worries you. Neither of you cares to answer to the other. Structure isn't necessarily a bad thing. It can allow you to be organized enough to enjoy freedom even more. A few rules help to define your romance adequately so you see that you are in a real relationship. Getting back to emotions for a moment (you probably hoped we were through with that subject), intimacy and passion thrive on the expression of your feelings. If you can forget your restless minds for a second and let each other into your inner world, you will discover even greater liberation. Challenge yourselves to inch closer. Distance can make you cold. Why not gather around the fire?

The *Herky-Jerky* game will be less prevalent when you warn one another before you make a sharp turn. Sudden change is to be expected in this relationship. Complete predictability didn't draw you here in the first place, did it? You can do a few things to make sure you don't lose one another. You are not mind readers. Tell each other in advance when you are about to overhaul the schedule or your entire life strategy! The element of surprise is a turn-on in your romance. The excitement you arouse in one another can be mental or sexual. Shock is another story. You might blow out a fuse in your lover's mind if you frequent the unexpected lane too much. Your commitment is strengthened by the effort you make to talk frankly. It may surprise both of you that your lover may not know you as well as you think. In your fast-paced life together, it may be challenging to keep up in the here and now. What was true about you yesterday may not be your reality today. Keep each other in touch with the latest in your developing story.

The Magic of Signmates

The Rainbow

Your Aquarius-Aquarius relationship is one of endless self-discovery. The directions you pursue together will take you to places that are wonderfully unique. The future calls to you to explore it. The doors you walk through as individuals and as a couple lead to adventurous growth. You have a romance that challenges you to keep up with it! Your shared insights can accelerate your achievement of personal goals. Freedom is in the heart and breath of being together. People will often see you as a lively duo. Put energy into your lover's dreams, and the love you seek is never far away.

An Aquarius man likes the mind of the Aquarius woman. She has that same predisposition to chase after new trends. The Aquarius man soon realizes that the two may not always agree on which traditions are worthy of time and respect. The Uranian man isn't bothered by this because it is obvious that she has a mind of her own. The Aquarius woman can cut through idle chatter quickly. The Aquarius man needs an inventive partner. This woman fits the program better than many. He wonders if they can find things in common that will hold their interest. Her thoughts seem to travel along the same unpredictable circuitry as his own. This woman exhibits an experimental nature. He is delighted to see that this freewheeling spirit can display a rebellious side. He is aware that she is an agent of freedom and the future just as he is. He hopes he has found someone who is able to live within the confines of the present. This is no easy task for him because his impulse is to question all new experiences thoroughly to be sure there are no hidden obligations. He perceives that her heart is as well insulated from emotion as his own. Even so, feelings of love and passion run through him when she looks at him. Her gaze is inviting yet warns him to be ready for anything. She beckons him to come along on the ride of their lives!

The Aquarius woman perceives the Aquarius man to be exciting. He bolts into action when he is inspired by his thoughts. It seems to happen so fast, but she also acts quickly when inspiration strikes. The Aquarius man is confident about his intelligence but removed from his emotions. He seems to have difficulty relating to emotions, but she observes that his feelings emerge when he talks about his goals. She puts as much stock in the future as he does. The Aquarius woman is glad to see he has ambition. Why? She doesn't really want to be the sole focus of his life. She needs a lover who has a rich, full life of his own. This man seems to share her belief that love is found through equality and independence. Freedom seems to be a central concept in their lives. The Aquarius man has an offbeat mind, but he can fit into the mainstream when he chooses. She can't help but wonder where his mind goes when he looks into the distance. Visions are the lifeblood of the Aquarius man and woman. Both are influenced by instinctual, rebellious natures. The Aquarius woman enjoys exploring interesting venues with the Aquarius man. She is exhilarated by his company as they seek adventures together. His vision extends beyond the distant horizon. How does she know? She, too, casts her vision ahead to challenge the unpredictable future. She thinks they make a fine team that can make the most of any expedition.

The reasons that brought you together will eventually give way to a much bigger picture. You tend to have a tremendous impact on each other's life. Sometimes, it may seem that you are on a wild roller coaster ride. The ups, downs, and sudden curves make your romance a thrilling adventure. If you want predictability, this may be the wrong place to look for it. Your commitment evens out and becomes an anchor of contentment when you cheer each other on to realize your greatest potentials. There is no need to look back when you are a lover with a sharp mind and a caring heart.

Aquarius-Pisces: The Dazzlers

Aquarius + Pisces = Magic

These two signs think as differently as they feel. How can you get along? You both have vivid imaginations. Aquarius relies on the bullet-like speed of its perceptions while Pisces leans on its creative intuition. Dreamy Pisces can benefit from the mental coolness of Aquarius. Pisces influences Aquarius to take a chance on feelings. The two of you work better together when you understand the motivating forces behind each other's actions. Life is not mundane for you. Romantic interludes may highlight innovative ideas. This sign duo can enjoy exploring new trends and all types of aesthetic interests. The individualistic drives of Aquarius don't necessarily clash with the escapism of Pisces. Both of you like to wander off into your own worlds. This is a relationship that gets better with time as you see that your own life mission can still flourish. The sign chemistry of this duo is fascinating.

Off-Key Game

The games played in your Aquarius-Pisces relationship are associated with talking about unrelated concepts and draining one another emotionally. When you are not really communicating, it might be due to the *Off-Key* game. This is a scenario in which you both try to make plain sense, but you soon see that you must be speaking in foreign languages. Your two signs filter the input of information quite differently. Aquarius screens everything through fine mental filters. The mind works fast and is ready to react at lightning speed. The Fish listens intuitively and logically and often switches between the two in mid-sentence. Pisces' first impulse is to react with feelings while Aquarius will choose logic at least nine out of ten times, so you have a person with a keen intellect trying to talk to someone whose feelings are off the Richter scale. Sounds like a challenge, doesn't it? It is! You both can be frustrated when you try hard to make your lover understand your reasoning. It's tempting to throw everything—from a tantrum to a dish. Finding harmony is agonizing. Impatience makes this game tough to master.

One-Way Street Game

The two of you can get extremely attached to your own plans. Aquarius can get downright stubborn in exerting its will. Pisces can grow solemn and project a "holier than thou" image when it pronounces its understanding of the truth. The *One-Way Street* game is one in which the two of you are not willing to compromise. When you refuse to consider opposing viewpoints the clash heats up. You are bound to get into some intense battles by not being tolerant. Aquarius can become belligerent and sarcastic when its insights are undervalued. This air sign will become chillingly cold. Pisces will show hurt feelings and may actually give its partner the silent treatment. The mood is not pleasant. You are uncomfortable when your lover withholds his or her love. The dilemma is at its worst when neither of you finds the wherewithal to rectify the situation. You are in a state of limbo.

Blown Fuses Game

When you can't see straight due to angry feelings and sense that a blowout is near, you are right smack-dab in the *Blown Fuses* game. Neither of you enjoys dealing with heated issues because the aftermath produces a disorienting sensation. By not dealing directly with a predicament, you tend to fuel your anger. You become exhausted through not letting your ire out in the open. (Remember, pulling a bandage off slowly can be excruciating while you won't feel a thing if you rip it off quickly.) Aquarius can find itself becoming tremendously nervous when holding back insights. Pisces becomes a wet dishrag when absorbing the confusion inherent in denial. The message here is that there isn't much love or passion when your time is occupied by emotional exchanges like this. By keeping how you really feel invisible, closeness is not evident either.

Strategies

How can you get past these Aquarius-Pisces games? In the *Off-Key* game, you may need to listen carefully to ascertain why you misinterpret what your partner says. Aquarius must slow down its mind so it can hear Pisces. Pisces must calm its emotions so it can listen dispassionately to Aquarius. Communication does not automatically happen just because two people talk. It takes effort to communicate clearly. You can get good at this if you make a bold attempt. You will notice how much better you make decisions together when your words hit the mark. You can learn how to talk on key when you really want to support one another's dreams.

The *One-Way Street* game urges you to be flexible. It's true that you may not think things through in the same fashion. It does not matter! You must let go of the need to be right. Aquarius will attract more support and love if it shows sensitivity to the ideas of a partner. Pisces will not turn off its lover if it avoids dogmatism. Present an atmosphere that invites free discussion. There is a payoff. You are very likely to receive valuable input when you encourage free interaction.

The *Blown Fuses* game asks you to stop denying the need to deal head-on with issues. It's okay if things get a little messy. Anger has a way of reshuffling your energies. You can't be close if there are unresolved differences between you. If you can find the courage to nip an oncoming obstacle in the bud, life will be a lot more enjoyable. You will have extra energy for romantic getaways and creative enterprises. The two of you become confused when ruled by what you fear. The shadow cast by doubt can keep your intimate moments few and far between. If you are able to take control of the situation and talk to (not at or around) each other, you will be surprised by how good you feel. It is tiring to run away from what makes you feel loved. The more quickly you deal with a problem, the faster it will disappear.

The Rainbow

Your Aquarius-Pisces relationship keeps you on your toes. The two of you can be ready to take off in a new direction quickly. Your ideals spark many of your ideas. The paths you seek as individuals and as a couple are filled with enriching opportunities. You will not always agree on what is best for your personal development. Let each other gravitate to those goals that add zest to your life. It is not impossible to combine your worlds into one powerful expression. You will interact with many others through your relationship. Each of you needs outside input to define your major purposes. You are a dynamic duo who could encourage others to change their lives for the better. Think the best of one another, and you will find the confidence to cross the hurdles that stand in your way.

When the Aquarius man meets the Pisces woman, he becomes unusually thoughtful and reflective. The Aquarius man tries to adjust his way of thinking to match the approach of the Neptunian woman. He surmises that her reasoning powers are based upon intuition. She seems to see right through him. Although he is most comfortable with the mind, the Aquarius man does have feelings, which the Pisces woman would like to share. The Aquarius man notices that she is a dreamer who seems to live according to her own rhythms. His own pace is upbeat while she almost appears to float through life. The Uranian man does not find this so strange because he has met all types. He likes the way she makes him feel accepted. He doesn't know how he will avoid disappointing this romantic woman. Then again, she seems to be quite aware that love is not always predictable. He is relieved because he knows himself to be as unpredictable as a shooting star. This Pisces woman seems to live among the stars. Her knowledge appears to come from beyond the boundaries of Earth. The Aquarius man knows a unique vision when he sees one. He wants to be with this sensitive, trusting woman.

The Pisces woman isn't sure how to sum up the Aquarius man. He fits the bill as far as her need for an independent partner. Dreamy lovers exhaust her. This Uranian man has a way with words and quickly spins out ideas. There is love in his devotion to causes. She has an attraction to causes of her own. They seem to share a fascination with the mysteries of life that occur as though they were preconceived events. She is delighted about their "accidental" meeting. The Neptunian woman waits to see if this Uranian man has even a trace of sensitivity. He is not quick to dip into his feelings (it is as though they are saved for special occasions). She hopes he sees her as a partner with whom he can share extraordinary days. He looks like someone who has fought conventions and still has that aura about him. This is not a problem. She is more interested in whether he can respond positively to a straightforward love. His voice is decisive and he seems to be fair. She appreciates his ability to differentiate the trivial from the real. Her idealism seems to take him out of his mind and into the surreal. "We make a fine pair," she thinks. If he doesn't make a move on her soon, she may surprise him.

The Aquarius woman finds the Pisces man to be an enigma. He can perform various roles without even thinking. When it comes to getting to the point in matters of the heart, he is elusive. She is not disturbed by this because there are times when she does the same to distract a lover from her feelings. This Neptunian man clearly loves his causes. The Uranian woman hopes he isn't so absorbed by his "mission" that he forgets to enjoy his personal life. The Aquarius woman is quick to notice that he showers her with attention. Her independent thinking brings out his passion. This feeling-oriented man keeps himself hidden behind a curtain. The Aquarius woman is happy to see that the Pisces man can make his own way in the world. She likes someone with a mind of his own. The Neptunian man has a heart that shines through when he thinks about romance. She looks forward to escapes to exotic places with him. Their love seems to flourish when they get away from the stress of everyday hassles. He appears to be a sensitive man whose feelings are easily hurt. She perceives him to be giving when life provides him with abundance. She wants him to realize she has added greatly to his good fortune. She doesn't want to tell him so but would rather he see this on his own. The sooner the better!

When the Pisces man comes into the presence of the Aquarius woman, he can't help but notice her air of knowledge. What she knows he is not so sure. Her mind can electrify his own like a bolt of lightning that brightens the night sky—even if only for a few seconds. This Uranian woman senses that he is trying to label her. He can tell that this makes her jumpy and apt to duck. The Neptunian man likes her exuberance. Her defiance of convention intrigues him. He usually evades what he doesn't like to face. This woman will challenge her adversaries openly. The Pisces man wants to show her that he can fight for his own beliefs. His faith is as strong as her mental vision. He thinks they would make an exciting team. They both want life to rise above the humdrum. He has a sense of divine discontent that seeks new inspiration. She seems to possess an intellect that tires of routines as soon as she finds herself in one. They share a passion for freedom and ideals. The Neptunian man notices that this Uranian woman likes it when he listens. So many must either fear her or think she is foolish and turn a deaf ear. To him, her voice is as refreshing as the spring in all its splendor. He only hopes she can see that he has the potential to be with her through the changing seasons. She certainly is already able to turn his attention away from despair toward a feeling of hope that was within him but he wasn't able to see.

Let the Games Begin

The connection you find in your romance keeps you from roaming elsewhere in search of love. The path to each other possibly found you struggling through past encounters that broke your hearts. The life you create together can be the answer to your quest to find a friend and lover. Keep renewing your commitment. Don't let it accumulate dust through inactivity. You don't need to take unnecessary risks. A special celebration of your personal and shared milestones is wise. When you look into your lover's eyes, don't forget the gift that you symbolize to each other. Your relationship is proof that there are mysterious ways by which the stars bring two hearts together.

Pisces-Pisces: The Dreamers

Pisces + Pisces = Out of This World Relationship

A Pisces-Pisces relationship engages in a true cosmic dance. The saying, "life is a play," must have been inspired by this sign combination. The two can lift one another through a show of faith. You are likely to share extraordinary idealism. Reality testing helps to keep things running with greater precision. You share great expectations of life. Following ideas may lead to great accomplishments. Imagination is readily available. The roles each chooses must lead to fulfillment. Falling in love over and over again keeps you close. You naturally read each other's moods. You probably feel like you already know one another. A mysterious set of circumstances might have introduced you. A belief in the invisible forces may be as real as what can be seen, tasted, or touched. You find it easier to coexist when you stay free of guilt and avoid an unrealistic pursuit of perfection.

Strawberry Fields Forever Game

The games played in your Pisces-Pisces relationship are linked to lapses in defining reality and unfounded expectations. When the two of you see the world through overly idealized lenses, the *Strawberry Fields Forever* game occurs. Your minds play tricks on you. Your perceptions are based more on what you would like to see rather than what is. Your expectations of each other could be as high as the Empire State Building. It is frustrating to try to measure up to perfection. Your faith in others could get you into trouble. If you don't keep your feet on the ground, you could lose money and time. It is tempting to criticize each other for not doing everything just right. Romance does not flow when you scrutinize each other's actions too closely. You deny your need to take a more sober approach. This is a case of overactive imaginations getting the best of you.

Eating Chicken Broth with a Fork Game

The two of you may feel that moving in step is awkward as is the case in the *Eating Chicken Broth with a Fork* game. Your ideas don't seem to translate into action. Results elude you because plans never really fully materialize. Emotional intensity may be the reason for this game. Feelings may outweigh thinking. Pisces is a water sign that needs structure. You may lack focus because you don't follow a sound blueprint. You choose to float ahead but may drift far off course into uncharted territories. You have the impression that you are lost in the Bermuda Triangle of relationships. Concrete ideas may be disregarded in favor of your intuitive impressions. Communication can be frustrating if it doesn't solve a problem. This is further compounded by exhibiting codependent behavior. Dependency needs must be balanced.

Guilt-Ridden Game

A nemesis of Pisces can be feeling responsible for the problems of others as in the *Guilt-Ridden* game. You are not going to have as much fun with each other when you act out this scenario. The two of you may blame yourselves for things that go wrong in each other's life. You can't save one another from growing pains. It's possible that you overidentify with what each goes through. Don't blame your lover if your life isn't trouble-free. You may forget that there are no perfect people. Others may make you feel responsible for their emotions. You are not happy when you allow people to pollute your waters with their problems. This game goes beyond the realm of caring. You are too affected by things over which you have no control. A loss of boundaries is often involved.

Strategies

How can you get around these Pisces-Pisces games? The *Strawberry Fields Forever* game could use your most sound reasoning powers. You will get better results when you balance your ideals with reality. There's nothing wrong with imagination, which is the source of your creative power. Make sure your perceptions of your partner are reasonable. You won't be able to do everything just the way the other would like.

Your business sense will be grounded when you take the time to think things through. Even in defining your relationship, your expectations will be clearer when you talk in pragmatic terms. Pisces is a deeply romantic sign. You don't have to sacrifice your instincts. Stay away from blaming each other for things you're not happy with in your life. Each of you makes a valuable contribution to the relationship by acting responsibly.

In the *Eating Chicken Broth with a Fork* game, you only need to put together a solid plan. If you rely on fate to make everything click, you will be disappointed. You may have a lot of faith that things will work out for the best with no structure. You don't have to stop dreaming. As a matter of fact, your dreams may come to fruition faster with careful planning. Creative impulses can benefit from discipline. You will be less frustrated with each other if you don't leave too much to chance. You may even find that you accomplish more with less stress. The decisions you make are likely to run more smoothly when you exercise a little organization. You are not so likely to anger one another by forgetting appointments or promises if you adopt a clear strategy. No one is asking you to give up your intuition. A balance between your feelings and thoughts is required.

If you want to free yourself from the *Guilt-Ridden* game, you must give yourself a break. It takes faith to believe in yourself and not to feel responsible for everybody else's troubles. You can exhibit extreme sensitivity to the point of berating yourself unnecessarily. You need to define your boundaries carefully. If you cross over into each other's territory unconsciously, you will become confused. You are so emotional that you may become disoriented if you don't keep your lives sorted out. You can be the greatest of lovers without trying to save one another. Blame only detracts from constructive interactions. Be reasonable in what you ask of yourselves. Don't go overboard in aiding others. The urge to help may be strong. Channeling this energy into appropriate causes or realistic activities is wiser than trying to do the impossible. If you're not careful, feelings of guilt may cause you to let others lean too heavily on you. Take the time to realistically assess situations.

The Rainbow

Your Pisces-Pisces relationship is full of faith that buoys you through difficult times. The belief you have to fulfill a dream is awesome. If you are dedicated to helping one another fulfill key goals, you will delight in being part of the same love. You are tremendously idealistic. You do need to keep reality testing in mind. Focusing your energies will save you time and energy in the long run. Your relationship is magical and the inspiration you share can lift others out of their doldrums. You have a desire to express creative talents. Aesthetic abilities may shine through you.

The Pisces man dances gently into the life of the Pisces woman. He is careful not to scare her or himself away. The Pisces man senses that her emotions are deep and powerful. The Neptunian man has idealism that surrounds him like a brightly colored aura. He wears his causes proudly. He notices that the Neptunian woman is attracted to his many life interests. Both are avid students of life. He thinks they share many of the same values. Their intuitive energies do appear to be similar. The Fish would like to swim with her to waters that provide an ultimate escape. The Neptunian man likes to think of himself as her *yang*. She is certainly his *yin*. The Pisces man thinks in symbols but isn't always aware of this tendency. He is easily distracted by responsibilities. The Pisces woman takes him back to his basic nature. She reminds him of his life mission. Love with her is easy. The Pisces man hopes this woman, who seems to have much to say, perceives him to be sincere. He likes the way she cares about him, and her intuition and sensuality match his own. Their sense of unity defies description. He is willing to take the time to understand her subtlest emotions. She can tempt him to come out to the deeper waters where her mind and feelings are one. The Neptunian man knows he has met his emotional match. He imagines what life will be like with her. It certainly is better than the alternative!

The Pisces woman senses something special in the Pisces man. He is mysterious yet simple. The Neptunian woman is entertained by the Pisces man's creative instincts. He displays a faith that isn't so different from her own. She feels that perhaps their spirits have encountered one another somewhere in the past. She has a sense of déjà vu when they meet. The Neptunian man sweeps the Pisces woman away with his idealism. Her own dreams seem made from the same fabric. She finds it hard to keep a secret from him. It is strange, but she is aware that he can't keep much hidden from her either. Their minds often blend as one. She doesn't want to be dependent on his strength any more than she wants him to lean too heavily on her. They find physical and emotional passion together. She marvels at his ability to understand her unspoken thoughts just as she is able to effortlessly tune in to his quiet moods. Silence is golden when they are together, though it is grounding to speak as well because it breaks the intuitive trance. She thinks their chemistry is uplifting. The Neptunian man and woman often confuse

The Magic of Signmates

others. They share the contemplative power of their Sun sign and cast a mesmerizing spell on each other.

Your relationship is like a fairy tale that sustains its dreams of love. The calmness of the emotional waters you share is easily rippled by the stones of reality you encounter. Riding out the waves of discontent takes faith. Your love can carry the two of you across the high seas. You gain power with each challenge you face. There is no need to run away when you have such a loving, supportive lover. You only need to ride your intuition to find the calm within the storm and to discover your way home. You are fortunate to have such a strong advocate to help you find your way. Your creative power reaches lofty heights when you learn to trust the love that brought you to each other in the beginning.

www.ingramcontent.com/pod-product-compliance
Lightning Source LLC
Chambersburg PA
CBHW081738100526
44592CB00015B/2224